The Actuarial Use of the MMPI with Adolescents and Adults

The Actuarial Use of the MMPI with Adolescents and Adults

Philip A. Marks, Ph.D.

Professor of Psychiatry and Psychology,
Ohio State University, Columbus, Ohio

William Seeman, Ph.D.

Professor of Psychology,
University of Cincinnati, Cincinnati, Ohio

Deborah L. Haller, B.A.

Research Associate
Department of Psychiatry,
Ohio State University, Columbus, Ohio

The Williams & Wilkins Company/Baltimore

Copyright ©, 1974
The Williams & Wilkins Company
428 E. Preston Street
Baltimore, Md. 21202, U.S.A.

Made in the United States of America

Reprinted 1975

Library of Congress Cataloging in Publication Data

Marks, Philip Andre.
    The actuarial use of the MMPI with adolescents and adults.

    Includes bibliographies.
    1. Minnesota multiphasic personality inventory.
2. Adolescent psychology. 3. Personality. I. See-
man, William, 1912–   joint author. II. Haller,
Deborah L., joint author. III. Title.
[DNLM: 1. MMPI. 2. Personality assessment. WM145
M346a 1974]
BF698.8.M5M37   155.2'83   73-22402
ISBN 0-683-05591-7

Composed and printed at the
Waverly Press, Inc.
Mt. Royal and Guilford Aves.
Baltimore, Md. 21202, U.S.A.

To Steff, Jeff, and Mark—
three adolescents

Foreword to
the Revised Edition

Readers familiar with the long out-of-print *Actuarial Description of Abnormal Personality* will be pleased to learn of the publication of the present volume. In it they will find an expanded and up-dated version of the discussion of actuarial versus clinical procedures which delighted Professor Meehl in that first edition, together with a reprinting of the data comprising the adult code types originally developed by the first two authors on their psychiatric cases from the University of Kansas Hospitals. They will be pleasantly surprised that these data are now in a narrative format with somewhat less stringent typal defining criteria. The real bonus for them in this edition, however, will be the totally new set of code types and descriptors for adolescent subjects. These latter categories were developed from a nationwide sample of adolescents who were tested with the MMPI while in treatment and described (blind to the test data) by their therapists after a period of close acquaintance with their problems and personalities. Thus, not only is an old standby of MMPI interpretation available again for a rising generation of clinicians but also a fund of new interpretive material never before available on teenagers is presented to the field for old hands and novices alike.

As the reader will soon learn, the issue of statistical versus clinical prediction and description from psychometric data is far from resolved into any generally accepted argument. For many reasons, the MMPI early became the psychometric axis of this ambivalent issue. Paul Meehl's propounding of the arguments of the controversy in 1954 rather clearly betrayed his identification with the MMPI as the source he considered most appropriate for the initial studies that were intended to give us the practical benefit of using the statistical method once we had become persuaded of its real promise. The original evidence for MMPI validity was conveyed in the so-called "Clinical *Atlas*" of Hathaway and Meehl which was an early prototype that presented personality descriptions that were derived independently of test data and latterly linked to the test through the classificatory power of the MMPI code. But, for many users, the "Clinical *Atlas*" vignettes, while evocative, were hard to apply since they lacked a summary of items that occur with convincing frequency among persons similar in code to those who were to be described.

The first Marks and Seeman *Atlas* in 1963 was the pioneer among the more mature actuarial descriptions that were partially successful in avoiding some of the defects of the original "Clinical *Atlas*". Marks and Seeman soon discovered, however, that while the results of their work were useful and stimulating, there were several obvious ways in which the power of the actuarial method could be enhanced. A first problem was the limitation in case coverage resulting from failure of the available code types to include enough cases. Users could often be discouraged by repeated failures to find a descriptive niche for profiles they were attempting to interpret. Also the actuarial items were stated in too telegraphic a form, making colorful personality descriptions difficult. Finally, the published work was restricted to adults, a limitation that was increasingly severe since the trend was so strong to be more and more concerned with younger subjects in early intervention to prevent delinquency and adult maladjustment problems.

It seems likely that the feature of this new version of the Marks and Seeman *Atlas* which will be the most noteworthy, and perhaps the most controversial, is the use of the MMPI with boys and girls as young as twelve or thirteen. The view that is generally held of the MMPI is that it is a special clinical instrument for use solely with seriously disturbed adult psychiatric patients. In many ways it is difficult to understand this stereotype since almost from its inception, the test was extended to young people, both for research and for clinical purposes. Even before the full standard set of scales had been developed, Dora Capwell took the early box form with her to test her charges at the Sauk Centre School for Girls, a Minnesota state reformatory for delinquents. Suspecting that the adult norms might not be entirely suitable for comparative purposes with these inmates, Capwell also gathered MMPI data on girls of the same age and general background who were attending the Sauk Centre High School at that time. Her preliminary findings, together with her follow-up testing of both groups, were reassuring in several respects. First, the normal high school girls gave profiles with elevations and patterns which were very similar to the scores (on the available scales) obtained from the Minnesota normal women in the Hathaway and McKinley standardization sample. (It is puzzling how few samples of teenage boys or girls studied since her original research have earned mean profiles as close to the Minnesota norms as Capwell's high school girls.) Secondly, the separation between non-institutionalized teenagers and the institutionalized delinquent girls was not only statistically stable but clinically useful on several of the clinical scales. Third, and perhaps most important for the present work of Marks, Seeman, and Haller, the patterns of scores on the available scales (and the remaining ones when they were subsequently scored) indicated that there were important subgroups of delinquents that could be identified by these configurations. These early successes of the Capwell investigations led directly to the extensive collaboration by Hathaway and Monachesi in the study of adolescents. Since few of the existing personality instruments had shown any dependable relationship to delinquent behavior, most workers in the field of delinquency had become convinced that these forms of social deviancy were virtually entirely attributable to social and familial circumstance. The Capwell data were a dramatic departure from these previous findings. But her research had first to be taken one step further to establish an etiological basis for personality variables in the initiation of a delinquent career: prospective data had to be obtained on adolescents prior to their apprehension, prosecution, and commitment to an institution to rule out these effects on their test scores. The predictive work of Hathaway and Monachesi, together with the efforts of many of their students and colleagues, was highly successful in documenting the personality of the child himself as an important source of variance in the delinquent acts which led so many youngsters into the hands of police and law enforcement authorities. The data that they gathered on urban ninth-graders in Minneapolis and Duluth, and on small town and rural ninth-graders around the state of Minnesota, not only provided the basis for numerous follow-up studies on delinquency, academic success, school conduct, school drop-out or later college attendance, marriage stability, and parental behavior, but also these same data comprise the bulk of the normative material used by the present authors in the special age norms for each sex that they include in Section III of this volume.

Although the applications of the MMPI to adolescents started with the problems of predicting, diagnosing, and planning rehabilitation programs for delinquents, the uses to which it was put by Dr. Reynald Jensen and his associates in the Child Psychiatric Services of the University of Minnesota Hospitals and by Mrs. Virginia Hathaway and others in the Child Study Service of the Minneapolis school system grew rapidly. Unexplainable school failures, school phobias, chronic truancy, kleptomanias, sexual identity problems, early forms of neurosis and psychosis, as well as emotional complications of various organic disorders, were all studied by means of the MMPI. These early case studies were carried out, however, without the necessary background of empirical findings on typical correlates of the various profile patterns and configurations that were encountered in their referrals. Although some of the MMPI patterns appearing in work with boys and girls as young as twelve years old were recognizable versions of common adult patterns, many were quite specific to these age levels and the clinical problems characteristic of this developmental stage. As the readers of this volume will discover as they proceed through the types in Section III, new configurations will be introduced and other relatively rare patterns in adult populations will be explicated in considerable detail. We can anticipate that the types summarized here for the first time will soon come to serve adolescent psychiatry as a clinico-descriptive framework in the way that MMPI-based types and patterns have been gradually supplanting more traditional psychiatric classifications in work-day clinical practice with adults. Something of this sort is now urgently needed in adolescent psychiatry (and child psychiatry generally).

More controversial than the recommendations made here to employ this personality instrument with patients in early adolescence, however, will be the suggestions that testing, whether with the MMPI or with almost any other kind of psychological instrument, should be employed for early identification of emotional and behavioral disorders in school systems across the country. In the relatively short period of time that the MMPI has been commercially available, a little over thirty years, there has been a dramatic alteration in the standing of expert, professional consultation by clinical psychologists in school-related problems that their pupils are manifesting. Wholesale attacks have been launched, by PTA groups, civil libertarians, veteran organizations, and federal agencies, on the legitimacy of school record-keeping, against the use of surveys of school populations by means of ability, achievement, or personality test batteries in order to identify potential problems and guide early intervention work, and even against consultation by professional psychologists with school officials or classroom teachers. Most of the general assumptions that were held when the MMPI was first applied to adolescent emotional problems about how to use historical material and personality test data to understand and guide students and how to employ psychological methods to individualize and maximize educational and training efforts in our schools have by now either been seriously questioned or rejected outright. Rather, these various efforts and techniques are often seen as part of some malicious conspiracy against the individual student. Part of the impetus to these present attacks stems from a violent reaction against and angry rejection of stereotypes based upon sex membership, ethnic background, or mistaken genetic theories. These reactions have led to an endorsement of extreme environmentalist theories of personality and behavior. Even the most extreme environmentalist psychologist, however, must concede that by the time a child has reached adolescence he has accumulated the effects of so wide and extensive an array of experiences that his behavior is already shaped and predictable to an important degree in many different situations. Use of tests like the MMPI can serve important purposes in assessing these existing patterns and anticipating their future development if circumstances are not altered. Properly employed, psychological assessment can further the proper recognition of important individual differences and help guide professional efforts to offset ominous trends in emotional and behavioral reactions. In the hands of properly trained psychologists and psychiatrists, the information provided in this volume can help assure that the MMPI assessments of adults and adolescents will meet these high standards of professional practice.

Starke R. Hathaway
W. Grant Dahlstrom

Minneapolis, Minnesota
June 6, 1974

Preface

In extending our studies to include adolescents, we are offering, for the first time, a comprehensive system of narrative-form, actuarial personality descriptions—a system derived from patients classified on the basis of the Minnesota Multiphasic Personality Inventory (MMPI). This book is designed for use in private practice, clinics, hospitals, and schools; its objective is to assist the psychologist, physician, or counselor in understanding and assessing the individual. We also envision that this work will be of value in the classroom, with particular focus on courses in abnormal and adolescent psychology, the psychology of personality, and psychological tests and measurement techniques. It is hoped that this approach to the assessment of personality will illuminate areas where clinical practice and personality theory may be better articulated.

Chapter 1 presents a description of the MMPI scales; those readers interested in obtaining information on the administration and scoring of the MMPI will find this in the *Revised Manual* (Hathaway and McKinley, 1967). In addition, an extraordinarily complete coverage of not only administration and scoring, but of many other aspects of the MMPI will be found in *An MMPI Handbook Volume I: Clinical Interpretation* (Dahlstrom, Welsh, and Dahlstrom, 1972); information specific to adolescents may be found in *Adolescent Personality and Behavior* (Hathaway and Monachesi, 1963).

Chapter 2 contains a discussion of some central issues concerning clinical and actuarial approaches to personality description as well as some comments designed to clarify a number of widely held and persistent misconceptions about the nature of actuarial description itself.

Chapters 3 and 5 describe in detail the procedures followed in developing, respectively, the 16 code types for adults and the 29 code types for adolescents.

Inspection of the statements which comprise one aspect of the personality descriptions which appear in Chapters 4 and 6, reveals that they operate at a variety of levels: some are purely descriptive (*e.g.*, "Is overanxious about minor matters and reacts to them as if they were emergencies"); some operate at the level of dispositional constructs, indicating tendencies to act in certain ways in the presence of specified stimulating circumstances (*e.g.*, "Resents authority figures and typically has impulses to resist and derogate them"); still others operate at a dynamic-causal level, considered by many clinicians and counselors to be the most significant and meaningful way in which one can characterize personality or behavior (*e.g.*, "Has a need to achieve," "Has inner conflicts about emotional dependency"). In another sense of the term dynamic, we are concerned with change over time and the potentialities of the ego as reflected in certain measures discussed in the text. It was our intent to provide a diversity and a range of complexity of personality descriptors which will permit readers of varying theoretical orientations and levels of training and sophistication to select and emphasize whatever aspects they consider most appropriate and significant.

Presented in Appendix A is a glossary of abbreviations and symbols. Appendix B provides, from our earlier work, the conceptual scheme we found helpful in organizing and clarifying the Q descriptors, which comprise one aspect of the narrative personality descriptions. Presented in tabular form in Appendixes C and D is an extensive summary of our findings. Appendix C provides frequencies of all descriptors for each of the 16 adult code types. Also given are the objective scoring procedures developed by Meehl and Dalstrom, and modified by Hendrichs to aid in differentiating adult neurotic and psychotic MMPI profiles. In Appendix D are given the instructions to participants in the adolescent studies, and the base rates of all descriptors for adolescents.

Support for our research with adults was provided by the Foundation for Research in Psychiatry and by the Smith, Kline and French Foundation. In this regard, we thank Donald C. Greaves, then Chairman of the Department of Psychiatry, University of Kansas School of Medicine. We also gratefully acknowledge the cooperation of the following students and colleagues from the University of Kansas: George B. Appleford, John T. Brauchi, Lyman W. Condie, Richard E. Davis, Edward A. Dreyfus, Adrian D. Duffy, Kathleen A. Dunn, Thomas O. Harries, James F. Hooke, Glen Hunt, Bernard Klappersack, Altan Kodanaz, Ruth M. Lapi, John F. Mardock, Clyde V. Martin, Arnold Moskowitz, Robert E. Ransmeier, Arlene Rigdon, Stanton L. Rosenberg, René A. Ruiz, Marion Sims, Sophie Stathopoulos, Janet Turk, James D. VanAntwerp, James W. Vaughn, and Linda L. Whitsell.

The adolescent studies began at The University of Kansas and were concluded at The Ohio State University. From 1964 to 1968 they were funded by the National Institute of Mental Health (MH 05833 and MH 12987), and from 1968 to 1974 by The Psychiatric Research Foundation of Columbus, The Ohio State University Medical Research Fund, and the College of

Medicine General Research Support Grant. Numerous individuals have been involved throughout all stages of our work and to each we are grateful. The rating forms were developed and normative MMPI data were collected with the assistance of our colleagues mentioned above; and, additionally, Allan G. Barclay, Joseph E. Brewer, Peter F. Briggs, Loretta K. Cass, Jeanne E. Fish, Raymond F. Fowler, Harrison G. Gough, A. Jack Hafner, Robert G. Harlow, Starke R. Hathaway, Paul C. Laybourne, Ted Leventhal, Hyman S. Lippman, Lovick C. Miller, Alan O. Ross, Jacob O. Sines, C. Leland Winder, Robert D. Wirt, Gerald H. Vandenberg, and the late Aldo Vigliano.

A real debt must be acknowledged to our research collaborators, many of whom also participated as psychotherapists and provided ratings on which our adolescent data are based. Our thanks are thus expressed to the following individuals and agencies:

Sander M. Abend, M.D., *Bronx Municipal Hospital Center, Bronx, New York.*

Henry E. Altenberg, M.D., *Child Guidance Clinic, Inc., New Britain, Connecticut.*

Robert C. Bennion, Ph.D., *Child Guidance and Mental Health Clinic, Provo, Utah.*

Ralph Bierman, Ph.D., *The Psychiatric Clinic, Inc., Buffalo, New York.*

Joseph E. Brewer, Ph.D., *Wichita Guidance Center, Wichita, Kansas.*

Normand J. Brochu, *Washington County Mental Health Services, Inc., Montpelier, Vermont.*

Charles M. Brodie, Ph.D., *University of Oklahoma Medical Center, Oklahoma City, Oklahoma.*

Herman T. Brown, Jr., Ph.D., *Pasadena Child Guidance Clinic, Pasadena, California*

Alvin G. Burstein, Ph.D., *University of Illinois Medical School, Chicago, Illinois.*

Mary Campbell, Ph.D., *Clinic 8, Seattle, Washington.*

Louis Centers, Ph.D., *Langley Porter Neuropsychiatric Institute, San Francisco, California.*

Lawrence Claman, M.D., *Dallas Child Guidance Clinic, Dallas, Texas.*

J. Frank Clark, Ph.D., *Children's Medical Center, Tulsa, Oklahoma.*

William G. Closson, Jr., M.D., *The Psychiatric Medical Group, San Jose, California.*

Jane E. Cooke, Ph.D., *Medical College of Virginia, Richmond, Virginia.*

Peter P. Coukoulis, Ph.D., *Southern Reception Center and Clinic, Norwalk, California.*

William Crow, *Rhyther Child Center, Seattle, Washington.*

Andrew S. Dibner, Ph.D., *Boston University, Boston, Massachusetts.*

Michael Dinoff, Ph.D., *University of Alabama, University, Alabama.*

O. C. Elsea, Jr., Ph.D., *Department of Public Welfare, Oklahoma City, Oklahoma.*

John A. Ewing, M.D., *University of North Carolina School of Medicine, Chapel Hill, North Carolina.*

Joseph A. Fitzgerald, M.D., *Larue D. Carter Hospital, Indianapolis, Indiana.*

C. J. Frederick, Ph.D., *Patton State Hospital, Patton, California.*

Paul D. Frederickson, Ph.D., *Child Guidance Clinic of Marion County, Indianapolis, Indiana.*

Virginia Fulcomer, Ph.D., *Child Guidance Center of Youngstown, Youngstown, Ohio.*

Ivan N. Mensh, Ph.D., *University of California at Los Angeles School of Medicine, Los Angeles, California.*

C. A. Galliani, Ph.D., *Delaware State Hospital, New Castle, Delaware.*

Alan Gessner, Ph.D., *Mental Health Clinic, Lakeland, Florida.*

Lothar Gidro-Frank, M.D., *New York State Psychiatric Institute, New York.*

Bernard C. Glueck, Jr., M.D., *Institute of Living, Hartford, Connecticut.*

Beverly Golden, Ph.D., *Community Guidance Center of Bexar County, San Antonio, Texas.*

Jacquelin R. Goldman, Ph.D., *University of Florida Medical Center, Gainesville, Florida.*

Harry A. Grater, Jr., Ph.D., *University of Florida, Gainesville, Florida.*

Elsa S. Greenberg, Ph.D., *Children's Hospital of the District of Columbia, Washington, D.C.*

Jack D. Hain, Ph.D., *University of Alabama Medical Center, Birmingham, Alabama.*

John E. Hannon, Ph.D., *Milledgeville State Hospital, Milledgeville, Georgia.*

Christina Herness, M.A., *Amherst H. Wilder Child Guidance Clinic, St. Paul, Minnesota.*

S. Otho Hesterly, M.D., *University of Arkansas Medical Center, Little Rock, Arkansas.*

John P. Hindley, Ph.D., *Eastern State Hospital, Medical Lake, Washington.*

Franz W. Husserl, M.D., *Monmouth Medical Center, Long Branch, New Jersey.*

Marvin Hyman, Ph.D., *Detroit Psychiatric Institute, Detroit, Michigan.*

Grace K. Jameson, M.D., *The Titus Harris Clinic, Galveston, Texas.*

Richard L. Jenkins, M.D., *University of Iowa State Psychopathic Hospital, Iowa City, Iowa.*

Donald F. Kausch, Ph.D., *University of Missouri School of Medicine, Columbia, Missouri.*

E. Walton Kirk, *Hilltop Professional Building, Walnut Creek, California.*
Geralann Kratz, M.A., *Children's Medical Center, Tulsa, Oklahoma.*
Martin Levine, Ph.D., *Community Child Guidance Clinic, Portland, Oregon.*
John V. Liccione, Ph.D., *Milwaukee County Mental Health Center, Milwaukee, Wisconsin.*
Bruce M. Lodewyk, M.S.W., *Flint Mental Health Clinic, Flint, Michigan.*
Gordon R. Loomis, M.D., *Cleveland Guidance Center, Cleveland, Ohio.*
David Markert, Ph.D., *Barron-Polk Guidance Clinic, Turtle Lake, Wisconsin.*
Beverly T. Meed, M.D., *Creighton University Medical School, Omaha, Nebraska.*
John E. Meeks, M.D., *University of Texas Southwestern Medical School, Dallas, Texas.*
Thomas D. Nelson, Ph.D., *Arapahoe Mental Health Center, Inc., Englewood, Colorado.*
Arthur Norman, Ph.D., *University of Oregon Medical School, Portland, Oregon.*
David R. Offord, M.D., *J. Hillis Miller Health Center, Gainesville, Florida.*
Gordon W. Olson, Ph.D., *Anoka State Hospital, Anoka, Minnesota.*
Gail Osborne, M.S.W., *Los Angeles County General Hospital, Los Angeles, California.*
Gene F. Ostrom, Ph.D., *Crownsville State Hospital, Crownsville, Maryland.*
D. A. R. Peyman, Ph.D., *Alabama State Hospital, Tuscaloosa, Alabama.*
Gordon J. Polder, Ph.D., *Northwest Psychiatric Clinic, Eau Claire, Wisconsin.*
Marion Powell, Ph.D., *Child Guidance Clinic of the Oranges, East Orange, New Jersey.*
Ronald S. Pryer, Ph.D., *Central Louisiana State Hospital, Pinesville, Louisiana.*
John M. Reisman, Ph.D., *Rochester Child Guidance Clinic, Rochester, New York.*
Patricia M. Renaud, Ph.D., *Sagamore Hills Children's Hospital, Northfield, Ohio.*
Alfred Rubinstein, Ph.D., *The Union County Psychiatric Clinic, Plainfield, New Jersey.*
Richard A. Sanders, Ph.D., *Norfolk State Hospital, Norfolk, Nebraska.*
Donald J. Shoemaker, Ph.D., *Southern Illinois University, Carbondale, Illinois.*
Hirsch L. Silverman, Ph.D., *Newark, New Jersey.*
Hans H. Stroo, M.D., *Roanoke Guidance Center, Roanoke, Virginia.*
Max Sugar, M.D., *Louisiana State University, New Orleans, Louisiana.*
Francis J. Tartaglino, M.D., *Fulton State Hospital, Fulton, Missouri.*

Allen W. Valcov, Ph.D., *Columbus State Hospital, Columbus, Ohio*.

Ernest J. White, M.D., *Las Palmas School for Girls, Los Angeles, California*.

Gerald Yagoda, Ph.D., *Middletown State Hospital, Middletown, New York*.

Our clerical, computer programming, and secretarial assistance in Kansas City was provided by John V. Bowser, Ruth Decker, Jane Jennings, John R. Kispaugh, Marion D. Lindblad, Susan L. Miller, and Carolyn S. Wright. In Columbus, Lynda Berkley, Regina Doll, Mary Heger, Linda Kerns, Richard North, and Janet Parker helped process and file the ratings and profiles and check and recheck the tabular materials. Special thanks to Eileen Merrick who typed the final draft of the manuscript.

Our discussions over the years with Jim Butcher, Alex Caldwell, Grant Dahlstrom, Ray Fowler, Ron Fox, Mal Gynther, Starke Hathaway, John Kangas, and Mark Lefkowitz were typically 'multi-fine,' always stimulating, and much appreciated. We are also most grateful to Ian Gregory, Chairman of the Department of Psychiatry, at the Ohio State University, for creating the atmosphere that made this work possible, and to Don Smeltzer, who not only wrote the programs for analyzing our data, but who was available when we needed him. We thank the OSU Instructional and Research Computer Center for contributing their time and facilities. Our debt to our Editor, G. James Gallager should be obvious to the reader!

Permission to quote from *Objective Approaches to Personality Assessment*, edited by Bernard M. Bass and Irwin A. Berg, was granted by D. Van Nostrand. The late Harold G. Seashore, director of the Test Division of The Psychological Corporation, was kind enough to permit us to reproduce a number of MMPI items which we borrowed from the *Manual*. Harrison G. Gough and Consulting Psychologists Press gave permission to reproduce *The Adjective Check List*. The University of Minnesota Press granted us permission to quote from *Clinical versus Statistical Prediction*, to reproduce the Henrichs rules and the adolescent T-score conversion tables which also appear in *An MMPI Handbook, Volume I: Clinical Interpretation*, and to condense the tables we used from *An atlas for the Clinical Use of the MMPI* and the *Handbook*. Permission to draw upon tabular material from other sources was provided by the authors, The American Psychological Association, and The McGraw-Hill Book Company.

Finally, we thank the over 3,000 people who, while serving as patients, permitted this book to happen.

January 1, 1974   Phil Marks
                                                     Will Seeman
                                                     Deb Haller

Contents

PART THREE

ADOLESCENT SECTION

PART FOUR

APPENDIXES

PART

ONE

INTRODUCTION

1

The MMPI

An intelligent and efficient use of this book will be promoted by an understanding of the kind of psychological test instrument which the MMPI is and by a knowledge of the specific procedures used in deriving the personality characterizations that this book contains. It will therefore be the purpose of this section to describe and discuss the MMPI, the nature of actuarial description, and the procedures by which the descriptions were derived.[1]

The MMPI

The MMPI belongs to that class of psychological or psychometric instruments which have been characterized as *structured* and as *inventory*-type tests. An inventory-type psychological test is one in which the items are answered *true-false, yes-no, agree-disagree*, etc. The concept of structure is usually invoked in this context (*i.e.*, in psychological tests) to denote the characteristics of the test's stimulus material; the more *ambiguous* a stimulus is said to be, the less structured it will be (Seeman and Marks, 1962). There is some question, however, whether the concept of stimulus structure in this sense can ever be adequately defined (Gibson, 1960). Attempts to define stimulus structure in psychological tests in terms of meaning have also been somewhat unsuccessful. It has frequently been said, for example, that a structured stimulus "means the same thing" to different people, whereas an unstructured stimulus has different and idiosyncratic meanings for different people. The difficulties involved in such

---

[1] The reader who needs information on the administration and scoring of the MMPI can readily obtain this from the Manual (Hathaway and McKinley, 1967), or from any one of several sources listed at the end of this chapter. Although neither the administration or scoring of the test, nor the classification of test profile by code type, may require special psychometric skill, it is certainly our view that the ultimate responsibility does devolve upon a highly trained professional person. An MMPI profile and its associated information is no less confidential than any other personal information about an individual. We take it as obvious that the responsibility for conveying this information to a person and discussing it with a person is at all times a *professional* one.

3

an attempt at definition have been analyzed by Meehl (1945), who has shown that items in personality tests usually regarded as structured, may, in fact, be subject to variable meanings from one individual to another. Cattell (1936), also, would almost certainly object to this view that stimuli which occur in inventory type tests "mean the same thing" to all persons. Indeed, Cattell argues that the *most valid* "projective" tests are likely to be precisely those in which the items are inventory-like in their format. Further, Zubin, Eron, and Schumer (1965) characterize as a "shibboleth" (*i.e.*, a slogan without much merit) the idea that standardized test items—which are mostly of the inventory or "structured" type—necessarily "mean the same thing" to all subjects.

The MMPI itself consists of 550 items which the subject is asked to assess as *true* or *false*; there is a *cannot say* category which the subject is encouraged to keep quite low. All subjects who participated in the studies leading to the development of this work were given the booklet or group form of the test,[2] and they were actively discouraged from using the *cannot say* category by omitting this category as a possible choice from the test instructions. The distribution of content of MMPI items with representative illustrative items is presented in Table 1. It should perhaps be made explicit that this is simply one of a number of possible ways of classifying the items, and that there is no standard nor uniform system of classification.

The overwhelming majority of MMPI items are obvious with respect to content in that they clearly deal with psychiatric, psychological, neurological, or physical symptoms. However, there are a number of items which appear innocuous but which are found on one or more of the clinical MMPI scales because, in the original scale construction, they appeared to be contributing validly to the scale. In some cases they appeared to be operating in psychologically obscure (not intuitively obvious) ways. For example, it is not at all clear why "I sometimes tease animals" should appear on a scale measuring depression (MMPI scale 2). It is a scale 2 item, however, because in the original empirical (*i.e.*, nontheoretical) derivation of the scale, the criterion depressed patients marked this item *true* more frequently than did the "normals" in the standardization sample. It thus happens that an item may be scored in the *abnormal* direction even though it is answered in the *normal* direction. How might such a seemingly paradoxical thing happen? Consider this: Suppose the item "What others think of me does not bother me" was answered *true* by 56% of people in general (*i.e.*, a majority of normal persons). Suppose, also, that it was answered *true* by 82% of patients diagnosed as "hysterical." The odds are greater, then, that the item will be answered in the *true* direction by a patient labeled "hysteric" than by a normal person even though the majority of normal persons do, in fact, respond to the item that way. Thus, it was argued, such

---

[2] Available from The Psychological Corporation, 304 East 45th Street, New York, New York 10017.

Table 1. *A Classification of MMPI Content with Illustrative Items*

Category	Representative Items	No of Items
Attitudes:		
Religious	I believe in the second coming of Christ.	19
Sexual	Children should be taught all the main facts about sex.	16
Social.	I like parties and socials.	72
Test-taking	I do not always tell the truth.	15
Education	I was a slow learner in school.	12
General health	I am very seldom troubled by constipation .	81
Masculine/Fem.	I very much like hunting.	55
Mood	I am happy most of the time .	56
Morale	I am entirely self-confident.	33
Occupation	I would like to be a soldier.	18
Phobias	I am afraid when I look down from a high place.	29
Preoccupations	Someone has control over my mind.	46
Miscellaneous	I like to read newspaper editorials .	98

items should be included in a scale even though there was not available a rationale, theory, or reason to *explain* the operation of such an item.

However, because of recent research and revision of thinking about psychological test items it seems necessary at least to qualify some aspects of this argument and of such an item selection procedure. The "meaning" and the utility of *some* of these so-called "subtle" items are now more controversial and perhaps more dubious than was the case 10 years ago. Whether this is attributable to unhappy consequences of correlation with unrecognized nuisance variables [as suggested by Meehl (1971) and by Jackson (1971)] whose influence might have been filtered out if keying of the MMPI items had included a requirement that in order to be included in a scale, an item must make "theoretical sense"; or whether they were *originally* valid but have yielded to changes in fashion and/or conceptions of psychopathology is not clear. Wales and Seeman (1969) also have raised questions about the meaning and the validity of such items, which, however, make up a small part of the total item pool. Further, we suggest that to the extent that some of these items *do* make theoretical sense on a *particular* scale (*e.g.*, scale 3, the Hysteria scale) they may be contributing validly to those scale scores.

Although the MMPI, as has been indicated, is an inventory-type instrument there is one significant property, *not* necessarily shared by all inventory-type tests, which is characteristic of it. For many years in the development of psychological tests of the inventory-type, it was assumed that the item content of the test could be regarded as a kind of surrogate for observed behavior. Thus, if one wished to know whether a person was easily embarrassed one very obvious procedure would be to observe the individual in a variety of social situations. A plausible alternative seemed to be a psychological test instrument loaded with items such as "I am easily embarrassed." Ultimately, however, it became clear that such items could not be taken at face value nor as surrogates for observed behavior, and for at least two reasons. In the first place, there is no good theoretical reason to suppose that individuals necessarily *know* such important things about themselves. And indeed, there are many important facets of their personalities and of their behaviors of which people remain wholly or partially unaware. In the second place, there is every reason to believe that even when people are aware of their attitudes they will often go to considerable lengths to conceal them from others. Thus, the interpretation of an MMPI personality profile does *not* involve an assumption of intrinsic truth or face validity for the item content. For example, the validity of an item like "My parents find more fault with me than they should" does not rest upon the behavior of the parents, but rather upon what things we know (or can find out) about people who mark the item as *true*. In the case of the MMPI, the items are grouped together in empirically derived scales based on known psychological and psychiatric characteristics of patients who respond to the items in certain ways.

The rationale for this extremely empirical approach to scale construction was first set forth in a now classic paper by Meehl (1945) who more recently characterized the procedure as "insufficiently theoretical and psychometrically simplistic" (Meehl, 1971, p. 245). It is an approach also severely taken to task recently by Jackson (1971). Of course, the effectiveness of any test-derivation procedure is at least, in part, subject to experimental investigation. In the only such investigation carried out thus far, Hase and Goldberg (1967) found it neither superior nor inferior to *rational* approaches to test or scale derivation of the sort advocated above by Jackson.

There are four validity scales and ten basic clinical scales which make up an MMPI personality profile. (It should perhaps be mentioned that there are a large number of experimental scales based on the MMPI and new scales are constantly being reported in the literature; Dahlstrom, Welsh, and Dahlstrom, 1972.) The basic MMPI scale names and numbers are presented in Table 2.

The scale numbers are particularly important in coding the personality profile, which is an essential step in using the second and third sections of this book. The function of coding is to provide a convenient means of identifying some of the salient characteristics of the profile, especially with respect to its pattern or type. It is widely recognized in the clinical use of the MMPI (as in many other psychological test instruments) that the "meaning" of a particular scale elevation may vary, depending on the magnitude and elevation of other scales on the profile. For example, in the two profiles in Figure 1, scale 4 (Pd) attains an identical magnitude; but the clinical consequences (*i.e.*, the interpretation) would be quite different for the two cases. This is analogous to saying in the Rorschach, for example, that zero M responses in a 15 response record must be interpreted differently from an absence of M in a 100 response record.

Table 2. *Basic MMPI Scales*

Validity Scales	No. of Items	Clinical Scales		No. of Items
? Cannot say		1 Hs Hypochondriasis.		33
L Lie .	15	2 D Depression .		60
F Frequency .	64	3 Hy Conversion hysteria.		60
K Correction.	30	4 Pd Psychopathic deviate .		50
		5 Mf Masculinity-femininity .		60
		6 Pa Paranoia .		40
		7 Pt Psychasthenia.		48
		8 Sc Schizophrenia .		78
		9 Ma Hypomania.		46
		0 Si Social introversion.		70

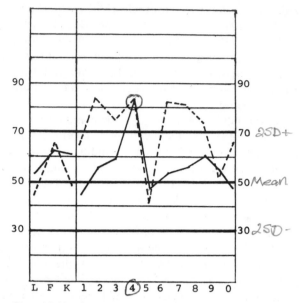

Fig. 1. MMPI profiles with identical scores on <u>scale 4</u> (Pd) which would be interpreted differently because of profile pattern differences.

In Figure 1, the *solid line* profile would indicate an individual superficially pleasant and affable, suffering no subjective distress, but quite easily angered when crossed; prone to acts of impulsivity some of which might be of an antisocial nature. The *broken line* profile would be more likely to indicate an overtly angry, consistently resentful person with an exaggerated need for affection, hypersensitive to criticism and generally mistrustful. The scores in Figure 1 are T scores (*i.e.*, standard scores) rather than raw scores. For some scales a given T score will correspond to a different raw score for male and female subjects. For example, on scale 2 (Depression) a T score of 60 for female subjects corresponds to a raw score of 22, whereas for male subjects the corresponding raw score is 26. The T score 50 is arbitrarily assigned the mean value, and the scores 70 and 30 represent two standard deviations from the mean in upper and lower directions, respectively. A "normal" MMPI personality profile is one which has no scale scores outside these limits. In practice, scores of 30 and below are encountered only rarely (with exception of scale 5 (Mf) for female subjects), and the significance of these has yet to be explored experimentally.

The procedure in coding the MMPI profile is quite simple. One uses the numbers assigned to the clinical scales as indicated in Table 2, writing the scale numbers in order of descending magnitude of elevation. Using the *broken line* profile in Figure 1, the method may be easily illustrated:

No.	1	2	3	4	5	6	7	8	9	0
Scale	Hs	D	Hy	Pd	Mf	Pa	Pt	Sc	Ma	Si
T-Score	66	83	76	85	40	85	80	74	52	68

Hathaway Code: 462738'01-5
Welsh Code: 4627"38'01-9/5

In the Hathaway (1947) code, all scale numbers precede a prime (') when the scale magnitudes are 70 or greater (T scores). Since scale 4 (Pd) has the highest T score in Figure 1 it is written first, and followed by scale 6 (Pa) which is next in magnitude. Scales with T scores lower than 70 and higher than 54 appear to the right of the prime and these are then followed by a dash (−); in this case, scales 0 (Si) and 1 (Hs). In the Hathaway coding system no scale is coded which has T scores within the range of 54 to 46. Thus, in the example, scale 9 (Ma) does not appear in the code. Following the dash the code continues with the *lowest* scale in the profile which has a T score value less than 46. It happens that in the example there is only one scale, 5 (Mf) which fulfills this requirement. Had any of the other scales been less than 46, they, too, would have followed the dash and in *ascending* order of magnitude, with the lowest scale immediately following the dash, as has already been indicated. In contrast to the Hathaway code, the Welsh (1948) code records *all* scales and omits none, and in descending order of magnitude throughout the entire code. In this coding system, an asterisk follows all scales at 90 or above; there are none in this profile. Scales between 89 and 80 are coded to the left of a double prime ("); in this case, scales 4, 6, 2, and 7. To the left of the single prime (') appear all scales between 79 and 70; in this case, scales 3 and 8. To the left of the dash (−) all scales between 69 and 60 are recorded; in this case, scales 0 and 1. Scales between 59 and 50 (scale 9 in this instance) are followed by a slash (/). Scales between 49 and 40 (scale 5 in this profile) are coded to the left of a colon (:), and scales below 40 to the left of a sharp (#); there are none in the example. Comparing the two coding systems, Dahlstrom, Welsh, and Dahlstrom (1972, p. 74) point out that the Hathaway code is a good deal more variable, since it omits scales with certain magnitudes, as indicated above; that the code order changes in the Hathaway code but remains constant for the Welsh system; that the position of the highest scale is variable in the Hathaway system (*e.g.*, it may be the *last* scale in a profile which has no elevations higher than 46), but constant in the Welsh system; and that the position of the lowest scale is comparably variable. It should perhaps be noted that in this book low scales as well as elevation symbols are ignored (in the code typing), and descriptions are presented in association with the first two or three scales in magnitude (*e.g.*, 2-7, 2-7-4, etc.).

THE VALIDITY SCALES

The function of the validity scales is to shed some light upon factors which permit one to accept the clinical profile with some confidence or indicate that extreme caution must be exercised in the profile interpretation. The first of these validity scales is the "cannot say" (?) scale. The raw score on the ? scale is made up of the number of items which are omitted from the answer sheet in the booklet or group form of the test or the number of items filed behind the "cannot say" category in the card form. Failure to answer an item which appears on one or more MMPI scales (not all items appear on the basic scales, and some items appear on more than one of the scales) has the effect of deleting the item from the scale. It can readily be seen that if enough items are omitted from any one of the scales the scale score is lowered, and in this way a piling up of ? items can contribute to profile invalidity. In construction of the present code-types, however, instructions to the patients did not include provision for failing to answer any item; that is, patients were instructed to answer all items.

Scale L

The L (Lie) scale is made up of 15 items which had been previously tested in research on deceit by Hartshorne and May (1928). In effect, these items (see Table 3) provide 15 opportunities throughout the test for the subject to lay claim to certain social virtues (*e.g.,* answering *false* to the item "I do not always tell the truth"). Since, presumably, individuals would be expected to entertain *some* feelings of virtue, one would expect a number of these items to be answered in the so-called "lie" direction by most people. And in fact the mean number of items answered in this direction by "normal" adults is 4, whereas 7 or more items are rarely so answered. The distribution of raw scores is decidedly skewed, the scores bulking at 4 and below. A high score on this particular scale reflects a tendency to put oneself in a favorable light; and it may be presumed that such a tendency would also operate in answering the items on the other scales. Thus, an elevated L score should alert one to the possibility that the individual is dissembling not only on that scale but on the clinical scales as well. However, there are other possibilities for interpretation of an elevated L scale. An individual who really believes in his own virtues might well record this perception of himself in an elevated score. It will be apparent that interpreted in this way the L scale ceases to be regarded as purely a validity indicator and takes on, additionally, the characteristics of a personality indicator. Thus, "rigidity,"

Table 3. *Illustrative L Items*

Item	Direction
Once in a while I think of things too bad to talk about .	F
I do not always tell the truth.	F
Sometimes when I am not feeling well I am cross .	F
I would rather win than lose a game .	F

"naivete," and "lack of insight" are characterizations often assigned to high L scale respondents. It is for this reason, no doubt, that Dahlstrom and Welsh (1960, p. 128) state that ". . . for many of these subjects the responses that they give on the L scale are not entirely the result of an artificial facade behind which they intend to evade the test, but in some important ways are a reflection of their own pervasive view of themselves." When answering the MMPI items under instructions which presumably induce a "set" to claim socially desirable characteristics, psychiatric patients will obtain higher L scores. More specifically, adult hospitalized patients obtain elevated L scores when following instructions to "answer these (MMPI) items as you expect to feel when you get out of the hospital." The clinical profile obtained under such instructions has been called the "projected discharge" profile. This projected discharge profile provides interesting and important information about the patient and is included in the actuarial descriptions which appear in the adult section.

A good deal remains yet to be learned about the deceptively simple looking L scale of the deceptively simple looking MMPI. That the consequences of an elevated L score are not simple and clear-cut is illustrated by the two personality profiles in Figure 2, both obtained from patients at the Kansas University Medical Center. The validity scales for these two patients are quite comparable and both have elevated L scores. The *solid line* represents the profile of a 64 year-old woman with 12 years of education who was diagnosed a "chronic brain syndrome"; the *broken line* profile, a 35 year-old secretary with 3 years of

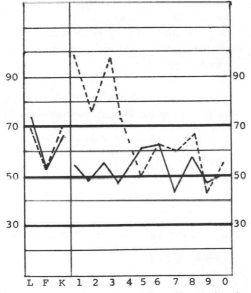

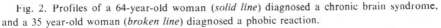

Fig. 2. Profiles of a 64-year-old woman (*solid line*) diagnosed a chronic brain syndrome, and a 35 year-old woman (*broken line*) diagnosed a phobic reaction.

business college, diagnosed a "phobic reaction." In the *solid line* profile the defensiveness and denial represented in the L scale elevation appear to permeate the entire clinical profile; *something*, surely, is being denied, although it is impossible to say what this is from the profile itself. About all that can be said is that the socially undesirable (and pathological) thoughts, behaviors, and dispositions are being consistently bypassed. In contrast, and notwithstanding the high L score, the *broken line* profile suggests that the patient was denying very little, admitting some rather unusual and odd things about herself.

Scale F

The origin of the choice of letter for the F scale is lost in the history of the MMPI. Possibly the "frequency" idea was involved. At any rate, such an idea would make sense in view of the nature and construction of the F scale. It consists of 64 items (one of the longest of the MMPI scales) which have a high community agreement; that is, items to which at least 90% of the normal subjects in the original standardization group respond in the same direction. It is irrelevant whether the item is answered *true* or *false*; the point is, that whatever the direction of response, the agreement is at least 90%. Thus, every time a subject answers in the rare direction he is deviating from the community on some subject in which it is in exceedingly high agreement. Therefore, a high raw score on the F scale is obtained when an individual answers the scale in a most unusual way as compared with people in general. Since the odds are 0.90 or better for any given item that the normal subject will answer in the popular direction, it is not surprising that the mean for the F scale is 3 items in the "abnormal" or "deviant" direction. Since the F scale was developed in this purely empirical fashion, it is hardly a matter for surprise that there should be no intuitively obvious psychological homogeneity in the item content (see Table 4).

A discussion of the kind of information which is contained in this scale might well begin with the profiles in Figure 3. Both profiles were obtained from the

Table 4. *Illustrative F Items*

Item	Direction
My father was a good man .	F
I have a cough most of the time.	T
It would be better if almost all laws were thrown away .	T
My soul sometimes leaves my body .	T
I like to study and read about things that I am working at .	F
It does not bother me particularly to see animals suffer .	T

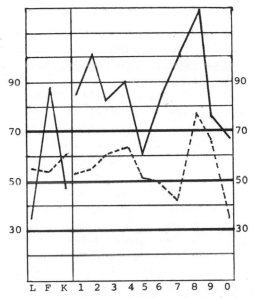

Fig. 3. Admission (*solid line*) and projected discharge (*broken line*) profiles of a 34-year-old schizophrenic man.

same patient, the second (*broken line*) within 6 days of the first (*solid line*), and illustrate quite dramatically the sensitivity of the F scale to the set assumed by the subject in responding to the test. The first (*solid line*) profile was obtained under "usual" conditions; that is, the test was administered as it is usually administered, with instructions simply to answer the questions. The set induced by the second set of instructions was quite different; these instructions required the patient to answer the questions the way she would expect to respond when she got out of the hospital. The profile obtained under these instructions we have labeled "projected discharge." If we now inquire what factors might have led to the initial elevations of the F score we can certainly eliminate one possibility with complete confidence. This particular F score (raw scores = 20), almost certainly did not come about as a consequence of inability to read or understand the items. This is one possibility, however, which must always be entertained in the presence of an elevated F score, although the value of F is likely to be somewhat higher than 20 in that event. That is, a subject who, as a consequence of low intelligence or reading deficit, cannot understand the content of the items will be responding to them in a somewhat random fashion; and this inevitably leads to an elevation of the F score. With such a radical change in clinical profile elevation resulting from the change in instructions, this possibility must be dismissed. This is, of course, no trivial matter in interpreting the MMPI clinical profile; for, if one were to decide that a particular F score was in fact produced by inability to understand the items, one would then have to regard the profile as invalid and devoid of useful information. One may also reject the hypothesis that the F scale elevation results from deliberate lack of cooperation. Such a lack of cooperation would result in the kind of profile which is obtained when responses occur to the items in a random fashion; and the result, again, is an untrustworthy clinical profile, along with an elevated F score. Evidence either against inability to understand the items or against noncooperation may be found in Figure 3 in the admission (*solid line*) profile; scale 5 (Mf) is too low and scales 2 (D), 4 (Pd), and 7 (Pt) are too elevated for the typical random response to the items (see Figure 5). In this case, the elevated F score most probably reflects the idiosyncratic, unusual, and "odd" character of the patient's thought processes. The diagnosis in this instance was schizophrenia.

In the more than 1200 profiles which, in one way or another, were studied in connection with the adult section of this book, the F scale overwhelmingly behaved in just the manner illustrated in Figure 3. However, there were discovered a small group of patients whose MMPI's were quite different. They appeared unable to "project" themselves into the future and to conceive of themselves in a more "normal" fashion. The profile of one such patient is presented in Figure 4. Here the F scale in the projected discharge (*broken line*) profile, and the clinical scales are, if anything, more deviant than before. Although we have not completed the careful studies such patients deserve, it is distinctly our impression that, on discharge from the hospital, they are rated as relatively unchanged or "worse" insofar as their psychological state is concerned. Interestingly, Grayson and Olinger (1957, p. 77) report a significant relationship between degree of improvement when simulating normalcy and hospital status 3 months later. In summarizing their findings they state that "Improvability on the (MMPI) test appears to be a favorable prognostic indication of early hospital discharge."

The F scale, in addition to being sensitive to random responding, instructional set, inability to comprehend the items, and failure to cooperate, will also reflect "faking bad" approaches to the test. That is, individuals who, for whatever reason, wish to convey an impression of being "emotionally disturbed" (*e.g.*, in attempting to obtain discharge from the armed services) will most frequently answer the items in a way which results in F scale elevation along with clinical scale elevations (see Figures 6, 7, and 9). It would appear that when nonpatients approach the MMPI with a view to conveying the impression of psychological illness they decidedly tend to overclaim symptomatology; and that, moreover, they include odd statements which do not appear on the clinical scales but which do contribute to F elevation. Here a strong note of caution is indicated against an oversimplified use of any "dissimulation index" to detect conscious authentic malingering (in contrast to "experimental malingering" induced by a set of instructions). It is not at all certain that an individual who deliberately sets out to fake an emotional disturbance in an attempt to obtain insurance damages following an accident will approach the test with the same set as the experimental subject instructed to fake such an emotionally disturbed state.

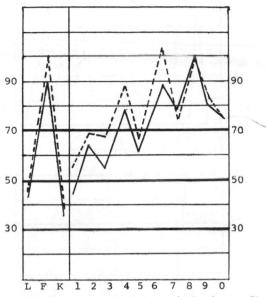

Fig. 4. Admission (*solid line*) and projected discharge (*broken line*) profiles of a 25-year-old schizophrenic woman.

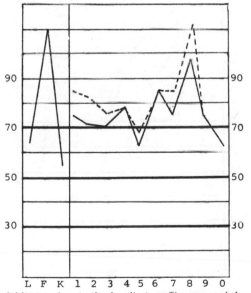

Fig. 5. Female (*solid line*) and male (*broken line*) profiles expected theoretically from a *random* response to the items.

The considerations thus far discussed do not exhaust all psychological sets which may affect the F scale of MMPI. It sometimes happens that a "bona fide" patient, that is, one with an authentic psychiatric and psychological

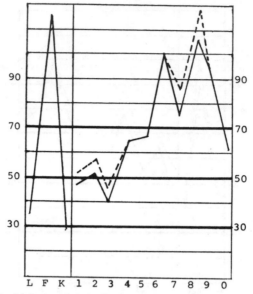

Fig. 6. Female (*solid line*) and male (*broken line*) profiles expected when answering each item *true*.

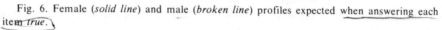

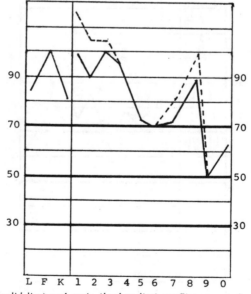

Fig. 7. Female (*solid line*) and male (*broken line*) profiles expected when answering each item *false*.

disturbance, overstates his case in a "flag waving" fashion. This overstatement of symptomatology, resulting in an elevated F and elevated clinical scales, appears to have as its objective a "loud" signaling for some kind of help. Although such

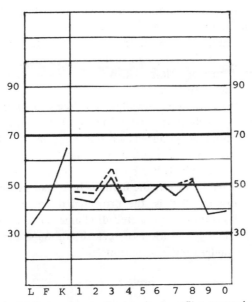

Fig. 8. Female (*solid line*) and male (*broken line*) profiles expected when answering each item in the direction of the *majority of normals*.

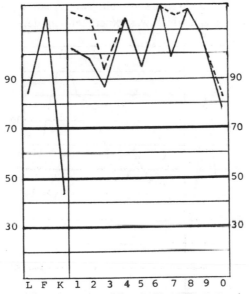

Fig. 9. Female (*solid line*) and male (*broken line*) profiles expected when answering each item in the direction *opposite to that of the majority of normals*.

profiles should be "underinterpreted," the profile itself probably cannot yield the crucial clue concerning the motivation of the patient. Rather, other knowledge of the patient and of the patient's situation is likely to provide this.

As an example, we may cite a young woman whose MMPI at the time she was discharged from the hospital yielded a markedly elevated F score and marked elevations on several clinical scales. Investigation revealed that the patient did not at all wish to leave the hospital and that she was being coerced to leave by her parents. She took this occasion to overstate her psychological state in an attempt to remain in the hospital.

The correlation between the F scale and scale 8 (the schizophrenia or Sc scale) in the individual case is nicely portrayed in Figure 10, which presents two MMPI profiles of a 21 year-old hospitalized schizophrenic male patient. The first profile (*solid line*) was obtained upon administration under usual conditions with the usual instructions. The other profile (*broken line*) was obtained when the patient was instructed to answer the items as he would expect to respond on discharge from the hospital; that is, the projected discharge instructions. The sharp decline in the F score with projected discharge set is accompanied by an extraordinary decline in the elevation of scale 8, although the profile remains clearly abnormal even under these instructions.

Scale K

The last of the validity scales to be considered is the K scale, which operates both as a correction scale for a number of the clinical scales and as an indicator of certain personality characteristics as well. The earliest versions of the MMPI did not include the K scale, which was experimentally developed later to meet

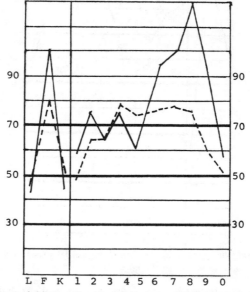

Fig. 10. Admission (*solid line*) and projected discharge (*broken line*) profiles of a 21-year-old schizophrenic man.

some of the difficulties and failures in identifying patients encountered when the MMPI began to be used. Experience with the early test revealed "test misses" in which adults with psychiatric disturbances, hospitalized on a psychiatric ward, achieved "normal" profiles. Fifty such profiles (25 male and 25 female) were selected for analysis and for comparison with the responses of the group from the general population which had been used in the original standardization. This analysis yielded 22 items which could operate to correct for certain test misses. High scores on these items helped to identify "false negatives"; that is, instances in which a patient who *should* have obtained an abnormal clinical profile actually obtained a normal one. Low scores on these items helped to identify "false positives"; that is, instances in which presumably normal persons obtained abnormal profiles. However, the success of the new scale was marred by failure to pick up many patients who were severely depressed as well as patients diagnosed as schizophrenic. In an attempt to correct this failure, 8 additional items were selected for inclusion in the scale. These items had to meet two criteria: (1) they had to be insensitive to changes in psychological set, so that they were answered in the same direction by subjects operating under "fake good" or "fake bad" experimental instructions; and (2) the responses to these items by normal subjects had to be different from responses by the schizophrenic and depressed criterion patients. These 8 items added to the 22 already mentioned form the 30 item K scale. The primary function of the K scale, then, is to improve the operation of the clinical scales. Responses to K items (see Table 5) indicate a tendency to deny problems, worries, and feelings of inferiority and a Pollyanna-like tendency to look at others (and at oneself) through rose-tinted glasses (*e.g.*, "I think nearly anyone would tell a lie to keep out of trouble" is scored for K if answered false).

The influence of the simultaneous operation of scale K with scales F and L is reflected in the MMPI profile of a 31 year-old schizophrenic woman presented in Figure 11. The clinical scales of the profile on admission (*solid line*) are markedly elevated in the context of low L and K scores which reflect a tendency

Table 5. *Illustrative K Items*

Item	Direction
I have very few quarrels with members of my family.	T
Criticism or scolding hurts me terribly .	F
I certainly feel useless at times .	F
I think nearly anyone would tell a lie to keep out of trouble	F
I worry over money and business .	F
I have never felt better in my life than I do now .	F

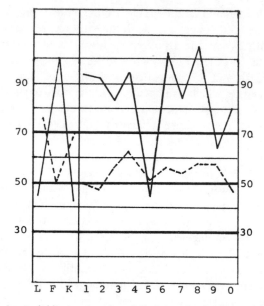

Fig. 11. Admission (*solid line*) and projected discharge (*broken line*) profiles of a 31-year-old schizophrenic woman.

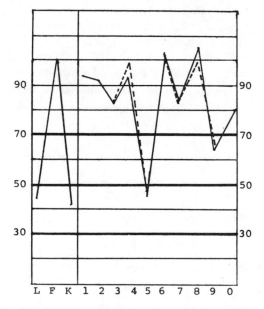

Fig. 12. K-corrected (*solid line*) and uncorrected (*broken line*) profiles of the patient depicted in Figure 11.

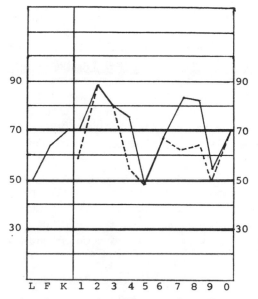

Fig. 13. Difference in code type and profile pattern between K-corrected (*solid line*) and uncorrected (*broken line*) profiles of a 41-year-old hospitalized woman.

to admit symptoms and worries quite freely, a tendency which is associated also with an elevated F score. The psychological set induced by the projected discharge instructions leads to symptom denial, resulting in the precipitous rise of L and K scores and the equally sharp decline in the F score—all this accompanied by a corresponding decline in the clinical scales. The influence of the K scale correction on the profile pattern and code-type is illustrated with the same patient in Figure 12. Since the K score operates statistically to correct some scales (1, 4, 7, 8, and 9) but not others (2, 3, 5, 6, and 0) and, moreover, corrects in differential proportions (0.5K on 1, 0.4K on 4, 1K on 7 and 8, and 0.2K on 9), the net effect is often to change the profile code. In the present case, the change from 8-6 (corrected) to 6-8 (uncorrected) has trivial psychological consequences since the two profiles share a common actuarial description. Not all pattern changes are so innocuous, however, and Figure 13 illustrates a code or pattern change which does have considerable psychological implications. The corrected 2-7-8 profile would, in this case, entail an actuarial description quite different from that of the uncorrected 2-3-6 profile.

Since, at the present state of development, experimental evidence provides no specific set of rules for identifying the MMPI variables which could tell the working clinician how he might use the K scale correction with maximal efficiency, we concur in the recommendations of Dahlstrom, Welsh, and Dahlstrom (1972, p. 129) ". . . that any MMPI worker who has the appropriate records, criterial data, and time . . . systematically compare MMPI profiles drawn in both ways with nontest information on the case." At the same time, we should remind the reader that in the adult section the codes were developed with K corrections.

The patterning of the validity scales L, F, and K is a matter of considerable interest. In our study of more than 1200 adult profiles, we found that only two of the code-types represented in this book were associated with a "V" pattern on the validity scales, all others being associated with an inverted "V" pattern (∧). One of the code-types associated with the "V" patterning of L, F, and K scales is the 3-1 (or 1-3). Patients of the 3-1 and 1-3 type tend to "funnel" their conflicts into somatic symptoms while at the same time denying subjective worries or problems, thereby obtaining higher L and K scores. The other code-type with this "V" pattern on the validity scales is the normal K+ code in which all clinical scales are kept below 70. These patients, although all hospitalized, manage to produce clinical profiles which do not *look* abnormal (though some may be borderline); and the same denial of symptoms which leads to this normal appearing profile also leads to elevations on the L and K scales.

THE CLINICAL SCALES

Scale 1

In first position on the clinical profile is the MMPI scale which was first to see the light of publication, and which was based on the responses of 50 cases of hypochondriasis. Such patients typically express their psychological and emotional conflicts through somatic channels, manifesting persistent and often extreme preoccupations concerning physical health. These 50 criterion patients were studied at great length as inpatients, and extreme care was exercised to eliminate persons who might be classified as psychotic as well as patients with evidence of some organic basis for their complaints. However, early forms of scale 1 yielded too many "false positives" (*i.e.,* high scores for patients who clinically betrayed no marked preoccupation with bodily health or bodily functions) and it became necessary to introduce a set of "suppressor" items to act as a correction for this tendency. These suppressor items constituted a correction scale within the hypochondriasis scale called C_H. The C_H score was subtracted from the original scale score to yield a final score for the entire scale. When the K scale was later developed as a correction scale, it performed the correction function, replacing C_H. Some illustrative items from the 33 item 1 scale are presented in Table 6. A quick reading reveals that their content is diffuse rather than localized in one or two body areas or systems, and that there is nothing subtle about items. Patients who have scale 1 as the highest peak of the profile are usually self-centered, focus heavily on their bodily symptoms, are reluctant to accept "psychological" sources of symptomatology, and demand a great deal of attention. High scale 1 scores usually are sufficient indication for therapeutic reassurance directed toward the relief of concern over physical health.

Table 6. *Illustrative Scale 1 Items*

Item	Direction
I have a good appetite .	F
I am bothered by acid stomach several times a week .	T
I hardly ever feel pain in the back of the neck.	F
I have a great deal of stomach trouble .	T
The top of my head sometimes feels tender.	T
I have never vomited or coughed up blood .	F

Table 7. *Illustrative Scale 2 Items*

Item	Direction
I am easily awakened by noise.	T
My judgment is better than it ever was .	F
I usually feel that life is worthwhile .	F
I don't seem to care what happens to me.	T
I enjoy many different kinds of play and recreation.	F
I brood a great deal .	T

Scale 2

Scale 2 (D), which is often characterized as a "mood" scale, is quite sensitive to momentary and transient emotional states. It was designed as a measure of "degree of depression," a psychological state expressing poor morale and feelings of hopelessness and sorrow, and as these vary the scale can be expected to fluctuate. The scale was derived with a criterion group of 50 patients described as relatively "pure cases of depression" (reactive depression; manic-depressive, depressed). Since unhappiness is one of the chief characteristics of the adult psychiatric patient, it is not surprising to find that scale 2 is the most frequently elevated scale on the MMPI, and that it is the most frequent high point in an adult psychiatric population. Among adolescent patients, scale 2 appears second only to scale 4 in high-point frequency. Table 7 presents illustrative content of the 60 item scale 2.

Patients with scale 2 as a high point readily recognize their own self-depreciation, their moodiness, and their disposition to worry even over small matters. Nevertheless, it cannot be said that an elevated scale 2 is always and

Table 8. *Illustrative Scale 3 Items*

Item	Direction
There seems to be a lump in my throat much of the time .	T
Much of the time my head seems to hurt all over.	T
I am worried about sex matters .	T
Most of the time I feel blue .	T
I like to read newspaper articles on crime .	F
I can be friendly with people who do things which I consider wrong .	T

necessarily a bad prognostic sign. To the extent that it reflects an unhappiness with one's self-concept and an attendant willingness to change, or to try to change, it may be a prognostically hopeful sign.

Scale 3

Quite early in the history of the MMPI an attempt was made to develop a scale which would be useful in the identification of patients suffering from conversion hysteria. The 59 items comprising scale 3 (Hy), differentiated a main criterion group of 50 hospital patients diagnosed under this clinical label. Table 8 presents some of these items.

An examination of scale 3 content reveals three clusters or groups: somatic items (*e.g.,* "There seems to be a lump in my throat much of the time"); items presenting a personality picture of superior adjustment, answered in the same direction as persons in general but with a much higher frequency rate (*e.g.,* "I can be friendly with people who do things which I consider wrong"); and, somewhat paradoxically, a subset of items reflecting sadness and lack of satisfaction, though not necessarily psychiatric involvement (*e.g.,* "I am worried about sex matters"). The rather distinctive psychology of the hysteric is reflected in the fact that the adjustment items and the somatic items are negatively correlated for normal subjects but highly positively correlated for hysterics. A significant positive correlation occurs between scale 1 and somatic scale 3 items not only because of item overlap but because of common mechanisms operating in the high 1 and 3 profiles. Perhaps the greatest difference between these two groups is to be found in their emotional tone or affect. The familiar and classical "belle indifference" of many hysterics constitutes a bland emotional reaction which is different from the dour, querulous picture presented by so many hypochondriacal patients. This association of bland affect with physical complaints is expressed in the MMPI in the 3-1/1-3 profile pattern which has become known in the literature as the "conversion V." The test counterpart of the clinical "belle indifference" is quite plausible; that is, there appear real somatic complaints (contributing to elevation of scale 1) together with bland emotional unconcern (keeping scale 2 down) and denial of anxieties and fears (by endorsing the subtle items and raising scale 3). Quite consistently such patients are perceived by others as immature and egocentric, and by clinicians as using their symptoms to evade responsibilities and to escape from stressful and unpleasant situations.

Scale 4

In discussing scale 4 (Pd), it would be quite possible to become lost in a long and probably fruitless discussion concerning the nature of the "psychopathic personality." Probably no diagnostic group, with the possible exception of the schizophrenias, has been the subject of such extensive discussion, including questions as to whether the diagnostic category is a "wastebasket" category or a meaningful one. We shall not enter into such a discussion but simply content ourselves with noting that the criterion subjects used in the derivation of scale 4 were probably as homogeneous as those used in developing some of the other scales and perhaps *more* homogeneous than the subjects used in developing scale 8 (the schizophrenic scale). The criterion group with which scale 4 was developed consisted of 100 subjects of both sexes ranging in age from 16 to 22, all of whom had histories of delinquency so characteristic of the psychopath. These subjects all had notable difficulties in maintaining satisfactory personal relationships, were superficially genial but easily angered or irritated, often acted hastily and impulsively, and, although quite bright in measured intelligence, were unable to profit from experience in the sense that other people do. It was as though, notwithstanding their intelligence, these individuals were unable to anticipate the consequences of their behavior, to predict the responses they would elicit from others, or to learn those anticipatory anxieties which operate to deter most people from committing antisocial behavior. This does not mean that terms like "guilt," "shame," and "embarrassment" were not in their vocabulary (although even this extreme phenomenon does occasionally occur); they were. But one gets the impression from such people that they "know the words but not the music." So far from experiencing authentic guilt or shame, they typically project the blame for the difficulties, in which they perennially get themselves involved with others, on their environment. In this way, they manage to convey a sort of paranoid tinge. In moments of genuine threat, as when facing the possibility of prison because of some violence to society, they typically betray nervousness and concern. Presented in Table 9 is the content of the 50 item scale 4. An inspection of this table reveals items covering several areas of behavior and affect: family disaffection ("At times I have very much

Table 9. *Illustrative Scale 4 Items*

Item	Direction
At times I have very much wanted to leave home.	T
I have never been in trouble with the law .	F
I am easily downed in an argument .	F
My daily life is full of things that keep me interested .	F
I am sure I get a raw deal from life.	T
My parents and family find more fault with me than they should.	T

wanted to leave home"), social maladjustment ("I have never been in trouble with the law"), freedom from worry or care ("I am easily downed in an argument"), boredom ("My daily life is full of things that keep me interested"), and paranoid proclivities ("I am sure I get a raw deal from life"). Among adolescents, scale 4 is the most frequently elevated scale on the MMPI, and it is also the most frequent high point in an adolescent psychiatric population.

Scale 5

Scale 5 (Mf), is comprised of 60 items which primarily reflect both masculine and feminine interest patterns. The scale was originally derived from the responses of a small but carefully selected group of 13 homoerotic male inverts who had been screened for their relative freedom of neurotic, psychotic, and psychopathic disorders. Retained were those items which were answered differently by the criterion subjects as compared with men in general. The items were also tested on groups of more feminine men as measured by the Terman Miles Attitude Interest Analysis. Although the responses of men and women were also compared, this was a less important consideration in scale 5 derivation. For either sex, high T scores indicate an interest pattern in the direction of the opposite sex; but, in themselves, they are *not* sufficient evidence of homosexual practices. High scoring men are usually passive and dependent, whereas high scoring women are usually dominant with marked masculine protest. Low scores for women may often represent an almost masochistic passivity.

Examination of scale 5 content (see Table 10) shows that the items cover several broad areas of interest and behavior: hobbies ("I like collecting flowers or growing house plants"), kinds of work ("I think I would like the work of a building contractor"), personal sensitivities ("I think that I feel more intensely than most people do"), social activities ("I like to go to parties and other affairs where there is lots of loud fun"), sexual proclivities ("I am very strongly attracted by members of my own sex").

Table 10. *Illustrative Scale 5 Items*

Item	Direction
I like collecting flowers or growing house plants .	T
I think I would like the work of a building contractor .	F
I very much like hunting.	F
I think that I feel more intensely than most people do.	T
I am very strongly attracted by members of my own sex .	T *a*
I like to go to parties and other affairs where there is lots of loud fun .	F

a Scored F (false) for females

Table 11. *Illustrative Scale 6 Items*

Item	Direction
No one seems to understand me .	T
Most people are honest chiefly through fear of being caught .	F
I believe I am being plotted against.	T
Someone has been trying to poison me.	T
Someone has control over my mind.	T
I have no enemies who really wish to harm me.	F

Scale 6

Scale 6 (Pa), is primarily an "obvious" scale of 40 items designed to measure thought characteristics labeled as paranoid. The criterion patients, although falling into more than one standard psychiatric category (primarily paranoid state, paranoid condition, and paranoid schizophrenia), did have in common the classical paranoid symptoms: ideas of reference, suspiciousness, interpersonal sensitivity, rigid and inflexible adherence to ideas and attitudes, feelings of persecution, grandiose ideas, and self-perceptions.

It will be apparent from Table 11 that some of the items are obviously bizarre in content; this is perhaps a weakness of the scale, since it would be a simple matter for an alert patient wishing to conceal his unusual thoughts to answer in the innocuous direction. And, indeed, 75% of the paranoid subjects in the Atlas of Hathaway and Meehl (1951) have T scores below 70 on this scale, whereas

Table 12. *Illustrative Scale 7 Items*

Item	Direction
I seldom worry about my health .	F
I cannot understand what I read as well as I used to .	T
I frequently find myself worrying about something .	T
Often I cross the street in order not to meet someone I see .	T
I have a habit of counting things that are not important such as bulbs on electric signs, and so forth .	T
I almost never dream .	F

30% of the paranoid patients have no scores at all above 70. This is perhaps surprising in the light of the kinds of patients paranoids *are*: suspicious and hypersensitive with a major propensity to being secretive. An interesting feature of some of items, however, lies in the fact that they are scored in the direction opposite to that which might at first be expected. For example: "Most people inwardly dislike putting themselves out to help other people," is an item scored for Pa if answered *false,* although naively one might expect this to be answered *true.*

Scale 7

Scale 7 (Pt) is a 48 item scale designed to measure personality characteristics subsumed under psychasthenia, a term introduced by Pierre Janet, and no longer widely used; included are phobic and obsessive-compulsive reactions. Persons in this category are characterized by excessive doubt, have great difficulty in making decisions, are plagued by a variety of fears, are given to obsessive preoccupation with thoughts which are often unwelcome, perform compulsive and ritualistic acts, and are often perfectionistic in their demands on themselves and others. A "psychasthenic tendency" may be manifested in the form of vague anxieties, insecurity, low self-confidence, and a view of the world as generally and diffusely threatening and hostile. Feelings of guilt constitute a pervasive affect in such people. Although the *specific* fears, preoccupations, and compulsive acts are different from individual to individual and are potentially innumerable, the personality makeup of such persons has sufficient homogeneity to comprise a recognizable common pattern. Probably only the more extreme cases find their way to a psychiatric clinic or hospital, and more are likely to be seen in a college counseling bureau. It is perhaps for this reason that there were only 20 patients in the original group with which the scale was derived. Because of the small criterion group, an item analysis was performed correlating each item with the total scale score in addition to the usual analysis which compared responses of the patient group with responses of the general population sample.

Presented in Table 12 are examples of scale 7 content. That a large number of specific phobias and compulsions do not appear on the scale can probably be accounted for on grounds already indicated; that is, the *specific* fears, preoccupations, etc., will vary from person to person and hence an item will not be endorsed with sufficient frequency to survive an item analysis. It is, therefore, the underlying personality structure which is reflected in the item content. As in other psychiatric populations, 7 is infrequently the peak score in our setting, and it is most frequently elevated in combination with scale 2.

Scale 8

Anyone familiar with the diversity of strange, odd, unusual, bizarre behavioral and thought phenomena which have been reported under the schizophrenias will recognize *a priori* the impossibility of formulating a scale designed to measure these which would be expected to have any considerable homogeneity in item content. Schizophrenia is itself exhibited in ways too complex and heterogeneous to expect this. Thus, although more research time was devoted to the development of scale 8 (Sc) than to any of the other clinical scales, it must still be considered as one of the weaker scales. Even with the introduction of the K scale correction, which materially improved the operation of scale 8, the detection rate for 50 criterion cases could not be improved beyond 60%. To the extent that anything can be said to be characteristic of the schizophrenic patient, the characteristic features are incongruity of affect and thought content and fractionation of the thought processes. As a result, the clinician talking to a schizophrenic patient often wonders "How did we get to this?" because progression toward a goal of thought is so devious and so frequently interrupted. Interest is withdrawn from the surrounding environment and these patients often give the impression of being "shut-in" and "out of this world."

Scale 8 has 78 items and is the longest of the clinical scales, yet, as has been indicated, one of the weakest. Some of the bizarre content (see Table 13) is classically associated with the general conception of schizophrenia, as is the emotional isolation (*e.g.*, "Most anytime I would rather sit and daydream than do anything else," "Even when I am with people I feel lonely much of the time"). The inadequate family relationships, also classically associated with schizophrenia, are represented in a number of the items (*e.g.*, "Once in awhile I feel hate toward members of my family whom I usually love"), as is apathy and indifference (*e.g.*, "I don't seem to care what happens to me"). Great caution should be exercised against a hasty diagnosis and labeling of patients as "schizophrenic" on the basis of scale 8 elevation, even when the magnitude of the score exceeds 70. Agitated neurotics, for example, not infrequently have

Table 13. *Illustrative Scale 8 Items*

Item	Direction
Most of the time I wish I were dead .	T
Sometimes I enjoy hurting persons I love .	T
Most any time I would rather sit and daydream than do anything else .	T
Even when I am with people I feel lonely much of the time	T
Once in a while I feel hate toward members of my family whom I usually love .	T
I don't seem to care what happens to me .	T

high scores on scale 8. Elevated 8 scores are also obtained by schizoid patients who may appear odd, eccentric, individualistic, or unconventional to their friends but who are able to maintain adequate social and vocational adjustment. In instances in which the diagnostic issue for adults is between neurosis and psychosis, the reader is advised to consult the "Rules for Profile Discrimination," in the Appendix.

Scale 9

Scale 9 (Ma), measures the milder aspects of the elevated mood in persons who have been diagnosed as manic-depressive, manics. This state (hypomania) is characterized by hyperactivity, restlessness, easy distractibility, unstable elation, insomnia, and overoptimism, accompanied occasionally by grandiosity, suspiciousness, and irascibility. Speech is usually rapid, reflecting a press of thought. The state is thought by some clinicians to be a defense against depression. The criterion group included only 24 cases, a consequence of the fact that "pure manics" are not frequently observed in the psychiatric population.

Some of the content of the 46 item 9 scale is presented in Table 14. A number of the items are face valid in the sense that they reflect characteristics in the classical description: hyperactivity (*e.g.*, "I sometimes keep on at a thing until others lose their patience with me"); press of thought (*e.g.*, "At times my thoughts have raced ahead faster than I could speak them"); and distractibility and restlessness (*e.g.*, "When I get bored I like to stir up some excitement"). There are, however, as in other MMPI scales, a number of subtle items which are not face valid and which are not theoretically explicable (*e.g.*, "I am afraid when I look down from a high place," is scored for 9 if answered *false*).

Table 14. *Illustrative Scale 9 Items*

Item	Direction
I sometimes keep on at a thing until others lose their patience with me .	T
I have never done anything dangerous for the thrill of it	F
At times my thoughts have raced ahead faster than I could speak them .	T
When I get bored I like to stir up some excitement .	T
I am afraid when I look down from a high place .	F
I don't blame anyone for trying to grab everything he can get in this world .	T

In the adult psychiatric population a low 9 score is frequently a concomitant of a high 2 score, though this is not always the case. Simultaneous elevation of 2 and 9 scores is not usual; when it does occur, the possibility of a brain syndrome should at least be considered, since about a third of adult patients with 9-2 or 2-9 profiles are ultimately so diagnosed.

Scale 0

Scale 0 (Si), is a 70 item scale measuring degree of social introversion-extroversion and is a late comer among the MMPI clinical scales. It is also the only clinical scale for which the criterion group was comprised of a nonpsychiatric (normal) sample. It was first published as the Social I. E. scale by Drake (1946). Fifty high scoring college women studied in 1944 and 1945 (men were not used in the validation study because of the danger that the war would most likely have left an extremely biased and atypical male sample on college campuses) revealed a decided tendency *not* to become involved in social groups and activities, whereas 50 low scoring college women tended to be involved in multiple groups and activities. Thus, elevation of scale 0 reflects social introversion in this sense of tending to withdraw from social contact and social activity.

Some of the scale 0 items are presented in Table 15. Items characterized by face validity would, of course, exhibit shyness, withdrawal from and/or uneasiness in social situations: (*e.g.*, "At parties I am more likely to sit by myself or with just one other person than join in with the crowd," "I find it hard to make talk when I meet new people"). It is clinically plausible that such people

Table 15. *Illustrative Scale 0 Items*

Item	Direction
At parties I am more likely to sit by myself or with just one other person than join in with the croud .	T
I wish I were not so shy .	T
I find it hard to make talk when I meet new people .	T
If given a chance I would make a good leader of people .	F
I brood a great deal .	T
Criticism or scolding hurts me terribly .	T

would also experience a more generalized brooding, uneasiness, and self-depreciation of the sort expressed in items like "I brood a great deal," and "Criticism or scolding hurts me terribly."

REFERENCES

CATTELL, R. B. *A guide to mental testing*. London: University of London Press, 1936.

DAHLSTROM, W. G., AND WELSH, G. S. *An MMPI handbook: A guide to use in clinical practice and research*. Minneapolis: University of Minnesota Press, 1960.

DAHLSTROM, W. G., WELSH, G. S., AND DAHLSTROM, L. E. *An MMPI handbook. Volume I: Clinical interpretation*. Minneapolis: University of Minnesota Press, 1972.

DRAKE, L. E. A social I. E. scale for the MMPI. *J. Appl. Psychol., 30*, 51-54, 1946.

GIBSON, J. J. The concept of the stimulus in psychology. *Amer. Psychol. 15*, 694-703, 1960.

GRAYSON, H. M., AND OLINGER. L. B. Simulation of "normalcy" by psychiatric patients on the MMPI. *J. Consult. Psychol. 21*, 73-77, 1957.

HARTSHORNE, H., AND MAY, M. A. *Studies in the nature of character. I. Studies in deceit*. New York: The Macmillan Co., 1928.

HASE, H. D., AND GOLDBERG, L. R. Comparative validities of different strategies of constructting personality inventory scales. *Psychol. Bull. 67*, 231–248, 1967.

HATHAWAY, S. R. A coding system for MMPI profiles. *J. Consult. Psychol. 11*, 334-337, 1947.

HATHAWAY, S. R., AND McKINLEY, J. C. *The Minnesota multiphasic personality inventory manual, revised*. New York: The Psychological Corporation, 1967.

HATHAWAY, S. R., AND MEEHL, P. E. *An atlas for the clinical use of the MMPI*. Minneapolis: University of Minnesota Press, 1951.

JACKSON, D. N. The dynamics of structural personality tests: 1971. *Psychol. Rev. 78*, 229-248, 1971.

MEEHL, P. E. The dynamics of "structured" personality tests. *J. Clin. Psychol. 1*, 296–303, 1945.

MEEHL, P. E. Prefatory comments to the dynamics of "structured" personality tests. In L. D. Goodstein and R. I. Lanyon (Eds.) *Readings in personality assessment*. New York: John Wiley and Sons, 1971, p. 245.

SEEMAN, W., AND MARKS, P. A. A study of some conceptions of "test" dimensions. *J. Project. Tech. 26*, 469-473, 1962.

WALES, B., AND SEEMAN, W. What do MMPI Zero items really measure: an experimental investigation. *J. Clin. Psychol. 4*, 420-424, 1969.

WELSH, G. S. An extension of Hathaway's MMPI profile coding system. *J. Consult. Psychol. 12*, 343-344, 1948.

ZUBIN, J., ERON, L. D., AND SCHUMER, F. *An experimental approach to projective techniques*. New York: John Wiley and Sons, 1965.

What Is Actuarial Description?

Many professional people have a major interest in understanding, predicting, or describing various aspects of human behavior. The politician is interested in knowing when a tempest is brewing in the polling place, how people plan to vote, and how he can influence their vote. The physician is interested not only in human illness and the probabilities of recovery (given certain treatment), but in how people cope with their illness. The clinical psychologist and psychiatrist are interested in how humans express their emotional conflicts in behavior, in problems of psychological diagnosis, in prognosis, and in remedial procedures. For the clinical psychologist and the psychiatrist there is perhaps no more important task than obtaining an accurate understanding of what his patients (or clients) are like. It is such an understanding which is conveyed when the psychologist or psychiatrist describes the personality of the patient or client. How does the clinical psychologist or the psychiatrist go about this descriptive task?

There is no question about how this has typically and historically been done. The psychologist or psychiatrist brings together data from interviews, from case history materials, from a variety of psychological tests (projective and non-projective) and organizes and integrates these data in the light of his knowledge, his experience, and his working theory. In a sense, then, we may say that all this is "funnelled or processed through his CNS (central nervous system)" and synthesized into some kind of coherent personality picture. Surely, this kind of operation is carried out hundreds or thousands of times weekly in the professional practice of clinical psychologists and psychiatrists throughout the United States.

Our concern here is in a special classification of the procedures by which the variety of data are processed so that they eventually emerge in the kind of *personality description* we have just mentioned. No doubt there are many ways in which one might classify such procedures, but the particular one of interest here is that which distinguishes them as "clinical" or "actuarial" (*i.e.*, "statistical"). In the clinical method the clinician proceeds in the manner indicated above. That is, he marshals his experience, mentally calls on explicit and/or implicit norms, and, using one or more theoretical systems, writes the personality description. We shall hereafter refer to this as clinical processing. In the actuarial method, by contrast, the transition from data to description (what we have called the processing) has a kind of mechanical quality in the sense that the descriptive statements can either be looked up in a book provided for this purpose (such a book may be characterized as a "cookbook or codebook") or can be printed out automatically by a computer which has been programmed appropriately.[1] Examples of such codebooks would be the first edition of this book (Marks and Seeman, 1963), Gilberstadt and Duker (1965), and Drake and Oetting (1959).[2]

Without prejudging the question "Must these two procedures, the clinical and the actuarial, necessarily be set in opposition to each other?" it is nevertheless possible to illustrate in a relatively clear-cut fashion how these two methods might differ procedurally. Assume that a clinical psychologist (or a psychiatrist, a resident, or a psychology intern) has some professional stake in understanding and describing a specific patient or client. He has the following information. He knows that the person in question is especially fond of cartoons which he, the clinician, would label as "hostile"; he knows, further, that this person is excruciatingly polite and deferential and is an avid collector of precious stones (being wealthy enough to indulge his tastes). Using such evidence the clinician might then formulate a miniature hypothesis to the effect that the patient is basically a hostile individual who is, however, unable to express his hostility in a forthright and direct manner, and hence needs to discharge it vicariously through the enjoyment of hostile cartoons (and probably other forms of hostile humor) and that he entertains deep-seated feelings of unworthiness which he attempts to combat (not very successfully) through his hobby of collecting precious stones. We are not concerned here with the *accuracy* of such an hypothesis nor even with the question of how one would test its accuracy, although neither of these is a trivial question. We simply wish to call attention to the nature of the procedure. The clinician makes use of his knowledge concerning some general principles, "laws," or "theories" concerning repression of hostility, the symbolic representation of personality conflict, and the like, and makes some decision in a

---

[1] The programs for any of these codebooks consist of sets of rules by which the input data classify the individual and the descriptions which are associated with the classifications. To take a deliberately absurd example, suppose a client or patient were classified: First born, IQ 135, mother had green hair. For *this* kind of person, the program might "instruct" the machine to print-out: "Person is highly introverted, prone to depression, and very self-critical." At this time, we would make a point which, because of the confusion in the literature, we may later repeat to the point of boredom: Whether we decide to call any set of descriptive statements "actuarial" has *nothing* to do with whether the statements are programmed for the computer.

[2] All of these are associated with the MMPI but obviously codebooks can be developed for any psychological test.

not wholly specifiable way concerning the manner in which the data on *this* man instantiates these general principles, laws, or theories. By instantiate, we mean represent an illustrative instance of. In this sense, for example, it could be said that the falling of a particular stone instantiates the laws of gravitational attraction, or the occurrence of a specific daydream instantiates the theory that daydreams are wish fulfillments.

An alternative procedure, however, could be pursued with these same data about the same patient. It might be that previous research had succeeded in classifying a number of individuals of this kind; that is, individuals who enjoyed hostile cartoons, collected items of high economic value, and manifested scrupulous courtesy even where others might become aggressive or disgruntled. Furthermore, quite independently and without access to these data, a number of independent judges might have described these people as "insecure" entertaining "feelings of unworthiness," and characterized them as having repressed hostility." In other words, previous experience and/or experimentation had permitted one to order such people as this patient to a *class* whose defining characteristics were precisely the behavioral characteristics manifested by this patient: enjoying hostile cartoons, etc. Thus, if there were available somewhere an "experience table" or a table in which there were recorded the adjectives and other data which were applied to persons of this class, it would be possible simply to look up these facts in the appropriate place. Given the data which specify the class, it is a simple and quite mechanical procedure to obtain the appropriate, corresponding adjectives. At risk of boring the reader we wish to repeat the point that we are not concerned here with the plausibility of the adjectives nor their accuracy; and we certainly hope that no collector of rare gems who might happen to pick up our example will be shaken thereby and feel the need for psychotherapy or analysis. We are simply interested in clarifying and illustrating, the salient differences between the two methods of procedure which have been called clinical and actuarial. In the actuarial method, the descriptive personality characteristics (*i.e.,* what we *say* about the person) are derived on the basis of specified experimental-statistical procedures which permit one to say with some degree of explicitness how the description is related to the data which classify the individual. It is these experimental-statistical procedures (which we shall hereafter refer to as actuarial processing) which are the defining property of the notion "actuarial"; and by definition any set of descriptions (irrespective of how interesting, accurate, or impressive they may be) which are derived or generated in other ways are *not actuarial.* Thus, *automated is not a synonym for actuarial;* and neither is *mechanical.* On this score the literature is unfortunately confusing. For this reason we plan later in this chapter to describe in some detail an experiment which illustrates how the statistical relationship between input data and output descriptions may be established.

The core conception of actuarial description, then, may be stated in the following way: *Actuarial descriptions consist of a set of descriptive attributes which are assigned to individuals on the basis of an explicit set of rules derived from experimentally-statistically demonstrated associations between the input data (e.g., MMPI profiles, Rorschach psychograms, word associations, birth order, socioeconomic status (SES), etc.) and the descriptive statements which constitute the output side.* Whether these descriptions are phenotypic or genotypic,[3] dynamic or static, behavioral or inferential, global or atomistic, is not at issue here although these are important considerations which we shall subsequently discuss.

To summarize, everything we shall have to say in this chapter has this central focus. There is available a set of data, which may take a variety of forms. The data are to be processed with the objective of providing either a prediction or a person description (and in either case there may be involved a decision to take some specified kind of action such as instituting psychotherapy, providing drug treatment, recommending parole, etc.). Those data may be processed through the CNS of a professional person (our primary concern will be with the clinician), who brings to bear his knowledge and experience. Or the data may be processed by being "plugged into" some actuarial (statistical) set of manipulations which will yield the required output information. We are interested in what constitutes the central features of such actuarial procedures and in what evidence may be available concerning the accuracy of such actuarial processing.

We do not, of course, presume to legislate the sense in which the phrase "actuarial description" may be used. We should, however, like at this point to indicate in greater detail how *we* use this term, what confusions exist in the literature in this area, and ways in which we believe such confusion can be cleared up.

We begin with the strongest possible recommendation that a careful distinction be maintained between the *data* which constitute the input and the *processing—i.e.*, how the data are *treated*. Much of the confusion which we shall describe appears to stem from a failure to maintain this distinction. Here are some citations which illustrate the confusion which flows from failing to separate the categories which characterize the data from the categories which characterize the processing of data:

> "The statistician argues, with good reason, that a clinician cannot hold in mind at one time all the diverse knowledge he has acquired about his patient . . . only an actuarial table or a regression equation can incorporate all the data and weigh them appropriately. Moreover, the fact that this chore can be done mechanically by a mere clerk is an unexpected but highly welcome bonus that leaves the clinician free to

---

[3] As used here, the term "phenotypic" means statements of the sort "This person cries easily," or "This person is given to frequent bursts of anger"; that is, statements about the person which require adequate *observation* but a minimum of *inference*. In contrast, "genotypic" statements might be of the sort: "This individual has a deep-seated need to fail," or "His frantic pursuit and persecution of persons he calls 'pornographers' represents a reactive defense against his own aggressively hostile sexual impulses." It seems clear that "deep-seated need to fail" and "reactive defense" are not *observed*, but rather inferred.

do what no *test* can do . . ." (Miller, 1962, p. 319) (Italics ours).

". . . in all but one of the studies (reviewed by Meehl) the statistical predictions based on the formula were equal to or superior to the predictions made by clinicians . . . . This support for *tests* (which permit arriving at scores that can be entered into formulas) . . ." (Hilgard, Atkinson, and Atkinson, 1971 p. 433) (Italics ours).

"Even factor analytic approaches, like Cattell's, are usually directed toward the construction of measuring instruments for evaluating the patterning of relevant forces or qualities that characterize particular persons. The same is true of *actuarial* devices, such as the MMPI . . . ." (Shontz, 1965, p. 8) (Italics ours).

"By opposing clinical judgment to such well developed *actuarial* techniques as the MMPI he (Meehl) at times comes dangerously close to denying any actuarial potential for the judgment approach" (Hunt, 1959, p. 175) (Italics ours).

"Extending the clinical-statistical distinction to modes of measurement suggests replacing the term *"statistical"* by the term *"mechanical"* . . . The crucial point, of course is not what the distinction is called but that the concept can be applied to measurement as well as to prediction" (Sawyer, 1966, p. 180) (Italics ours).

"There is a very important confusion in the use of computer aids for interpretation in personality assessment . . . many of the advantages which have been attributed *to computers* are in fact due to the application of *actuarial methods*" (Lanyon and Goodstein, 1971, p. 211) (Italics ours).

Careful reading of these citations indicates that the following notions or words are sources of confusion: mechanical, statistical, actuarial, psychometric (*i.e.*, tests), automated (*i.e.*, computers), presence of explicit rules, and we might add "normative." We propose to analyze these in the context of Figures 1 and 2, which present a schematic representation which can provide a guide and aid to clarifying the notions which have now become associated with the clinical-actuarial distinction.

The misunderstanding illustrated in the first two citations above (Miller and Hilgard, Atkinson and Atkinson) represents a confusion of *type of data* (*i.e.*, tests) with *method of processing*. There is an implicit logical error here; once stated explicitly there should be no further confusion. Figure 1 clearly indicates that tests are on the *data input* side and not on the *processing* (clinical-actuarial) side. The logic appears to run as follows: (1) Meehl's reviews of empirical studies indicate a general superiority in predictive accuracy for the actuarial processing of the data. (2) Many of the studies involve psychometric data on the input side, probably because the quantitative data yielded by tests led themselves easily to actuarial processing. (3) Therefore, Meehl appears to be arguing for the superiority of test over nontest data on the input side. It is, however, clearly invalid to argue from "actuarial processing of data leads to greater accuracy" to "tests are the optimal input on the data side." Similarly, it is invalid to argue from "actuarial procedures incorporate and weight the data optimally" to "psychometric data are the most powerful predictors." It would, however, be a misunderstanding of our position to interpret us as insisting that there are no legitimate questions about whether clinicians or actuarial rules perform more effectively with some kinds of data than with others. Clinicians may or may not be more effective with psychometric data. Actuarial processing may or may not be more effective with nonpsychometric data. There may be some special combination of psychometric and nonspychometric data which the clinician is especially effective in processing and this may be a different combination from that which renders the actuarial techniques more powerful either in describing persons or in predicting outcomes. These are questions which must be settled experimentally by suitably ingenious experimental designs. We shall say more about this later in connection with Sawyer's paper, already mentioned. Thus, the summary statement to this point may be put in the following way: *The general superiority of actuarial processing (as revealed in Meehl's review of the studies) does not in itself speak to the issue of what kinds of input data provide either the clinical or the actuarial processing with its most powerful data.*

A somewhat different misunderstanding is presented in the citations from Shontz and from Hunt. Both of these refer to the MMPI as an "actuarial device." In so doing they have transferred a *processing* category (see Figure 1) to the *data input* side. The MMPI is a *psychometric* device (see Figure 1) on the data

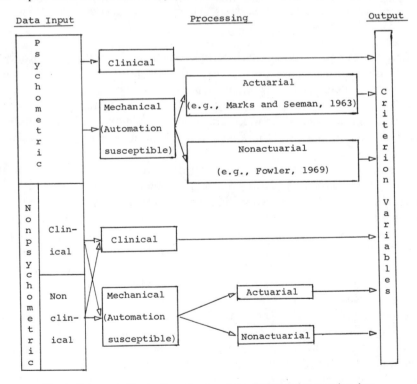

Fig. 1. Schematic illustration of ways of classifying and processing data.

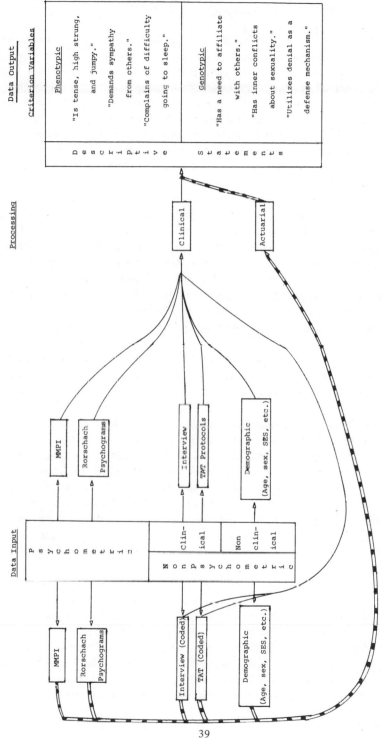

Fig. 2. Schematic illustration of types of data input processed clinically and actuarially and of types of data output or criterion information.

side. Instruments of this sort ordinarily yield as data a set of scores *which may or may not be processed actuarially*. That is, the scores may be converted to descriptive statements by the *clinician* (indeed, this is probably the most frequent procedure) or may be processed in an automatic manner through the application of a set of statistically-derived rules for assigning attributes. A very simple illustration of such an actuarially derived rule might be: "If MMPI scale 9 $<$ 45 and scale 0 = 65 to 75, assign test subject an *introversion* value of 7.5 where a value of 10 means *extremely introverted*." How such a rule might itself have been previously worked out we shall describe when we discuss the now classic actuarial-description study by Halbower.

These misconceptions are puzzlingly persistent and we can only guess at the reasons. We are reluctant to invoke a simple associationism; yet it is true that tests do yield quantitative scores and it may somehow appear more "natural" for such measures to be incorporated into an actuarial (and hence quantitative) formula or set of rules.[4] Second, it is of course, quite true that item analysis, factor analysis, and other statistical techniques are involved in psychological test development and validation. Since however, we take it as obvious that test development procedures are irrelevant to the actuarial processing of test scores *taken as data*, it becomes confusing to use the term actuarial to characterize the data.

It is possible, also, that some of the confusion is generated by the fact that in the process of deriving, of searching out, of inventing and/or selecting and adapting, and ultimately arriving at the most suitable kinds of subsequently-to-be-used descriptive statements—in this process the investigator will use highly intuitive methods. Determining the functional relationships between the data (*e.g.*, interviews, psychological test profiles, and word associations) and the descriptions to be associated with them is an experimental task; and no rules yet have been discovered or evolved for directing a researcher to bring to bear creativity and ingenuity on the task. Furthermore (and this continues to be a source of confusion) at some time prior to formulation of the rules and prior to the experimental determination of the association between data and personality description (in this sense, at a "lower" level) there may, indeed, occur one or more clinical judgments. Suppose, for example, that we were interested in assigning a numerical value to the following definition of "bacon": "that part of a pig associated with breakfast"; and that this numerical value was intended to locate this particular utterance (say by a psychiatric patient) on a "scale of autism." That is, the number is to indicate on a scale "how autistic" (how subjective and unrealistic) this statement is. Suppose, further, it was found that after considerable training a number of clinicians could reach a high reliability (a high degree of agreement) on this judgment. Our point is that *no matter how impressive the reliabilities of such judgments, they do not constitute actuarial description in the sense in which we have defined it here*. Thus, Meehl (1954*b*, p.

---

[4] The citation from Hilgard, Atkinson, and Atkinson suggests that this may be so.

17) comments that the scoring of a Stanford-Binet response involves "a process of human judgment which, no matter how reliable it can be made by short training, is still not quite clerical or mechanical in character." We labor this point because William Hunt (1959), in an otherwise penetrating and stimulating discussion of actuarial procedures and clinical judgment appears unwilling to accept this distinction. Thus, it is a confusing issue to argue, as Hunt does, for the "actuarial potentialities of clinical judgment itself" (p. 175), as it is confusing to say: "... clinical judgment is qualitatively related to psychophysical judgment, that the differences are one of quality rather than kind, that they are contrasting in amount rather than conflicting in nature, and that clinical judgment is a culturally and educationally handicapped country cousin of the psychophysical judgment, and not a different species of being" (pp. 171-172). To support his position Hunt presents good interjudge reliabilities in the judgment of "autistic" characteristics of Wechsler-Bellevue vocabulary responses ("how schizophrenic each of these responses is"). *But this is not actuarial description in our sense.* We may, perhaps, clarify this if we were to ask: Once these highly reliable judgments of the vocabulary items are given, how might the clinician then, on this evidential basis, go about describing some of the personality characteristics of the individuals who gave these responses? *It is in getting from these judgments of vocabulary items to the personality attributions that one would proceed by actuarial or by clinical methods.* Thus, the clinician might sit back and reflect on the significance of these "highly autistic" vocabulary definitions, and decide that adjectives like "shy, inhibited, withdrawn, poorly socialized" are appropriate, on the basis of his previous experience. Or, alternatively, he might reach for a "cookbook" which might assign a mean Q-sort placement of these adjectives for individuals giving vocabulary responses which are judged to fall at the high end of a rating scale of "autistic thinking." It should be clear that we are not here discussing a *factual* issue, but rather attempting to clarify a distinction in concepts; *i.e.*, we are not arguing that it is "wrong" to use the term actuarial in the sense in which Hunt uses it, but wish only to emphasize that it is important to distinguish this sense from the sense in which the term is used here in the phrase "actuarial description."

We turn next to a consideration of the concept of *mechanical*. We have already seen above that Sawyer (1966, p. 180) proposed that the term "statistical" (and hence, presumably, "actuarial") be replaced by the term "mechanical." At the same time he proposed that identical categories be adopted on the data side as well as the processing side. Thus, he would characterize the *data* as clinical or mechanical to parallel the processing side. Although in general we regard Sawyer's analysis as a valuable contribution in some ways, we find these particular suggestions (because they add to the confusion) unacceptable and we recommend against their adoption. In the first place, to say as Sawyer does, that the term "mechanical" fits all data combinations (what we have called processing) is like saying all animals are horses. For, while it is true that all actuarial procedures render the processing (what Sawyer calls combination) mechanical, it is *not* true that every set of mechanical rules must be actuarially derived. To take but two examples: At the Mayo Clinic, Pearson *et. al.* (1964) developed a set of rules which provided for the mechanical (in this case, computerized) transition from MMPI test scores to descriptive statements. No experimental-statistical derivations were involved. Hence, this represents a *mechanical* but *not an actuarial* processing of MMPI scores. A widely used automated (hence, mechanical) print-out by Roche Psychiatric Service Institute represents, again, not an actuarial derivation of rules but the distilled experience of one clinician, Fowler (1964). We are not concerned here with whether such nonactuarially derived rules might be in some instances more *accurate* (a matter for experimental investigation, and on which there are no data), but rather with maintaining conceptual clarity. We shall never understand actuarial description if we allow it to fuse with the concept of mechanical processing. With respect to the second recommendation, that identical categories be adopted on the data side and the processing side, we are again in disagreement. Not clarity but confusion appears to flow from using the *same words* to characterize what appear to be at least somewhat *different processes*. Optimally, we would prefer completely different label categories for the data from those used to characterize the data *processing*. Nevertheless, we have felt compelled to include a "clinical" subcategory on the data side for one subset of nonpsychometric data (see Figures 1 and 2). We shall say more about this later.

We next consider the role of automation as it relates to actuarial processing of data. We have already seen that "mechanical" cannot be substituted as a synonym for "actuarial." And neither can "automated" nor "computerized." Of the four most widely known and widely used automated programs and delivery systems for processing MMPI scores (the Roche Psychiatric Service Institute program (Fowler, 1964, 1969), the Mayo Clinic Program (Pearson *et. al.*, 1967), the program of Finney Institute of Human Behavior, Inc. (Finney, 1966, 1969), and Caldwell's program of Medical Psychological Services (Caldwell, 1970) *none* are actuarially derived. Such automation, of course, vastly expands the service delivery capacities. There is, however, an additional sense in which the *programming* of any set of rules so that the processing *can* be rendered automatic, guarantees that the process is mechanical. To indicate this, we have introduced into Figure 1 the phrase "automation susceptible." Our purpose is to make clear two points: (1) a truly actuarial set of rules for processing the data is totally susceptible to automation and (2) automation itself is nevertheless not a defining property of "actuarial" but of "mechanical."[5] It is this point which is made in the citation above from Lanyon and Goodstein.

We now summarize again:

1. The defining character of *actuarial description* lies in the set of rules for

---

[5] We know that in a sense a processing procedure is mechanical if it is automated. It is, however, possible to refer to a mechanical procedure which involves having a clerk look up a set of rules for interpreting scores.

processing the data, which rules express an *empirical-statistical relationship* between the output descriptions and the input data.

2. While these rules are "computer susceptible" (in the sense already indicated), whether they are *in fact* processed by a computer has no bearing on their actuarial character.

3. There are already available *nonactuarial* rules and programs some of which are processed by computer. Thus, they process data *mechanically,* but *not actuarially*. They may represent the distilled experience of a single clinician. There are at this writing to our knowledge no experimental data on their accuracy as compared with actuarially derived programs.

The relationships among types of data, methods of processing, and output descriptions have hardly been studied at all experimentally. The complexity which such relationships may take on is suggested in Figure 2. Our objective now is to examine these relationships in some detail. We are perhaps unnecessarily cautious in the first place (because it may already be obvious) in noting that Figure 2 is illustrative, not exhaustive. We could not begin to list all psychometric and all nonpsychometric sources of data which are characteristically used by the clinician. Thus, only the MMPI and the Rorschach psychograms are listed as instances of psychometric data; and similarly, the interview, TAT protocols, and demographic data as instances of nonpsychometric data. Further, there are other clinical-nonpsychometric data sources than the interview and the TAT, as there are other nonclinical-nonpsychometric types of data than demographic. Also, with respect to processing, Figure 2 is not concerned with *nonactuarial*-mechanical or automated procedures. Including the latter would multiply the complexities of data processing output relationships. Mainly, then, Figure 2 is intended: (1) to throw some light on how certain types of data can be processed with certain kinds of descriptive outputs; and (2) to suggest what interesting experimental questions might be raised. Thus, it is clear from this figure that the clinician can process a single psychometric data source (*e.g.,* the MMPI scores), a single nonpsychometric data source (*e.g.,* the interview), several psychometric types of data (*e.g.,* the MMPI and the Rorschach psychogram), several nonpsychometric types of data (*e.g.,* the interview, the TAT protocols, and various demographic facts), or any combination of these types of data. Similarly, one may elect to process actuarially only a single psychometric data source (*e.g.,* the MMPI scores), a single nonpsychometric type of data (*e.g.,* scored or coded TAT protocols), several types of psychometric data (*e.g.,* MMPI and Rorschach psychogram scores), a variety of nonpsychometric data (*e.g.,* coded interview, coded or scored TAT stories along with demographic data), or any combination of these. Figure 2 further illustrates the concept of *levels* indicated by Meehl:

> "Thus, we have immediately a question of levels, in the sense that the transition from a certain class of statements, scores, or behavioral adjectives to the prediction proper may be purely mechanical, following explicit rules; whereas this evidential class itself may consist

of members all, some, or none of which were arrived at by human judgment, at least partly inexplict. There is no need for persistent ambiguity here, since in any real case we can specify the level of data with respect to which the query "Clinical or statistical?" is being raised. That the answer varies as we treat different levels or stages of the same total predictive process is only to be expected" (Meehl, 1954, p. 17).

This concept of levels is exhibited in the coding of both the interview and the TAT stories. For the actuarial processing of such data requires, as a prior step, the transformation of the "raw material" to either a set of scores or a set of categories. And *this* step may involve a set of human judgments which, however reliable, may be partly or totally inexplicit hence, "clinical."[6] It is also obvious (see Figure 2) that although this transformation of data to coded categories is required by the nature of actuarial processing, it by no means follows that such coded data are *restricted* to the actuarial procedures. Thus, one may make available to the clinician who may have conducted the interview, all the coded data as well. Whether doing so has any *payoff* is an experimental question for which there are at this time no available data. And the criteria for payoff themselves present complex problems, for presumably there arise questions about how much time and money we are willing to commit for a specified increase in accuracy. And, as if things were not already sufficiently complicated, there are additional questions concerning the competitive power of different coding or scoring categories for the same clinical material. Meehl (1959), for example, suggests Q-sorting based on interviews as one possible coding technique. There are a number of other already developed interview coding systems and one could derive still others. It is impossible to guess how many experimental man-hours would be required to give us dependable answers about the comparative power of these coding systems. Yet one's curiosity may be piqued by all these problems because, for some persons at least, they have an intrinsic interest. It is a little like saying: There is a mountain that asks to be climbed; there are questions which beg for experimental answers.

A little reflection over Figure 2 will reveal that there are instances in which *identical* data cannot be processed both actuarially and clinically. When the clinician is processing the TAT stories and/or the interview, he has available to him *all* the raw data—the entire interview and all the protocol material. It is not so with the actuarial processing. What can be processed actuarially is only what has been transformed (or reduced) to the scores or the attribute categories. We cannot be certain, of course, of how much or what aspects of the raw material the clinician is in fact attending to or processing. And we must be cautioned against supposing that more is necessarily *better*. That is, in reducing (coding) the data for actuarial processsing we have in some sense not only abstracted but

---

[6] Thus, in the sense that this coding or scoring process by the clinician is a prerequisite for and must precede the actuarial processing, the clinical coding may be said to be at a "lower level."

subtracted so that the clinician has more material available, in that sense, then has the formula. But, to repeat: We do not know that more is better. Indeed, the very necessity of trying to "juggle" so much material and to assign optimal weights to various events (which surely means *different* weights for some events than for others!) *may* clog the clinical pipeline. Nor do we know what advantages or disadvantages may affect the clinician's ability to specify what cues are influencing his clinical processing.

As we have already indicated, the considerable number of possible data processing combinations illustrated in Figure 2, almost automatically raises experimental questions about the relative *power* of these combinations. We are not interested merely in "horserace" designs that is, in experimental designs which pit clinician against actuarial processing. Although there are occasions when it would appear legitimate to ask: given X, Y, and Z are our objectives better promoted by having the clinician reflect upon the data or by actuarial processing of those data; there are other questions at least equally important. With what kinds of data is the clinician most effective?[7] Assuming that a given variable (*e.g.*, "anxiety") plays a crucial role in the clinician's theory, do we serve the clinician better by supplying on the data side a *test* measure of that variable or a clinical judgment—or both? Does the actuarial process become more powerful when both kinds of measures are used? And, most important, what kinds of data produce *incremental* power for either the actuarial or the clinical processing? That is, starting with "minimal" data (*e.g.*, no more than certain demographic information, which is routinely and easily gathered in all cases) what increased descriptive power can be obtained by either processing method as we add one data source after another? And at what cost in time and money? Does it make a difference who picks up the tab? In private practice the bite is on the patient or client—in publicly supported clinics, not. Should the same criteria of efficiency be invoked? (We should perhaps note that the latter questions are pragmatic, administrative, policy questions which are in some sense "philosophic" rather than experimental.)

However, the fact that we do not limit our experimental questions to horserace designs which pit actuarial formula against the clinician does not mean that there may not be some important instances in which we very much want to assess the relative power of the two processes. We judge from Figure 2 that nothing would appear more natural than to ask that kind of question with respect to the processing of psychometric data and perhaps with respect to demographic data, since such data are already presented in or can easily be adapted to a format especially suitable for actuarial processing. The classic study

---

[7] But this question has not always been asked in the clinical-actuarial context. For example, Kostlan (1954) varied the data sources for his experimental clinician-subjects and found that a combination of case history and MMPI as data sources proved more powerful than combinations involving Rorschach, sentence completion, or TAT data sources. He was, however, not interested in the clinical-actuarial dialogue, and all data were clinically processed.

of this sort is one we have already mentioned and plan later to discuss, the Halbower study on interpretation of the MMPI.

We should like, now, to turn to certain considerations which might lead some clinicians to reject, out of hand, the actuarial description of personality on the assumption that such descriptions *necessarily* violate or lack certain desired essential qualities, certain properties which (they feel) can be found only in the kinds of clinical, or case study techniques which are the more conventional modes of operation in daily clinical practice. Earlier we raised the question whether such traits, dispositions, or structures as we attribute to the individual might be genotypic or phenotypic, dynamic or static, global or atomistic. We take it that any broad survey of psychiatrists and clinical psychologists with respect to desired characteristics of the descriptive language would reveal decidedly strong preferences for the genotypic over the phenotypic, for the dynamic over the static, for the global over the atomistic. That the concepts embodied in these words have strong ideological and emotive appeal and are at the core of actuarial-clinical controversies is strongly suggested by Meehl's (1954*b*, p. 5) citations on the subject. Without prejudging issues which may have tremendous (and as yet unknown) empirical weights with respect to the efficacy of certain kinds of descriptive terms, as compared with other kinds (*e.g.,* global versus atomistic), we can nevertheless examine the question of whether and to what extent the actuarial descriptive process *necessarily* and *logically* excludes certain thought-to-be-desirable characteristics. In other words, the question we are asking is this: Are there impressive or convincing reasons for assigning actuarial description (as opposed to clinical description) to a lower rank on a rating scale anchored to "dynamic" at one end and "static" at the other? In order to answer such a question we must, of course, reach some decision concerning what kinds of statements we shall be willing to admit as dynamic. It is, of course, possible to set up the actuarial in opposition to the dynamic notion by fiat, and it does seem to us that this is often done. The only appeal from such a procedure is to call attention to the inconsistencies generated when such a definition is set beside certain empirical procedures. It may be that here we are dealing again with a *sociological* cluster; that is, it may be that those clinicians who strongly favor dynamic concepts in characterizing people also happen to have little interest in or find actively distasteful and repugnant, anything which smacks of the actuarial. But, there is no logical implication from one set of notions to the other, and we shall be misled if we take these empirical correlation clusters as grounds for argument. For this reason we ask: Is there anything about the concept of dynamics in human personality which has *intrinsic* implications for actuarial procedures? The meaning given for the word "dynamic" in *Webster's New International Dictionary* (1967) is: "Belonging to, or characterized by, energy or effective action." Also: "Pertaining to change or process (regarded as a manifestation of energy or agency); involving or producing alteration; esp. viewing or designating physical phenomena with reference to the grounds of their origin and manifestation rather than in their presentational character." More succinctly, Hinsie and Campbell in their *Psychiatric Dictionary* (1960), state that in psychiatry the concept of dynamic refers to "the operation of mental forces"—an obvious parallel to the use of this term in physics. These correspond, clearly, to the ways in which the construct dynamic is most frequently used in psychology: that is, in terms of psychological "forces" or "energizers"—*e.g.,* drives, motives, needs, demands; in terms of causal agents; and in terms of changes over time. Is there some reason to believe that descriptive personality statements exhibiting these defining characteristics of the dynamic concept must be excluded from or by a set of explicit rules of attribution? Here are some examples of such statements: "He reacts against his dependency needs by manifesting a façade of superindependence and by rejecting all dependency relationships"; "He is plagued by unconscious homoerotic impulses against which he defends by constant pursuit of women"; "His Tarzan-like supermasculinity constitutes a defense against his inner uncertainty about his masculine role"; "He has strong oral-dependent needs." We can see no reason why descriptive-dynamic statements of this kind should be excluded on logical grounds from a set of descriptive statements for which explicit rules and numbers have been devised which tell the clinician under what circumstances such descriptive statements may appropriately be attributed to individual X. We are not concerned here with whether such a set of rules and numbers can, *in fact,* be derived for the MMPI or for any other psychological instrument; this question can be answered only by experimental attempts with specific psychological instruments. It might very well be that the necessary correlations could be obtained, for example, with the Cattell 16 PF but not with the MMPI, or vice versa, or with both instruments or neither instrument. Or, it might turn out that only for Rorschach psychograms could the stable correlations be generated between psychogram and sets of descriptive-dynamic statements. The essential point is that we are not permitted to decide *on logical grounds* that all possibilities of establishing or deriving specification rules are excluded. We conclude, therefore, that actuarial means of arriving at descriptive statements do not, in principle, exclude the possibility that some of these statements may have dynamic properties when these properties are defined in terms of psychological forces, causal agents, or changes over time.

It is this important point (*i.e.,* that in principle any set of data which can generate genotypic, descriptive-dynamic statements as well as phenotypic ones out of the head of the clinician, can generate them also via the actuarial pipeline) which we try to present on the illustrative output side of Figure 2. Thus, if there are in the MMPI (to take only one example) any data (*e.g.,* combined elevation of scales F, Pt, and Sc) which lead the *clinician* to conclude that the test-taker "exhibits cognitive slippage," then that conclusion can also be processed by the actuarial procedure. Similarly, if there is something in the MMPI which leads the clinician to decide the test-taking subject is struggling with "reaction formation against dependency needs" then that (genotypic) comment too can be processed by the actuarial formula. Whether such statements can be generated *accurately* by *either* clinical or actuarial processing of MMPI data is a question about experimental demonstration of test validity, a quite separate issue. And, to the extent that is is more difficult to establish the accuracy of a statement such as "The patient is driven to testing limits of love" than the accuracy of "Patient exhibits cognitive slippage," validity problems will be more troublesome for the former than for the latter kind of statement. In short, as Marks and Sines (1969) have said, our preference for "deep" and "dynamic" concepts may lead us to sacrifice validity evidence for dynamic language. Moreover, there is a growing group of behavioristically oriented clinicians (behavior therapists) who would prefer to banish these "dynamic ghosts" from the human organism. Their preference presumably would be for the phenotypic, descriptive language which leaves little room for the notion that something "underlies" the behavior. *Chacun a son gout!*

We are led, by some discussions, to understand that if actuarial methods are prejudicial to dynamic descriptions of people, these methods are even more prejudicial to *global* description. (Other terms closely associated in meaning with global are "holistic," "gestalt," and "configural.") Thus, for these clinicians, clinically-arrived-at descriptions would be rated at the global end of the global-atomistic scale, whereas actuarial descriptions would be rated at the atomistic end. What is the justification for such a position?

If one observes the behavior of the psychologist or the psychiatrist interpreting an interview or a test protocol then it seems clear that one meaning of global is an essentially *impressionistic* one. For example, most clinical psychologists working with the Rorschach, according to Hertz (1951, p. 311), "take the intuitive configural approach when they interpret a record, studying the various Rorschach scores as interrelated and interacting configurations." That is, the clinician inspects the record and the significant factors and determinants; he notes the form level (F + %), the number of populars, the ratio of movement to color (M: Σ C), etc.; he notes especially the deviations from the optimal which occur in the record; he assesses the qualitative characteristics of the responses; and, after balancing these factors against each other intuitively, he emerges with a kind of total impression of the person. In *this* sense of global, it is, of course, true that actuarial descriptions not only do not possess this quality; they are expressly designed to *eliminate* the conditions by which there appear no formal rules for arriving at the final description *i.e.,* they aim at formulating precise rules and associations which specify just *what combinations of data* permit the psychiatrist or psychologist to attribute what personality characteristics, dynamic or otherwise. Another sense in which the term global is used occurs in the context of discussion of the "whole organism" or of the "total personality." It would appear that the distinction made here is rather close to Tolman's (1949) distinction between *molar* and *molecular* levels of analysis. Yet this notion of globality is subject to some ambiguity of understanding. It is often stated, for example, that the Rorschach yields a picture of the "total personality"; yet no one would be likely to deny that some other test of personality (*e.g.*, the TAT) *adds something* to the personality picture. In what sense, therefore, can this Rorschach picture be "total?" It is perhaps for this reason that Hutt (1945, p. 125) asserts: "unfortunately, despite some claims to the contrary, the Rorschach does not yield a total clinical picture . . . ." In making this point we do not intend in any sense to cast doubt upon the Rorschach, but rather to understand what it means to have a global picture of a personality in order that we may determine whether actuarial methods of description are capable of capturing that quality. To complicate matters further, Wechsler (1958, p.7) uses the term in his definition of intelligence as the ". . . global capacity of the individual to act purposefully, to think rationally, and to deal effectively with his environment." Yet the method of achieving the global quality in the Wechsler-Bellevue and in the WAIS is "additive" in the sense that the subscale scores are added to yield a score corresponding to the IQ; and this is the procedure definitely *rejected* by many clinicians, who argue that "the whole is greater than the sum of its parts."

The essential character of the concept global as it is widely used by clinicians involves organization and interrelatedness that is, traits, dispositions, needs, etc., which are attributed to a person by a clinician in complex conjunctions and disjunctions as in the following:

1. There is a tendency to subordinate impulses in the interest of long-range goals and values, with overinhibition of the acknowledgement and expression of impulses.

2. Although there is some awareness of conflict, the defense mechanisms seem to be working effectively to protect the person against too painful an awareness of conflict . . . .

3. There is considerable affectional anxiety, with much emphasis upon introspection as a method of dealing with it. However, it is suggested that the person's insight is limited, at present, chiefly by fear of seeing relationships between various aspects of experience.

Psychologists who are acquainted with reports which are typically written in clinical settings will be familiar with this kind of personality description. (The above represents, of course, an extremely limited sampling of statements from a complete report.) In order to make such descriptions amenable to quantitative measurement and study, such descriptions have been adapted to Q-sort technique. Although Q characterizations preserve the global character of the personality *in the sense just indicated,* they do *not,* as Meehl (1954*b*, p. 13) points out, represent configuration or patterning in another sense *i.e.,* in the sense that an increment in any personality variable is itself dependent upon another variable—a fact which becomes apparent in the wide use of the Pearsonian *r* in much Q research. In the sense in which globality is represented in the typical clinical report, then, it can also be represented in the actuarial description. Thus, Klopfer *et al.* (pp. 607-608) state no objections to such Q-sort description clusters.

The typical clinical report contains phenotypic statements (*i.e.*, statements attributing certain dispositions for the person to behave in specified ways: *e.g.*, "is shy," "is extrapunitive," and the like) and genotypic statements (*i.e.*, statements concerning inferred causal agents: *e.g.*, "unconscious homoeroti-cism," "strong anal-retentive needs," and the like). There are no obvious reasons which preclude mixed statements of this sort in actuarially derived descriptions. It could, of course, be the case that certain genotypic inferential statements might be so far from their evidential behavioral base that their Q-sort placement would vary widely from one clinician to another. Clearly, however, such interjudge unreliability would not be a function of actuarial description: *i.e.*, such variability in attribution of genotypic inner psychological states or events would presumably obtain in descriptive paragraphs of the sort composed typically in clinical fashion. The Q-sorting technique might *reveal* the unreliability without itself being the source of such unreliability. We do not, as yet, have much evidence on this point. Interestingly, in Meehl's (1960, pp. 21-22) report on "The Cognitive Activity of the Clinician" the Q correlations, between the therapist's sort after 24 hours of patient contact and his earlier sorts, are higher for the genotypic items than for the phenotypic ones, although probably not significantly so.

Summarizing this part of the discussion, it may be said that:

1. There are no convincing reasons to suppose that the method of arriving at the descriptions (clinical or actuarial) necessarily places any limits on the *kinds of descriptive language* employed. In either case the description may be couched in dynamic language or not, may be global or not, may include phenotypic (descriptive-behavioral) or genotypic (inferential) terms. There is, indeed, some reason to question whether, given a descriptive paragraph, it would be possible to determine *how the description was arrived at.*

2. The ultimate choice of output language, either clinical or actuarial, will depend upon the theoretical preferences of the clinician. A strong preference for psychoanalytic kinds of formulation will undoubtedly be correlated with the presence of dynamic terms and statements, whereas a strong behavioristic commitment will in all likelihood lead to a preference for behavior-descriptive kinds of statements.

3. Whether any psychometric instrument or, indeed, any set of data of any sort can validly generate certain kinds of statements is an experimental question to be answered in the context of established procedures for demonstrating construct validity. In general, it would appear that the "deeper" the constructs of the descriptive language the greater will be the difficulties in establishing validity and perhaps the more ingenious the validating procedures required.

With this as a background, one might ask a seemingly simple question: Does one of these two procedures (the clinical or the actuarial processing) have a marked advantage over the other in the sense that it yields a more *accurate* description as judged by some relevant criterion? Asked in this particular form the question does, indeed, appear to be oversimplified, in that it fails to take into account the many possible combinations of types of data and kind of processing reflected in Figure 2 and already discussed above. In his earlier book, Meehl (1954) analyzed 20-odd studies which combined a variety of data types in clinical and actuarial processing. Those studies involved, however, problems of *prediction* (*e.g.,* of relatively straightforward outcomes such as success in college, response to shock therapy, etc.) as opposed to clinical and actuarial *personality description* (*i.e.,* the description of persons). Summarizing the results of these studies Meehl said: "In about half of the studies, the two methods were equal; in the other half, the clinician is definitely inferior. No . . . fully acceptable study puts him clearly ahead" (Meehl, 1954, p. 119). Twelve years later, Sawyer (1966) published an analysis of 45 studies, many of these explicitly designed to make experimental comparisons between the two processing methods *and* the variety of data types. The results of that analysis substantiated and extended Meehl's earlier conclusions in that the actuarial processing maintained superiority with *all* types of data. Beyond that Sawyer also found:

1. There were no data type processing procedure interactions which should lead one to expect better results for one kind of data processing combination than for another. Put another way, it would appear that there is no processing method which will maximize predictive power of psychometric data on the input side while the other processing method is maximizing predictive power of clinical data.

2. Incremental predictive power (*i.e.,* improving prediction with more varied data) was revealed for only the *actuarial*[8] processing. Not only did such data-addition fail to promote the clinicians' predictive power, but clinical *data* on the input side actually proved *less* powerful in the clinical processing of the data.

3. The actuary is of greater assistance to the clinician than is the clinician to the actuary. That is, the clinician's predictive power is increased when he knows what the formula predicts (though this may be mainly because the clinician's *initial* processing is so modest in power). The predictive power of actuarial processing is *not* improved by "knowing" what the clinician has said.

4. It would appear that preferences among processing methods bear little relation to experimentally demonstrated predictive power. One of the more discouraging findings here is that, what Sawyer calls the "clinical composite" (which illustrates what the clinician does *typically*)[9] is so modest in its predictive power. As authors deeply involved in and committed to the clinical

---

[8] Sawyer, as we have already indicated (see p. 180) confused "mechanical" with "actuarial" and thus wrote of "mechanical" combination instead of "actuarial."

[9] That is, the clinician typically operates with a *battery* of tests, interview material, and demographic data. These he synthesizes, calling on his experience and his theoretical knowledge in arriving at a person prediction.

enterprise, we take some solace from the fact that the clinician in over half these studies was not a trained clinical psychologist or psychiatrist. Perhaps *experts* would do better. At the same time, scientific candor perhaps compels us to say that it is not possible to be dogmatic about this in the light of our present knowledge.

It is perhaps not surprising, in the light of this evidence that Meehl, reviewing the situation 16 years after his 1954 book, makes these comments about the scientific status of the clinical-actuarial problem:

> "*It is difficult to come up with so much as one single well-designed research study in which the clinician's predictions are better than the statistical table or formula; in most studies the clinician is significantly worse.*[10] There are very few domains of social science in which so sizeable a body of evidence is so consistently in the same direction" (Meehl, 1970, p. 9).

However, notwithstanding this strong statement, this interpretation has been challenged, notably by Holt (1958), on the ground that some of the studies were really tangential to the basic issue. Holt is especially critical of attempts to predict criteria where no "job analysis" has been carried out to ascertain what variables might be crucial in making these predictions; for example, attempting to predict "success in flight training" without having any experience in learning to fly, without studying flight trainees and what they have to do, and without determining what kinds of failures occur. As an illustration of what *can* be accomplished in clinical predication when the criterion is carefully and extensively analyzed, Holt cites data on the selection of residents in psychiatry, some of which evidence contains correlation coefficients which are of some moment. Furthermore, Holt argues (and so, for that matter, do others) that it is a mistake in the first place to formulate the issues in such a manner as to set the clinical and actuarial methods in opposition to each other, thereby creating controversy where it might have been avoided.

Whatever the status of the issue with respect to *prediction* we feel this to be only tangential to the task with which we are concerned in this book, namely, the actuarial derivation of *personality descriptions*. For this reason, we would like to turn our attention to a piece of research which is aimed specifically at comparing the relative efficiency of the clinical and actuarial methods of arriving at personality descriptions on the basis of an MMPI personality profile, and in a situation where it would be difficult to argue that the clinicians were not

---

[10] Italics in the original. Incidentally, a somewhat interesting division of opinion may be worth noting with respect to a study by Lindzey (1965) which received comment by Meehl (1965) and by Goldberg (1968). It involved a diagnostic postdiction of homosexuality from TAT stories. Lindzey's initial impression, concurred in by Meehl, was that the study revealed, in this instance, the superior power of the clinician. Goldberg, in a careful analysis, raised serious doubts about whether the study could be listed as a definitive victory for the clinician.

acquainted with either the task or the criterion. The research in question was carried out by Halbower (1955) and cited at length by Meehl (1956*a*).

The task which Halbower set for himself was that of (1) deriving sets of descriptive statements which were statistically associated with specified kinds of MMPI profiles or profile types, and then (2) comparing the accuracy of these descriptive statements (when accuracy is defined as agreement with a specified criterion set of descriptions) with descriptions which were clinically derived, *i.e.*, descriptions obtained by clinicians who studied the MMPI profiles and who, after reflecting about them, described the persons they felt would be likely to produce such results. Yielding to the quantification requirements in research of this sort and following procedures frequently used, Halbower (1955; Meehl, 1956*a*) converted descriptive-dynamic statements into Q-sort form. His Q array consisted of 154 items representative of the kinds of statements which one typically finds in psychological reports: For example, "Is rebellious toward authority figures, rules, and other constraints," "Utilizes intellectualization as a defense mechanism," "Manifests inappropriate affect," and the like. Halbower set himself the task of deriving experimentally a set of specification rules to indicate how these descriptive statements could be optimally applied to patients with certain kinds of MMPI profile codes; the specifications being in the form of mean Q-sort placements in an 11-category distribution following normal curve frequency and ranging from most characteristic to least characteristic of the person described. He selected four MMPI code types specified in terms of two-digit or three-digit high points (*cf.* Chapters 1, 3 and 5 from a discussion of coding and code types). The four code types were 1-2-3′, 1-3′, 2-7′, and 8-7′. The first three indicate primarily psychoneurotic profiles, whereas the fourth is more representative of profiles obtained by psychotic patients. The subjects were all male patients treated at the Minneapolis Mental Hygiene Clinic. Examples of additional rules similar to those originally developed for our adult codes, are the following, for the 1-3′ code type: 1 and 3 ⩾ 70; 2 < 1 and 3 by at least 10 T score points; K or L >? and F; F ⩽ 65; scales 4, 5, 6, 7, 8, 9, and 0 all ⩽ 70. For each of these four code types nine patients were randomly selected from each of the four lists as the subjects on whom the actuarial descriptions were to be derived. In each case the patient's psychotherapist (who had the most extensive contact and presumably knew the patient better than anyone else in the clinic) was asked to describe the patient, using the Q statements in the 11-category arrangement already described. In those instances in which a patient was no longer in psychotherapy, another clinician was assigned to study the available information in the case folder (from which, of course, the MMPI had been removed, as it had been from all folders of subjects in the study) that contained therapists' notes and psychological test data other than the MMPI. The clinician then carried out the Q sorting of the patient. The nine sorts yielded by this procedure for each of the code types were then pairwise intercorrelated, providing four sets of 36 coefficients. For each code type, the 10 highest intercorrelated sorts were then selected, representing the five most homogeneous patients for each type. Such a procedure was calculated to capitalize on code "purity" by omitting less representative (less homogeneous) descriptions. Then, for each of the code types, Halbower computed the mean placement of each of the 154 items used in his pool. These mean placements thus constituted the actuarially derived descriptions considered applicable to patients representative of each of the four code types. This is precisely the procedure used in the derivation of the adult Q-sort descriptions in this book.

How efficient is such an actuarial procedure in arriving at descriptions of patients representing Halbower's four code types? (It should be clear that we are not concerned here with the prediction of gross categories such as success-failure, recidivism-nonrecidivism, and the like, but with what is called "personality description" which attempts to state both surface characteristics of the person and some of the dynamic-causal features which purport to account for these surface characteristics.) To test this, it was necessary to apply the actuarially-arrived-at descriptions to new cases corresponding to the code types. That is, the actuarial descriptions were correlated with the Q characterizations of new patients for whom these Q sorts were provided by their therapists. Furthermore, if these same therapist Q sorts for the new patients were correlated with Q-sort descriptions provided by clinicians who described the patient on the basis of the MMPI only, then the magnitudes of *these* correlations would, on inspection, furnish some basis for deciding whether the clinically derived descriptions or the actuarial descriptions were a better approximation of the criterion descriptions— *i.e.,* the psychotherapists descriptions of the new patients. This is the paradigm actually carried out by Halbower. Eight new patients were then selected, four from the outpatient service. The inpatients, being from a different population, (though representing the same four code types) would provide a test of the degree to which the actuarial descriptions could be extended to inpatients with these code types. Psychotherapists then compiled descriptions of the eight patients in the absence of any knowledge about the patients' MMPI's. These therapist descriptions, as has been indicated, constituted the criteria which the actuarial descriptions and the clinical descriptions were to approximate. Thus, the actuarial description previously derived for a given code type was arbitrarily assigned to each of the new patients with that MMPI code, and the accuracy of this description was measured by the magnitude of the correlation coefficients obtained when the description was correlated with the therapist criterion sorts. And, of course, the accuracy of the clinical descriptions was assessed in the same way.

The relevant data for comparing the accuracy of the two methods are presented in Table 1. The clinically derived Q descriptions were compiled by clinicians of widely varied experience ranging from less than 1 year (for first year clinical psychology trainees) to 6 years (for Ph.D. staff psychologists). *No validity coefficient for the clinical descriptions equaled the magnitude of the*

Table 1. *Validity Coefficients for Actuarial and Clinical Descriptions of Eight Cross-validation Cases*[a]

| Description | MMPI Code Types | | | | | | | | Mean r | | Total Range |
| | 123' | | 27' | | 13' | | 87' | | | | |
	Op	Ip	Op	Ip	Op	Ip	Op	Ip	Op	Ip	r
Actuarial	.88	.63	.69	.64	.84	.36	.68	.70	.78	.60	.36-.88
Clinical	.75[b]	.37/.49[c]	.50[b]	.29/.42[c]	.50[b]	.30/.30[c]	.58[b]	.50/.50[c]	.48	.41	.29-.75

[a]Adapted from Meehl (1956)

[b]Mean coefficients

[c]Two readers

actuarial description for the same profile type! For the actuarial descriptions the validity coefficients ranged from 0.36 to 0.88, for the clinical descriptions the validities ranged from 0.29 to 0.75. For the outpatients (on whom the actuarial description had been derived) the difference in magnitude of mean *r's* corresponds to a 38% superiority for the actuarial over the clinical description; for the inpatients, this superiority is reduced to 19%. (One would predict that an actuarial description derived on inpatients would improve this superiority to something like the outpatient.) In short, there can be no question that the superiority of these actuarial descriptions for these MMPI code types and for this kind of psychiatric population (with this Q array) has been conclusively demonstrated.

Does this demonstrated superiority arise from the stereotypic conception of the "average psychiatric patient" by taking advantage of the fact that there may be a valid stereotype of the "average psychiatric patient?" In dealing with this question, Meehl (1956a, pp. 269-270) writes: ". . . let me say first that to the extent the cookbook's superiority did arise from its actuarially determined tendency to 'follow the base rates,' that would be a perfectly sound application of the inverse probability considerations I at first advanced. For example, most psychiatric patients are in some degree depressed. Let us suppose the mean Q-sort placement given by therapists to the item 'depressed' is seven. 'Hysteroid' patients, who characteristically exhibit the so-called 'conversion V' on their MMPI profiles (Halbower's cookbook code 13), are less depressed than most neurotics. The clinician, seeing such a conversion valley on the Multiphasic, takes this relation into account by attributing 'lack of depression' to the patient. But maybe he overinterprets, giving undue weight to the psychometric finding and understressing the base rate. So his rule-of-thumb placement is far down at the nondepressed end, say at position three. The cookbook, on the other hand, 'knows' (actuarially) that the mean Q placement for the item 'depression' is at five in patients with such profiles—lower than the over-all mean seven but not displaced as much in the conversion subgroup as the clinician thinks. If patients are so homogeneous with respect to a certain characteristic that the psychometrics ought not to influence greatly our attribution or placement in defiance of the over-all actuarial trend, then the clinician's tendency to be unduly influenced is a source of erroneous clinical decisions and a valid argument in favor of the cookbook." By "base rates," Meehl here is referring to the frequencies with which specific behavior classifications occur in the population. Examples of base rates would be the incidence of brain damage in a population, the incidence of schizophrenia, the incidence of suicide, anxiety, depression, etc. It has become increasingly evident that the efficiency of any clinical instrument is considerably affected by these rates. A discussion of the problem can perhaps best be clarified with the aid of Table 2. In this table, ++ represents those instances in which some test indicator predicts an event (*e.g.,* suicide) which actually occurs; *i.e.,* ++ equals valid positives. Similarly, −− represents those instances in which the absence of the test indicator corresponds to the absence of the event (*e.g.,* no suicide)—valid negatives. In column 1, −+ refers to instances in which the event does not occur but the test indicator is present—*i.e.,* false positives. In column 2, +− refers to the occurrence of the event when there is no test indicator for the event—*i.e.,* false negatives. Clearly, if the sum of the ++ and −− frequencies (*i.e.,* the successful predictions) are no better than could be obtained by chance, the indicators are invalid. It does not follow, however, that if the indicators are valid that they are necessarily clinically useful. For example, even if a "suicide indicator" predicted the ++ and −− frequencies well beyond chance, the incidence of −+ (false positives) would be likely to be so high (since so few persons in the population actually commit suicide) that over-all clinical efficiency would be reduced by use of the test. Of course, a clinical inefficiency of this sort would be of incomparably less consequence than would a clinical inefficiency deriving from false negatives where the test indicator would fail to alert the clinician when there was a danger of suicide. The very crux of this base rate problem is perhaps best stated in the following sentence by Meehl: "Probably most surprising is the finding that there are quantitative relationships between the base rates and test validity parameters such that the use of a 'valid' test will produce a net rise in the frequency of clinical mistakes" (p. 266). (There is, incidentally, no good logical reason to believe that nontest cues used as indicators—*e.g.,* as derived from observation or interview—are exempt from this base rate problem; and some day it will be

Table 2. *Relationship between the Occurrence of an Event and the Test Indicator for the Event*

Criterion Event	Test Indicator	
	Present (+)	Absent (−)
Occurs (+)	++	+−
Does not occur (−)	−+	−−

necessary for clinicians to become more sophisticated with respect to the ways in which base rate considerations ought to influence their daily practice.)

An example of how a valid "sign" or indicator may nevertheless mislead the clinician into erroneous decisions is offered in a paper by Hall and LaDriere (1969). In an attempt to discover or identify indicators which would enable them to diagnose brain damage in children, these two authors reported what they regarded as encouraging results using "conceptually inadequate" responses on the Similarities of the Wechsler Intelligence Scale for Children (WISC). These signs were, indeed, "valid" in the sense that they statistically differentiated the brain damaged and nonbrain damaged children. However, if it were assumed that 25% of the children seen in child guidance clinics were *in fact* brain damaged (and this is almost certainly an overestimate) and the WISC cutting score was employed as recommended by Hall and LaDriere, only 37% of the diagnostic decisions would be correct; decisions would be incorrect about 63% of the time *even though the WISC "conceptually inadequate"* indicators were valid. Incidentally, Hall and LaDriere cite a study by Spence (1963) using analogous diagnostic indicators. Analysis of data in *that* study also leaves one pessimistic; for there, too, the "valid" indicators would lead to extensive diagnostic error. However, it should be noted that, unlike Hall and LaDriere, Taylor made no claims for the diagnostic efficacy of these test indicators.

However, there is a sense in which the base rate problem as it affects the actuarial descriptions in this book is a tangential one rather than a direct one. That is, once it is accepted, by any given installation, that the MMPI has a sufficient degree of intrinsic validity to be adopted as an instrument for measuring personality, the central issue then becomes what is the most efficient way to "read" the test? Naturally, any decisions concerning the intrinsic validity of the MMPI must themselves rest upon experimental evidence. We take it as obvious that we believe the MMPI to possess sufficient intrinsic validity for certain clinical tasks to merit the considerable effort that goes into the construction of an actuarial book of this sort. All subsequent use in this book, of the phrase base rates will refer to the average frequencies which appear in the "Total" and "BR" columns of the Appendices. For a further and more detailed discussion of the relation of base rates to clinical efficiency the reader should consult the original article by Meehl and Rosen (1955).

There is, however, adequate evidence that the actuarial descriptions compiled by Halbower by the methods described did *not* rely upon stereotypic conceptions of the "average psychiatric patient." If it were true that validity depended on such a stereotype, then this would be reflected in the dispersion of items; specifically, the items would show little change in placement along the 11-category distribution. For example, if it were true that most psychiatric patients were "dependent" (and if the actuarial descriptions were taking advantage of this), then an item like "has strong dependency needs" would be placed at the "most descriptive" end of the sorting continuum for all four of the codes studies, and indeed, for most patient descriptions. Or, if it were true of few patients that they take a dominant ascendant role in interaction with others, then the item "takes a dominant, ascendant role . . ." would be consistently placed at the "least descriptive" end of the sorting continuum. In other words, such items would show little variation in placement from patient to patient over a wide range of patient types. But this is precisely one of the phenomena which Halbower experimentally controlled by eliminating from his Q array items which, in pretesting, were invariant. Secondly, an inspection of item placements for the four actuarial descriptions indicates that items *did*, in fact, vary considerably from one code tc another; only 2 items of the 154 appeared in the top quartile of the four codes involved. Furthermore, if the validity of the actuarial descriptions could be attributed to a valid stereotype, then it would follow that the stereotypes actually described in Halbower's experiment (clinicians were instructed to sort their conception of the "average patient")— would necessarily correlate highly with the four criterion descriptions. This was not the case; the criterion descriptions of three of the four codes correlated very poorly with the "average patient" descriptions of Halbower's clinicians (see Table 3). Moreover, when a composite description was compiled of the mean item placements for each clinician describing *his* own stereotype, this "mean average patient" description fared no better; three of the four validity coefficients were extremely poor. *All four* actuarial descriptions were significantly better than the individual stereotypes at the 0.001 level of significance and better than the composite stereotype as well.

   Closely associated with problems involving base rates is the notion of the "Barnum effect." This phrase was proposed by Meehl to characterize "pseudo successful clinical procedures" in which the apparent success actually derives from base rates. For example, if a psychiatrist or a psychologist were to say of a given patient on the basis of an MMPI profile, a Rorschach protocol, or a set of Thematic Apperception Test (TAT) themes that he "has fluctuating moods," the likelihood of his being "correct" would be extraordinarily high. The point is, however, that mood fluctuation as a phenomenon is so widespread that it can be as accurately attributed to a person without the test. In a previous paper by Marks and Seeman (1962) nine heterogeneous patients were characterized by Q sort as having mood fluctuations. Now, as has been indicated, if a clinician on the basis of any psychological test were to describe any one of these patients as

Table 3. *Validity Coefficients for Stereotype and Actuarial Descriptions*[a]

MMPI Code Types	Stereotype Range r	Mean r	Actuarial Mean r	MMPI Code Types	Stereotype Range r	Mean r	Actuarial Mean r
123'	.63 - .69	.74	.88	13'	.25 - .37	.32	.84
27'	-.03 - .20	.09	.69	87'	.25 - .35	.31	.68

[a]Adapted from Meehl (1956)

subject to mood fluctuations, this attribution would have the semblance of "success." Thus, in this instance, "Has fluctuating moods" would be characterized as a Barnum statement because it could be made with equal "success" simply with knowledge of the base rate; and indeed any test which persuaded the clinician to depart from the rate would decrease the frequency of this success. However, where a test-induced departure, even from a relatively high base rate, actually resulted in greater success in characterization, that characterization would not constitute a Barnum description. For example, the case history data in the adult section indicate that the base rate for depression is 73%. Any clinician armed with this knowledge could achieve a respectable success in attributing depression to patients drawn from this population without any test. However, the data also reveal that the incidence of depression varies widely over the adult codes from a high of 100% (*cf.* 2-3-1 code) to a low of 22% (*cf.* 4-9 code). Under these circumstances the potentialities for improving success by using the test seem quite clear. And it is in this kind of situation that the power of actuarial description may be manifested. For, presumably, successful departure from relatively high base rates requires an optimal assignment of weights to those indicators which should serve as a guide to such departures. And, it is precisely one of the very important functions of the actuarial description to assign optimal weights to such indicators. The evidence from Halbower's study indicates indeed that the actuarial description is more successful than is the clinician in assigning these optimal weights.

In discussing the usefulness of cookbooks, Towbin (1960) has argued that the use of such cookbooks necessarily defines the role of the clinician in relation to the referral; that only when the clinician is functioning as a *technician* as distinguished from a *consultant* will he consider the actuarial description appropriate. In Towbin's own words: "It is this *role*, so to speak, that requires the use of cookbooks. . . . the tester's role is that of a technician. Perhaps the most important feature of that role is the tester's disavowal of interest in the purpose of the referring person" (p. 121). In other words, as Towbin sees it, the clinician does not ask whether the initial referral questions are appropriate, does not discuss with the referring person what the implications might be for various answers to the questions asked by the referring person, does not discuss what other questions might fruitfully be asked—but simply proceeds in routine and mechanical fashion to the testing procedure. Then, on viewing the test results, he reaches for his handbook of actuarial descriptions and reads off the corresponding personality description. The complex issues imbedded in this question are beyond the scope of this book, and we shall therefore restrict ourselves to the comment that the implications of actuarial description are by no means as straightforward as those described by Towbin. It may indeed be the case that in fact some clinicians operate in this relatively mechanical fashion whether they use actuarial or clinical methods or both. As we understand it, however, it is the function of the consulting clinician to decide whether the questions which are asked can reasonably be answered by actuarial descriptions;

and whether such descriptions are likely to be more accurate than clinically derived descriptions. Answers to such questions are dependent upon empirical evidence, of course. It has never been contended that actuarial codebooks are useful for all tasks, but rather that for some kinds of tasks which are currently being discharged in far less efficient ways.

REFERENCES

CALDWELL, A. B. Recent advances in automated interpretation of the MMPI. Paper read at the Fifth Annual Symposium on Recent Developments in the Use of the MMPI, Mexico City, February, 1970.

DRAKE, L. E., AND OETTING, E. R. *An MMPI codebook for counselors.* Minneapolis: University of Minnesota Press, 1959.

FINNEY, J. C. Programmed interpretation of the MMPI and CPI. *Arch. Gen. Psychiat. 15,* 75-81, 1966.

FINNEY, J. C. *Manual for psychiatrists and psychologists: psychodiagnostic service.* Lexington, Ky.: Finney Institute for the Study of Human Behavior, 1969.

FOWLER, R. D. The automated cookbook. In Computer processing and reporting of personality test data. Symposium presented at Annual Meetings of the American Psychological Association, Los Angeles, September, 1964.

FOWLER, R. D. Automated interpretation of personality test data. In J. N. Butcher (Ed.) *MMPI: Research developments and clinical applications.* New York: McGraw-Hill Book Co., 1969.

GILBERSTADT, H., AND DUKER, J. *A Handbook for clinical and actuarial MMPI interpretation.* Philadelphia: W. B. Saunders Co., 1965.

GOLDBERG, L. R. Methodological critiques Seer over sign: The first "good" example? *J. Exp. Res. Personal. 3,* 168-171, 1968.

HALBOWER, C. C. A comparison of acturial versus clinical prediction to classes discriminated by MMPI. Ph.D. dissertation, University of Minnesota, Minneapolis, Minn., 1955.

HALL, L. P., AND LA DRIERE, L. Patterns of performance on WISC similarities in emotionally disturbed and brain damaged children. *J. Consult. Clin. Psychol. 33,* 357-364, 1969.

HERTZ, M. R. Current problems in Rorschach theory and technique. *J. Project. Techn. 15,* 307-338, 1951.

HILGARD, E. R., ATKINSON, R. C., AND ATKINSON, R. L. *Introduction to psychology.* New York: Harcourt, Brace, Jovanivich, Inc., 1971.

HINSIE, L. E., AND CAMPBELL, R. J., *Psychiatric dictionary, third edition.* New York: Oxford University Press, 1960.

HOLT, R. R. Clinical and statistical prediction: A reformulation and some new data. *J. Abnorm. Soc. Psychol. 56,* 1-12, 1958.

HUNT, W. A. An actuarial approach to clinical judgment. In B. Bass, and I. A. Berg (Eds.) *Objective approaches to personality assessment.* New York: Van Nostrand, 1959.

HUTT, M. L. The use of projective methods of personality measurement in army medical installations. *J. Clin. Psychol. 1,* 123-140, 1945.

KLOPFER, B., FOX, J., AND TROUP, E. Problems in the use of the Rorschach technique with children. In B. Klopfer (Ed.) *Volume II Developments in the Rorschach technique.* New York: World Book, 1956.

KOSTLAN, A. A method for the empirical study of psychodiagnosis. *J. Consult. Psychol. 18,* 83-88, 1954.

LANYON, R. I., AND GOODSTEIN, L. D. *Personality assessment.* New York: John Wiley and Sons, 1971.

LINDZEY, G. Seer versus sign. *J. Exp. Res. Personal. 1,* 17-26, 1965.

MARKS, P. A., AND SEEMAN, W. On the Barnum effect. *Psychol. Rec. 12,* 203-208, 1962.

MARKS, P. A., AND SEEMAN, W. *The actuarial description of abnormal personality: An atlas for use with the MMPI.* Baltimore: Williams & Wilkins Co., 1963.

MARKS, P. A., AND SINES, J. O. Methodological problems in cookbook construction. In J. N.

Butcher (Ed.) *MMPI: Research developments and clinical applications*. New York: McGraw-Hill Book Co., 1969.

MEEHL, P. E. Comments on analyzing the clinical process. *J. Counsel. Psychol. 1*, 207-208, 1954*a*.

MEEHL, P. E. *Clinical versus statistical prediction: A theoretical analysis and a review of the evidence*. Minneapolis: University of Minnesota Press, 1954*b*.

MEEHL, P. E. Wanted—a good cookbook. *Amer. Psychol. 11*, 262-272, 1956.

MEEHL, P. E. Some ruminations on the validation of clinical procedures. *Can. J. Psychol. 13*, 106-128, 1959.

MEEHL, P. E. The cognitive activity of the clinician. *Amer. Psychol. 15*, 19-27, 1960.

MEEHL, P. E. Psychology and criminal law. *Univ. Richmond Law Rev. 5*, 1-30, 1970.

MEEHL, P. E., AND ROSEN, A. Antecedent probability and the efficiency of psychometric signs, patterns, or cutting scores. *Psychol. Bull, 52*, 194-216, 1955.

MILLER, G. A. *Psychology the science of mental life*. New York: Harper & Row, 1962.

PEARSON, J. S., AND SWENSON, W. M. *A user's guide to the Mayo Clinic automated MMPI program*. New York: The Psychological Corporation, 1967.

PEARSON, J. S., SWENSON, W. M., ROME, H. P., MATAYA, P., AND BRANNICK, T. L. Further experience with the automated MMPI. *Proc. Mayo Clin. 39*, 823-829, 1964.

SAWYER, J. Measurement *and* prediction, clinical *and* statistical. *Psychol. Bull. 66*, 178-200, 1966.

SHONTZ, F. C. *Research methods in personality*. New York: Appleton-Century-Crofts, 1965.

SPENCE, J. T. Patterns of performance on WAIS similarities in schizophrenic, brain-damaged and normal subjects. *Psychol. Rep. 13*, 431-436, 1963.

TOLMAN, E. C. *Purposive behavior in animals and men*. Los Angeles: University of California Press, 1949.

TOWBIN, A. P. When are cookbooks useful? *Amer. Psychol. 15*, 119-123, 1960.

Webster's new international dictionary, seventh edition. Springfield: G. & C. Merriam Co., 1967.

WECHSLER, D. *The measurement of adult intelligence, fourth edition*. Baltimore: The Williams & Wilkins Co., 1958.

PART
TWO

ADULT SECTION

3

The Development of Code Types

SELECTION OF CASES

The actuarial data for adults were derived from patients seen at the Department of Psychiatry of the University of Kansas Medical Center during the years 1960 to 1962. The psychiatry inpatient service then provided for about 45 beds. Wards were open and patients were admitted to this service almost exclusively on a voluntary basis. The range in degree and extent of psychological disability was considerable; some patients were able to live and work outside of the hospital a good deal of the time, whereas others were so severely disturbed that they required constant supervision. The psychiatry outpatient clinic provided services for patients who were considered likely to benefit most from short term treatment; patients believed to require long term treatment typically were referred elsewhere. The clinical emphasis was on treatment rather than diagnosis and every patient received psychotherapy of some variety. The sample also included patients who received, from the faculty, private treatment of the sort characteristically found in private practice. The patient population was considered to be fairly representative, then, of both clinic and hospitalized patients in other medical settings and in private practice as well. A more complete description of the sample is given in the Appendix.

The procedure followed in the selection of cases and identification of codes was a contingency method similar to that of Halbower (1955), Meehl (1959), and Meehl and Dahlstrom (1959), and which was also adopted by Gilberstadt and Duker (1960). This configural procedure relies heavily on the investigator's clinical experience with the MMPI, including his knowledge of the reliability of scales over time and of frequencies of single and multiple scale high points. Of the available methods of profile analysis, the evidence at that time suggested that this was probably the most promising (Meehl and Dahlstrom, 1960). Since 1960, however, work by Goldberg (1965, 1969, 1972) and by others (*e.g.,* Stilson and Astrup, 1966) report no improvement of configural over linear methods. We have decided at this time to adopt a simple two-point or simple three-point system, which we regard as a move in the linear direction. For a few of our code types we have adhered to the original classification rules, and thus we should first like to describe the development of our original system.

On the basis of 165 female and 83 male MMPI profiles obtained during 1960 to 1961, it was possible to identify nine preliminary high point codes: 2-3-1, 2-7, 2-7-8-, 2-8, 3-1, 4-6, 4-8-2, 8-6, and a "normal" profile (*i.e.,* all clinical scale T scores below 70) with an elevated K score. These codes were determined following the procedure for coding a profile described in Chapter 1. Having identified these reference codes for men and women combined, we then proceded to compute various difference scores and other quantitative criteria which would provide trial rules for specifying each type. For example, we began with the 2-3-1 code requiring that scales 2, 3, and 1 be above 70 T scores. Then, by requiring that scale 2 minus 1 be greater than 5 T-score points, we introduced more specific patterning specifications. Following this procedure it was possible to produce a preliminary set of rules for the 2-3-1 type. The nine codes already indicated were derived in this way.

We then proceeded to examine 257 female and 130 male profiles for patients seen during the following year to test the applicability of the rules and to refine them. With this increased size of our sample we identified seven additional high point codes: 2-7-4, 3-2-1, 4-6-2, 4-9, 8-3, 8-9, and 9-6. For each code, the numeric arrangement is based on the relative size of the two or three high-point combinations. For example, if there were more 2-3-1 than 2-1-3 profiles, the high-point sequence would be 2-3-1/2-1-3.

Initially a minimum of 25 patients (of either sex) was required to constitute a code type, a requirement which was later changed when it was found that a specific code might have a low representation of males or females. On examination it was found that some codes were *primarily but not exclusively* represented by women and others by men. It was only subsequently, however, when correlations were available for the Q-sort data, that it became apparent that male and female subjects for a given code were described quite similarly.

Having specified and refined the rules for 16 code types, we took a subsequent 2-year sample of 556 females and 270 males and determined that the codes were stable over this period, requiring a minimum of 20 patients for each type. Following this procedure, 87% of the profiles for women and 45% of the profiles for men could be classified. It should be emphasized, however, that this low frequency for men obtains only when the requirement stipulates a minimum of 20 men to define a type; permitting a code to be defined by 20 *patients* (*i.e.*, both men and women), accounted for 75% of the male profiles. The distribution of males and females for each of the 16 codes is presented in Table 1. Table 1 also presents classification rates using the Marks-Seeman system for patients in other similar settings as reported by Briggs, Taylor, and Tellegen

Table 1. *Classification Rates[a] for Four Similar Clinical Settings*

Code Type	Males			Females			M+F		M+F	M+F
	A		B	A		B	A		C	D
	N	%	%	N	%	%	N	%	%	%
2-3-1	20	7.4	0.4	29	5.2	0.4	49	5.9	0.6	0.5
2-7	31	11.5	1.6	34	6.1	0.8	65	7.9	2.1	2.7
2-7-4	21	7.8	1.9	25	4.5	0.4	46	5.6	1.2	1.4
2-7-8	29	10.7	0.7	29	5.2	0.9	58	7.0	1.4	1.1
2-8	14	5.2	2.4	26	4.7	2.1	40	4.8	0.3	2.2
3-1	2	0.7	0.9	29	5.2	1.3	31	3.7	0.8	0.5
3-2-1	5	1.8	3.3	36	6.5	3.3	41	4.9	1.0	0.5
4-6	5	1.8	0.1	24	4.3	0.2	29	3.5	0.1	0.3
4-6-2	0	0.0	0.3	23	4.1	0.6	23	2.9	0.8	0.6
4-8-2	17	6.3	1.4	28	5.0	2.5	45	5.4	1.0	0.9
4-9	18	6.7	0.4	26	4.7	0.2	44	5.3	0.3	0.1
8-3	6	2.2	0.6	26	4.7	0.9	32	3.9	0.8	0.4
8-6	9	3.3	0.1	28	5.0	1.3	37	4.5	0.0	1.4
8-9	5	1.8	6.2	29	5.2	5.2	34	4.1	4.4	1.8
9-6	0	0.0	0.0	25	4.5	0.1	25	3.0	0.1	0.1
KI	21	7.8	8.1	24	4.3	6.2	45	5.4	6.8	2.3
Totals	203	75.2	28.4	441	79.3	26.4	644	78.0	21.7	16.8

[a]Based on the original system.

Note: A (Marks & Seeman, 1963), B (Owen, 1970), C (Briggs, Taylor & Tellegen, 1966), D (Meikle & Gerritse, 1970).

(1966), Meikle and Gerritse (1970), and Owen (1970). Later in this chapter we will comment on the discrepencies in coverage reported in Table 1.

With the considerably enlarged N of the 2-year sample just described, it proved possible to identify four additional code types: 1-2-3, 2-0, 4-3, and 8-7, which, however, were represented by fewer patients. In a sense, it might be said that we were rapidly reaching the point of diminishing returns, for these new codes accounted for only an additional 7% of the women and 8% of the men in our adult sample (see Table 2). However, since these codes do occur in the adult psychiatric population, and since they occur with sufficient frequency to be included in our system for adolescents, we feel it worth while to present the mean profiles for both samples in Figures 1 through 4. *It is especially important to note that throughout this book all adolescent profiles have been plotted using adolescent norms without the K correction for scales 1, 4, 7, 8, and 9.*

The procedure thus far may be summarized as follows:

1. Tabulation of high point frequencies of all K-corrected MMPI profiles for adults over a 1-year period (N = 165 women and 83 men).

2. Grouping of profiles on the basis of two-digit or three-digit high points, irrespective of sex.

3. Identification of nine preliminary code types: 2-3-1, 2-7, 2-7-8, 2-8, 3-1, 4-6, 4-8-2, 8-6, and a normal K+, with a requirement of at least 25 patients per type.

4. Inspection of all profiles for "goodness of fit" in grouping, and further specifying conditions for homogeneity within type (*e.g.*, in the case of the 2-3-1, scales 2, 3, and 1 above T score 70; scales 2 minus 1 greater than 5 T scores).

5. Computation of difference scores and other criteria to maximize within-type homogeneity and between-type distinctiveness (*e.g.*, $[7 + 8] - [1 + 2]$; $[4 + 6] - [1 + 3]$; etc.).

6. Refining of specification rules on the basis of step 4 above.

Table 2. *Distributions for Similar Adult (Unclassifiable)[a] and Adolescent (Classifiable)[b] Code Types*

Code Type	Adults (N=826)						Adolescents (N=834)					
	Male		Female		Totals		Male		Female		Totals	
	N	%	N	%,	N	%	N	%	N	%	N	%
1-2-3	6	2.2	7	1.3	13	1.6	c		c		c	
2-0	5	1.8	13	2.3	18	2.2	10	2.0	12	3.7	22	2.6
3-4	4	1.7	15	2.7	19	2.3	29	5.7	23	7.1	51	6.1
7-8	8	2.9	7	1.2	15	1.8	21	4.1	10	3.1	31	3.7

[a]Fewer than 20 cases on the 2-year sample.

[b]As plotted without K correction (see text).

[c]Information not available for three-digit codes.

7. Testing of newly refined specification rules on profiles for the following year (N = 257 women, and 130 men).

8. Identification of seven additional code types: 2-7-4, 3-2-1, 4-6-2, 4-9, 8-3, 8-9, and 9-6.

9. Revision and refinement of rules (e.g., in the case of 2-3-1, scale 7 greater than 8 or 8 minus 7 less than 5 T scores).

10. Testing of most recently refined specification rules on subsequent 2-year sample (N = 556 women, and 270 men).

11. Identification of four additional code types: 1-2-3, 2-0, 3-4, and 8-7.

12. Setting the requirement of N = 20 for including a code type.

We have already indicated that we are introducing a change in our classification procedure. We believe this is desirable in view of the difficulties reported in applying our system in other settings. The research since the original publication of our book has rather consistently indicated (1) that too few profiles could be made to fit the original rules (see e.g., Beckett, Grisell, and Gudobba, 1964; Cone, 1966; Fowler and Coyle, 1968a; Huff, 1965; Lachar, 1968; Shults, Gibeau, and Barry, 1968; Sines, 1966; Webb, 1970) although, under more optimal testing conditions there have been some interesting exceptions (Herrell, 1971; Newmark and Finkelstein, 1973; and Wilcox and Krasnoff, 1967); (2) that in too many instances a given profile could be classified by more than one type (Fowler and Coyle, 1968b; Gynther, Altman, Warbin, and Sletten, 1972; Meikle and Gerritse, 1970; and Rosman, Barry, and Gibeau, 1966); and (3) that the relaxation of rules permitted classification of many more profiles (Briggs, Taylor, and Tellegen, 1966; Owen, 1970; Pauker, 1966; and Payne and Wiggins, 1968). Furthermore, in a series of papers, Gynther (1972) and Gynther et al., (Gynther, Altman, Warbin, and Sletten, 1972, 1973a;

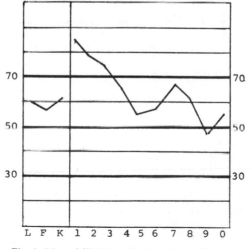

Fig. 1. Mean MMPI profile for 1-2-3 code type.

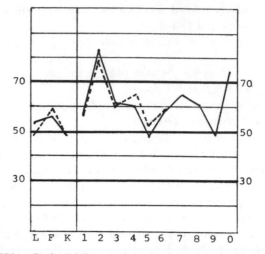

Fig. 2. Mean MMPI profile for 2-0/0-2 code type (adults, *solid line;* adolescents, *broken line*).

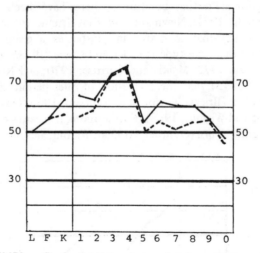

Fig. 3. Mean MMPI profile for 3-4/4-3 code type (adults, *solid line;* adolescents, *broken line*).

Gynther, Altman, and Warbin, 1972, 1973*b*, 1973*c*, 1973*d*, 1973*e*, 1973*f*; Altman, Gynther, Warbin, and Sletten, 1972, 1973; Gynther, Altman, and Sletten, 1973 and Warbin, Altman, Gynther, and Sletten, 1972) together with Lewandowski and Graham (1972) and Graham (1973) have presented cogent if not convincing evidence that a two-digit high-point classification system is not only powerful but has many advantages beyond the rather complex configural system which we originally employed. A review of our original profiles revealed that despite our numerous contingency rules, 80% or more of the profiles within

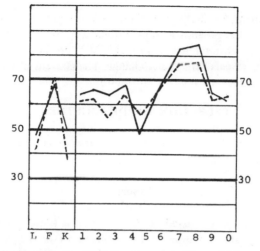

Fig. 4. Mean MMPI profile for 7-8/8-7 code type (adults, *solid line;* adolescents, *broken line*).

12 of our 16 codes could in fact be classified following slight modification[1] of a simple two-digit or three-digit high-point procedure. A comparison of the average intersort correlations (in Table 3, p. 74) for those 12 codes with the remaining 4 codes shows no significant difference (r's = 0.48 and 0.49, respectively). We interpret this to mean there is no appreciable loss of accuracy in shifting from our original system of profile classification to this new procedure. Thus, for the following 12 codes we shall use the simplified high-point system advocated by Gynther and others: 2-3-1/2-1-3, 2-7, 2-7-4/2-4-7/4-7-2, 2-7-8/8-7-2, 2-8/8-2, 3-1/1-3, 3-2-1, 4-6/6-4, 4-9, 8-6/6-8, 8-9/9-8, 9-6/6-9. For the remaining 4 codes: 4-6-2/6-4-2, 4-8-2/8-4-2/8-2-4, 8-3/3-8, K+ we will employ the original classification rules.

It should be clear that the procedure described and summarized above was designed to provide the MMPI profile codes which would guide the investigation of patient descriptions. In principle it would have been possible to classify these patients by a variety of other systems such as Rorschach variables or the nosology in the Statistical Manual of the American Psychiatric Association. The value of an MMPI code type (*e.g.*, 2-7 or 2-8) as a construct, like the value of a Rorschach variable (*e.g.*, M:ΣC or F + %) or a diagnostic variable (*e.g.*, conversion hysteria or schizophrenia), is determined empirically by its ability to generate a wide variety of *other* correlated information. For example, one of the values (presumably) of grouping patients under the rubrics of conversion reaction or schizophrenia is that it would have consequences for

---

[1] By disregarding certain scale high points. Specifically, in the case of 2-7-4/2-4-7/4-7-2 and 2-7-8/8-7-2, by disregarding scale 0; in the case of 3-2-1 and 8-9, by disregarding scale 7; and in the case of 4-6/6-4, by disregarding scale 8.

differential treatment. Similarly, one of the values of grouping patients by MMPI code type is that it has prognostic implications; *e.g.*, the 2-7 patient typically on discharge from the hospital has a normal MMPI profile, whereas for the 2-8 patient the profile reveals little if any change. The content of this book provides just such correlated test and nontest information.

SELECTION OF DESCRIPTORS

The descriptors or output used in the study of adults consisted of Q-sort, case history, and psychometric data.

Q-Sort

The Q-sort descriptors consisted of 108 phenotypic (descriptive or observable) and genotypic (dynamic or inferential) statements (see the Appendix). These statements had previously been selected for their representative coverage of the personality domain, and had then been empirically screened for applicability to both sexes, clinical pertinence, interpatient variability, and other variables; and by the time of the study they had accumulated a sizeable amount of research data (Marks, 1961; Marks and Seeman, 1962*a*, 1962*b*, 1962*c*; Marks and Seeman, 1963*a*, 1963*b*). The Q statements constitute, in effect, the results of an exceedingly fine screening and sifting process which began with over 2,000 statements compiled from various sources (see Marks, 1961). All sorting was done in a nine category, rectangular, forced distribution with 12 statements placed in each category.[2] Sorters were instructed to place in category 1 those 12 statements "least descriptive" of the patient, and in category 9 those 12 statements "most descriptive" of the patient. The remaining statements were distributed among categories between these two extremes, corresponding to the degree of judged "descriptiveness." In this way, the statements in categories 1, 2, and 3 represented the least characteristic or least salient aspects of the patient, whereas the statements in categories 7, 8, and 9 represented the most characteristic or most salient aspects. Special care was taken to keep from all sorters any information about the MMPI profile or the code type to which the patient belonged. In addition, all reference to psychiatric nosology was removed from the information available to the sorters, and they were specifically instructed to "sort the *patient* and not a diagnostic stereotype."

The clinicians who described the patients using the Q statements were 13 psychiatrists (4 staff psychiatrists and 9 second and third-year residents) and 6 psychologists (5 staff psychologists and 1 third-year intern with over 2-years

---

[2] The decade prior to this study had seen considerable controversy over the specific form (unimodal, U-shaped, or rectangular; forced, semiforced, or unforced) the Q distribution should take (*e.g.*, Block, 1956, 1961; Cronbach, 1953; Stephenson, 1952). Our own preference for a rectangular distribution was based on the findings of Livson and Nichols (1956).

clinical experience). Information available to all clinicians at the time of sorting consisted of social, personal, and medical history, as well as extensive results of psychological tests (MMPI excluded, of course).

Before sorting, the participating clinicians were asked to submit the names of patients whom they had treated in psychotherapy for a minimum of 15 hours.[3] From these lists, 9 or 10 patients were selected as representative of each MMPI code type, the selection being made by inspection of individual profiles for "best fit" to the mean profile for each type. There were thus available a total of nine or ten Q-sort descriptions for each code type. These descriptions were then pairwise correlated for each code type and the resulting matrices inspected for "maximum patient similarity" (homogeneity) on the basis of the coefficients' magnitudes. This procedure yielded information permitting selection of the five (in one instance six) "most homogeneous patients" for each type. It also enabled us to eliminate patients with atypical sortings, thereby reducing errors of clinical judgment. The mean category placement of each item was then computed for patients of each code; these average item placements were to constitute the actuarial Q descriptions for each of the 16 code types.

Table 3 presents product-moment correlation coefficients which reflect a number of facets of reliability of the Q descriptors. The coefficients in column 2 are means for the 5 "most representative" female patients, selected in a manner already described; the grand mean is 0.50 for all code types. Comparable data for males are found in column 3. Resorting by therapists was not possible for all code types. Some reliability coefficients are missing (for some code types) for correlations of psychiatrists with psychologists (column 6) and (for some code types) for coefficients indicating agreement of psychologists and psychiatrists resorting the same patient 1 week later (columns 4 and 5) because attempts to secure them proved unrealistic in light of the fact that they were constant demands on the clinicians's time.

The omissions from column 3 of Table 3 are of significance and require some consideration. Essentially, these omissions are occasioned jointly by the severe limitations on clinical time to which we have already referred and the strategy adopted to deal with these limitations. In the early stages of sorting it became obvious that the descriptions for men and women of a given code type could not be differentiated statistically. That is, when the correlations for a code were arranged in a matrix it proved impossible to separate the r's for men from the r's for women on inspection of the magnitudes of the coefficients. In other words, the correlations were not such as to permit identification of clusters of male or female descriptions. Confronted with this evidence for the codes we studied, we subsequently used patients more easily available—*i.e.*, female. We believe, both on the basis of the evidence just mentioned and on the basis of their use in this clinical setting, that the Q descriptors are equally applicable to male and female patients. In a sense it may be said that this constitutes empirical

---

[3] A rationale for a 10-hour criterion was developed subsequent to the adult study and will be discussed in the section on adolescents.

Table 3. *Q Correlations (Reliability Coefficients)[a] of Therapists' Patient Descriptions*

Code Type	Intersort r Females[e]		Intersort r Males		Intrasort r Pso		Intrasort r Psi		Pso and Psi	
	Mean	Range	Mean	Range	Mean	Range	Mean	Range	Mean	Range
2-3-1[b]	40	25–59	41[c]	25–61					64	
2-7[b]	52	41–64	53[d]	48–61	80		91			
2-7-4[b]	51	36–66	54[c]	47–66						
2-7-8[b]	65	43–82	50[c]	26–73	78					
2-8[b]	46	27–64	43[c]	23–56						
3-1[b]	44	33–63							45[d]	43–47
3-2-1[b]	45	33–80			72		79		59	
4-6[b]	41	25–71								
4-6-2	57	32–82					87		51	
4-8-2	44	33–55			76					
4-9[b]	54	46–73	56[c]	47–71	83		83			
8-3	52								50	
8-6[b]	51	29–66							63	
8-9[b]	60	49–72			67[d]	65–79				
9-6[b]	43	30–64					82			
K+	37	13–56	34[d]	14–50						
Totals	50	13–82	48	14–73	75	65–83	85	79–91	54	43–64

[a] Decimal points omitted. All mean r's significantly greater than zero (P. = .001). Pso = psychologists, Psi = psychiatrists.

[b] Classified only by two-digit or three-digit high point.

[c] Based on three sorts.

[d] Based on two sorts.

[e] Based on five sorts, except for 2-7 where N = 6.

evidence in support of the hypothesis initially made when items were selected. It should be recalled that one of the original criteria for screening the items was their applicability to both sexes. (One could think of an extreme item such as

"Is pregnant" which would obviously *not* be applicable to both sexes!)
extreme item such as "Is pregnant" which would obviously *not* be applicable to both sexes!)

This procedure for deriving the actuarial Q-sort descriptions, using the 108 item array, for each of the 16 code types may now be summarized:

1. For each code type a sample of 9 (or 10) patients was selected, all of whom had been treated in psychotherapy for a minimum of 15 hours.

2. For each of these patients a 108 item rectangular Q description was compiled, based on psychotherapy notes, social, personal, and medical histories, and psychological test data (MMPI excluded).

3. This yielded a minimum of nine Q descriptions for each code type.

4. Pairwise correlations yielded a matrix of 36 (or more) product-moment coefficients for each code type.

5. By inspection of the *r* magnitudes, the five "most homogeneous patients" for each code were selected as most representative of that type.

6. For each code type the mean of the Q-statement placements based on these five patients constitutes the actuarial Q-sort description for that code type.

Table 4 reports data on typological relationships within our original system. The Q correlations were computed between average sorts of the 16 code types and average sorts of four stereotypic descriptions (Nor = normal, Pso = psychotic, Psn = psychoneurotic, PD = personality disorder). Each stereotype was derived from the five most highly intercorrelated sorts of 9 skilled clinicians—5 psychologists and 4 psychiatrists (Marks and Seeman, 1962*b*, 1962*c*; Marks and Sines, 1969).

It is of some interest that the code types with the highest incidence of a psychotic clinical diagnosis (8-6, 8-9, 9-6) correlate most highly with the psychotic stereotype (*r*'s = 0.83, 0.77, and 0.75, respectively). Similarly, the code types having the highest incidence of neurotic membership (2-3-1, 2-7, 3-1) show the same relationship to the neurotic stereotype (*r*'s = 0.68, 0.71, and 0.66, respectively). And essentially the same correlations obtain for the personality disorder stereotype and the codes with personality disorder as the primary clinical diagnosis (4-6, *r* = 0.56; 4-9, *r* = 0.64). Of greater interest, however, is the magnitude of intercorrelations for common families of codes (*e.g.*, see 4-6 versus 4-8-2, 4-6-2, and 4-9; also 2-3-1 versus 2-7, 2-7-4, and 2-8). Other relationships, such as those between code types having no common scale elevations (*e.g.*, 3-1 versus 4-6, *r* = 0.16; 2-7 versus 8-9, *r* = 0.01), provide evidence of between-type distinctiveness or discriminant validation for these constructs.

Case History Data

A promising array of case history and clinical descriptors was suggested by a rating schedule and record form used by Schofield, Hathaway, Hastings, and Bell

Table 4. *Q Correlations of 16 Adult Code Types and 4 Stereotype Personality Descriptions* [a]

Type	2-7	2-7-4	2-7-8	2-8	3-1	3-2-1	4-6	4-6-2	4-8-2	4-9	8-3	8-6	8-9	9-6	K+	Nor	Pso	Psn	PD
2-3-1	62	64	37	61	72	49	12	12	06	22	33	09	-01	27	28	-17	15	68	-15
2-7		39	62	50	52	55	-15	-15	04	-33	45	14	01	41	44	-21	26	71	-51
2-7-4			57	69	52	58	44	50	44	50	44	40	37	51	34	-47	44	53	15
2-7-8				68	25	84	23	20	54	14	78	69	60	79	66	-74	80	53	-24
2-8					49	70	42	32	46	28	59	54	38	56	58	-49	55	57	01
3-1						36	16	20	06	21	17	-02	-16	18	23	01	01	66	-08
3-2-1							33	29	56	24	73	62	51	66	66	-67	72	48	-12
4-6								66	68	57	36	48	45	43	35	-26	37	07	56
4-6-2									62	79	25	31	39	36	06	-27	29	04	61
4-8-2										49	59	72	72	47	59	-49	65	05	41
4-9											15	16	32	25	02	-26	20	08	64
8-3												70	67	79	60	-62	74	32	-12
8-6													80	61	71	-69	83	12	12
8-9														71	54	-62	77	03	20
9-6															65	-63	75	38	-06
K+																-43	59	38	-11
Nor																	-77	-21	12
Pso																		21	-09
Psn																			-33

[a] Stereotypes represent average sorts of five most homogeneous (of nine) descriptions (see Marks & Seeman, 1962b, 1962c). Nor = Normal, Pso = Psychotic, Psn = Psychoneurotic, PD = Personality Disorder. Reprented from Marks and Sines (1969).

(1954) and originally developed by Dahlstrom (1949). A checklist of descriptive terms (symptoms and complaints) empirically derived by Cantor (1952) and reported by Gilberstadt and Duker (1960) also provided a variety of items. From these sources over 300 descriptors were pretested on female subjects in the first 2-year sample by having three raters (senior medical students) independently rate the items on the basis of hospital records, case summaries, and therapy notes. In addition, raters were instructed to record any high frequency items not included in the original lists. For this pretesting, 5 female patients were randomly selected from each code type. On the basis of the records described above, the three raters indicated the presence or absence, or the degree of a phenomenon. The criteria for survival of any descriptor required (1) sufficient data for ratability; and (2) sufficient agreement for reliability of the rating. For example, it turned out that "urban-rural" (one of the items reported by Schofield *et al.*) was so frequently left blank by the raters that the conclusion was inevitable that the information in the folders was not sufficient to rate the item. (It should be clear that it is most undesirable to force a rating on any item for which sufficient information is not available, since such forcing would contribute to lowering reliability of the rating.) The reliability criterion required agreement by 2 of 3 raters for survival of any descriptor. Using this procedure some 225 descriptors were retained following a second series of ratings (by 3 staff psychologists) on the subsequent 2-year sample of female patients (5 from each code), the criterion group. This final list includes the new items reported and reliably rated, and the surviving original items in modified form. An example of a new item is "hysterectomy," which, interestingly, differentiates among the female codes. That is, 60% of the 3-2-1 female patients "lose their uterus" as compared with 5% of the 8-6 group, a difference significant well beyond the 0.01 level. All ratings were not only independent, but were carried out in the absence of any knowledge of either the MMPI profile or the code type to which the patient belonged.

Psychometric Data

The psychometric descriptors associated with each of the codes consist of an IQ estimated on the basis of the Shipley Institute of Living Scale[4] as well as a Conceptual Quotient (CQ) derived from that test instrument. Full scale Wechsler Adult Intelligence Scale (WAIS) IQ's are also provided, as are Verbal and Performance scale scores. Where available, WAIS subscale scores are also included. Finally, the routine admission and discharge or dismissal MMPI scores and profiles are given along with the projected discharge profiles.

These data, then, were culled from the psychological test folders of over 500 female clinic and hospitalized patients. The N's on which the data are based will vary for the different instruments because all tests were not routinely administered to all patients. With exception of the admission MMPI scores for eight of the codes (2-3-1, 2-7, 2-7-4, 2-7-8, 2-8, 4-8-2, 4-9, and normal K+), there are no scores for male subjects included in the psychometic data because the N's for the majority of variables were simply too small. For female patients, there were 310 Shipley scores available, 231 WAIS, 441 admission MMPIs, 258 projected discharge MMPIs, and 320 actual discharge MMPIs. For male patients, there were 175 admission MMPI scores available. Considering the *total* projected discharge data (where the N for men was sufficiently large), a comparison of admission with projected discharge profiles yields similar results for men and women. For both sexes, 12 of the 13 scales are different for the two profiles, all except scale 9 being significant at the 0.001 level. Comparing the projected discharge with the actual discharge profiles, scales L, F, 1, 6, 8, 9, and 0 behave

---

[4] Available from The Institute of Living, Hartford, Connecticut 06106.

alike for men and women. Scales 2, 3, 4, 5, and 7 are somewhat different for the sexes. For men, scales 2, 3, 4, and 5 are *not* different when actual and projected discharge scores are compared; for women, these scales differ for the two profiles. On scale 7, the scores differ significantly for male, but not for female patients.

Finally, as in the case of the Q-sort data, all psychometric data are uncontaminated by knowledge of the admission MMPI profile or by knowledge of the patient's code type.

ORGANIZATION OF DATA

For each adult code type a corresponding set of actuarial descriptions has been made available consisting of intelligence test scores, psychiatric diagnoses, and a narrative summary of significant Q-statement, mental status, and case history information. The code type itself is identified by two-digit or three-digit high points. Immediately below the code for each type appears the representative MMPI mean profile at time of admission (*i.e.*, the profile corresponding to the type), at time of projected discharge, and at time of actual discharge or termination of treatment. Next are given some descriptive characteristics of the patients included in that code type. For example, appearing below the profiles for the 2-3-1/2-1-3 are the following:

	Admission			Projected (broken line) 17ds++					
Female (solid line)	45ys+	30:69		3:35ds	36% T ≥ 70	0% Code−			
Male (broken line)	42ys	27:64		Discharge (solid line)	35ds				
* Classified by high-point code				20:176ds	67% T ≥ 70	25% Code			
Shipley	IQ	113	95:126	CQ 66 − − − 56:93					
WAIS IQ	FS	114+	96:128						
	VS	110	95:123	12+	13	9	11	7−	13
	PS	116+	93:131	11+	12+	7−	9	14+	

Below "Admission" the data represent, for "Females" and "Males" respectively, the mean age (45 and 42 years) and the age range (30 through 69 years for females and 27 through 64 years for males). Appearing next are the rules for profile classification. In the case of the 2-3-1/2-1-3, the profile is classified simply by reference to the three highest scales of the profile, which, in descending order may be either 2, 3, 1 or 2, 1, 3. "Projected" and "Discharge" refer, respectively, to the *projected* and *actual* discharge MMPI data (for females only). The projected discharge MMPI data were obtained shortly after admission under instructions "to answer the items as you expect to be when you get out of the hospital." For the 2-3-1/2-1-3 code, the projected discharge profile was obtained an average of 17 days (ds) after admission (range from 3 to 35 days); the actual, discharge profile, an average of 35 days (range from 20 to 176 days). The next entry refers to the percentage of profiles in which *any* clinical scale score equalled or exceeded 70 Ts (36% of the projected and 67% of the actual discharge profiles). Following this is given the percentage of profiles in which the code type itself remained unchanged. Thus, no patient in the 2-3-1/2-1-3 group obtained a 2-3-1/2-1-3 projected discharge profile; whereas 25% retained the 2-3-1/2-1-3 pattern on actual discharge.

Appearing next is the Shipley mean IQ (113), followed by the IQ range (95 through 126). Next appears the Shipley mean conceptual quotient CQ (66), followed by the CQ range (56 through 93). The mean and the range of scores below these are for the WAIS Full Scale IQ (FS), the WAIS Verbal Scale IQ (VS), and the WAIS Performance Scale IQ (PS). The figures to the right of these are median scaled scores for the Verbal and Performance WAIS subtests for the code type. These are given from left to right in the order in which they appear in the Record Form, that is, Information, Comprehension, Arithmetic, Similarities, Digit Span, Vocabulary. Below these are the Performance subtests: Digit Symbol, Picture Completion, Block Design, Picture Arrangement, Object Assembly.

The intelligence test scores are followed by psychiatric diagnoses. Presented in order of frequency are the major syndromes followed by the most frequently occurring subcategory or categories within the broader classification. In the case of the 2-3-1/2-1-3, 54% were diagnosed psychoneurotic, of whom the majority were either depressive or psychophysiologic reactions. Psychotic disorders were the next most prevalent, with depressive again the most frequent subtype. Next were brain syndromes, with the most frequent subtype (chronic), and last were personality disorders which, in the case of 2-3-1/2-1-3, were 0%.

Psychoneurosis	54%+	Depressive/psychophysiologic
Psychosis	30%	Depressive
Brain syndrome	17%+	Chronic
Personality disorder	0%	

Significant deviations from the average or base rate values of female data are expressed by + and − symbols. For example, in the case of the 2-3-1/2-1-3, the mean age (45) is above the third quartile (Q3) for all codes, and is hence followed by a +. Similarly for the 2-3-1/2-1-3, the incidence of psychoneurotic disorders (54%) is higher than the third quartile for all codes. Double plus signs (++) indicate values at least twice the difference between the base rate and the lowest frequency in the fourth quarter of codes, and triple plus signs (+++), values at least three times that difference. Similarly, double minus signs (−−) indicate values at least half the difference between the base rate and the highest frequency in the first quarter of codes, and triple minus signs (−−−) values at least one-third that difference.

The personality descriptions appearing next are narrative summaries of data selected on the basis of the preceding analysis. Included are descriptors (yielding ++, +++, −−, and −−− values) significant in this sense.

We should perhaps mention a problem introduced in connection with some of the significant "least descriptive" descriptors. An examination of the various codes revealed that certain items, in spite of their quartile designation, did not differentiate; *e.g.,* "Is normal, healthy, symptom-free" appeared as "least characteristic" of all code types, as might be expected in a psychiatric population. The astute reader will recognize such statements as "Barnum" in the sense previously defined in Chapter 2. And, indeed, it is hardly necessary to administer an MMPI or any other psychological test to ascertain this about a psychiatric patient. However, in selecting an adequate Q-item array, one is confronted with the necessity of including items which are sensitive to change in a person's psychological state over time. In other words, such item content is essential in order to express the dynamic characteristics of psychological states in this sense. Hopefully, subsequent descriptions of these patients after therapy would reveal a change in the placement of items such as these.

PREPARING AND CLASSIFYING THE PROFILE

It is important that the person who is to code and classify the MMPI profile be thoroughly familiar with the administration and scoring procedures in the Manual (Hathaway and McKinley, 1967).[5] It should be recalled that the adult data were derived on literate persons over 18 years of age[6] voluntarily seeking professional help for problems of personal adjustment. In particular, a very high F score (say greater than 26) may reflect violation of one or more of these criteria. For example, the lowest WAIS Full Scale IQ represented here is 65; consequently, it would be incorrect to use the data to interpret a profile where the question of mental deficiency is involved. Furthermore, the patient's motivation must be accounted crucial in classifying the test profile. In certain settings (*e.g.,* the criminal court) malingering may well occur with far greater frequency than in a typical psychiatric setting. Finally, it should be noted that the data for adults were derived mainly on females, and that some unspecifiable proportion of these are inappropriate for males. This system is not appropriate, therefore, for routine screening of presumably normal individuals who are largely symptom free. It should not be used for any nonclinical purpose.

The fundamental step preparatory to using the actuarial descriptive data (once the MMPI has been administered and scored, and the scores plotted on the profile) involves classification of the coded MMPI profile. Essentially, coding consists of writing the scale numbers from left to right in order of descending scale magnitudes (see Chapter 1); *e.g.,* a 2-3-1 code indicates scale 2 is highest in the profile, scale 3 is next, etc. Prior to entering the code-type section certain precautionary measures should be carried out to ensure the accuracy of classification. In the first place, the sex of the patient should correspond to that indicated on the profile sheet; that is, male profiles should be plotted on the side

[5] Available from The Psychological Corporation, 304 East 45th Street, New York, New York 10017.

[6] The adult data may be appropriate for some 17 or 18 year-olds, although the reader should consult the adolescent data first.

of the profile sheet indicated for men and female profiles on the side of the sheet indicated for women. Since all profiles in the *adult section* are K-corrected, it is important to ascertain that the K-correction has been accurately recorded and totaled for the five scales involved. A check should next be made to make certain that the scores plotted on the profile are actually those reported in the scoring. That is, the raw score totals recorded at the bottom of the profile sheet should correspond to the values on the respective scales in the body of the profile. *In the event that the raw F score exceeds 26, the clinician is advised to read the discussion of scale F in Chapter 1 before proceeding further.*[7] Next the user is to make certain that the first two or three digits in the code correspond, in fact, to the order of elevation and arrangement of the corresponding scales. That is, if a profile has been coded 2-3-1/2-1-3 then scale 2 should be highest or equal to scales 3 and 1, scale 3 or 1 should be next or equal to each other, and the remaining scale (1 or 3) should be last.

The steps required preparatory to entering the code-type section may be summarized as follows:

1. Care should be exercised to plot the scores on the side of the profile sheet indicating "Males" for men, and "Females" for women.

2. The raw score totals should be checked particularly with attention to accuracy on the five scales where K is added.

3. The raw score totals at the bottom of the profile sheet should correspond to the figures on the respective scales in the body of the profile sheet.

4. When the raw F score exceeds 26, consult the discussion of scale F in Chapter 1.

5. The first two or three digits of the code should be recorded in the order of descending magnitudes of the corresponding scales.

Once these steps have been completed the next procedure is to ascertain which of the code types most closely corresponds (*i.e.*, "fits") the individual patient's profile. Following the "average" patient description, the codes are arranged in numerical order beginning with profiles which have 2 as the highest scale and ending with the profile which has 9 as the highest scale; except that the normal K+ code follows these and is the last code type in the adult section. In the case of seven of the codes (2-3-1/2-1-3, 2-7, 2 8/8-2, 3-1/1-3, 4-9, 8-6/6-8, and 9-6/6-9),[8] the profile may be classified simply on the basis of the first two or three high points (*i.e.*, by the code type). Five of the codes require a slight modification of this procedure. Thus, in the case of 2-7-4/2-4-7/4-7-2 and 2-7-8/8-7-2, scale 0 is disregarded in making the classification; for the 3-2-1 and 8-9/9-8, scale 7 is disregarded, and for the 4-6/6-4, scale 8 is disregarded. The remaining four codes (4-6-2/6-4-2, 4-8-2/8-4-2/8-2-4, 8-3/3-8, and K+) require the application of the original contingency rules.

---

[7] We recommend this simply as a precautionary measure. The code types themselves were actually derived without regard to F-scale elevation.

[8] The within type high-point arrangement is based on the frequency of occurrence. *E.g.*, in the case of 2-3-1/2-1-3, there were more profiles coded 2-3-1 then there were coded 2-1-3.

If the reader is in doubt about classifying a profile, he should turn to the "Mean Profile Index"[9] and inspect all profiles with a first digit high point corresponding to that of the patient's code; for example, if the patient's high point digit is 2, inspect all profile types coded 2. There are five such combinations in which 2 appears as the first digit (2-3-1/2-1-3, 2-7, 2-7-4/2-4-7, 2-7-8, and 2-8). The second digit in the code should next be considered for fit (*e.g.,* 2-3, 2-7, etc.) and then the third digit. In the case of the four types which require contingency rules, visual configural properties of the profile can serve as a guide in addition to the code digits. An estimate of fit for these types can then be obtained by comparing the individual profile curve with the mean profile curve for the specified code type. However, "goodness of fit" is judged by additional criteria stated below the profile curve for the code type. In other words, an individual patient's MMPI profile fits one of these types if it fulfills the specifications set down by these rules. The decision concerning profile fit should be made with extreme care since misclassification would obviously have serious consequences. Once the profile has been classified, all descriptive data for the type may be read as equally applicable to the individual patient.

While many adult MMPI profiles can be classified simply by reference to high points, there are the four types already mentioned for which it is considered advisable to permit some "degrees of freedom" for defining the code in order to encompass enough patients to render the system maximally useful.

To illustrate what this means, consider the *broken line* profile in Figure 5. The high points in this profile are 8 and 1. There is, however, no 8-1 (or 1-8) adult code type. Nonetheless, visually the profile in Figure 5 is similar to the mean profile (*solid line*) of the 8-3 and *no other code type.* Examining the specification rules for the 8-3 one finds:

> 8, 3, and 1 above 70 Ts (97, 87, and 92, respectively)
> 3 minus 1 less than 10 T-scores (87 − 92 = −5)
> 3 minus 2 more than 5 T-scores (87 − 68 = 19)
> 8 greater than 3 (97 > 87)
> 8 minus 7 more than 5 T-scores (97 − 82 = 15)
> 8 minus 9 more than 10 T-scores (97 − 70 = 27)
> 9 greater than 0 (70 > 58)
> 0 below 70 Ts (0 = 58)

Thus, the MMPI profile in Figure 5 meets all requirements of the 8-3/3-8 specification rules, and may be subsumed under this code type.

---

[9] This Index and the other mean profiles are plotted mainly for convenience to the clinician. Most users of the MMPI are more accustomed to viewing the curve than reading the actual scores.

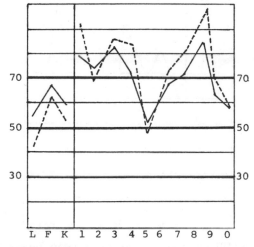

Fig. 5. Individual MMPI profile (*broken line*) coded 8-1 and mean profile (*solid line*) of the 8-3/3-8 adult code type.

Now, consider the patient profile in Figure 6. Since the two scales most elevated are 8 and 4, the first two digits of the code are 8-4. An inspection of the adult Mean Profile Index reveals no 8-4 code. There are, however, five code types in which 8 appears as the highest scale (8-2, 8-3, 8-4-2, 8-6, and 8-9). In this instance, it is necessary to examine the Mean Profile Index in order to decide on the code of best fit. The configural properties both of the 8-6 and of the 4-8-2 (or 8-4-2) most closely approximate the pattern of the patient's profile. Under these circumstances, it is necessary to consult the rules if, as in the case of the 4-8-2 (8-4-2), there are rules to apply. Consider these:

> 4, 8, and 2 above 70 Ts (90, 98 and 80, respectively)
> 4 minus 2 less than 15 T-scores (90 − 80 = 10)
> 4 greater than 7 (90 > 85)
> 8 minus 2 less than 15 T-scores (98 − 80 = 18)
> 8 minus 7 more than 5 T-scores (98 − 85 = 13)
> 8 minus 9 more than 10 T-scores (98 − 60 = 38)
> 9 below 70 Ts (9 = 60)
> L and K less than F (43 and 40 < 80+)
> F below 80 Ts (F = 80+)

Clearly, the patient's profile violates rules 4 and 9 for this code type. Since there are no rules for the 8-6/6-8, and since the patient's profile has only one scale (4) greater than 6, the profile may be subsumed under this code for purpose of the actuarial description. A somewhat different classification problem is presented by the patient's profile in Figure 7. Is the MMPI profile here an 8-6/6-8, 8-9/9-8, or 9-6/6-9 code type? Considering *only* the two digit code, any one of these is possible, since 6, 8, and 9 all are elevated and at approximately

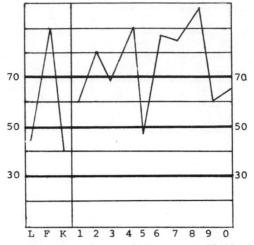

Fig. 6. Individual MMPI profile coded 8-4 which can be classified by the 8-6/6-8 adult code
type.

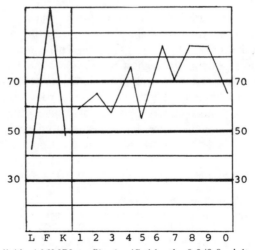

Fig. 7. Individual MMPI profile classified by the 8-9/9-8 adult code type.

identical magnitudes. Consultation of the adult Mean Profile Index reveals these
to be among the last three code types listed. What strikes the eye immediately in
the 8-6 profile is the difference between scales 8 and 9. For the patient's profile
in Figure 7, scales 8 and 9 are equal. The patient's profile is thus quite different
in configuration. Next, the 9-6 code (the next to final code in the adult Mean
Profile Index) again reveals a considerable difference between scales 8 and 9.
But, as we have already seen, the difference between 9 and 8 in the patient's
profile is 0. The third mean profile to be considered in the Index is the 8-9/9-8.
On inspection, it is apparent that the patient's profile is indeed most similar to

the 8-9/9-8 and thus this code type would yield the most appropriate actuarial description.

The next illustrative case is the patient's profile in Figure 8, in which scale 0 attains the highest elevation. However, no 0 high point in *any* combination appears among the adult codes (see Mean Profile Index). An absolute and rigid adherence to the rules, therefore, would make this an unclassifiable profile insofar as this system is concerned. One can ask: Discounting scale 0, could the profile be classified? Reference to the Mean Profile Index and the next three high points indicates that by disregarding scale 0, the profile may be classified by the code 2-7-4/2-4-7/4-7-2. We would thus be inclined to classify the profile by this type, apply the corresponding personality description, but include some scale 0 modifications. A review of the discussion of scale 0 in Chapter 1 reveals that 0 scale elevation is an indicator of shyness, social withdrawal, brooding, uneasiness, and self-deprecation. Hence, these descriptive terms, in addition to the 2-7-4 actuarial data, could be said to characterize the patient represented in Figure 8.

A somewhat complicated problem is presented by the profile in Figure 9. In this instance, rigidly applying the high-point system would eliminate the profile from classification for there is no 1-2 or 1-2-3 code among any of the adult types. The question arises, should this profile be eliminated from classification or can it be adapted to the actuarial descriptions of, say, the 2-3-1/2-1-3 and 3-2-1, to which it is visually similar. To this question, there is as yet no definitive answer; this is a question to be answered by future research. On the other hand, an inspection of the "most descriptive" Q statements (see Appendix) of both the 2-3-1/2-1-3 and 3-2-1 code types reveals eight items in common. It seems clinically plausible to accept these as descriptive of the patient represented in

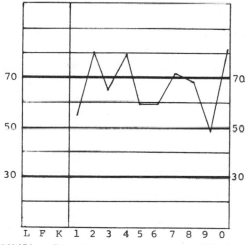

Fig. 8. Individual MMPI profile coded 0-2-4 which can be classified by the 2-7-4/2-4-7/4-7-2 adult code type.

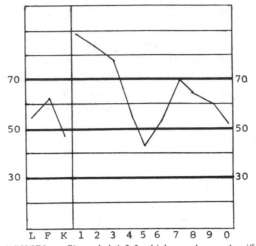

Fig. 9. Individual MMPI profile coded 1-2-3 which can be co-classified by the 2-3-1 and 3-2-1 adult code types.

Figure 9. In addition, the experienced clinician would be aware that scale 1 (which is the most elevated scale in the profile) taps concern about bodily health. Thus, he would "over interpret" this aspect for the profile in question, as he would in the case of the scale 0 modification discussed above.

This, of course, raises the broader question of how deviations from the code-type specifications are to be dealt with in the general case. It is unfortunately not possible to state a set of rules for abrogating the code-typing rules. And, rather than misclassify the profile by type, the clinician is well advised to consult Chapter 1 to obtain clinical descriptive data for single scale elevations.

A word needs to be said about the "Normal K+" profile, the last adult code type. The most important thing to be said about this code is that it was developed exclusively on *hospitalized* psychiatric patients (*i.e.,* inpatients on a psychiatry service), and it would, therefore, be inappropriate to apply the actuarial descriptive data to *any other group.* It might also be pointed out that the specification rules make no stipulations concerning the magnitude of the clinical scales relative to each other. That is, the highest elevations can occur on *any* of the scales in any combination. We hasten to add that for this reason the average profile has unknown clinical meaning.

The steps in classifying an individual adult MMPI profile may be summarized as follows:

1. Code the profile following the system described above and in Chapter 1.

2. If the individual profile is that of a *hospitalized* psychiatric patient, and if all clinical scale scores are below 70, refer to the Normal K+ profile appearing as the last code in the adult section.

3. If the individual profile has at least one clinical scale score above 70,

consult the Mean Profile Index and inspect all code types with high points corresponding to the high point of the individual profile.

4. If the first two or three high points of the individual profile correspond to those of a code type, refer to the adult code section for further instructions. If the individual profile can be classified by the high points, the corresponding actuarial description may be used.

5. If the first two or three digits do not *fully* correspond (*e.g.,* a 2-3-4 rather than a 2-3-1), consider the configural properties (shape) of all code types with corresponding high points (*i.e.,* consider all 2's, all 3's, etc.).

6. Refer to the specification rules of those code types indicated by Step 5 above. If the individual profile fulfills all rules for a code type, the corresponding actuarial description may be used.

7. When the procedures followed above do not lead to classification under one of the codes, find in the Mean Profile Index those profiles which have configural properties (shape) similar to those of the individual profile.

8. Refer to the specification rules of all code types considered in Step 7 above. If the individual profile fulfills all rules for a code type, the corresponding actuarial description may be used.

9. When the foregoing procedures have not led to classification under one of the code types, refer to the discussion in connection with Figure 8 above.

10. For descriptive data on unclassifiable profiles, refer to the discussion of scales in Chapter 1 and to the material in the Appendix.

It is hoped that the preceding discussion and illustrations have contributed to some clarification of the rules governing the code types and of the procedures involved in classifying an individual MMPI profile. It cannot be emphasized too strongly, however, that the only way to become familiar with these procedures is through continued practice and use.

A comparative study of descriptive characteristics across code types is made possible by the data presented in the Appendix. For example, the data on "system involvement" reveal that only 10.0% of the 2-7 patients exhibit "musculoskeletal" complaints and 5.0% of the 2-7-4 patients present "gastrointestinal" complaints; in contrast, 60.0% of the 3-1 and the 8-3 patients present "musculoskeletal" complaints with 65.0% of the 3-1 patients indicating "gastrointestinal" complaints. At a rather low theoretical level the association of scale 3 with these kinds of symptomatic expressions of illness makes sense in the light of known characteristics of the patients on whom scale 3 was derived. Across other code types there are some interesting differences in age of onset. Scales 4 and 9 appear to be "young" scales in the sense that psychological disorder in general appears to occur earlier in the life of those patients for whom these scales are prominent. The average age of onset for the 4-9 code is 22.6, in contrast to age 49.0 for the 2-7. In addition, it is well known that elevation on scales 4 and 9 is exceedingly frequent for adolescents.

Presented in Table 5 are some selected personal history characteristics which

Table 5. *Comparison of Selected Personal History Characteristics for Various Code Types* [a]

Characteristic	High Frequency		Low Frequency	
	Code	%	Code	%
Sibling status				
Youngest	2-7-4	44	3-2-1	7
Middle	3-2-1	67	2-7-4	17
Oldest	K+	50	3-2-1	7
Childhood health				
Behavior problem	4-9	61	2-7-4, 2-8	0
School achievement				
Above average	2-7, 3-2-1	50	2-3-1, 4-8-2, 8-6	10
Below average	4-8-2	40	2-7	0
Social				
Withdrawal	2-7-8	80	4-9	18
Delinquency				
Sexual	4-9	56	2-7, 3-1	0
Education				
College (combined)	K+	61	2-8	6
Parental home				
Death (combined)	3-1	60	4-8-2, 8-6	10
Paternal relations				
Affection	3-1	77	2-3-1	13
Indifference	4-9	53	2-7-4	7
Maternal relations				
Affection	8-9	60	4-8-2	0
Domination	4-9	56	4-6-2	7

[a] As reported in the Appendix.

illustrate differences across codes. This list by no means exhausts such differences and there may be other characteristics which may be of greater interest to the reader.

REFERENCES

ALTMAN, H., GYNTHER, M. D., WARBIN, R. W., AND SLETTEN, I. W. A new empirical automated MMPI interpretive program: The 6-8/8-6 code type. *J. Clin. Psychol. 28*, 495–498, 1972.

ALTMAN, H., GYNTHER, M. D., WARBIN, R. W., AND SLETTEN, I. W. Replicated empirical correlates of the MMPI 8-9/9-8 code type. *J. Personal. Assess.*, in press.

BECKETT, P. G. S., GRISELL, J. G., AND GUDOBBA, R. Psychiatric attributes of MMPI profiles. Paper presented at the Sixth Annual Meetings of the IBM Medical Symposium, Poughkeepsie, New York, October, 1964.

BLOCK, J. A comparison of the forced and unforced Q-sorting Procedures. *Educational and Psychological Measurement, 16*, 481-493, 1956.

BLOCK, J. *The Q-sort method in personality assessment and psychiatric research.* Springfield: Charles C Thomas, 1961.

BRIGGS, P. F., TAYLOR, M., AND TELLEGEN, A. A study of the Marks and Seeman MMPI profile types as applied to a sample of 2,875 psychiatric patients. Research Laboratories Report No. PR-66-5, Department of Psychiatry, University of Minnesota, 1966.

CANTOR, J. M. Syndromes found in psychiatric population selected for certain MMPI code endings. Doctoral dissertation. University of Minnesota, Minneapolis, Minn., 1952.

CONE, J. D. A note on Marks' and Seeman's rules for actuarially classifying psychiatric patients. *J. Clin. Psychol. 22*, 270, 1966.

CRONBACH L. J. Correlations between persons as a research tool. In O. H. Mowrer (Ed.) *Psychotherapy theory and research.* New York: Ronald Press, 1953.

DAHLSTROM, W. G. An exploration of mental status syndromes by factor analytic techniques. Doctoral dissertation, University of Minnesota, Minneapolis, Minn., 1949.

FOWLER, R. D., AND COYLE, F. A. A comparison of two MMPI actuarial systems in classifying an alcoholic outpatient population. *J. Clin. Psychol. 24*, 434-435, 1968a.

FOWLER, R. D., AND COYLE, F. A. Overlap as a problem in *Atlas* classification of MMPI profiles. *J. Clin. Psychol. 24*, 435, 1968b.

GILBERSTADT, H., AND DUKER, J. Case history correlates of three MMPI profile types. *J. Consult. Psychol. 24*, 361-367, 1960.

GOLDBERG, L. R. Diagnosticians vs. diagnostic signs: The diagnosis of psychosis vs. neurosis from the MMPI. *Psychol. Monogr. 79*, 1965.

GOLDBERG, L. R. The search for configural relationships in personality assessment: The diagnosis of psychosis vs. neurosis from the MMPI. *Multivariate Behav. Res. 4*, 523-536, 1969.

GOLDBERG, L. R. Some recent trends in personality assessment. *J. Personality Assess. 36*, 547-560, 1972.

GRAHAM, J. Behavioral correlates of simple MMPI code types. In J. N. Butcher (Chm.), MMPI symposium. Presented at the Eighth Annual Symposium on Recent Developments in the Use of the MMPI, New Orleans, February, 1973.

GYNTHER, M. D. A new replicated actuarial program for interpreting MMPI's of state hospital patients. In J. N. Butcher (Chm.), MMPI symposium. Presented at the Seventh Annual Symposium on Recent Developments in the Use of the MMPI, Mexico City, February, 1972.

GYNTHER, M. D., ALTMAN, H., AND SLETTEN, I. W. Development of an empirical interpretive system for the MMPI: Some after-the-fact observations. *J. Clin. Psychol. 29*, 232-234, 1973.

GYNTHER, M. D., ALTMAN, H., AND WARBIN, R. W. A new empirical automated MMPI interpretive program: The 2-4/4-2 code type. *J. Clin. Psychol. 28*, 498-501, 1972.

GYNTHER, M. D., ALTMAN, H., AND WARBIN, R. W. A new actuarial-empirical automated MMPI interpretive program; The 4-3/3-4 type. *J. Clin. Psychol. 29*, 229-231, 1973.

GYNTHER, M. D., ALTMAN, H., AND WARBIN, R. W. Behavioral correlates for the Minnesota Multiphasic Personality Inventory 4-9, 9-4 code types: A case of the emperor's new clothes? *J. Consult. Clin. Psychol. 40*, 259-263, 1973a.

GYNTHER, M. D., ALTMAN, H., AND WARBIN, R. Interpretation of uninterpretable Minnesota Multiphasic Personality Inventory profiles. *J. Consul. Clin. Psychol. 40*, 78-83, 1973*b*.

GYNTHER, M. D., ALTMAN, H., AND WARBIN, R. W. A new empirical automated MMPI interpretive program: The 6-9/9-6 code type. *J. Clin. Psychol.*, in press.

GYNTHER, M. D., ALTMAN, H., AND WARBIN, R. W. A new empirical automated MMPI interpretive program: The 2-7/7-2 code type. *J. Clin. Psychol.*, in press.

GYNTHER, M. D., ALTMAN, H., WARBIN, R. W., AND SLETTEN, I. W. A new actuarial system for MMPI interpretation: Rationale and methodology. *J. Clin. Psychol. 28*, 173-179, 1972.

GYNTHER, M. D., ALTMAN, H., WARBIN, R. W., AND SLETTEN, I. W. A new empirical automated MMPI interpretive program: The 1-2/2-1 code type. *J. Clin. Psychol.*, in press.

HALBOWER, C. C. A comparison of actuarial versus clinical prediction to classes discriminated by MMPI. Doctoral dissertation, University of Minnesota, Minneapolis, Minn., 1955.

HATHAWAY, S. R., AND MCKINLEY, J. C. *The Minnesota multiphaseic personality inventory manual, revised.* New York: The Psychological Corporation, 1967.

HERRELL, J. M. Administrative variables affecting the utility of an MMPI Atlas. *J. Consult. Clin. Psychol. 37*, 302-303, 1971.

HUFF, F. W. Use of actuarial description of abnormal personality in a mental hospital. *Psychol. Rep. 17*, 224, 1965.

LACHAR, D. MMPI two-point code-type correlates in a state hospital population. *J. Clin. Psychol. 24*, 424-427, 1968.

LEWANDOWSKI, D., AND GRAHAM, J. R. Empirical correlates of frequently occurring two-point MMPI code types: A replicated study. *J. Consult. Clin. Psychol. 39*, 467-472, 1972.

LIVSON, N. H., AND NICHOLS, T. F. Discrimination and reliability in Q-sort personality descriptions. *J. Abnorm. Soc. Psychol. 52*, 159–165, 1956.

MARKS, P. A. An assessment of the diagnostic process in a child guidance setting. *Psychol. Monogr. 75*, 1961.

MARKS, P. A., AND SEEMAN, W. On the Barnum effect. *Psychol. Rec. 12*, 203-208, 1962*a*.

MARKS, P. A., AND SEEMAN, W. The heterogeneity of some common psychiatric stereotypes. *J. Clin. Psychol. 18*, 266-270, 1962*b*.

MARKS, P. A., AND SEEMAN, W. A study of stereotype conceptions of psychological disorders. *J. Clin. Psychol. 18*, 507-510, 1962*c*.

MARKS, P. A., AND SEEMAN, W. Academic knowledge and clinical concepts of medical students in psychiatry. *J. Kans. Med. Soc. 64*, 101–103, 1963*a*.

MARKS, P. A., AND SEEMAN, W. *The actuarial description of abnormal personality: An Atlas for use with the MMPI.* Baltimore: Williams & Wilkins, 1963*b*.

MARKS, P. A., AND SINES, J. O. Methodological problems in cookbook construction. In J. N. Butcher (Ed.) *MMPI: Research developments and clinical applications.* New York: McGraw-Hill Book Co., 1969.

MEEHL, P. E. A comparison of clinicians with five statistical methods of identifying psychotic MMPI profiles. *J. Counsel. Psychol. 6*, 102-109, 1959.

MEEHL, P. E., AND DAHLSTROM, W. G. Rules for profile discrimination. Mimeographed manuscript, Authors, 1959.

MEEHL, P. E., AND DAHLSTROM, W. G. Objective configural rules for discriminating psychotic from neurotic MMPI profiles. *J. Consult. Psychol. 24*, 375, 1960.

MEIKLE, S., AND GERRITSE, R. MMPI "cookbook" pattern frequencies in a psychiatric unit. *J. Clin. Psychol. 26, 82-84, 1970.*

NEWMARK, C. S., AND FINKLESTEIN, M. Maximizing classification rates of Marks and Seeman code types. *J. Clin. Psychol. 29*, 61-62, 1973.

OWEN, D. R. Classification of MMPI profiles from non-psychiatric populations using two cookbook systems. *J. Clin. Psychol. 26*, 79-82, 1970.

PAUKER, J. D. Identification of MMPI profile types in a female, inpatient, psychiatric setting using the Marks and Seeman rules. *J. Consult. Psychol. 30*, 90, 1966.

PAYNE, F. D., AND WIGGINS, J. S. The effects of rule relaxation and system combination on classification rates in two MMPI "cookbook" systems. *J. Consult. Clin. Psychol. 32*, 734–736, 1968.

ROSMAN, R. R., BARRY, S. M., AND GIBEAU, P. J. Problems in Atlas classification of MMPI profiles. *J. Clin. Psychol. 22*, 308-310, 1966.

SCHOFIELD, W., HATHAWAY, S. R., HASTINGS, D. W., AND BELL, D. M. Prognostic factors in schizophrenia. *J. Consult. Psychol. 18*, 155-166, 1954.

SHULTS, T. D., GIBEAU, P. J., AND BARRY, S. M. Utility of MMPI "cookbooks." *J. Clin. Psychol. 24*, 430-433, 1968.

SINES, J. O. Actuarial methods in personality assessment. In B. A. Maher (Ed.) *Volume 3: Progress in experimental personality research*. New York: Academic Press, 1966.

STEPHENSON, W. Some observations on Q technique. *Psychol. Bull. 49*, 483-498, 1952.

STILSON, D. W., AND ASTRUP, C. Nonlinear and additive methods for long-term prognosis in the functional psychoses. *J. Nerv. Ment. Dis. 141*, 468-473, 1966.

WARBIN, R. W., ALTMAN, H., GYNTHER, M. D., AND SLETTER, I. W. A new empirical automated MMPI interpretive program: 2-8 and 8-2 code types. *J. Personal. Assess. 36*, 581-584, 1972.

WEBB, J. T. The relation of MMPI two-point codes to age, sex, and education level in a representative nationwide sample of psychiatric outpatients. Paper presented at the Annual Meetings of the Southeastern Psychological Association, Louisville, April, 1970.

WILCOX, R., AND KRASNOFF, A. Influence of test-taking attitudes on personality inventory scores. *J. Consult. Psychol. 31*, 188-194, 1967.

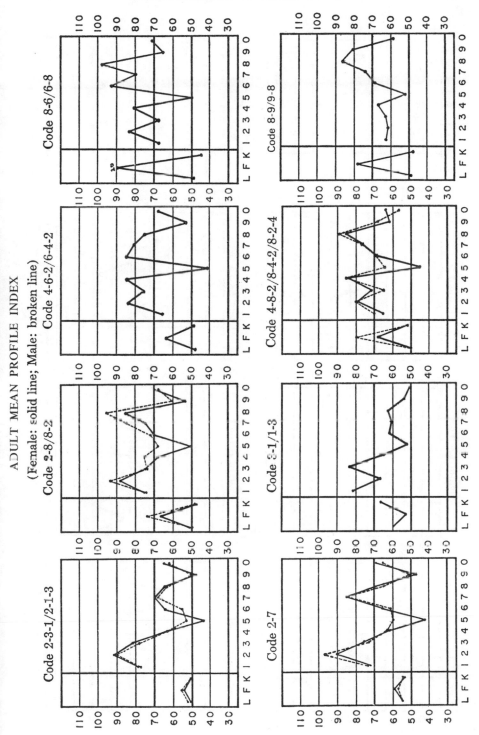

ADULT MEAN PROFILE INDEX

(Female: solid line; Male: broken line)

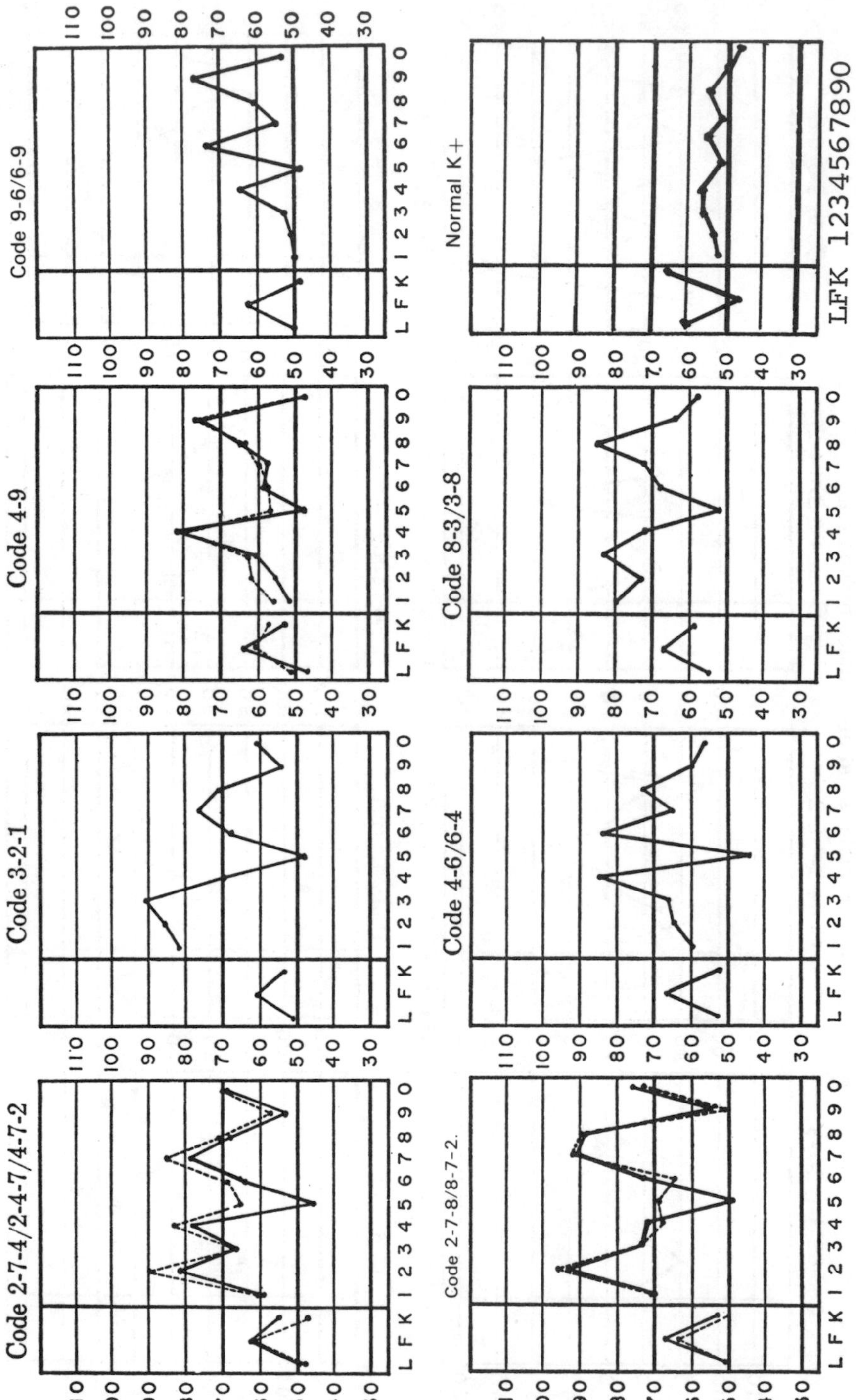

Code 9-6/6-9
Code 4-9
Code 3-2-1
Code 2-7-4/2-4-7/4-7-2
Normal K+
Code 8-3/3-8
Code 4-6/6-4
Code 2-7-8/8-7-2.
L F K 1 2 3 4 5 6 7 8 9 0
110
100
90
80
70
60
50
40
30

4

Characteristics of Adult Codes

THE AVERAGE KUMC ADULT FEMALE PSYCHIATRIC PATIENT

In referring to the "average patient" we do not wish to suggest that there exists a person or group of persons who "fit" a certain set of descriptive statements. Rather, we are suggesting that there may be a useful fiction or stereotype which incorporates the base rates of certain facts relevant to this patient. We expect no broad consensual agreement on the usefulness of such a concept; indeed, we suspect that there might be a range of opinion from angry rejection, through indifference, to friendly receptivity. At any rate, our intention in presenting a picture of the "average patient" is to answer this question: Given a set of descriptors (such as our Q statements), what are the base rates which express clinicians' assessments of psychiatric patients? The relevant data (the base rates) are those which appear in the "Total" and "BR" columns of the Appendix. A number of studies have indicated that patients in other psychiatric settings may, in some respects, be different from those at KUMC (*e.g.*, see Briggs *et al.*, 1966; Gynther *et al.*, 1972; Lachar, 1968; Meikle and Gerritse, 1970).

AVERAGE ADULT PATIENT

Mean Profiles

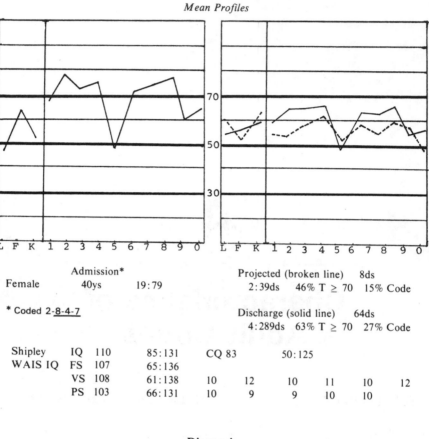

	Admission*	
Female	40ys	19:79

* Coded 2-8-4-7

Projected (broken line)   8ds
    2:39ds   46% T ≥ 70   15% Code

Discharge (solid line)   64ds
    4:289ds   63% T ≥ 70   27% Code

Shipley	IQ	110	85:131	CQ 83		50:125			
WAIS IQ	FS	107	65:136						
	VS	108	61:138	10	12	10	11	10	12
	PS	103	66:131	10	9	9	10	10	

Diagnosis

Psychosis	46%	Schizophrenic/paranoid
Psychoneurosis	28%	Depressive
Personality disorder	20%	Trait/aggressive
Brain syndrome	6%	Chronic

Personality Description

It seems clear that the characteristic expression of the average patient's unhappiness is via depressive mood, despondency, and feelings of hopelessness. This clinical assessment is in accord with the frequent elevation of scale 2 for both inpatients and outpatients. A correlate of this depression is the intropunitive disposition of the patient, that is, the tendency to turn blame and punishment inward against the self rather than outward against others. It may also be that the complaints of weakness and easy fatigability are somatic counterparts of subjective depression. Closely comparable in ratings by clinicians are the propensity for persistent worrying and a tendency to overreact to what is perceived as threat. Unfortunately, those things that others perceive as mere irritants are seen as dangerous by the patient; minor discomforts are reacted to as emergencies. A variety of fears and phobias are present. Anxious, tense, high-strung, and jumpy are adjectives characteristically applied to this patient, who has difficulty sleeping as well. One of the most pervasive aspects of the behavior is lack of modulation—an inability to maintain an emotional balance. Thus, it may be said that the defenses which ordinarily relieve psychological distress are not adequately functioning.

The average patient seems basically insecure and has exaggerated needs for attention and affection. These needs, the inner conflicts about dependency, and the fear of emotional involvement with others, lead the patient to keep others at a distance and to make close personal friendships very difficult. The ratings also indicate distrust of people, doubt about the motivations of others, and sensitivity to anything that can be construed as a demand. It follows that a person with these conflicts would also entertain sexual conflicts.

The average patient is considered to be more than normally ruminative and obsessional and to display stereotyped rather than flexible approaches to the solution of problems. Resentment and irritability are manifested, though at what might be characterized as a moderate level.

The average patient is a hospitalized 40 year old. Her personal history places her as a middle child in a disrupted home. Her academic history is about average and she has a high school education. Although withdrawn, the average patient dated frequently and married at age 20, with parental consent. The areas most affected by the patient's disturbance appear to be "personality" and "home." There is generally only small improvement with treatment, which tends to be "psychotherapy only," and the prognosis is poor.

ADULT CODE: 2-3-1/2-1-3*

Mean Profiles

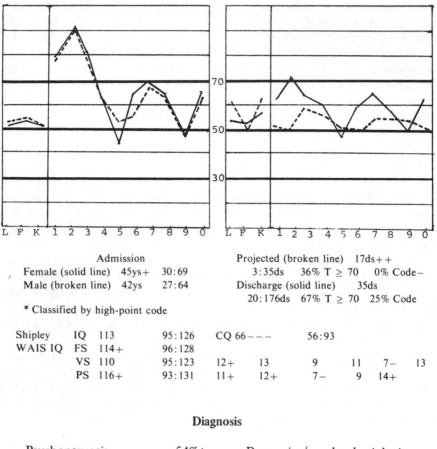

	Admission	
Female (solid line)	45ys+	30:69
Male (broken line)	42ys	27:64

Projected (broken line)   17ds++
    3:35ds   36% T ≥ 70   0% Code−
Discharge (solid line)   35ds
    20:176ds 67% T ≥ 70 25% Code

* Classified by high-point code

Shipley	IQ	113	95:126	CQ 66 − − −	56:93				
WAIS IQ	FS	114+	96:128						
	VS	110	95:123	12+	13	9	11	7−	13
	PS	116+	93:131	11+	12+	7−	9	14+	

Diagnosis

Psychoneurosis	54%+	Depressive/psychophysiologic
Psychosis	30%	Depressive
Brain syndrome	17%+	Chronic
Personality disorder	0%	

Personality Description

    People who generate this profile are likely to perceive themselves as physically ill. Their complaints are hypochondriacal; that is, they represent the displacement of psychic conflicts in the somatic domain. The personality may be characterized as "hysteroid." A variety of complaints are to be expected, with about 50% of these patients reporting gastrointestinal problems; the musculo-skeletal and cardiorespiratory systems are also frequently implicated. Specific symptoms include headache, nausea and vomiting, chest and heart pain, fatigue, weakness, tremor, ulcers, weight loss, paresthesia, loss of interest, impaired sleep, and forgetfulness. Alcoholism is also more frequent among this group than among the total psychiatric population. Such people may derive appreciable secondary gain from their symptoms as well as from the sympathy they demand and often elicit from others. The duration of their disability is generally longer than a year and previous similar episodes are reported in 50% of the cases. Adjectives used most often to describe these patients are tense and nervous.

People with this profile also typically exhibit depression (manifest sad mood), impaired morale, and multiple neurotic complaints. They tend to be self-depreciating, self-punishing (intropunitive), rather than blame others for their misfortunes. They are vulnerable to threat—sometimes real and sometimes fancied; they are generally fearful and given to constant worrying. These patients have considerable internal conflict over self-assertion and dependency. Psychomotor retardation is evident from the general slow tempo of these people and also from their depressed speech rate which, in turn, reflects a slowing of thought processes.

About 70% of the case histories studied report parental indifference or rejection (especially by fathers)—a figure significantly higher than the base rate for the psychiatric population. Sixty per cent of these patients come from disrupted homes; 55% were subjected to a death in their immediate family during childhood. Typically these patients are not the youngest child. It is not surprising, then, that these people report subjective emotional deprivation and lack of parental affection. Their therapists see them as insecure and possessing a basic need for attention.

People with this profile are pessimistic about the benefits of treatment and about the future, perhaps even more so that are people with the 2-7 profile type; scale 2 (Depression) is more elevated for the 2-3-1 (by a half a standard deviation). Treatment outcomes, however, do not indicate that this super-pessimistic attitude is justifiable—either in terms of discharge MMPI (obtained at the termination of therapy) or therapists' ratings uncontaminated by the MMPI. With respect to the latter, only 7% were rated "no change" and none were rated "worse." The typical diagnosis for these patients included depression (about 85%); 50% also had psychophysiological concomitants.

It would be *atypical* for people yielding this profile to exhibit such grossly psychotic features as delusional thinking or schizoid 'cognitive slippage.' It is *not* likely that they would be distrustful of people in general, nor is it likely that they would question the motivation of others. Neither is it probable that psychopathic features would be present; these people tend *not* to be flippant in word or gesture and do *not* take the attitude that the world owes them a living. They also do *not* undervalue or derogate the opposite sex. Clinical judgments by their therapists suggest that intellectualization is *not* at all prominent in the armamentarium of defense mechanisms for people with this profile type.

ADULT CODE: 2-7*

Mean Profiles

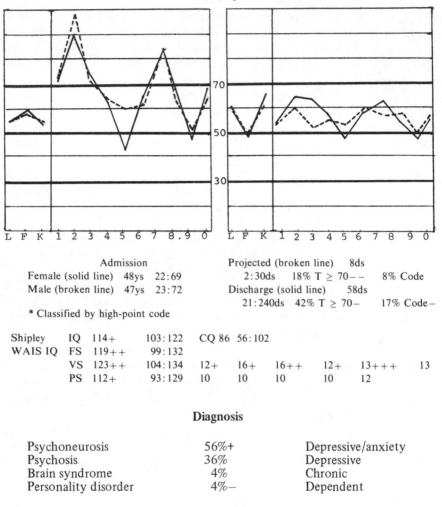

Admission
Female (solid line) 48ys   22:69
Male (broken line)   47ys   23:72

* Classified by high-point code

Projected (broken line)   8ds
2:30ds   18% T ≥ 70– –   8% Code
Discharge (solid line)   58ds
21:240ds   42% T ≥ 70–   17% Code–

Shipley	IQ	114+	103:122	CQ 86	56:102			
WAIS IQ	FS	119++	99:132					
	VS	123++	104:134	12+	16+	16++	12+	13+++	13
	PS	112+	93:129	10	10	10	10	12

Diagnosis

Psychoneurosis	56%+	Depressive/anxiety
Psychosis	36%	Depressive
Brain syndrome	4%	Chronic
Personality disorder	4%–	Dependent

Personality Description

The most salient descriptive feature of persons yielding this profile is depression. The personal tempo is slowed, as is the rate of speech. Although thought processes are retarded, there is no noticeable cognitive slippage; that is, the thoughts, phrases, and ideas are "glued" together in appropriate sequence and in a grammatically and semantically sound fashion. These people are likely to express feelings of pessimism, hopelessness about the future, and even the futility of any treatment. Nevertheless, it is significant that the "projected discharge" profile for this group is within normal limits with no T-score over 70. This constitutes a prognostically hopeful sign which contradicts the gloomy attitude so characteristic of these patients. Furthermore, the discharge MMPIs at termination of therapy conform, in large, to the "projected discharge" profile—indicating improvement. This is consistent with independent clinical ratings by therapists who judged improvement from "some" to "considerable" and reported an 85% remission rate.

The mean age of onset of disturbance was 49 years; this is significantly older than for any other profile type. In general, the disorder took somewhere from 1 month to 1 year in developing and, in 70% of the cases, there were no previous episodes. Eighty-four per cent of these patients reported having dated frequently, 78% were married, 87% of those married reported good marital adjustment, and none were divorced. Courtship is typically short for these people and 60% married within 1 month's time.

These patients should be expected to exhibit compulsive, meticulous, and perfectionistic trends. A variety of fears and phobias are possible, as is obsessive thinking. Among multiple neurotic manifestations frequently observed are strong conflicts about self-assertion and a decided tendency toward self-blame and self-punishment. In psychoanalytic terminology, they may be said to be dominated by severe superego constraints. Indeed, they are the most rigid and the most devoutly religious of the profile types.

Tense, high-strung, nervous, anxious, and jumpy are adjectives often applied to these people. Thus, it is not surprising to observe trembling and sweating. Sleep difficulties are characteristic and should be expected. Often these patients are anorexic as well.

There are a variety of ways in which people presenting this profile express their psychological difficulties in a somatic, hypochondriacal fashion. A wide array of body symptoms may be presented; weakness and fatigue, chest pain, constipation, dizziness, and neurasthenia are some of the more common complaints.

These individuals, too, are constant worriers and are very vulnerable to threat—real or imagined. The 2-7 individual is a serious person who is given to anticipating problems and difficulties—the proverbial "crosser-of-bridges-before-the-bridges-have-materialized."

The scholastic history of these patients is average or above. Twenty-eight per cent have a college education; 84% have at least a high school education. In fact, the average IQ for this group is 114 on the Shipley and 119 on the WAIS. They place value on intellectual and cognitive activities, skills, and attitudes.

Behavioral or psychological characteristics very *unlikely* to be encountered in persons with this profile are flippant manner, speech, or resentment of authority figures. Adjectives used *infrequently* to describe them include self-centered and egocentric. Deliberately argumentative behavior or deliberately provocative behavior, verbal or nonverbal, is *not* likely.

ADULT CODE: 2-7-4/2-4-7/4-7-2*

Mean Profiles

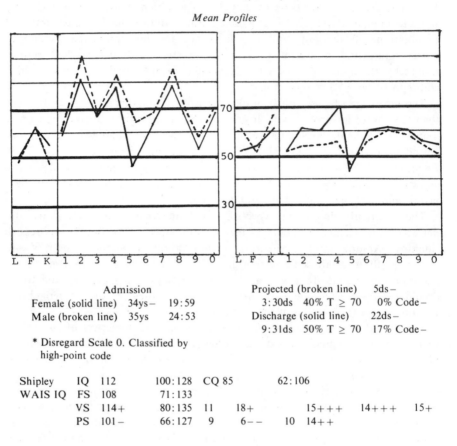

	Admission	
Female (solid line)	34ys–	19:59
Male (broken line)	35ys	24:53

* Disregard Scale 0. Classified by
high-point code

Projected (broken line) 5ds–
3:30ds   40% T ≥ 70   0% Code–
Discharge (solid line)   22ds–
9:31ds   50% T ≥ 70   17% Code–

Shipley	IQ	112	100:128	CQ 85		62:106			
WAIS IQ	FS	108	71:133						
	VS	114+	80:135	11	18+		15+++	14+++	15+
	PS	101–	66:127	9	6– –	10	14++		

Diagnosis

Psychoneurosis	43%+	Depressive
Personality disorder	33%+	Passive-aggressive
Psychosis	19%–	Mixed
Brain syndrome	0%–	

Personality Description

Patients who present this profile are, like patients with the 2-7 profile, fearful and worrisome. Because their threshold for threat is exceedingly low, they are vulnerable to it—both real and imagined; what to others might appear as trivial or minor irritants become "federal cases" for them. They tend to overreact and almost everything seems to be an emergency. Depression (manifest sad mood) is a predominant feature of the symptom picture—hence morale is impaired. Many of these patients are tearful and cry openly. Complaints of weakness and easy fatigability are reported with high frequency. Adjectives used by their therapists to describe them are excitable, tense, nervous, sweating, and high-strung—all indicators of anxiety-proneness. Strong emotional reactivity is noted, such that these patients seem unable to control, to adapt, to modulate, or to "tone down" their behavior. With scale 7 part of the defining code, it is hardly surprising that therapists note the presence of phobic reactions and find ruminative, obsessional ideation characteristically present. Therapists also judge them to derive appreciable secondary gain from their symptoms, which represent essentially the somatic expression of psychological conflicts.

These patients are perceived by clinicians as suffering from basic insecurity, unfulfilled needs for attention, and exaggerated needs for affection. Conflict is generated when these magnified needs collide with fears of emotional dependency. Seventy-one per cent of these patients express feelings of inferiority. In addition, clinicians are impressed with the presence and role of internal conflicts about sexuality.

The reader who is interested in the theory underlying MMPI variables might find it instructive to study the differences in traits and dispositions of persons yielding this code and those yielding the Adult 2-3-1 and 2-7 profiles. (See Meehl, 1972, on a "theory-sketch of the basic temperamental parameters" underlying the scale 4 *construct*.) Scale 4 is a construct related to (1) undercontrol of impulses, (2) poor socialization, and (3) irritable rebelliousness. Its influence can be noted when patients generating the 2-7-4 profile are compared with those of other code types. The Q statement "Is argumentative" appears at the *low* end of the 1 to 9 Q-sort scale (mean placement 2.8) for patients with the 2-7 profile, this is to say that this statement is "least characteristic" for this type. The same statement appears at the *high* end of the scale (mean placement 7.2) for patients with the 2-7-4 configuration; this is to say that this statement is "most characteristic" for this type. For the 2-7-4 type, "Is irritable" has a mean placement of 7.4, while for the 2-7, the placement drops to 5.8 and for the 2-3-1, to 5.4. The statement "Undercontrols own impulses, acts with insufficient thinking and deliberation" has a mean rating of 7.6 for the 2-7-4 type and yet drops to 3.3 for the 2-7 type, although these two groups share two scales in common. Consider further, "primary narcissism" as part of the theory-sketch for the scale 4 construct; for the 2-7 patient, the item "Is egocentric, selfish" is sorted low (mean placement 3.0), while for the 2-7-4 patient, the rating given is 6.8.

While 78% of the 2-7 type are married, none are divorced; 80% of the 2-7-4 type are married, yet 15% are divorced. While 84% of the 2-7 patients report having dated frequently, 63% of the 2-7-4 patients never dated or did so only on rare occasions.

ADULT CODE: 2-7-8/8-7-2*

Mean Profiles

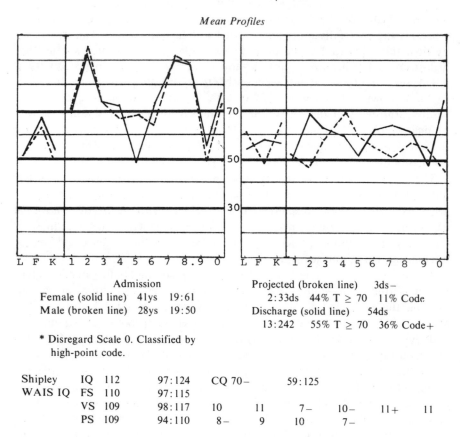

Admission
Female (solid line) 41ys 19:61
Male (broken line) 28ys 19:50

Projected (broken line) 3ds−
    2:33ds 44% T ≥ 70 11% Code
Discharge (solid line) 54ds
    13:242 55% T ≥ 70 36% Code+

* Disregard Scale 0. Classified by
  high-point code.

Shipley	IQ	112	97:124	CQ 70−		59:125			
WAIS IQ	FS	110	97:115						
	VS	109	98:117	10	11	7−	10−	11+	11
	PS	109	94:110	8−	9	10	7−		

Diagnosis

Psychosis	58%	Schizophrenic
Psychoneurosis	33%	Anxiety/obsessive-compulsive
Personality disorder	4%−	Schizoid
Brain syndrome	4%	Acute

Personality Description

As befits people with scale 2 so elevated, these patients are depressed. The despondency and pessimism may be expressed in feelings of hopelessness and about 65% of these patients verbalize their suicidal ruminations. The typical somatic symptoms of weakness and easy fatigability found in depression also occur. However, depression does not occupy the central focus in the total psychological status that it does for either the 2-3-1 or 2-7 types; the picture is more varied and more diffuse. The flow of thought, as revealed in speech, may be disturbed. In our own patient group and in that of Gilberstadt and Duker (1965), these people are frequently termed schizoid or schizophrenic; they seem unable to express their emotions in any modulated or adaptive way. Reports of difficulty in thinking and in concentration are quite common.

Patients with this profile have a long history of personal isolation. One-fourth of them were only children and one-fourth describe their parents attitude toward them as rejecting. There were deaths in the immediate family of 45% of these patients; later, 11% were widowed. Too, there is a trend of physical illness in the parental home of these patients; 15% of fathers and 20% of mothers were not well and 25% of these patients themselves were sickly during childhood.

The 2-7-8 patient is likely to be guilt- and worry-ridden, generally fearful, and vulnerable to minimum threat. What others are likely to view as no more than an irritant, is usually perceived by them as a major threat. Further, they frequently make emergency responses when no ostensible or "objective" reason can be discerned. Terms often used in describing these patients are tense, nervous, trembling, sweating—all indicators of anxiety or fear. Shy and inhibited are also characteristic descriptive adjectives, with 80% being perceived as withdrawn. Persons with this profile generally have a long history of poor interpersonal relations. Inner conflicts about emotional dependency are frequent and emotional involvement of any sort poses threats. They withdraw and keep others at a distance. They perceive themselves as blameworthy people, often express feelings of doubt, self-accusation, and self-condemnation. Sexual conflicts are pervasive and the heterosexual relationships of these patients are notoriously poor; 50% report extramarital relations.

Many of the complaints and behaviors associated with scale 7 elevation are reported for these patients. Perfectionistic tendencies and compulsively meticulous behaviors occur. Indecisiveness is characteristic as is the tendency to delay or avoid actions, or to commit oneself to a definite course. Obsessional, ruminative preoccupations are to be expected; these may occur in the form of interest in and exploration of various "philosophic" notions of an unusual or odd sort. Phobias are also commonly encountered in the 2-7-8 profile type.

Intellectually, these patients are above average. Their mean IQ obtained on the Shipley is 112 and the mean on the WAIS is 110. This high average intelligence test performance is also consistent with that reported for this code by Gilberstadt and Duker.

ADULT CODE: 2-8/8-2*

Mean Profiles

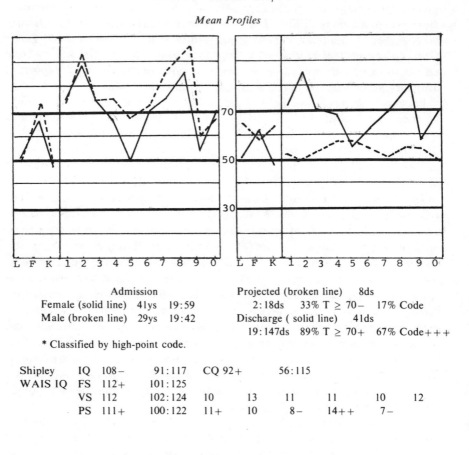

	Admission		Projected (broken line) 8ds
Female (solid line)	41ys	19:59	2:18ds 33% T ≥ 70– 17% Code
Male (broken line)	29ys	19:42	Discharge (solid line) 41ds
			19:147ds 89% T ≥ 70+ 67% Code+++

* Classified by high-point code.

Shipley	IQ	108–	91:117	CQ 92+		56:115			
WAIS IQ	FS	112+	101:125						
	VS	112	102:124	10	13	11	11	10	12
	PS	111+	100:122	11+	10	8–	14++	7–	

Diagnosis

Psychosis	70%+	Schizophrenic/schizo-affective
Brain syndrome	15%+	Acute
Psychoneurosis	10%	Mixed
Personality disorder	5%	Schizoid

Personality Description

Patients with this code are manifestly depressed individuals who are likely to express their sadness and despondency in open tearfulness. About half the patients with this profile report suicidal thoughts and 15% make threats, although nowhere near that proportion carry such thoughts and threats into action. Disturbance of sleep is part of the depressive component of the psychological picture, as is the retarded stream of thought. While some of these patients are diagnosed as suffering from involutional depression, a diagnosis of schizophrenia is far more common; 70% are judged to be psychotic and another 15% are classified as organic brain syndrome.

The expression of psychological conflict through somatic channels is encountered frequently among patients generating this profile. Often, they view their problems and their disorder as "being physically ill" and they are quite defensive about admitting any possible psychological component. Typically they experience dizziness, blackout spells, nausea, and vomiting. Warbin *et al.* (1972) report somatic delusions among their 2-8 sample.

The avoidance of close interpersonal relationships is a cardinal characteristic of these patients, the majority of whom come from "broken" homes; they strive to keep people at a distance. Involvement of any intimate sort with others is threatening, yet 70% are married; it is interesting to note that 45% of those married report a courtship period of 1 week or less. Others are likely to be regarded by the 2-8 patient with mistrust and their motivations are likely to be questioned. Conflict about emotional dependency is probable, as is inner conflict about sexuality. A generally irritable and resentful manner or tone is also characteristic of 2-8 patients. Most frequently, they are described as tense, high-strung, anxious, and jumpy.

These patients are given to obsessional thinking and to repeated ruminative preoccupation. Thinking is unoriginal and problem-solving is stereotyped rather than flexible. Although 63% finished high school, fewer of these patients than any other group have advanced education. Too, these patients are more forgetful than any other group. There frequently appears to be a fear in these patients of losing control; emotional "letting go" thus seems to be impossible for them. At the same time, self-assertion is just as difficult. The prognosis for patients with this profile is generally poor (60%) and the response to treatment in 85% of the cases studied is judged to be "no change" or "small improvement."

ADULT CODE: 3-1/1-3*

Mean Profiles.

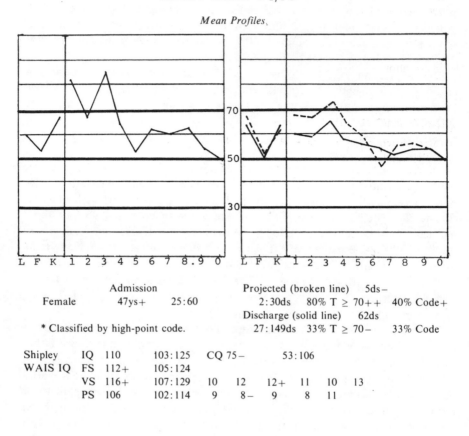

	Admission	
Female	47ys+	25:60

Projected (broken line)   5ds−
2:30ds   80% T ≥ 70++   40% Code+
Discharge (solid line)   62ds

* Classified by high-point code.

27:149ds   33% T ≥ 70−   33% Code

Shipley	IQ	110	103:125	CQ 75−		53:106			
WAIS IQ	FS	112+	105:124						
	VS	116+	107:129	10	12	12+	11	10	13
	PS	106	102:114	9	8−	9	8	11	

Diagnosis

Psychoneurosis	77%+++	Conversion/psychophysiologic
Psychosis	14%−	Mixed
Personality disorder	5%	Dependent
Brain syndrome	5%	Acute

Personality Disorder

The predominant clinical features presented by these patients correspond to what has become characterized as "the conversion V" formed by the three scales of the so-called "psychoneurotic triad" (scales 1, 2, and 3). These are the features subsumed under the heading conversion reaction or (in the revision of the *Diagnostic Manual* of the American Psychiatric Association, 1968) Hysterical neurosis, conversion type. The classical picture, then, is one in which these patients present themselves as physically ill, while denying that their symptomatology is an expression (*i.e.,* a conversion) of psychological conflict. Under the influence of psychoanalytic thinking, the symptoms are sometimes said to be "speaking" in a symbolic "body language." The mechanism of repression is commonly regarded as the major defense. Weakness and easy fatigability are frequently heard complaints. Other symptoms include back pain, headache, neurasthenia, dizziness, numbness, paresthesia, blurred vision, tremor, genital pain, insomnia, and anorexia; 25% of these women have had hysterectomies. It should be noted that although the classical symptoms of hysteria affect the voluntary muscles, a number of these patients suffer gastrointestinal disturbances such as nausea, vomiting, and ulcers. These are likewise reported by Gilberstadt and Duker (1965) and suggested by Lewandowski and Graham (1972).

The clinicians who studied this group concur in the general notion that hysterical patients garner considerable secondary gain from their symptoms. The 3-1 patients are characterized as demanding sympathy, and harboring considerable needs for attention (needs correlated with basic insecurity), as well as exaggerated needs for affection. At the same time, their emotional dependency is seen as a source of inner conflict for them.

As reported by other clinicians studying hysterical patients, we found that they differ from the modal patient in that they are generally socially adaptable and socially appropriate; they are also viewed as "getting along well" in the world outside the hospital. Nevertheless, their emotions are not well modulated and there is a certain exaggerated, histrionic character which colors their behavior.

The 3-1 patients also deviate from the modal psychiatric patient in the obvious intactness of their logical thought processes as reflected in their stream of speech. This is the type, for example, which serves as the anchor at the low end of the 1 to 9 Q-sort scale on the statement "thinks and associates in unusual ways, has unconventional thought processes"; for these patients to obtain a mean rating of 1.0 requires the unanimity of at least five clinicians' opinions. Thinking difficulties and concentration difficulties are also virtually absent. These patients do, however, tend to be forgetful and appear perplexed.

The role of genetics and its contribution to disturbed behavior and disturbed functioning is not well understood—certainly not agreed upon. Nevertheless, in the case of this functional disorder, there appears to be substantial agreement in the emphasis on environmental factors. Gottesman's (1962) study using a large number of monozygotic twins reports a small genetic loading—a finding consistent with this view of the primary contribution of learning. The personal history of these patients demonstrates this as well. Although the age of onset of disorder is 47 years (one of the oldest of all groups studied), previous episodes were reported in 75% of the cases. As children, 30% of these patients were ill and 30% had mothers who were also ill. In fact, death of one or both parents was noted in 60% of all cases (40% father, 35% mother).

ADULT CODE: 3-2-1*

Mean Profiles

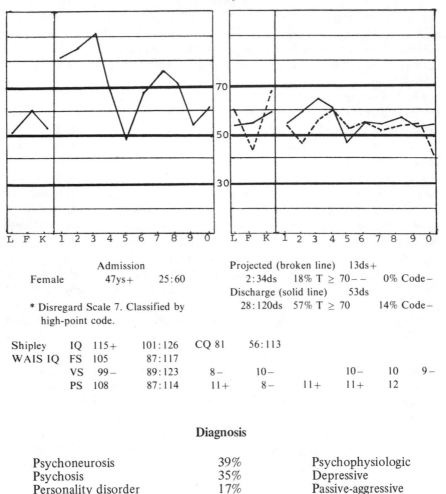

	Admission	
Female	47ys+	25:60

* Disregard Scale 7. Classified by
high-point code.

Projected (broken line)   13ds+
2:34ds   18% T ≥ 70– –   0% Code–
Discharge (solid line)   53ds
28:120ds   57% T ≥ 70   14% Code–

Shipley	IQ	115+	101:126	CQ 81	56:113				
WAIS IQ	FS	105	87:117						
	VS	99–	89:123	8–	10–		10–	10	9–
	PS	108	87:114	11+	8–	11+	11+	12	

Diagnosis

Psychoneurosis	39%	Psychophysiologic
Psychosis	35%	Depressive
Personality disorder	17%	Passive-aggressive
Brain syndrome	9%	Chronic

Personality Description

The most prominent feature of patients with this profile is manifest depression expressed in feelings of hopelessness, feelings of inferiority and perplexity. As might be expected of scale 3 and scale 1 elevations, hypochondriacal tendencies and complaints are characteristically observed.

Seventy per cent have somatic symptoms ranging from back pain, stiffness, weakness, tremor, hypertension, fatigue, blackout spells, and blurred vision to constipation, diarrhea, nausea, vomiting, genital pain, anorexia, and weight loss. About 40% of these patients are diagnosed as suffering from psychophysiological disorders; a considerable number are also characterized as basically hysteroid in personality makeup.

One of the most frequent areas of manifestation of the disorder is sexual. Sexual delinquency is reported with high frequency as is sexual difficulty. Twenty per cent of these women have had abortions and 60% have had hysterectomies! It is no wonder that genitourinary discomfort is often one of the presenting symptoms and complaints.

Disturbances of sleep is commonly observed in patients who generate this profile. Thinking and concentration difficulties are also frequently heard complaints. Typically, these patients react to frustration in an intropunitive manner—punishing themselves consistently rather than blaming others. They are seen as self-defeating and prone to placing themselves in an obviously bad light. Easily threatened, these individuals might be characterized as emotional and unable to tone down or modulate their behavior. Adjectives frequently applied to them include tense, anxious, and nervous.

Although scales 3, 2, and 1 are the most elevated (and thus define the code), scale 7 is commonly above 70 T-scores (and may in fact be the highest or among the highest scales) for patients of this type. Consequently, our 3-2-1 patients were characterized as obsessional, as well as compulsive and perfectionistic. The terms "schizoid" and "paranoid" also are applied to these individuals. Close personal relationships appear to present problems for these patients who tend to keep others at an emotional distance. Thus, about 65% are indicated to be withdrawn.

These patients tend to come from families where the father is dominating and strict and where the mother, although affectionate, is also said to be strict. Ten per cent of the fathers were physically ill and another 10% were mentally ill during the patient's childhood. Most often, these patients were middle children (67%); another 20% were only children. School achievement was generally above average and more than one-third of the patients with this profile were educated beyond the high school level. This group presented the highest mean IQ on the Shipley (115).

Eighty per cent of these patients are seen on an inpatient basis, and 63% have had previous episodes of one sort or another. Although the prognosis for these women was considered generally quite good at the time of the study, subsequently about 25% committed suicide while in the course of outpatient treatment. In each such instance the suicide was obviously unpredictable and the patient was over 45 years of age. Marital status seemed to have little bearing on this outcome.

ADULT CODE: 4-6/6-4*

Mean Profiles

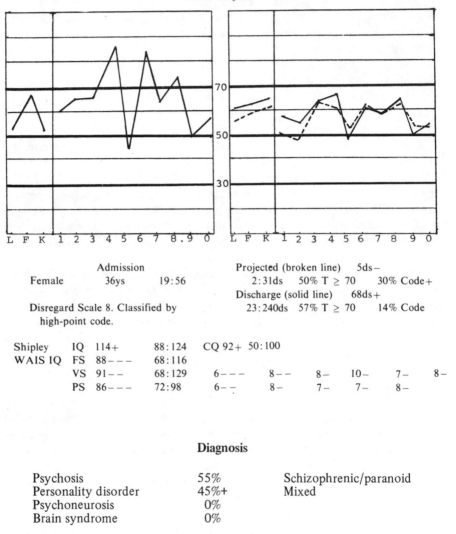

	Admission		Projected (broken line) 5ds−
Female	36ys	19:56	2:31ds 50% T ≥ 70 30% Code+

Discharge (solid line)   68ds+

Disregard Scale 8. Classified by
high-point code.

23:240ds   57% T ≥ 70   14% Code

Shipley	IQ	114+	88:124	CQ 92+ 50:100
WAIS IQ	FS	88 − − −	68:116	
	VS	91 − −	68:129	6 − − − 8 − − 8 − 10 − 7 − 8 −
	PS	86 − − −	72:98	6 − − 8 − 7 − 7 − 8 −

Diagnosis

Psychosis	55%	Schizophrenic/paranoid
Personality disorder	45%+	Mixed
Psychoneurosis	0%	
Brain syndrome	0%	

Personality Description

The characteristics of patients yielding profiles with primary elevations on scales 4 and 6 may be explained through understanding of the constructs underlying these scales; they involve rebelliousness and hostility. Hence, it is not surprising to find that these patients are described as irritable, aggressive, egocentric, and self-indulgent. They have been perceived, virtually unanimously by our clinicians, as evasive and consistently resentful and argumentative. These patients also exhibit their rebelliousness in a persistent disposition to derogate authority figures.

These patients are not likely to admit readily their own responsibility for their difficulties; they are seen as defensive and tend to deny psychological conflicts and psychological problems. They rationalize these difficulties in an attempt to make them appear reasonable and justifiable. Alternatively, or concurrently, they readily project the blame for their troubles on others. They resent and are especially sensitive to anything that may be construed to be a demand made on them. At the same time, they are likely to demand sympathy from others. Patients who present this profile are, in general, immature, insecure, indecisive, and passively manipulative. They exhibit poor judgment, are suspicious, and have exaggerated needs for affection and attention. These needs and the egocentric self-indulgent behavior already indicated appear consistent with the narcissism ascribed to these patients by the clinicians who had the opportunity to observe them.

As children, these patients were typically behavior problems. They were often delinquent, sexually and criminally. A number of fathers of patients generating this profile were alcoholic (20%) or mentally ill (15%); they were characterized as permissive and either rejecting or indifferent in their attitude toward the children. The mothers were very similar; 63% were reported to be strict, rejecting, or indifferent.

Marriage and sex seem to be areas particularly affected by these patients' disorders. Twenty-five per cent are either divorced or separated. Thirty per cent have had abortions and 15% have given birth to illegitimate children. Another 17% are alcoholic and 28% report drug abuse. Nearly 40% have attempted suicide. Somatic symptoms most often reported include headaches, blackout spells, amnesia, delusions, and cardiac complaints. These patients tend not to respond to treatment; the prognosis is considered poor in 64% of the cases.

ADULT CODE: 4-6-2/6-4-2*

Mean Profiles

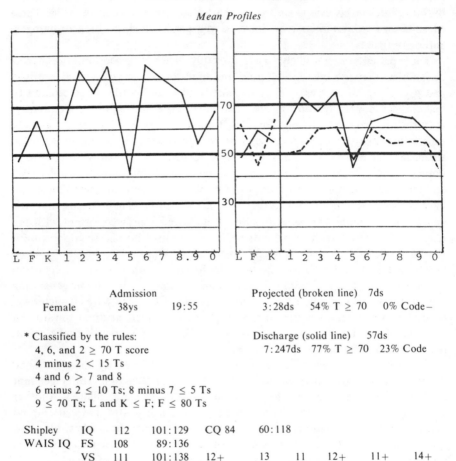

	Admission		Projected (broken line) 7ds
Female	38ys	19:55	3:28ds 54% T ≥ 70 0% Code–

* Classified by the rules: Discharge (solid line)   57ds
  4, 6, and 2 ≥ 70 T score   7:247ds 77% T ≥ 70 23% Code
  4 minus 2 < 15 Ts
  4 and 6 > 7 and 8
  6 minus 2 ≤ 10 Ts; 8 minus 7 ≤ 5 Ts
  9 ≤ 70 Ts; L and K ≤ F; F ≤ 80 Ts

Shipley	IQ	112	101:129	CQ 84	60:118			
WAIS IQ	FS	108	89:136					
	VS	111	101:138	12+	13	11	12+	11+	14+
	PS	103	77:127	9	10	9	8	9

Diagnosis

Personality disorder	60%++	Passive-aggressive
Psychoneurosis	30%	Mixed
Psychosis	10%–	Mixed
Brain syndrome	0%–	

Personality Description

The characterization of these patients as depressed is consistent with the elevation of scale 2 in the profile. This depression is manifested in open tearfulness, negativisim, and in suicidal threats and attempts. Nevertheless, it is the characterological features of these patients rather than their depressive mood which dominate the psychological picture and which present a striking contrast between the 4-6-2 type and other depressed patients (*e.g.,* the 2-7 or the 2-3-1 types). The central personality traits are consistent with the basic character of the constructs underlying scale 4 and scale 6. It is interesting that clinicians characterize these patients as "psychopathic" (consistent with scale 4) and as "paranoid" (consistent with scale 6). Correspondingly, the defense mechanisms of rationalization and projection are rated as typical of the operating style exhibited by these patients.

The 4-6-2 patients' lack of ego control of impulses—leading to hasty, impulsive, and thoughtless action, is also consistant with the underlying scale 4 construct. These people project a self-dramatizing, histrionic quality. They convey the impression of egocentricity, and are seen as self-centered, and self-indulgent. They are given to forceful comments and assertions, sometimes very provocative. Adjectives often ascribed to them are resentful, irritable, excitable, and argumentative. They rate generally low in trust of others and tend to question their motivations. The underlying rebelliousness of scale 4 is reflected in the consistent resentment manifested with respect to authority figures and a tendency to derogate them. They are critical, skeptical, and not easily impressed as well as sensitive to anything that might be construed as a demand. Consistant, too, is the "acting out" of conflicts by these patients in impulsive and antisocial ways; if, in a loose sense, one may talk meaningfully about the locus of psychopathology—then it might be said that in the 4-6-2 patient the locus is in the behavior rather than in the mental or physical domain. They undercontrol their impulses and act without sufficient foresight or deliberation.

One psychodynamic view of the kind of aggressive or passive-aggressive behavior characteristically displayed by these patients is that such behavior is essentially a defense against inner conflict revolving around strong dependency needs. Whatever the status of the theory, it remains an empirical fact that clinicians consistently judge these patients to be suffering from such conflict about emotional dependency. Correlated with this are feelings of basic insecurity, excessive needs for attention, exaggerated needs for affection, and a generally demanding orientation ("the world owes me a living").

These patients are often the "baby" of the family. Although their school achievement is typically below average, 32% of them eventually receive a college education. Eighty-four per cent are married and there is conflict in 82% of these marriages. One in six of these patients has an alcoholic and/or mentally ill father. Nevertheless, paternal relations during childhood are described as having been affectionate (60%), while maternal relations were described as having been indifferent or rejecting (67%). Both parents are typically said to have been permissive.

ADULT CODE: 4-8-2/8-4-2/8-2-4*

Mean Profiles

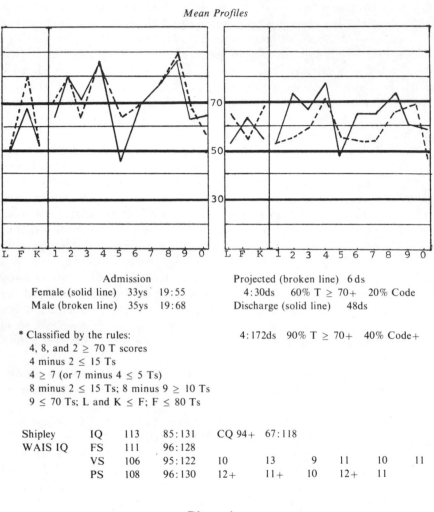

Admission
Female (solid line)   33ys   19:55
Male (broken line)   35ys   19:68

Projected (broken line)   6 ds
   4:30ds   60% T ≥ 70+   20% Code
Discharge (solid line)   48ds

                            4:172ds   90% T ≥ 70+   40% Code+

* Classified by the rules:
   4, 8, and 2 ≥ 70 T scores
   4 minus 2 ≤ 15 Ts
   4 ≥ 7 (or 7 minus 4 ≤ 5 Ts)
   8 minus 2 ≤ 15 Ts; 8 minus 9 ≥ 10 Ts
   9 ≤ 70 Ts; L and K ≤ F; F ≤ 80 Ts

Shipley	IQ	113	85:131	CQ 94+	67:118			
WAIS IQ	FS	111	96:128					
	VS	106	95:122	10	13	9	11	10	11
	PS	108	96:130	12+	11+	10	12+	11	

Diagnosis

Psychosis	71%+	Schizophrenic/paranoid
Personality disorder	21%	Sociopathic/antisocial
Psychoneurosis	8%−	Mixed
Brain syndrome	0%−	

Personality Description

These patients have in common a general distrust of people, a suspicious questioning of their motivations, and a fear of emotional involvement with others. They are consistently perceived by clinicians as maintaining an emotional distance from people and avoiding close personal relationships. Notwithstanding this rejection of emotional ties, the 4-8-2 has an exaggerated need for affection, is weighted down with basic insecurity and needs for attention, and harbors conflict over emotional dependency.

Described as resentful, irritable, moody, argumentative, and hostile, these patients are emotionally inappropriate and given to ideas of reference. These are all characteristics which are consistent with the label "paranoid." Gilberstadt and Duker (1965, p. 76), in fact, use the diagnostic term "paranoid personality" in connection with these patients. That the defense mechanism of projection is rated quite high for these patients is also consistent with this clinical characterization. They are also judged high on "rationalization"; that is, they try to justify as logical what is clinically rated as "psychopathological." Evident also, is the tendency of these patients to "act out" and manipulate both objects and others. The difficulties revolving around interjudge reliability of psychiatric diagnosis may be illustrated here in that nearly three-fourths of our 4-8-2 patients are diagnosed paranoid schizophrenic rather than paranoid personality and yet gross or florid thought disorder is less salient and less prominent than in the mental status of patients yielding other profiles in which scale 8 predominates (e.g., 8-3, 8-6, and 8-9).

People with this profile are sensitive to anything that can be construed as a demand upon them. Inner conflicts about sexuality exceed in frequency even the high base rate of the population in general. No doubt, this is related to the unusually high frequency of endorsement of "single" marital status. Gilberstadt and Duker (1965) report a majority of their 4-8-2 patients to be unmarried, and in our sample, 50% are unmarried. Of those who are married, 70% report discord.

Clinicians observing and/or treating our 4-8-2 patients found their behavior to be erratic and unpredictable. Their ego controls are weak and they seem unable to express their emotions in any modulated or adaptive way.

About 75% of these patients report histories of parental rejection or parental domination; none reported that their parents were affectionate during their childhood. Ten per cent of these patients were of illegitimate birth. Throughout their childhood, they were labeled as "behavior problems" and their school work was almost always below average; in fact, 35% had received only a grade school education.

ADULT CODE: 4-9*

Mean Profiles

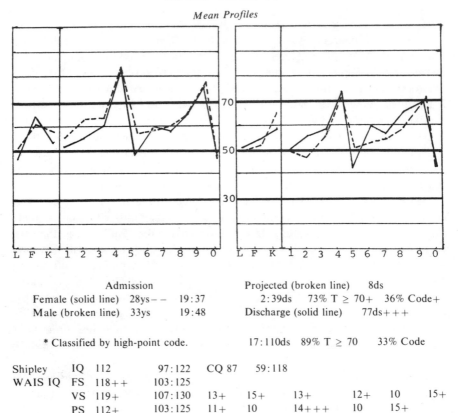

	Admission	
Female (solid line)	28ys--	19:37
Male (broken line)	33ys	19:48

Projected (broken line)   8ds
    2:39ds   73% T ≥ 70+   36% Code+
Discharge (solid line)   77ds+++

* Classified by high-point code.   17:110ds   89% T ≥ 70   33% Code

Shipley	IQ	112	97:122	CQ 87	59:118			
WAIS IQ	FS	118++	103:125					
	VS	119+	107:130	13+	15+	13+	12+	10	15+
	PS	112+	103:125	11+	10	14+++	10	15+

Diagnosis

Personality disorder	80%+++	Sociopathic/emotionally unstable
Psychosis	15%-	Mixed
Psychoneurosis	0%-	
Brain syndrome	0%-	

Personality Description

To understand the 4-9 type, it helps to have some grasp of what Meehl (1972, p. 139) calls a "theory-sketch" of the basic psychological structure. For one thing, it is important to distinguish between the characteristic life history of delinquency and/or persistent antisocial behavior, and the personality construct. The point here is that people get labeled *legally* as delinquent or become entangled with the law for *psychologically* different reasons. In our patient group, as in others, the 4-9 individual is likely to be diagnosed as an "antisocial personality"—the earlier terms are sociopathic or psychopathic personality. Whether for primarily constitutional genetic reasons or as a result of a learning history (and these are unlikely to be mutually exclusive since the 4-9 personality is a phenotype resulting from submitting an endowed genotype to a learning history) the 4-9 individual appears to have an abnormally low capacity to experience anxiety or stress. This, in turn, leads to a deficiency in acquiring what are characterized as ego and superego controls normally developed during the socialization process and induced, at least in part, by aversive stimulation; people who generate this profile just do not learn from aversive experiences. Consistently, they rate low on adjectives like tense, nervous, high-strung, anxious, shy, and inhibited. When they get into difficulty, they rationalize; always it is someone else's fault.

The 4-9 type is distinctive in that it is the only one which maintains its code under all instructional sets (admission, projected discharge, and discharge). In other words, on entering the hospital or when beginning outpatient treatment, these patients obtain 4-9 profiles; when asked to take the test as they would like to be at the conclusion of treatment, the profiles are unaltered (though sometimes they are less elevated); and when they do, in fact, leave the hospital or conclude outpatient treatment, their profiles remain 4-9 and in general are still elevated. It is as though they are announcing: "I am a 4-9; I plan to remain a 4-9." And, in fact, they do! No other code type behaves in this way.

The 4-9 seems incapable of controlling impulses and acts with insufficient deliberation and poor judgment. In psychoanalytic terms it might be said that while in most people the reality principle governs behavior, for these individuals the pleasure principle dominates. To have an impulse is to act it out where others might first monitor that impulse. The 4-9 is histrionic, self-dramatizing, egocentric, self-centered, selfish, narcissistic, and self-indulgent. Although some of them may react with (subjective) depression to being in a psychiatric hospital, (objective) depressive affect has a *low* incidence in these individuals. Indeed, they tend to be restless and have a rapid personal tempo.

People with this profile appear incapable of establishing the kind of emotional contact and commitment which characterizes friendship. They keep others at a distance and avoid the ties of close interpersonal relationships. Nevertheless, they are perceived by clinicians as insecure, conflicted about emotional dependency, wanting if not demanding attention, and harboring exaggerated needs for affection. They are sensitive to anything that can be construed as a demand on them. Their rebelliousness is exhibited in their antagonism to and resentment of authority figures whom they characteristically deride and oppose. They are immature, resentful, easily irritated—though there may be a thin facade of sociability—and highly provocative people. Their quick antagonisms are often reflected in flippant manner, blatant manipulations, and in caustic comments. Seventeen per cent are reported to be homicidal.

This type is the youngest of all codes studied (mean age of 28 years). As children, these patients were typically behavior problems and although they were quite bright and test intelligent (mean WAIS IQ 118), their school achievement was generally below average. Invariably, the 4-9 is an under-achiever! Though deficient in judgment and in social learning, thinking is intact in the sense that thought disorder is absent as reflected in speech.

Frequent or steady dating is common for people with this profile. Many do marry, but over one-third are later separated or divorced, and two-thirds have extramarital relations. Marital discord is indeed reported in 100% of the cases. Delinquency of some sort is to be expected; 56% of that reported was sexual in nature, 39% of these patients were described as amoral, and 17% took other forms—drug abuse or alcoholism both occurred in about 25% of the cases. It is interesting that while 11% of these patients were born illegitimately (the highest percentage of any type), 33% later gave birth to illegitimate children themselves, while another 22% had illegal abortions.

Many 4-9's come from homes where the fathers were indifferent and permissive while the mothers were dominating and permissive. Seventeen per cent of their fathers and 6% of their mothers were reported to have been alcoholic.

Eighty per cent of these patients received only psychotherapy, while 20% also received tranquilizers. Unfortunately, there is typically reported "no response" to treatment. When there is improvement, it is only minimal. Consistent with this is the generally poor prognosis these patients receive. As many as 38% terminate treatment prematurely against their therapists' advice.

ADULT CODE: 8-3/3-8*

Mean Profiles

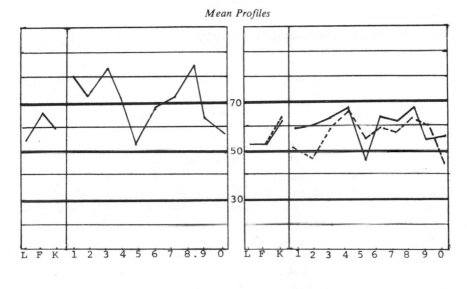

	Admission		Projected (broken line)	8ds
Female	39ys	19:71	4:31ds	50% T ≥ 70 20% Code

* Classified by the rules:
  8, 3, and 1 ≥ 70 T score
  3 minus 1 ≤ 10 Ts; 3 minus 2 ≥ 5 Ts
  8 ≥ 3 (or 3 minus 8 ≤ 5 Ts)
  8 minus 7 ≥ 5 Ts; 8 minus 9 ≥ 10 Ts
  9 ≥ 0; 0 ≤ 70 Ts

Discharge (solid line) 80ds+++
8:289ds 67% T ≥ 70 25% Code

Shipley	IQ	109	96:130	CQ 80		50:107			
WAIS IQ	FS	104−	72:130						
	VS	105	74:127	10	10−	9	11	10	12
	PS	101−	74.131	9	8−	10	8	11	

Diagnosis

Psychosis	48%	Schizophrenic/manic depressive
Psychoneurosis	43%+	Dissociative/mixed
Personality disorder	10%	Schizoid
Brain syndrome	0%−	

Personality Description

Quite prominent in the psychological status of the 8-3 patient is a notable disorder in the thought process as reflected in the flow of speech. The clinicians who observed this group characterized their thinking as unconventional, unusual, schizoid, and autistic; often what is said seems irrelevant or incoherent. Thinking and concentration difficulties are also subjectively reported. Twenty-five per cent of these patients further report that lapses of memory pose a problem for them. Delusions and hallucinations are frequent, but by no means always present.

Depression is a dominant feature in the emotional tone of these patients. Consistent with this, the typical reaction to frustration is intropunitive (self-punishing). Feelings of hopelessness are openly expressed. Adjectives used to describe the 8-3 are resentful, anxious, tense, and nervous. Also seen as ruminative and obsessional, these patients are easily threatened, generally fearful, and constantly worrying. Phobias are present in about 30% of the cases. This makes for strong overreaction to minor irritants which are often interpreted as major threats. Thus, there is a lack of emotional balance—a characteristic lack of adaptability. Patients who obtain this profile tend to be indecisive and immature. Sleep difficulties are reported frequently.

These patients possess a basic insecurity, inner conflict about sexuality, excessive needs for attention, and exaggerated needs for affection. There is a stereotyped and unoriginal quality in their approach to problems. They are viewed as evasive, uninvolved, apathetic, and passively resistant. The degree of clinically rated regression is well beyond the base rate for our psychiatric population.

Although 8-3's are *not* perceived by clinicians as "somatizers," they do report a fair amount of physical distress; 60% claim musculoskeletal difficulties and 25% say they experience genitourinary problems. One-third have blurred vision. Other complaints include dizziness, chest pain, genital pain, headaches, numbness, and paresthesia.

Typically, patients with this profile are *not* the oldest child—often they are the youngest. Childhood health is generally good, as is academic achievement; half of these people do above average work in school and 42% are educated beyond the high school level. Although an unusually small percentage of these patients come from disrupted homes, 30% report one or both parents alcoholic with 25% of all fathers being alcoholic. Fifteen per cent of the parents also had known mental illness. Fathers tended to be affectionate yet dominating, while mothers, if not affectionate, were not neglecting.

The 8-3 patient tends *not* to be "psychopathic." They are neither poised in social situations nor are they provocative. Their tempo is not particularly rapid and their speech and manner are neither flippant nor flighty. Neither are they likely to be viewed as suspicious, skeptical, or critical. In many cases, there is no response to treatment and when there is improvement, it is only minimal. The prognosis for these patients is fair to poor.

ADULT CODE: 8-6/6-8*

Mean Profiles

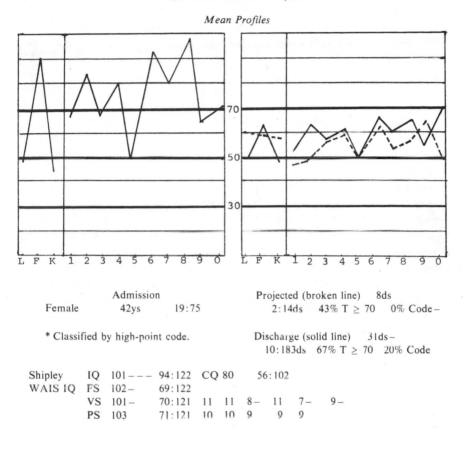

	Admission	
Female	42ys	19:75

* Classified by high-point code.

Projected (broken line)   8ds
2:14ds   43% T ≥ 70   0% Code−

Discharge (solid line)   31ds−
10:183ds   67% T ≥ 70   20% Code

Shipley	IQ	101 − − −	94:122	CQ 80	56:102
WAIS IQ	FS	102 −	69:122		
	VS	101 −	70:121	11 11 8− 11 7− 9−
	PS	103	71:121	10 10 9 9 9

Diagnosis

Psychosis	68%	Schizophrenic/paranoid
Personality disorder	18%	Paranoid
Brain syndrome	14%	Chronic
Psychoneurosis	0%−	

Personality Description

The pattern of the validity scales L, F, and K indicates honesty in responding to the test questions and a tendency toward self-derogation; this lack of self-confidence and low self-esteem is also commented on by Gilberstadt and Duker (1965). The low K corresponds to decompensation of the patient's defenses, accompanied by florid psychological symptomatology. The extreme elevation on scale F reflects confusion and considerable ego disorganization. These patients subjectively report difficulty in thinking and in concentration. Clinicians unanimously concur that these patients think in a disordered, unusual, unconventional, and autistic way. Thinking is also characterized as obsessional and suicidal ruminations are frequent. Delusions, grandiose ideas, excessive fears, and phobias are all common. Clinicians are also impressed that the 8-6 patient spends a great deal of time in personal fantasy and in daydreaming. It is not surprising that the majority of these patients are diagnosed as paranoid schizophrenics, their predominant defense mechanism being projection.

The general orientation of these patients toward others is one of suspicion and distrust; the motivations of others are regarded as questionable and highly suspect. Avoidance of close interpersonal relationships and hence, emotional distance from others, is a typical pattern for patients who obtain this profile. The 8-6 patient is described as schizoid, inhibited, shy, withdrawn as well as irritable, resentful, anxious, and sensitive to anything that can be construed as a demand. These are descriptive adjectives also applied to the 8-6 patient studied by Gilberstadt and Duker (1965). The erratic character of these patients' behavior has led clinicians to view them as unpredictable. They tend to be moody, rigid, negativistic, manipulative, emotionally immature, and emotionally inappropriate; they exercise poor judgment and are generally uncooperative and apathetic. Feelings expressed by the 8-6 patient include inferiority, guilt, and unreality. It is no wonder that they do not arouse liking and acceptance in others.

Patients with this profile were quite often either an only child, or the youngest in the family. Both parents were characterized as rejecting or indifferent at best. School achievement was frequently below average which is consistent with our findings that these patients obtained the second lowest IQ scores of any group studied on both the Shipley and WAIS (mean full scale IQ's of 101 and 102, respectively).

The onset of their disorder is typically quite short. Their prognosis is fair to poor, regardless of the fact that 85% demonstrate at least some positive response to treatment with about 50% showing decided improvement.

ADULT CODE: 8-9/9-8*

Mean Profiles

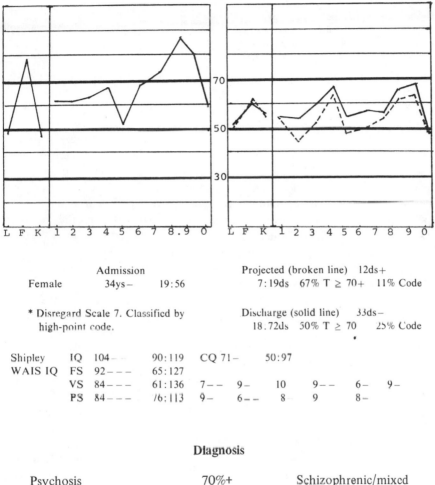

	Admission	
Female	34ys–	19:56

* Disregard Scale 7. Classified by high-point code.

Projected (broken line) 12ds+
7:19ds 67% T ≥ 70+ 11% Code

Discharge (solid line) 33ds–
18.72ds 50% T ≥ 70 25% Code

Shipley	IQ	104–	90:119	CQ 71–		50:97			
WAIS IQ	FS	92– – –	65:127						
	VS	84– – –	61:136	7– –	9–	10	9– –	6–	9–
	PS	84– – –	76:113	9–	6– –	8–	9	8–	

Diagnosis

Psychosis	70%+	Schizophrenic/mixed
Psychoneurosis	17%	Depressive
Brain syndrome	9%	Acute
Personality disorder	0%–	

Personality Description

The typical validity scale pattern of the 8-9 type (low L and K with elevated F) indicates a candid, honest approach to the test questions in the context of feelings of inferiority and inadequacy, low self-esteem, and a disorganization of thought processes. Consequently, it is not surprising that this code represents primarily an inpatient rather than outpatient group; 85% of the patients with this profile were hospitalized on a psychiatric service.

Mean clinical ratings indicate extraordinarily high agreement that the 8-9 patient is likely to be grossly delusional (hence paranoid) and to reflect the emotional inappropriateness that is a cardinal symptom of a schizophrenic disorder. In fact, 70% are diagnosed psychotic. Grandiose ideas and hallucinations are frequently noted and projection is seen as a major mechanism of defense—second only to regression! Clinicians judge these patients to spend a good deal of time in personal fantasy and in daydreaming. Not only are there reports of difficulty in concentration and thinking, but the structure of the thoughts—as revealed in speech—indicate an unusual, odd, autistic association process. Thus, the impression is one of considerable regression insofar as the thinking and behavior of these patients is concerned. Their behavior is endowed with a generally erratic character so that they are often seen as unpredictable. They appear unable to modulate or tone down their behavior in any adaptive way. Attempts at problem-solving fall into ineffectual, stereotyped, and unoriginal approaches. Patients with this profile are often agitated, uncooperative, irritable, indecisive, hostile, restless, impulsive, and negativistic. They express feelings of unreality, perplexity, and are often disoriented for place and time. Fifteen per cent report alcoholism with 10% reporting drug abuse.

Insofar as their relation to others is concerned, they are distrustful, suspicious, and questioning of their motivations. Being afraid of emotional involvement, they manage to avoid close interpersonal contacts and to keep people at a distance. Inner conflicts about sexuality are strong and stressful; only 55% of these patients are married.

Most of our 8-9 patients have elevations on scale 7 (or scale 7 is the highest of the profile) which accords with the clinical judgment that they are ruminative, overideational, and obsessional. Many have a schizoid component to their personality; they feel isolated and are socially withdrawn. Nearly half report that dating is a rare or nonoccurrent event.

Most often, the 8-9 patient was a middle-child. School achievement followed a normal curve and 24% have a college education despite the fact that this is one of the least test intelligent groups studied; the mean WAIS IQ is 92, while the Shipley is 104.

The onset of this disorder is typically quite rapid, the duration is somewhat shorter than for other codes, and previous episodes of some sort were reported in 60% of the cases.

ADULT CODE: 9-6/6-9*

Mean Profiles

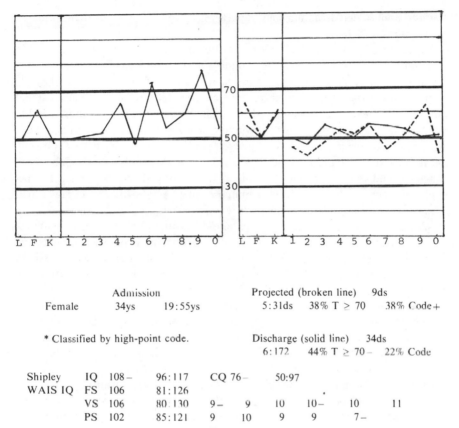

	Admission		Projected (broken line) 9ds
Female	34ys	19:55ys	5:31ds 38% T > 70 38% Code+

* Classified by high-point code.

Discharge (solid line) 34ds
6:172 44% T ≥ 70– 22% Code

Shipley	IQ	108–	96:117	CQ 76–	50:97				
WAIS IQ	FS	106	81:126						
	VS	106	80.130	9–	9	10	10–	10	11
	PS	102	85:121	9	10	9	9	7–	

Diagnosis

Psychosis	85%	Schizophrenic/paranoid
Psychoneurosis	10%	Mixed
Personality disorder	5%	Sociopathic
Brain syndrome	0%–	

Personality Description

Thought disorders are characteristic of patients yielding this profile. They subjectively report difficulty concentrating and difficulty thinking. They are ruminative, overideational, and obsessional. What they say is frequently irrelevant or incoherent. The stream of thought is retarded. These patients tend to be disoriented and appear perplexed; often they are delusional and hallucinatory. Clinicians judge them to spend a good deal of time in personal fantasy and in daydreaming and report regression as one of their principle mechanisms of defense.

Patients with this profile are also described by clinicians as tense, high-strung, and jumpy; they are nervous, they tremble and sweat, and show various other signs of anxiety. They are sometimes tearful and cry openly. Because they are overanxious, they tend to make emergency responses to any perceived threat and to overreact to minor matters. They are impulsive, unpredictable, changeable, and restless, as well as vulnerable to real or imagined threat. They tend to be uncooperative and yet they are readily dominated by others—possibly because of their exaggerated needs for affection. Typically, they exhibit poor judgment and their approach to problems is stereotyped and unoriginal. Ten per cent are seen as homicidal. In summary, they are unable to express their emotions in any modulated or adaptive way.

This profile is also indicative of paranoid features. Indeed, 9-6 patients are hostile, irritable, and moody; they are given to having grandiose thoughts and ideas of reference. Twenty-five per cent describe themselves as excessively religious. They are generally distrustful and constantly question the motivations of others. Projection is often employed as their major defense.

These patients are afraid of emotional involvement of any sort. They are also conflicted over sexual matters; their heterosexual adjustment is described by clinicians as poor. They judge themselves and others in terms of popularity, and although they are somewhat ambitious and would like to get ahead, their prevailing mistrust of people leads them to keep others at a distance and prevents them from establishing close and meaningful relationships.

The parents of patients who present this profile were not consistent in their disciplinary actions. The fathers tended to be permissive while the mothers were strict. Fathers were also viewed as indifferent, rejecting, or even neglecting; mothers were described as affectionate and overprotective. Fewer than half of these parents were seen as affectionate by the 9-6 patients.

People with this profile are generally inpatients who have been diagnosed as psychotic (85%). The presenting disorder seems to permeate nearly all areas of the patient's life, but those most frequently affected are home, occupation, and social relations. These patients are quite young (mean age 26 years) at the onset of the disorder, and have often had previous episodes of one sort or another. Unfortunately, the prognosis for these patients is considered poor.

ADULT CODE: NORMAL K+*
Mean Profiles

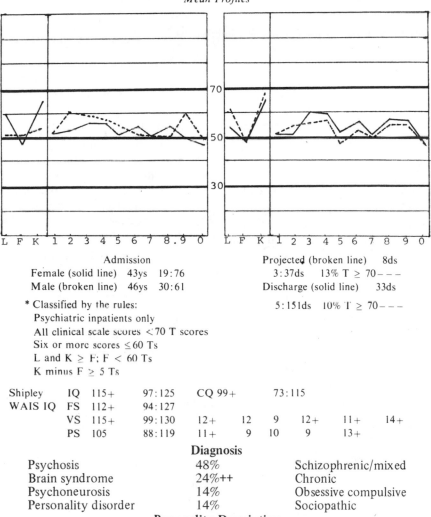

Admission
Female (solid line)   43ys   19:76
Male (broken line)   46ys   30:61

Projected (broken line)   8ds
3:37ds   13% T ≥ 70– – –
Discharge (solid line)   33ds
5:15lds   10% T ≥ 70– – –

* Classified by the rules:
Psychiatric inpatients only
All clinical scale scores < 70 T scores
Six or more scores ≤ 60 Ts
L and K ≥ F; F < 60 Ts
K minus F ≥ 5 Ts

Shipley	IQ	115+	97:125	CQ 99+		73:115			
WAIS IQ	FS	112+	94:127						
	VS	115+	99:130	12+	12	9	12+	11+	14+
	PS	105	88:119	11+	9	10	9	13+	

Diagnosis

Psychosis	48%	Schizophrenic/mixed
Brain syndrome	24%++	Chronic
Psychoneurosis	14%	Obsessive compulsive
Personality disorder	14%	Sociopathic

Personality Description

These patients who have in common their hospitalization on a psychiatric inpatient unit are shy, anxious, inhibited, and defensive about admitting the possibility that their problems could be psychological in nature. Basically withdrawn and uncooperative, they are afraid of emotional involvement with others and tend to keep people at a distance, thus avoiding close interpersonal relationships. At the same time, they are readily dominated by others and overly responsive to their evaluations; they are suggestable and submissive and conflicted about emotional dependency. Possibly because of these feelings people who generate this profile tend not to become involved in activities—they are passively resistant. They also avoid situations where their own performance may be inferior to that of others. It seems impossible for them to express their emotions in any modulated or adaptive way; in fact, they tend toward overcontrol of needs and impulses. There is a definite schizoid component to the personality structure of these patients. Clinicians judge them to spend a good deal of time in fantasy and daydreaming. Their stream of thought is often incoherent and they quite frequently appear perplexed.

The K+ patients are described as genotypically paranoid. They are suspicious and fearful and sensitive to anything that may be construed as a demand. In general, they are constant worriers; they are therefore vulnerable to both real and imagined threat. Phobic reactions are reported in about 40% of the cases.

It is significant that approximately one-fourth of these patients are diagnosed as suffering from a chronic brain syndrome. Symptoms which are reported with this diagnosis include loss of consciousness, amnesia, paresthesia, loss of memory, and eye complaints. Ironically, perhaps, these patients are quite bright in test intelligence; their mean IQ on the Shipley is 115, while on the WAIS, it is 112. The CQ, obtained on the Shipley, is 99—the highest for all codes studied. The patients also have a history of above average school achievement. Over 60% are educated beyond the high school level.

About one-fifth of these patients come from poverty ridden homes. Most frequently, K+ patients were the oldest child and very rarely were they the youngest or only child. The fathers of these patients were deceased in 33% of the cases and physically ill in another 11%. They were characterized as affectionate. Mothers were described as dominating.

If these patients receive any treatment beyond psychotherapy, it most likely is ECT (18%). Fifty-six per cent of these patients show small improvement, while another 19% show decided improvement. The prognosis is considered fair to good for the majority of the sample.

REFERENCES

AMERICAN PSYCHIATRIC ASSOCIATION, COMMITTEE ON NOMENCLATURE AND STATISTICS. *Diagnostic and Statistical Manual of Mental Disorders, second edition.* Washington, D.C.: APA, 1968.

BRIGGS, P. F., TAYLOR, M., AND TELLEGEN, A. *A study of the Marks and Seeman MMPI profile types as applied to a sample of 2,875 psychiatric patients.* Research Laboratories Report No. PR-66-5, Department of Psychiatry, University of Minnesota, 1966.

GILBERSTADT, H. AND DUKER, J. *A handbook for clinical and actuarial MMPI interpretation.* Philadelphia: W.B. Saunders Co., 1965.

GOTTESMAN, I. I. Differential inheritance of the psychoneuroses. *Eugen. Quart. 9*, 223–227, 1962.

GYNTHER, M. D., ALTMAN, H., WARBIN, R. W., AND SLETTEN, I. W. A new actuarial system for MMPI interpretation: Rationale and methodology. *J. Clin. Psychol. 28*, 173–179, 1972.

LACHAR, D. MMPI two-point code-type correlates in a state hospital population. *J. Clin. Psychol. 24*, 424–427, 1968.

LEWANDOWSKI, D., AND GRAHAM, J. R. Empirical correlates of frequently occurring two-point MMPI code-types: A replicated study. *J. Consult. Clin. Psychol. 39*, 467–472, 1972.

MEEHL, P. E. Reactions, reflections, projections. In J. M. Butcher (Ed.) *Objective Personality Assessment.* New York: Academic Press, pp. 131–189, 1972.

MEIKLE, S., AND GERRITSE, R. MMPI "cookbook" pattern frequencies in a psychiatric unit. *J. Clin. Psychol. 26*, 82–84, 1970.

WARBIN, R. W., ALTMAN, H., GYNTHER, M. D., AND SLETTEN, I. W. A new empirical automated MMPI interpretive program: 2–8 and 8–2 code types. *J. Personal. Assess. 36*, 581–584, 1972.

PART

THREE

ADOLESCENT SECTION

5

The Development
of Code Types

The studies reported in this section constitute an extension of our earlier work with adults. Our objective is to present a systematic array of social, personal, and psychological-psychiatric information about emotionally disturbed youth. Apart from the delinquency studies of Hathaway and Monachesi (1953), Wirt and Briggs (1959), and Ball (1962) and the works on normal adolescents by Hathaway and Monachesi (1961, 1963), the present studies represent the largest MMPI-related research on teen-age boys and girls. In this instance, we have opted for an empirical study of a large number of adolescents using a variety of data in preference to an "in depth" clinical approach limited to a very small sample (see Meehl, 1972). We also report MMPI scores (in Tables 1 and 2) for over 1,800 normal adolescents, since we believe that such data will help the reader better understand adolescent emotional disturbance; it is these norms on which our classification system is based.

At this point, we remind the reader that MMPI code types are a taxonomy, the value of which is determined by its usefulness in bringing together a variety of (uncontaminated) non-MMPI information of an empirical and theoretical sort. The content of the next chapter includes just such correlational data. We now wish to describe our procedure in selecting cases, in selecting personality descriptors, in relating these descriptors to the MMPI, and in assigning an individual test profile to one of the adolescent codes.

SELECTION OF CASES

The Normal Samples

The MMPI data reported here for normal adolescents were collected during the decades 1940, 1950, and 1960. The largest group of profiles was provided by Peter F. Briggs who selected cases from the original Minnesota state-wide sample reported by Hathaway and Monachesi (1963). This sample was comprised of

3,971 Minneapolis public school ninth graders who were tested during the 1947 and 1948 school year. An additional 11,329 ninth graders, who were tested in 1954, completed the sample. This combined sample was comprised of both rural and urban youngsters from 92 schools situated in 86 communities, in 47 of Minnesota's 87 counties. In describing their sample, Hathaway and Monachesi (1963) state that "The schools were selected to represent so far as possible Minnesota's diverse economic and geographic areas . . . (the cases were described as) mostly average boys and girls, normal or near it, who did not need special help" (p. 17). This sample actually represented 28% of the entire ninth grade public school population of Minnesota in 1954 and 36% of all ninth graders outside the Minneapolis and St. Paul public school systems. Although the subjects ranged in age from 13 to 18 years, 91% of the boys and 96% of the girls were 14 or 15 years old. For a detailed description of these cases, the reader should consult the original source (Hathaway and Monachesi, 1963).

For purpose of the present study, Briggs selected from these profiles, samples of 100 boys and 100 girls 14, 15, and 16 years of age and 80 boys and 40 girls, 17 years of age. In order to obtain a larger and more nationally representative sample, 1,046 additional profiles were collected in 1964 and 1965 from both rural and urban, public and private school youngsters living in Alabama (N = 129), California (N = 189), Kansas (N = 230), Missouri (N = 108), North Carolina (N = 225), and Ohio (N = 165). To the best of our knowledge, all profiles were obtained from white boys and girls who, at the time of testing, were neither institutionalized, nor being treated for an emotional disturbance.

Tables 1 and 2 present, for the combined sample, raw score means and standard deviations for boys and girls in four age groups.[1] It is important to note that these norms were derived from all profiles regardless of L, F, or K scale elevations. No profiles were eliminated from analysis because of *any* scale values. At this point, we should also note that all adolescent profiles (both normal and abnormal) are scored and plotted *without* the K correction. There are at least three reasons for this: (1) K was developed on a small sample of adults (see Meehl, 1945), and hence its applicability to adolescents is at best questionable; (2) Welsh and Dahlstrom (1956) and Dahlstrom, Welsh, and Dahlstrom (1972) have repeatedly cautioned against its use with samples different from those from which K was developed; and (3) Marks and Seeman (1962a) found a negative correlation (-0.53, p = 0.05) between validity coefficients (based on psychotherapist descriptions) and K score magnitude for an adolescent sample. Moreover, additional support for such a procedure is found in a recent study by Berry (1972). Employing a modification of the procedure proposed by Campbell and Fiske (1959), Berry examined the efficiency of five multivariate classification methods in identifying discriminable subgroups of adolescent MMPI profiles with and without K, and reported superior results for the cluster

---

[1] Although some of our subjects were as young as 9 years of age, and as old as 18, the number of subjects below 14 and age 18 was too small to warrant our presenting separate age norms.

Table 1. *Raw Score Means and Standard Deviations without K-corrections for Normal Male Adolescents*

Age	N	L	F	K	Hs	D	Hy	Pd	Mf	Pa	Pt	Sc	Ma	Si
14[a]	271	3.7	7.2	13.2	5.3	17.9	17.5	17.6	20.9	10.3	14.4	16.4	17.7	28.9
		2.06	5.03	4.84	3.39	4.50	4.51	4.31	4.23	3.67	7.30	9.33	5.10	7.39
15	265	3.9	8.1	13.4	5.7	18.3	17.8	18.3	21.3	11.0	14.5	16.9	18.4	29.2
		2.33	5.97	4.77	4.26	4.41	4.87	4.67	4.79	4.78	7.04	10.00	5.23	7.44
16	250	4.3	8.5	13.3	5.9	18.4	18.2	18.4	20.8	11.5	14.6	17.3	18.5	29.5
		2.21	5.77	4.43	3.55	4.45	4.58	4.63	4.22	6.78	6.77	9.24	4.66	7.05
17[b]	166	4.8	8.2	13.5	5.9	19.1	19.3	18.9	20.8	10.4	14.9	17.8	18.1	28.9
		2.40	4.60	4.54	3.99	5.51	5.26	4.36	4.59	3.39	6.48	9.11	4.70	6.63

aIncludes a few subjects less than 14 years of age.

bIncludes a few subjects over 17 years of age.

Table 2. *Raw Score Means and Standard Deviations without K-corrections for Normal Female Adolescents*

Age	N	L	F	K	Hs	D	Hy	Pd	Mf	Pa	Pt	Sc	Ma	Si
14[a]	280	4.0	5.5	13.5	5.5	18.5	19.6	16.6	35.2	10.4	14.9	14.5	16.3	28.6
		2.15	3.99	4.48	4.01	4.75	4.50	4.66	4.55	4.58	7.00	8.18	4.74	7.90
15	277	4.2	6.1	13.4	5.9	19.2	20.1	17.7	34.3	10.5	15.4	15.6	17.0	28.8
		2.32	4.40	4.60	4.47	4.63	4.87	4.77	4.86	4.57	7.40	9.31	5.37	7.75
16	158	4.7	6.8	12.9	6.5	20.7	20.2	17.6	33.9	10.9	16.8	16.8	16.8	31.6
		2.27	4.44	4.56	4.30	4.89	5.07	4.58	4.33	3.86	7.56	9.49	4.45	8.07
17[b]	139	5.1	7.2	12.6	8.0	21.2	21.4	18.4	33.5	10.1	16.8	17.6	16.2	32.0
		2.41	4.06	3.98	4.37	4.66	5.02	4.33	4.46	3.46	6.86	8.77	4.63	7.49

aIncludes a few subjects less than 14 years of age.

bIncludes a few subjects over 17 years of age.

of profiles scored *without* the K correction. Thus, these norms differ slightly from those reported by Hathaway and Monachesi (1963) and are probably more truly representative of a cross-section of caucasion United States youth.[2] Approximately 10% of the subjects in the 17 year-old group are actually 18 years of age. However, we included an 18 year-old *only* if the youngster was still living in his or her parental home. Conversely, about 20% of the cases in the 14 year-old group are as young as 9 years of age. Finally, some unknown small percentage of the sample were subjects who had dropped out of school prior to the time of testing; in some instances they were siblings of youngsters involved in treatment who themselves were not emotionally disturbed.

The T-score conversion tables which were compiled from these norms and first published in Dahlstrom, Welsh, and Dahlstrom (1972) appear in our discussion of profile classification. The effect of age on the MMPI is shown in Figure 1 where mean scores for normal adolescents are plotted against adult norms.

The Abnormal Samples

The main sample from which the adolescent code types and their descriptions were derived consists of 834 teen-agers who, during the period of study (1965 to

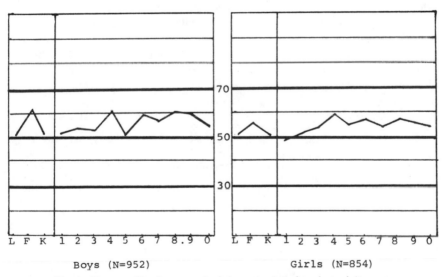

Boys (N=952)   Girls (N=854)

Fig. 1. Mean profiles for normal adolescents plotted against adult norms.

[2] We are in basic agreement with the recommendation by Hathaway and Monachesi (1963) that one should view adolescent MMPI scores against an adult norm background. Nevertheless, it still appears to us that the meaning "disturbed" or "abnormal" adolescents is established against an adolescent normative view. We do not find these two sets of norms mutually exclusive.

1970), were involved in psychotherapy of one form or another.[3] They comprise
the "treatment" sample of a larger investigation of over 3,000 emotionally
disturbed youth. This project began early in 1964, with an attempt to collect
information regarding MMPI usage from all clinics, hospitals, and individual
practitioners throughout the United States who provided psychological services
to adolescents. Included as survey resources were the then recent directories of
the American Psychological Association, the American Psychiatric Association,
the American Board of Psychological Services, Exceptional Children, the
Association of American Medical Colleges, the American Association of
Psychiatric Clinics for Children, and Resources for Mentally Ill Children in the
United States; in addition, contacts were also made with the directors of APA
approved doctoral programs in clinical and counseling psychology, APA
approved internship programs for doctoral training in clinical psychology,
members of Section 1-Division 12 of APA, chief psychologists in state mental
health programs, and private practitioners suggested to us by various colleagues.
In two surveys (the first conducted in 1964 and the second in 1965), we
contacted 638 individuals and agencies in the 48 continental states. As a result
of these preliminary contacts, some 74 agencies and 172 psychotherapists from
30 states participated in this study. Data collected from the first survey (2, 242
"general referrals," *i.e.,* patients from whom we collected MMPI and intake
information only) as well as frequency tables for each adolescent code developed
from the second, or "treatment," sample will be reported in another
publication. The "treatment" sample, for which extensive data are reported
here, consists of white boys and girls, 12 through 18 years of age, who were *not*
mentally deficient or retarded, but who had some adjustment problem and were
either seeking professional help or had been referred for it by others. In
addition, only those patients were included who had completed the MMPI,
answered a personal data schedule, remained in therapy for a minimum of 10
hours, and whose therapists' had completed an extensive set of ratings. Although

---

[3] In studying adolescents during recent years, we have noticed sharp increases in the
frequencies of certain behaviors which were not at all prevalent at the time we collected our
original data. To take some outstanding examples, drug use and abuse, premarital sex,
pregnancy, and violence appear much more often in the case histories of youth seen in
psychotherapy in the 1970's than they did for those seen during the 1960's. In an attempt
to "update" our earlier findings, we drew another abnormal sample consisting of 419
inpatients and outpatients seen at The Ohio State University Health Center during the
period 1970-73. For 22 of our 29 adolescent code types we located 10 or more additional
cases; from these, we extracted information of a sort *not* investigated in the earlier study.
These findings are reported in the final paragraphs of the narrative descriptions of these 22
codes. It should be noted that the frequencies reported may well be *underestimates* since
there was no way of knowing whether some behavior did not appear in the chart because it
did not occur, or whether its occurrence was simply unknown to the clinician writing the
summary. It should also be noted that the characteristics reported for this later sample have
been neither replicated nor statistically tested against the base rates of the larger group.
Also, 61 cases (15%) included in this sample are black adolescents. While we are well aware
of the cautions required and the warnings given in the MMPI literature when including
blacks (*e.g.,* Gynther, 1972), we make a special point of noting that we found few
black-white differences among the descriptions of the adolescents studied.

various forms of the MMPI were used, the "cannot say" alternative was eliminated from the instructions and the patients were encouraged to answer every question; they were also encouraged to answer all items on the personal data schedule. Any subject who left 50 or more MMPI questions unanswered, exhibited poor vision, refused to cooperate, or showed gross mental confusion, was either retested or excluded from the study. Table 3 reports the distribution of cases by age and sex for the "treatment" sample. Additional characteristics of the sample appear in the description of the "average adolescent patient" and in Appendix D.

Of the 172 psychotherapists who provided patient ratings,[4] 116 were either board certified psychiatrists, Ph.D. level clinical psychologists, or MSW level social workers with 2 additional years of therapy experience. These "experienced" therapists rated 746 patients or 90% of the cases; an additional 24 therapists who were either third- or fourth-year clinical psychology interns, third-year psychiatry residents, or recent MSW graduates rated 83 patients or 10% of the cases. Table 4 presents descriptive data on the participating psychotherapists; a more complete description is given in Appendix D.

The instructions to therapists (see Appendix D) requested that they complete, in order, a case data schedule, an adjective check list, and a Q-sort. All ratings were to be based on available evidence, including informants reports, interview notes, chart notes, case history materials, psychological test reports, etc., with the critical exception of the MMPI; ratings were *not* to be influenced either

Table 3. *Distribution of "Treatment" Cases*

Age	N Boys	N Girls	Total
12	25	11	36
13	73	26	99
14	95	39	134
15	120	76	196
16	92	78	170
17	76	63	139
18	28	32	60
Totals	509	325	834

[4] All psychotherapists were paid for their ratings from NIMH and other grants.

Table 4. *Therapist Descriptive Data*

Variable	Per Cent	Variable	Per Cent
Sex		Years of psychotherapy	
Male	68	experience	
Female	32	1 to 5 years	58
Educational degree		6 to 10 years	22
M.D.	29	11 to 15 years	14
M.S W.	27	16 to 20 years	6
Ph.D.	20	(Mdn = 5 years)	
M.A.,M.S.,M.Ed.	19	Psychotherapy hours	
B.A.,B.S.	4	per week	
Ed.D.	1	1 to 10 hours	22
Profession		11 to 20 hours	40
Psychologist	36	21 to 30 hours	21
Social worker	33	31 to 40 hours	11
Psychiatrist	29	41 to 50 hours	6
Psychoanalyst	2	(Mdn = 18 hours)	

directly or indirectly by this test instrument.[5] A minimum of 10 diagnostic and/or treatment interviews of 45 to 60 minutes duration with frequency of not less than one session every 2 weeks were prerequisite to these ratings. The 10-hour minimum was adopted on the basis of several considerations and in light of the fact that a large number of cases were needed as were quality ratings. While it seemed reasonable to assume that increasing the hours might increase the quality of ratings, it seemed even more certain that an increase in required prerating interviews would result in substantially fewer cases being collected. In effect, extending the time would not only tend to exclude early therapy drop-outs, but would also eliminate patients who terminate following rapid improvement. Another consideration was a finding reported by Meehl (1960).

[5] In 90% of the cases, psychotherapists reported compliance with this requirement that ratings be kept free of MMPI contamination. And in the remaining 10% of cases, there were instances in which a therapist may have seen an MMPI but paid little attention to it.

By correlating Q-sorts following successive interviews with a terminal Q-sort description, Meehl explored the rate at which a psychotherapist's image of his patient converged over time. It was clear from his data that this image crystalizes quite early, "so that somewhere between the second and fourth therapeutic hour it has stablized approximately to the degree permitted for the terminal sort-resort reliabilities" (p. 21). Figure 2 presents some of our own data on the rate of convergence using the Marks 108 Q-Item pool.

The therapists for this convergence study were four clinical psychology interns who had described four different patients following varying numbers of consecutive interviews. Plotted at "P" are correlations of pretherapy average patient (stereotype) descriptions with terminal patient descriptions for three of the four therapists. The *solid line* (x) connects Q correlations of sorts completed following the first, second, third, and fourth interview hours. In this instance, the fifth hour description was the terminal sort correlated with each earlier description, as well as with the therapists' pretherapy patient stereotype. The *solid line,* which appears as an extension of this, represents data for a different therapist-patient combination; in this case, the therapist's first sort followed his fifth interview hour and successive sorts followed each interview hour up to the 20th interview. Here the 20th-hour description was correlated with each earlier sort. The *dotted line* connects correlations of earlier sorts with a 20th-hour terminal description. The *broken line* represents correlations of a ninth-hour terminal sort with earlier sorts. These findings, based on inexperienced

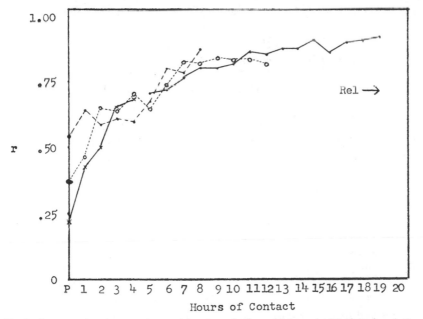

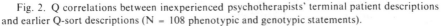

Fig. 2. Q correlations between inexperienced psychotherapists' terminal patient descriptions and earlier Q-sort descriptions (N = 108 phenotypic and genotypic statements).

Table 5. *Interview Hours Prior to Ratings*[a]

	Boys		Girls	
Age	Mdn	Range	Mdn	Range
12	21	10–150	20	15–34
13	18	10–77	14	10–50
14	21	10–110	20	10–72
15	18	10–168	22	10–153
16	19	10–64	24	10–203
17	20	10–200	21	10–129
18	14	10–187	21	10–111

[a]Minimum of 10 hours (11% of cases)

therapists using a different pool of statements, are quite similar to those reported by Meehl. Together they suggest that a therapist's patient-image stabilizes (*i.e.,* the *r*'s reach as asymptote) somewhere between the 8th and 10th hour; they also indicate rather promising sort-resort reliabilities for this particular Q-item pool. Table 5 presents age-sex data on the number of interview hours that were actually held prior to rating. The mean number of hours for boys and girls is approximately 19 and 21, respectively, with only 11% of the cases rated at the 10-hour minimum.

SELECTION OF DESCRIPTORS

The goal of this study, from the outset, was to obtain comprehensive information about emotionally disturbed adolescents. We developed and employed several rating forms which contained both phenotypic and genotypic descriptor content (Marks and Sines, 1969). These forms comprised a preliminary pool of 2,302 descriptors which, in effect, "covered the waterfront."

The first of these, the Personal Data Schedule (PDS), is a self-administered objective questionnaire of 72 items plus Gough's 300 adjectives; it is completed by the patient. The content of the items, suggested from the work of Barrington (1963), Bell (1938), Gilbert (1931), Gough (1960), Hildreth (1933), Jackson and Getzel (1959), Mather (1934), Mooney (1950), Ramsey (1943), Roeber and Garfield (1943), Symonds (1936), Wilson (1959), and the authors, covers attitudes and feelings towards self, others, home, school, work, health, religion, dating, sex, and leisure time. A preliminary form of the PDS was pretested with a heterogeneous group of 20 boys and girls, both patients and normals, who ranged in age from 12 to 18 years. The revision is comprised of items that were judged to be readable, rateable, reliable, and easily understood (see Appendix D).

The Q-sort array, one of the therapists' rating materials, consists of 108 penotypic (descriptive) and genotypic (dynamic) statements of personality structure and function. The statements were originally selected for their representative coverage of the personality domain from a pool of over 12,000 items. They were then empirically screened for sex and age nonspecificity, for clinical pertinence, ratability, and interpatient variability; they have since accumulated a sizeable amount of research data (see Marks, 1959, 1961; Marks and Seeman, 1962a, 1962b, 1962c, 1962d, and 1963; Coyle, Fowler, and Marks, 1967; Woodward, 1968; Berry, 1972; and Marks and Sines, 1969). The content of the item pool covers attitudes towards self, attitudes towards others, motivational needs, areas of conflict, mechanisms of defense, types of control, character traits, ego strengths, ego weaknesses, and openness to personality change. (See Appendices B and D.)

The Case Data Schedule (CDS) is an objective questionnaire consisting of 174 items concerning personal and family history, relations with others, school achievement, social adjustment, psychological status, and nature, course, and progress of treatment. The CDS, which was also developed specifically for this project, was inspired by the works of Briggs (1957), Buss and Gerjudy (1957), Dahlstrom (1949), Lewinsohn, Nichols, Pulos, Lomont, Nickel, and Siskind (1964), McNair and Lorr (1964), Marks and Seeman (1963), Mayfield and Strupp (1961), Miles, Barrabee, and Finesinger (1951), Patterson (1964), Peterson (1961), Schofield, Hathaway, Hastings, and Bell (1954), Wirt (1964). A preliminary form of the CDS was also pretested empirically for coverage, clarity, and ratability by 22 highly experienced medical and nonmedical psychotherapists who rated adolescent patients who had been in therapy for 10 hours or more. Retained in the revised form (see Appendix D), are the items which survived this screening procedure.

The Adjective Check List (ACL) is a list of 300 adjectives developed and reported by Gough (1960), and commonly used to describe individual attributes. This is the same adjective check list that appears in the PDS for patient self-ratings.

Once the ratings for the 834 cases had been completed, the descriptors used in all subsequent analyses were selected as follows. The sample was divided by sex and then subdivided by age. Cases were then alternately assigned to one of two subgroups. This yielded two samples of boys and two of girls equally matched for age and presumably randomly matched for other variables. This procedure was followed because there were too few cases to classify boys and girls separately and to facilitate replication of the findings. Next, t or chi-square (with Yates' correction) analyses were performed to test for sex differences for each descriptor; those which yielded alpha values of 0.10 (with the difference in the same direction) for each half of the sample—with the resulting joint probability of 0.01—were identified and deleted from further analyses. The remaining descriptors were then examined for items having exceedingly high (≥90%) or low (≤10%) base rate frequencies; these descriptors were also eliminated. (However, it should be noted that exceptions were made for certain descriptors with such important content as "suicide attempts.") The reader will recognize these latter items as Barnum in the sense discussed in Chapter 2. Conversely, a number of non-Barnum descriptors were also eliminated where their content was of little interest or relevance. Table 6 reports the results of this procedure. All subsequent analyses were performed on the revised pool of 1,265 descriptors. Appendix D presents base rates for the original descriptors. Separate means and percentages are given for sex specific descriptors and results are combined where no significant differences exist.

RELATING DESCRIPTORS TO CODES

Some comments concerning our search for an optimal procedure for grouping profiles and relating descriptors to codes are in order. Since, as Meehl points out (Marks and Seeman, 1963, p. viii) there exists no straightforward actuarial searching technique for grouping profiles, we have, over the years, explored a variety of methods[6]; finally, we decided to adopt the two-point system recently recommended by Gynther (1972) and Lewandowski and Graham (1972). This system is simple, relatively objective, and in principle can accommodate all MMPI profiles.

Raw scores *without* K corrections are first converted to T-scores using the appropriate sex-age conversion tables which appear below (see Tables 10 through 17). The scores for each case are plotted on standard profile sheets and the points connected in the usual manner. Each profile is next coded, following the procedure described in Chapter 1. The profiles are then sorted by two-point code using the 10 standard MMPI scales. When ties between high scale scores occur, the profile is coded on the basis of the scale with the lowest numeric value, reading from left to right. For example, if scales 1, 3, and 6 are the high points and have identical T values, the profile is coded 1-3. Similarly, if scale 2 is the high point and scales 1, 7, and 8 are tied for second, the profile is coded 2-1. For the 10 scales taken two at a time, there are 90 possible two-point combinations; and by pairing two scales (*e.g.,* 1-2s) with their reversals (2-1s), there are 45 possible two-point permutations. Table 7 indicates the distribution of cases following the "original" and "substitute" (discussed below) coding systems. It should be noted that the use of this method may increase the number of profiles assigned to code types with low numeric values. For example, given a profile in which scales 2, 7, and 8 are of equal elevation, coding it 2-7, as

---

[6] See Marks (1967, 1971), Marks and Sines (1969), Persons and Marks (1970, 1971), and Berry and Marks (1972). See, also, Goldberg's (1972) *Recent trends in personality assessment,* and Dahlstrom's (1972) *Personality systematics and the problem of types.*

Table 6. *Selection of Personality Descriptors*

Descriptors	Rating Forms							Totals	
	ACL		PDS		CDS		Q Sort		
	N	%	N	%	N	%	N	N	%
Original sample	300	100	990	100	904	100	108	2,302	100
Sex disciminating	61	20	200	20	102	11	a	363	16
≤10% or ≥90%	72	24	194	20	283	31	a	549	24
Low relevance[b]	-	-	82	8	43	5	a	125	5
Revised pool	167	56	514	52	476	52	108	1,265	55

[a] Excluded during selection of Q-item pool.

[b] Applied to PDS (Personal Data Schedule) and CDS (Case Data Schedule) descriptors only. Note: ACL (Adjective Check List) was excluded from this analysis. Eliminated were PDS Item Nos. 6,7,10,11,12,13, 20,21,24,25,34,35,36,37,45,46,48,49,50,52,53,54,56,57,59,60,61,62; and CDS Item Nos. 1,2,3,4,5,6,10,12,13,14,19,22,25,26,33,34,35,44, 45,54,55,56,63,89,122,125,154,164,165,166,167,168,169, and 170.

Table 7. *Distribution of Cases by Original and Substitute Two-Point System*[a] *Using Adolescent Norms*

Code	Original			Substitute			Code	Original			Substitute			Code Type	Substitute		
	M	F	T	M	F	T		M	F	T	M	F	T		M	F	T
1-2	4	3	7	5	6	11	2-1	5	6	11	6	6	12	1-2/2-1	11	12	23
1-3	13	13	26	17	13	30	3-1	7	7	14	7	7	14	1-3/3-1	24	20	44
1-4	10	4	14	11	5	16	4-1	5	3	8	5	3	8	1-4/4-1	16	8	24
1-5	5		5	6		6	5-1	5	4	9	5	4	9	1-5/5-1	11	4	15
1-6	4		4	4		4	6-1	7		7	7		7	1-6/6-1	11		11
1-7*	3	1	4				7-1*	3	1	4				*			
1-8	14	1	15	17	2	19	8-1	3	4	7	6	4	10	1-8/8-1	23	6	29
1-9*	2	1	3				9-1*	2	2	4	1		1	*			
1-0*	2	2	4				0-1*	3		3				*			
2-3	15	7	22	15	8	23	3-2	8	7	15	8	7	15	2-3/3-2	23	15	38
2-4	11	18	29	12	19	31	4-2	16	13	29	16	13	29	2-4/4-2	28	32	60
2-5	11	2	13	12	2	14	5-2	8	2	10	8	2	10	2-5/5-2	20	4	24
2-6*	4	2	6				6-2*	1	1	2	1		1	*			
2-7	9	7	16	9	7	16	7-2	2	1	3	2	1	3	2-7/7-2	11	8	19
2-8	2	9	11	3	9	12	8-2	2	2	4	2	2	4	2-8/8-2	5	11	16
2-9*							9-2*							*			
2-0	6	8	14	6	8	14	0-2	4	4	8	4	4	8	2-0/0-2	10	12	22
3-4	19	10	29	19	11	30	4-3	10	12	22	10	12	22	3-4/4-3	29	23	52
3-5	5		5	5		5	5-3	8		8	8		8	3-5/5-3	13		13
3-6	2	2	4	2	2	4	6-3	4	4	8	4	4	8	3-6/6-3	6	6	12
3-7*		2	2		1	1	7-3*	2		2				*			
3-8*		1	1				8-3*	1		1				*			
3-9*	1	1	2				9-3*	4	3	7	1		1	*			
3-0*	2		2	1		1	0-3*							*			
4-5	8	5	13	8	5	13	5-4	19	3	22	20	4	24	4-5/5-4	28	9	37
4-6	14	22	36	14	22	36	6-4	7	4	11	9	5	14	4-6/6-4	23	27	50
4-7	12	7	19	12	7	19	7-4	2		2	4		4	4-7/7-4	16	7	23
4-8	12	16	28	12	16	28	8-4	4	11	15	4	11	15	4-8/8-4	16	27	43
4-9	34	27	61	34	27	61	9-4	13	13	26	16	17	33	4-9/9-4	50	44	94
4-0	10	3	13	10	3	13	0-4	4	1	5	7	2	9	4-0/0-4	17	5	22
5-6	4		4	6		6	6-5	5		5	5		5	5-6/6-5	11		11
5-7*	1	2	3		1	1	7-5*	3		3	1		1	*			
5-8*	5		5				8-5*		1	1				*			
5-9	8	1	9	9	1	10	9-5	5	2	7	7	3	10	5-9/9-5	16	4	20
5-0	4		4	6		6	0-5	5		5	5		5	5-0/0-5	11		11
6-7*	4	2	6	1	1	2	7-6*							*			
6-8	7	2	9	9	2	11	8-6	1	3	4	2	4	6	6-8/8-6	11	6	17
6-9*	1		1				9-6*	2		2				*			
6-0*	2		2				0-6*	4	2	6				*			
7-8	15	3	18	16	4	20	8-7	5	6	11	5	6	11	7-8/8-7	21	10	31
7-9	4	1	5	4	2	6	9-7	10	1	11	10	1	11	7-9/9-7	14	3	17
7-0	4	1	5	5	1	6	0-7	4		4	4	1	5	7-0/0-7	9	2	11
8-9	5	6	11	8	7	15	9-8	5	2	7	12	6	18	8-9/9-8	20	13	33
8-0*							0-8*	2		2				*			
9-0*	1	1	2				0-9*	4	2	6	1	1	2	*			

[a]See text for explanation.

*Excluded from analysis. See text on substitutions.

Note: M (male), F (female), T (total) Ns.

146

opposed to 2-8, increases disproportionately the 2-7 group size. Thus, the frequencies reported may be somewhat different from those actually obtained.

The cases reported in columns 2, 3, and 4 of Table 7 under the "original" heading were derived by the procedure just described. The number of cases vary, for example, from 0 for the 2-9 to 34 M (males) and 27 F (females) for a T (total) of 61 cases for the 4-9s. In the paired reverse-code columns of "original" data, there were no cases of 9-2s, 0-3s, or 7-6s; on the other hand, there were as many as 29 4-2s. We next set N = 10 as the minimum number of cases needed to establish a code type for the purpose of statistical analysis. This reduced the number of paired two-point codes from 45 to 29 and the number of classifiable cases from 834 to 749. While we could row classify these 749 cases, or 90% of our sample, we would be losing 85 cases for which we had high quality ratings. Rather than discard this many cases, we followed an alternative in which we disregarded the second highest scale and substituted the third. Applying this procedure (*i.e.*, recoding and reclassifying) to these 85 profiles where the original coding had yielded groups with Ns of less than 10, resulted in the frequencies reported under the "substitute" columns of Table 7. Thus, for the 1-7/7-1s there were a total of 8 cases of which all 8 could be reclassified by a substitute code. Similarily, for the 1-9/9-1s in which there were 7 cases, 6 could be reclassified by a substitute code. Table 8 gives the two-point redistributions following the third-scale substitutions.

Table 8 shows there were 8 cases in which the original profiles were coded either 1-7 or 7-1. By disregarding scale 7 of the 1-7s (N = 4) and substituting the third highest point in its place, there was thus available one additional 1-2, 1-4, 1-5, and 1-8.[7] These latter profiles were than added to their respective prototype codes increasing the number of cases per type. For example, following substitutions, the number of "original" 1-2s appearing in Table 7 increases from 4 to 5 for "M" (males) and from 3 to 6 for "F" (females); the number of 2-1s increases from 5 to 6 for males but remains the same for females. The corresponding totals become 11 and 12 for males and females or 23 "T" (total) cases for the 1-2/2-1 code type.

Inspection of Table 7 also reveals that some code types are either totally 'pure' (*e.g.*, 1-6/6-1, 4-8/8-4) or have little second-scale 'noise' or saturation (*e.g.*, 1-4/4-1 = 8%, 2-4/4-2 = 3%). For other codes, the substitutions vary from 24% in the case of the 6-8/8-6 to a high of 46% for the 8 9/9 8. The total number of cases that could *not* be classified by this procedure was 13, or less than 2%. In these latter cases, substituting the third digit placed the profile in one of the other low frequency, hence unclassifiable codes. Thus, one of the 9-1 profiles, in which the third highest point was 3, became a 9-3, which would have also required substitution. We therefore excluded from further grouping all cases in which a profile could not be classified by substituting the third highest scale.

---

[7] Again in the case of ties the scale with the lowest numeric value was used in the two-point code.

Table 8. *Substitutions for Low Frequency Two-Point Codes*

Original Code	N Cases	N Cases (Substitute Code)
1-7 or 7-1	8	1(1-2), 1(1-4), 1(1-5), 2(1-8), 1(7-8), 1(7-9), 1(7-0)
1-9 or 9-1	7	1(1-2), 1(1-3), 1(1-4), 2(9-4), 1(9-8), 1(NC)
1-0 or 0-1	7	2(1-2), 2(1-3), 2(1-8), 1(0-4)
2-6 or 6-2	8	1(2-1), 1(2-3), 2(2-4), 1(2-5), 1(2-8), 1(6-4), 1(NC)
3-7 or 7-3	4	1(3-1), 2(7-4), 1(NC)
3-8 or 8-3	2	1(3-4), 1(8-1)
3-9 or 9-3	9	3(9-4), 1(9-5), 4(9-8), 1(NC)
3-0	1	1(3-6)
5-7 or 7-5	6	2(7-1), 1(5-4), 1(7-8), 2(NC)
5-8 or 8-5	6	1(8-1), 1(5-4), 2(5-6), 1(5-9), 1(5-0)
6-7	6	2(6-4), 1(6-8), 1(8-6), 2(NC)
6-9 or 9-6	3	1(9-4), 1(5-9), 1(9-8)
6-0 or 0-6	8	3(0-4), 1(6-8), 1(0-7), 3(NC)
0-8	2	1(8-1), 1(8-6)
9-0 or 0-9	8	1(9-4), 1(9-5), 4(9-8), 2(NC)

Note: NC (Not classifiable by code substitution)

What effect this may have on the validity of our system is not empirically known. However, we found no significant relationship ($r = -0.18$) between the percentage of saturation and the number of significant descriptors for the 29 code types.

Following the procedure described by Gynther[8] (1972), both within and between code-type comparisons of means or percentages—whichever was the appropriate measure—were made for each descriptor where the groups contained 10 or more cases. If the number of cases per group was 20 or more, the sample was randomly divided and separate comparisons were made in an effort to replicate the findings. In each grouping, cases were assigned so that age and sex were represented equally in each half of the sample. Chi-square with Yates' correction was used with frequency data and Students' t-tests were used with means for all group comparisons. These data were processed through an IBM 370/175 computer.

Table 9 reports the results of our descriptor analysis. There were 14 code types where N permitted a comparison between the high and low profiles. For purpose of this analysis, the two scores comprising the code were averaged for each profile and the profiles ranked from high to low for the type. The distribution was divided at the median and a comparison was made between the two groups on every descriptor. Only those descriptors with alpha values $\leqslant 0.01$ or 0.02 ("a"), or 0.04 through 0.06 ("b") were then identified for use. Included were descriptors from one-sample comparisons with alpha values of 0.04 or less and descriptors from two-sample replicated comparisons where alpha values yielded a joint probability of 0.06 or less.

Reference to Table 9 shows, for example, that the N for the 1-4/4-1 code type was sufficiently large to permit a one-sample comparison between the high and low profiles. This yielded a total ("ab") of 16 descriptors which significantly differentiated the highs from lows; 7 of these had associated probability values $\leqslant 0.01$ and 0.02, and 9 had values between 0.04 and 0.06. Similarly, in the case of the 1-3/3-1 code type, there were sufficient cases to compare high 1-3s with low 1-3s "Left" refers to the 1-3 subgroup (the group to the left of the slash) of profiles within the 1-3/3-1 code type. Since there were insufficient 3-1 profiles to be included in the analysis, the comparison was limited to the 1-3s. Conversely, for the 4-5/5-4 code type, where the high versus low comparison was performed only for the 5-4s, the corresponding results appear in the column under "Right." It can be seen that for the 4-9/9-4s, there were sufficient cases to analyze high versus low 4-9s and high versus low 9-4s separately, as well as to cross-validate the results of the 4-9s. In this instance, there were a total of 27 replicated descriptors which differentiated high from low 4-9s; yet there were only 22 descriptors which separated high from low 9-4s—in a one-sample comparison.

The figures appearing under the "Left vs Right" columns of Table 9 indicate

---

[8] The authors are indebted to Dr. Malcolm D. Gynther who kindly provided us with his original PL/I program which we then rewrote for our own analyses.

Table 9. *Significant Descriptors Derived from an Analysis of Adolescent Codes*[1]

Code Type	High vs Low[2] Code Type			Left			Right			Left vs Right[3]			Type vs Other[4]			Case Total N
	a	b	ab	a	b	ab	a	b	ab	a	b	ab	a	b	ab	N
1-2/2-1*										3	18	21	15	22	37*	23
1-3/3-1*				3	10	13				8	10	18	25	19	43*	44
1-4/4-1*	7	9	16										30	27	57*	24
1-5/5-1													43	41	84	15
1-6/6-1													14	21	35	11
1-8/8-1*				14	19	33				11	17	28	31	33	64*	29
2-3/3-2*										5	13	18	21	27	48*	29
2-4/4-2*				9	25	34	5	21	26	8	13	21*	18	20	38*	60
2-5/5-2*										6	14	21	28	38	66*	24
2-7/7-2													61	47	108	19
2-8/8-2													25	43	68	16
2-0/0-2*	10	12	22										112	34	146*	22
3-4/4-3*				11	21	32	7	13	20	6	10	16*	24	20	44*	52
3-5/5-3													18	28	46	13
3-6/6-3													9	21	30	12
4-5/5-4*							4	10	14	9	15	24	29	32	61*	37
4-6/6-4*				19	38	57				17	19	36	87	41	128*	50
4-7/7-4*	12	10	22										13	13	26*	23
4-8/8-4*				14	23	37				27	35	62	49	28	77*	43
4-9/9-4*				13	14	27*	8	14	22	5	13	18*	126	41	167*	94
4-0/0-4*	5	15	20										11	22	33*	22
5-6/6-5													10	23	33	11
5-9/9-5*										7	7	14	8	16	24*	20
5-0/0-5													42	35	77	11
6-8/8-6													65	55	120	17
7-8/8-7*	3	12	15							11	20	31	9	33	42*	31
7-9/9-7													13	19	32	17
7-0/0-7													23	30	53	11
8-9/9-8*							19	25	44	13	24	37	13	17	30*	33

[1] Subgroup Ns will vary in size with a minimum of 10 cases per group required for each statistical analysis. These Ns appear in Chapter 6.

[2] Comparison of profiles above and below the median for the combined two-point code (e.g., 1-2s and 2-1s).

[3] Comparison of profiles coded left of the slash (e.g., 1-2s) with profiles coded right of the slash (e.g., 2-1s).

[4] Comparison of all profiles for a given code (e g., 1-2s and 2-1s) with all remaining profiles.

a=N descriptors significant at≤.01 or .02 levels.

b=N descriptors significant between .04 and .06 levels

ab=Total significant descriptors.

*Cross validated descriptors.

the number of significant descriptors resulting from reverse scale comparisons (*e.g.*, 1-2s versus 2-1s) within the same code type. That is, N was sufficiently large for the 1-2/2-1 code to permit a comparison of all profiles coded 1-2 with all profiles coded 2-1. This analysis yielded a total of 21 significant descriptors. Similarly in the case of the 2-4/4-2 code, the results were replicated and there were 21 significant descriptors.

The "Type vs Other" heading of Table 9 lists the major results of our system analysis. Reported are the number of significant descriptors resulting from comparisons of each code type with the remainder or "Other" profiles. The asterisks indicate cross-validated findings; thus, the Ns were sufficiently large to permit replication of 18 (or 62%) of the 29 code types. The number of descriptors per type (*i.e.*, the "ab" totals) range from 24 for the 5-9/9-5s to 167 for the 4-9/9-4s. The question may now arise as to how many significant descriptors might be expected to emerge simply by chance? Gynther, Altman, and Sletten (1973), recently found, for example, that 3 of their 17 code types were "failures"; and that, of the remaining 14, 3 were only "marginally successful" in generating correlates beyond chance results. The problem of evaluating multiple statistical tests and the presence or absence of nonchance relationships is unsettled though well-known. Block (1960) found that the statistical model most commonly used was overly conservative. In a series of empirical analyses comparing criterion groups assembled by a randomizing procedure, he reported that considerably fewer items emerged as significant than convention would have presumed—convention being 5% at the .05 level, and 1% at the .01 level. Thus, the over-all mean percentage of items that reached significance at the .01 level was actually 0.36; at the .05 level, the mean percentage was 2.08. Applying these findings to the present data suggests that approximately 5 descriptors at the .01 level and 26 at the .05 level might occur on a chance basis. We mention this because the reader may wish to compare these estimates with the number of significant descriptors actually obtained. In so doing, the reader should note that Block set significance levels at 0.01 and 0.05, whereas the descriptors reported in Table 9 reached significance between levels 0.01 and 0.06. Thus, there are some code types—especially those derived from a single sample comparison, (*e.g.*, 3-6/6-3, 5-6/6-5), which may be less reliable than those which were replicated (*e.g.*, 4-6/6-4, 4-9/9-4). At the same time, some code types are more robust than others in generating a large number of descriptors (*e.g.*, 2-7/7-2, 6-8/8-6).

The relationship between number of significant descriptors and number of cases per code type is not immediately clear! While the correlation between "Type vs Other" totals and "Case Totals" of Table 9 is 0.39, which *is* significant ($p < .05$) and similar to the findings reported for Gilberstadt and Duker (*Rho* = 0.45, $p < .05$) and for Lewandowski and Graham (*Rho* = 0.68, $p < .01$), it is unlike that reported by Gynther, Warbin, and Sletten (1973, p. 233) who found *no* significant relationship. For our own data, a comparison of number of *replicated* descriptors with number of cases per code failed to show a significant relationship (*Rho* = 0.29), although a similar comparison involving only the *most* significant descriptors (*i.e.,* those with *p* values ≤0.01 or 0.02) yielded *Rho* = 0.33. That factors other than sample size are involved is indicated by the findings for the 2-0/0-2 code, where an N of only 22 yielded as many as 146 *replicated* descriptors. In contrast, an N as large as 60 for the 2-4/4-2 code yielded only 38 replicated descriptors. We concur with Gynther, Altman, and Sletten (1973), that the lower limit for N would appear to be about 10, and that the specific code type investigated seems more predictive of correlates than the number of cases per code.

The procedure described above may be summarized as follows:

1. Collecting MMPI profiles from a national sample of 1,766 normal adolescents.

2. Constructing norms and developing separate T-score conversion tables for boys and girls, ages 14 through 17.

3. Collecting MMPI profile and Case Summary Data from a national sample of 2,242 emotionally disturbed youth.

4. Developing objective rating forms consisting of a Personal Data Schedule, Case Data Schedule, Q-Sort, and Adjective Check List, consisting of 2,302 descriptors.

5. Collecting MMPI profiles, self-ratings, and therapists' ratings for a national sample of 834 adolescents in treatment.

6. Selecting from the descriptor pool 1,265 frequently occurring, nonsex discriminating, and clinically relevant descriptors for code-type analysis.

7. Converting all MMPI raw-scores without K corrections to T-scores using the tables developed in step "2" above.

8. Coding the profiles and grouping them irrespective of age or sex by two-point code using the 10 standard MMPI scales.

9. Combining profiles with two-point reversals (*i.e.,* 1-2s with 2-1s).

10. Setting N = 10 as the minimum for code-groupings and for statistical analyses.

11. Inspecting groups where N ≤ 10 and recoding profiles by substituting the third highest digit for the second.

12. Reclassifying profiles by their substitute code and adding these cases to the remaining code types.

13. Identifying 29 adolescent code types with N = 10 or more cases per type.

14. Performing both within (high versus low, left versus right) and between (the combined code versus remainder) type statistical analyses for each descriptor where subgroup N = 10 or more, replicating findings where N = 20 or more.

15. Reporting results at the ≤0.01 to 0.02 levels and at the 0.04 and 0.06 levels for each of the 29 code types.

16. Collecting MMPI profile and additional case summary information from a local sample of 419 emotionally disturbed youth.

17. Identifying for 22 of the 29 code types, an N = 10 or more cases per type.

18. Abstracting and reporting information to supplement the narrative, description for these 22 codes.

ORGANIZATION OF DATA

For each adolescent code type appearing in Chapter 6 a corresponding narrative actuarial description is available consisting of the descriptors significantly associated with that code type. The code type itself is identified by a two-digit high point. Immediately below that code appear representative MMPI mean profiles obtained at the time of admission or prior to treatment. The profiles are averaged and only in the case of scale 5 (masculinity-femininity) are separate scores plotted for boys and girls, except for those code types where scale 5 is one of the two defining high points. We should mention that the scores for scale 5 are so arranged that an elevated score (above T-score 50) is always in the direction of the opposite sex.

Separate mean profiles are given for each code-type subgroup whenever a statistical analysis is performed on the data. In the case of Adolescent Code 1-2/2-1, for example, the N is sufficiently large to compare 1-2s (N = 11) with 2-1s (N = 12), and thus separate mean profiles are reported. Appearing below the profiles are the corresponding ages of each group, which are 15.2 years and 14.7 years for the 1-2s and 2-1s, respectively. The second adolescent code is the 1-3/3-1 type, where both high and low mean profiles are given for the 1-3s together with the corresponding average subgroup ages and numbers of cases. Since there are only 14 3-1 cases, a single 3-1 mean profile appears.

Reported next are the interpretive narrative personality descriptions. These narratives are comprised of the descriptors of Table 9 which reached significance at levels ≤0.06 for each of the 29 code types. In some instances, where code types for which relatively few significant descriptors were found, a few statistically nonsignificant but highly rated Q-sort items were also included[9] in the personality description; these are designated by an asterisk immediately following the descriptor. In the case of the 1-2/2-1s, "basically insecure and possesses a great need for attention*," is an example of a statement of this type. In addition, a few nonsignificant but highly interesting items were included when their frequency of endorsement for a particular code type was far beyond the base rate for all other codes (e.g., the item "suicidal thoughts" for the 2-7/7-2s).

Because of the difficulty encountered in collating the descriptors by data source (i.e., grouping together all Personal Data Schedule descriptors, all Case Data Schedule descriptors, etc.), the data are rather grouped according to content area. Thus, all items referring to relations with others, regardless of what data source they appeared in originally, are grouped together. Descriptors

---

[9] But only where the mean rating was 2.5 or less, or 7.5 or more, indicating either "least" or "most" characteristic extremes, respectively.

significantly associated with either high or low profiles, or with profiles coded left (*e.g.,* 1-2) or right (*e.g.,* 2-1), are incorporated with those which discriminate a particular code type from all others. In order to reduce possible confusion about the person endorsing the items, such phrases as "these adolescents state" and "their therapists say" are introduced to designate whether the information came from one of the therapist rating forms or from a patient's self-description. Occasionally, a percentage is reported to emphasize the magnitude of a descriptor's endorsement. Our goal throughout writing these personality narratives is to avoid stilted phraseology while adhering closely to the actual content of the original items.

For 22 of the 29 codes, the last paragraph summarizes the unique descriptive characteristics of The Ohio State University sample collected during 1970 to 1974.

PREPARING AND CLASSIFYING THE PROFILE

It is important that the person who is to code and classify the individual MMPI profile be thoroughly familiar with the administration and scoring procedures in the *Manual* (Hathaway and McKinley, 1967),[10] and with the coding procedure described in Chapter 1.[11] It should be recalled that the adolescent data were derived from literate, white boys and girls, ages 12 through 18, who were not organically brain damaged, and who were having emotional problems for which they were either seeking professional help or had been referred for it by others. The also were living in their parental or adoptive homes at the time of contact. Consequently, it may be inappropriate to use the data where these conditions do not pertain. Certainly it would be inappropriate to use this system for routine screening purposes. We also remind the reader that we have already noted (Chapter 3, Footnote 6) instances in which the clinically observed behavior of a 17 or 18-year-old was more congruent with the adult description of that code type than with the adolescent description. In such instances, the user might be better advised to refer to the adult description.

The first step, once the MMPI has been administered and scored, involves the conversion of raw scores to T-scores using the appropriate sex and age Tables 10 through 17. Assume, for illustrative purposes, that the following raw scores—*without the K additions*—were obtained from a 14 year-old female:

Scale	L	F	K	1	2	3	4	5	6	7	8	9	0
Raw Score	1	8	8	23	36	35	20	37	18	27	32	13	42

Reference to the table for 14 year-old females (Table 14) shows that a raw score of 1 for the L scale converts to a T-score of 36. Similarly, a raw score of 8 on

---

[10] Available from The Psychological Corporation, 304 East 45th Street, New York, N.Y. 10017.

[11] See Footnote 1, Chapter 1.

Table 10. *T-Score Conversions without K Corrections for Adolescent Males Age 14 and Below*

Raw Score	L	F	K	1	2	3	4	5	6	7	8	9	0	Raw Score
0	32	36	23	34	9	10	10	0	23	30	32	15	11	0
1	37	38	25	37	12	13	12	3	25	32	33	17	12	1
2	42	40	27	40	15	16	14	5	27	33	35	19	14	2
3	46	42	29	43	17	18	16	8	30	34	36	21	15	3
4	51	44	31	46	19	20	18	10	33	36	37	23	16	4
5	56	46	33	49	21	22	21	12	35	37	38	25	18	5
6	61	48	35	52	23	25	23	15	38	38	39	27	19	6
7	66	50	37	55	26	27	25	17	41	40	40	29	20	7
8	71	52	39	58	28	29	28	20	44	41	41	31	22	8
9	76	54	41	61	30	31	30	22	46	43	42	33	23	9
10	80	56	43	64	32	33	32	24	49	44	43	35	24	10
11	85	58	45	67	35	36	35	27	52	45	44	37	26	11
12	90	60	48	70	37	38	37	29	55	47	45	39	27	12
13	95	62	50	73	39	40	39	31	57	48	46	41	28	13
14	100	64	52	76	41	42	42	34	60	49	47	43	30	14
15	105	66	54	79	43	44	44	36	63	51	48	45	31	15
16		68	56	82	46	47	46	38	65	52	50	47	33	16
17		70	58	84	48	49	49	41	68	54	51	49	34	17
18		71	60	87	50	51	51	43	71	55	52	50	35	18
19		73	62	90	52	53	53	46	74	56	53	52	37	19
20		75	64	93	55	56	56	48	76	58	54	54	38	20
21		77	66	96	57	58	58	50	79	59	55	56	39	21
22		79	68	99	59	60	60	53	82	60	56	58	41	22
23		81	70	102	61	62	62	55	84	62	57	60	42	23
24		83	72	105	63	64	65	57	87	63	58	62	43	24
25		85	74	108	66	67	67	60	90	65	59	64	45	25
26		87	76	111	68	69	69	62	93	66	60	66	46	26
27		89	79	114	70	71	72	65	95	67	61	68	47	27
28		91	81	117	72	73	74	67	98	69	62	70	49	28
29		93	83	120	75	75	76	69	101	70	63	72	50	29
30		95	85	123	77	78	79	72	104	71	65	74	51	30
31		97		126	79	80	81	74	106	73	66	76	53	31
32		99		129	81	82	83	76	109	74	67	78	54	32
33		101		132	83	84	86	79	112	75	68	80	56	33
34		103			86	87	88	81	114	77	69	82	57	34
35		105			88	89	90	83	117	78	70	84	58	35
36		107			90	91	93	86	120	80	71	86	60	36
37		109			92	93	95	88	123	81	72	88	61	37
38		111			95	95	97	91	125	82	73	90	62	38
39		113			97	98	100	93	128	84	74	92	64	39
40		115			99	100	102	95	131	85	75	94	65	40
41		117			101	102	104	98		86	76	96	66	41
42		119			103	104	106	100		88	77	98	68	42
43		121			106	107	109	102		89	78	100	69	43
44		123			108	109	111	105		91	80	101	70	44
45		125			110	111	113	107		92	81	103	72	45
46		127			112	113	116	109		93	82	105	73	46
47		129			115	115	118	112		95	83		75	47
48		131			117	118	120	114		96	84		76	48
49		133			119	120	123	117			85		77	49
50		135			121	122	125	119			86		79	50
51		137			123	124		121			87		80	51
52		139			126	126		124			88		81	52
53		141			128	129		126			89		83	53
54		143			130	131		128			90		84	54
55		145			132	133		131			91		85	55
56		147			135	135		133			92		87	56
57		149			137	138		135			93		88	57
58		151			139	140		138			95		89	58
59		153			141	142		140			96		91	59
60		155			143	144		143			97		92	60
61		157									98		93	61
62		159									99		95	62
63		161									100		96	63
64		163									101		98	64
65											102		99	65
66											103		100	66
67											104		102	67
68											105		103	68
69											106		104	69
70											107		106	70
71											108			71
72											110			72
73											111			73
74											112			74
75											113			75
76											114			76
77											115			77
78											116			78

Table 11. *T-Score Conversions without K Corrections for Adolescent Males Age 15*

Raw Score	L	F	K	1	2	3	4	5	6	7	8	9	0	Raw Score
0	32	37	22	36	9	12	10	06	27	29	33	15	10	0
1	37	38	24	39	11	15	13	8	29	31	34	17	12	1
2	42	40	26	41	13	17	15	10	31	32	35	19	13	2
3	46	41	28	44	15	20	17	12	33	34	36	21	15	3
4	50	43	30	46	18	22	19	14	35	35	37	22	16	4
5	55	45	32	48	20	24	22	16	37	37	38	24	17	5
6	59	46	34	51	22	26	24	18	40	38	39	26	19	6
7	63	48	37	53	24	28	26	20	42	39	40	28	20	7
8	67	50	39	55	27	30	28	22	44	41	41	30	21	8
9	72	52	41	58	29	32	30	24	46	42	42	32	23	9
10	76	53	43	60	31	34	32	26	48	44	43	34	24	10
11	80	55	45	62	33	36	34	28	50	45	44	36	25	11
12	85	57	47	65	36	38	37	31	52	46	45	38	27	12
13	89	58	49	67	38	40	39	33	54	48	46	40	28	13
14	93	60	51	69	40	42	41	35	56	49	47	42	30	14
15	98	62	53	72	43	44	43	37	58	51	48	43	31	15
16		63	55	74	45	46	45	39	60	52	49	45	32	16
17		65	58	76	47	48	47	41	63	54	50	47	34	17
18		67	60	79	49	50	49	43	65	55	51	49	35	18
19		68	62	81	52	52	52	45	67	56	52	51	36	19
20		70	64	84	54	54	54	47	69	58	53	53	38	20
21		72	66	86	56	57	56	49	71	59	54	55	39	21
22		73	68	88	58	59	58	51	73	61	55	57	40	22
23		75	70	91	61	61	60	53	75	62	56	59	42	23
24		77	72	93	63	63	62	56	77	64	57	61	43	24
25		78	74	95	65	65	64	58	79	65	58	63	44	25
26		80	76	98	67	67	66	60	81	66	59	65	46	26
27		82	78	100	70	69	69	62	83	68	60	66	47	27
28		83	81	102	72	71	71	64	86	69	61	68	48	28
29		85	83	105	74	73	73	66	88	71	62	70	50	29
30		87	85	107	77	75	75	68	90	72	63	72	51	30
31		88		109	79	77	77	70	92	73	64	74	52	31
32		90		112	81	79	79	72	94	75	65	76	54	32
33		92		114	83	81	81	74	96	76	66	78	55	33
34		93			86	83	84	76	98	78	67	80	56	34
35		95			88	85	86	79	100	79	68	82	58	35
36		97			90	87	88	81	102	81	69	84	59	36
37		98			92	89	90	83	104	82	70	86	60	37
38		100			95	91	92	85	106	83	71	87	62	38
39		102			97	94	94	87	109	85	72	89	63	39
40		103			99	96	96	89	111	86	73	91	64	40
41		105			101	98	99	91		88	74	93	66	41
42		107			104	100	101	93		89	75	95	67	42
43		108			106	102	103	95		90	76	97	69	43
44		110			108	104	105	97		92	77	99	70	44
45		112			111	106	107	99		93	78	101	71	45
46		114			113	108	109	101		95	79	103	73	46
47		115			115	110	111	104		96	80		74	47
48		117			117	112	114	106		98	81		75	48
49		119			120	114	116	108			82		77	49
50		120			122	116	118	110			83		78	50
51		122			124	118		112			84		79	51
52		124			126	120		114			85		81	52
53		125			129	122		116			86		82	53
54		127			131	124		118			87		83	54
55		129			133	126		120			88		85	55
56		130			135	128		122			89		86	56
57		132			138	131		124			90		87	57
58		134			140	133		127			91		89	58
59		135			142	135		129			92		90	59
60		137			145	137		131			93		91	60
61		139									94		93	61
62		140									95		94	62
63		142									96		95	63
64		144									97		97	64
65											98		98	65
66											99		99	66
67											100		101	67
68											101		102	68
69											102		103	69
70											103		105	70
71											104			71
72											105			72
73											106			73
74											107			74
75											108			75
76											109			76
77											110			77
78											111			78

Table 12. *T-Score Conversions without K Corrections for Adolescent Males Age 16*

Raw Score	L	F	K	1	2	3	4	5	6	7	8	9	0	Raw Score
0	31	35	20	33	8	10	10	0	34	28	30	11	8	0
1	35	37	22	36	11	12	12	3	35	30	32	13	10	1
2	40	39	24	39	13	15	15	5	36	31	33	15	11	2
3	44	40	27	42	15	17	17	8	37	33	35	17	12	3
4	49	42	29	45	18	19	19	10	39	34	36	19	14	4
5	53	44	31	47	20	21	21	12	40	36	37	21	15	5
6	58	46	33	50	22	23	23	15	42	37	38	23	17	6
7	62	47	36	53	24	26	25	17	43	39	39	25	18	7
8	67	49	38	56	27	28	28	20	45	40	40	28	20	8
9	71	51	40	59	29	30	30	22	46	42	41	30	21	9
10	76	53	42	62	31	32	32	24	48	43	42	32	22	10
11	80	54	45	64	33	34	34	27	49	45	43	34	24	11
12	85	56	47	67	36	37	36	29	51	46	44	36	25	12
13	89	58	49	70	38	39	38	31	52	48	45	38	27	13
14	94	60	51	73	40	41	41	34	54	49	46	40	28	14
15	99	61	54	76	42	43	43	36	55	51	48	43	29	15
16		63	56	78	45	45	45	39	57	52	49	45	31	16
17		65	58	81	47	47	47	41	58	54	50	47	32	17
18		66	60	84	49	50	49	43	60	55	51	49	34	18
19		68	63	87	51	52	51	46	61	56	52	51	35	19
20		70	65	90	54	54	53	48	63	58	53	53	37	20
21		72	67	93	56	56	56	50	64	59	54	55	38	21
22		73	70	95	58	58	58	53	66	61	55	58	39	22
23		75	72	98	60	61	60	55	67	62	56	60	41	23
24		77	74	101	63	63	62	57	68	64	57	62	42	24
25		79	76	104	65	65	64	60	70	65	58	64	44	25
26		80	79	107	67	67	66	62	71	67	59	66	45	26
27		82	81	109	69	69	69	65	73	68	61	68	46	27
28		84	83	112	71	71	71	67	74	70	62	70	48	28
29		86	85	115	74	74	73	69	76	71	63	73	49	29
30		87	88	118	76	76	75	72	77	73	64	75	51	30
31		89		121	78	78	77	74	79	74	65	77	52	31
32		91		124	80	80	79	76	80	76	66	79	54	32
33		92		126	83	82	82	79	82	77	67	81	55	33
34		94			85	85	84	81	83	79	68	83	56	34
35		96			87	87	86	84	85	80	69	85	58	35
36		98			89	89	88	86	86	82	70	88	59	36
37		99			92	91	90	88	88	83	71	90	61	37
38		101			94	93	92	91	89	85	72	92	62	38
39		103			96	96	95	93	91	86	74	94	63	39
40		105			98	98	97	95	92	87	75	96	65	40
41		106			101	100	99	98		89	76	98	66	41
42		108			103	102	101	100		90	77	100	68	42
43		110			105	104	103	103		92	78	103	69	43
44		112			107	106	105	105		93	79	105	71	44
45		113			110	109	107	107		95	80	107	72	45
46		115			112	111	110	110		96	81	109	73	46
47		117			114	113	112	112		98	82		75	47
48		118			116	115	114	114		99	83		76	48
49		120			119	117	116	117			84		78	49
50		122			121	120	118	119			85		79	50
51		124			123	122		121			86		81	51
52		125			125	124		124			88		82	52
53		127			128	126		126			89		83	53
54		129			130	128		129			90		85	54
55		131			132	130		131			91		86	55
56		132			134	133		133			92		88	56
57		134			137	135		136			93		89	57
58		136			139	137		138			94		90	58
59		138			141	139		140			95		92	59
60		139			143	141		143			96		93	60
61		141									97		95	61
62		143									98		96	62
63		144									99		98	63
64		146									101		99	64
65											102		100	65
66											103		102	66
67											104		103	67
68											105		105	68
69											106		106	69
70											107		107	70
71											108			71
72											109			72
73											110			73
74											111			74
75											112			75
76											114			76
77											115			77
78											116			78

Table 13. *T-Score Conversions without K Corrections for Adolescent Males Ages 17 and 18*

Raw Score	L	F	K	1	2	3	4	5	6	7	8	9	0	Raw Score
0	30	32	20	35	16	13	6	05	19	27	31	12	6	0
1	34	34	23	38	17	15	9	7	22	28	32	14	8	1
2	38	36	25	40	19	17	11	9	25	30	33	16	9	2
3	43	39	27	43	21	19	13	11	28	32	34	18	11	3
4	47	41	29	45	23	21	16	13	31	33	35	20	12	4
5	51	43	31	48	24	23	18	16	34	35	36	22	14	5
6	55	45	34	50	26	25	20	18	37	36	37	24	15	6
7	59	47	36	53	28	27	23	20	40	38	38	26	17	7
8	63	50	38	55	30	29	25	22	43	39	39	28	18	8
9	68	52	40	58	32	30	27	24	46	41	40	31	20	9
10	72	54	42	60	34	32	29	26	49	42	41	33	21	10
11	76	56	45	63	35	34	32	29	52	44	43	35	23	11
12	80	58	47	65	37	36	34	31	55	45	44	37	24	12
13	84	60	49	68	39	38	36	33	58	47	45	39	26	13
14	88	63	51	70	41	40	39	35	61	48	46	41	27	14
15	93	65	53	73	43	42	41	37	64	50	47	43	29	15
16		67	56	75	44	44	43	40	67	52	48	45	30	16
17		69	58	78	46	46	46	42	70	53	49	48	32	17
18		71	60	80	48	48	48	44	72	55	50	50	33	18
19		73	62	83	50	49	50	46	75	56	51	52	35	19
20		76	64	85	52	51	52	48	78	58	52	54	36	20
21		78	67	88	54	53	55	50	81	59	53	56	38	21
22		80	69	90	55	55	57	53	84	61	55	58	39	22
23		82	71	93	57	57	59	55	87	62	56	60	41	23
24		84	73	95	59	59	62	57	90	64	57	62	42	24
25		87	75	98	61	61	64	59	93	65	58	65	44	25
26		89	78	100	63	63	66	61	96	67	59	67	45	26
27		91	80	103	64	65	69	63	99	69	60	69	47	27
28		93	82	105	66	67	71	66	102	70	61	71	49	28
29		95	84	108	68	68	73	68	105	72	62	73	50	29
30		97	86	110	70	70	75	70	108	73	63	75	52	30
31		100		113	72	72	78	72	111	75	64	77	53	31
32		102		115	73	74	80	74	114	76	66	79	55	32
33		104		118	75	76	82	77	117	78	67	82	56	33
34		106			77	78	85	79	120	79	68	84	58	34
35		108			79	80	87	81	123	81	69	86	59	35
36		110			81	82	89	83	126	82	70	88	61	36
37		113			83	84	91	85	128	84	71	90	62	37
38		115			84	86	94	87	131	86	72	92	64	38
39		117			86	87	96	90	134	87	73	94	65	39
40		119			88	89	98	92	137	89	74	96	67	40
41		121			90	91	101	94		90	75	99	68	41
42		124			92	93	103	96		92	77	101	70	42
43		126			93	95	105	98		93	78	103	71	43
44		128			95	97	108	100		95	79	105	73	44
45		130			97	99	110	103		96	80	107	74	45
46		132			99	101	112	105		98	81	109	76	46
47		134			101	103	114	107		99	82		77	47
48		137			102	105	117	109		101	83		79	48
49		139			104	107	119	111			84		80	49
50		141			106	108	121	114			85		82	50
51		143			108	110		116			86		83	51
52		145			110	112		118			88		85	52
53		147			112	114		120			89		86	53
54		150			113	116		122			90		88	54
55		152			115	118		124			91		89	55
56		154			117	120		127			92		91	56
57		156			119	122		129			93		92	57
58		158			121	124		131			94		94	58
59		161			122	126		133			95		95	59
60		163			124	127		135			96		97	60
61		165									97		98	61
62		167									99		100	62
63		169									100		101	63
64		171									101		103	64
65											102		104	65
66											103		106	66
67											104		107	67
68											105		109	68
69											106		110	69
70											107		112	70
71											108			71
72											109			72
73											111			73
74											112			74
75											113			75
76											114			76
77											115			77
78											116			78

Table 14. *T-Score Conversions without K Corrections for Adolescent Females Age 14 and Below*

Raw Score	L	F	K	1	2	3	4	5	6	7	8	9	0	Raw Score
0	31	36	19	36	11	7	14	126	28	29	32	16	13	0
1	36	39	22	39	13	9	16	124	30	30	34	18	15	1
2	41	41	24	41	15	11	19	122	32	32	35	20	16	2
3	46	44	27	44	17	13	21	120	34	33	36	22	18	3
4	50	46	29	46	20	15	23	118	36	34	37	24	19	4
5	55	49	31	49	22	18	25	115	38	36	38	26	20	5
6	59	51	33	51	24	20	27	113	40	37	40	28	21	6
7	64	54	35	54	26	22	29	111	43	39	41	30	23	7
8	69	56	38	56	28	24	31	109	45	40	42	32	24	8
9	73	59	40	59	30	27	34	107	47	42	43	35	25	9
10	78	61	42	61	32	29	36	104	49	43	45	37	26	10
11	83	64	44	64	34	31	38	102	51	44	46	39	28	11
12	87	66	47	66	36	33	40	100	54	46	47	41	29	12
13	92	69	49	69	38	35	42	99	56	47	48	43	30	13
14	97	71	51	71	41	38	44	97	58	47	49	45	32	14
15	101	74	53	74	43	40	46	95	60	50	51	47	33	15
16		76	56	76	45	42	49	92	62	52	52	49	34	16
17		79	58	79	47	44	51	90	65	53	53	51	35	17
18		81	60	81	49	46	53	88	67	54	54	54	37	18
19		84	62	84	51	49	55	86	69	56	56	56	38	19
20		86	65	86	53	51	57	84	71	57	57	58	39	20
21		89	67	89	55	53	59	81	73	59	58	60	40	21
22		91	69	91	55	55	61	79	75	60		62	42	22
23		94	71	94	59	58	64	77	78	62	60	64	43	23
24		96	73	96	62	60	66	75	80	63	62	66	44	24
25		99	76	99	64	62	68	73	82	64	63	68	45	25
26		101	78	101	66	64	70	70	84	66	64	70	47	26
27		104	80	104	68	66	72	68	86	67	65	72	48	27
28		106	82	106	70	69	74	66	89	69	67	75	49	28
29		109	85	109	72	71	76	64	91	70	68	77	51	29
30		111	87	111	74	73	79	62	93	72	69	79	52	30
31		114		113	76	75	81	59	95	73	70	81	53	31
32		116		116	78	78	83	57	97	74	71	83	54	32
33		119		118	80	80	85	55	99	76	73	85	55	33
34		121			83	82	87	53	102	77	74	87	57	34
35		124			85	84	89	51	104	79	75	89	58	35
36		126			87	86	92	48	106	80	76	91	59	36
37		129			89	89	94	46	108	82	77	94	61	37
38		131			91	91	96	44	110	83	79	96	62	38
39		134			93	93	98	42	113	84	80	98	63	39
40		136			95	95	100	40	115	86	81	100	64	40
41		139			97	98	102	37		87	82	102	66	41
42		141			99	100	104	35		89	84	104	67	42
43		144			102	102	107	33		90	85	106	68	43
44		146			104	104	109	31		92	86	108	69	44
45		149			106	106	111	29		93	87	110	71	45
46		151			108	109	113	26		94	88	113	72	46
47		154			110	111	115	24		96	90		73	47
48		156			112	113	117	22		97	91		75	48
49		159			114	115	119	20			92		76	49
50		161			116	118	122	18			93		77	50
51		164			118	120		15			95		78	51
52		166			120	122		13			96		80	52
53		169			123	124		11			97		81	53
54		172			125	126		9			98		82	54
55		174			127	129		7			99		83	55
56		177			129	131		4			101		85	56
57		179			131	133		2			102		86	57
58		182			133	135					103		87	58
59		184			135	138		-2			104		88	59
60		187			137	140		-4			106		90	60
61		189									107		91	61
62		192									108		92	62
63		194									109		94	63
64		197									110		95	64
65											112		96	65
66											113		97	66
67											114		99	67
68											115		100	68
69											117		101	69
70											118		102	70
71											119			71
72											120			72
73											121			73
74											123			74
75											124			75
76											125			76
77											126			77
78											128			78

Table 15. *T-Score Conversions without K Corrections for Adolescent Females Age 15*

Raw Score	L	F	K	1	2	3	4	5	6	7	8	9	0	Raw Score
0	31	36	21	27	6	9	13	120	26	29	32	19	13	0
1	36	38	22	39	11	11	15	118	29	31	34	20	14	1
2	40	41	25	41	13	13	17	115	31	32	35	22	15	2
3	45	43	27	43	15	15	19	113	33	33	36	24	17	3
4	49	45	29	46	17	17	21	111	36	35	37	26	18	4
5	53	47	32	48	19	19	23	109	38	36	39	28	19	5
6	58	50	34	50	21	21	25	107	40	37	40	29	21	6
7	62	52	36	52	24	23	27	105	42	39	41	31	22	7
8	66	54	38	55	26	25	29	103	44	40	42	33	23	8
9	70	57	40	57	28	27	32	101	47	41	43	35	24	9
10	75	59	42	59	30	29	34	100	49	43	44	37	26	10
11	79	61	45	61	32	31	36	98	51	44	45	39	27	11
12	83	63	47	64	34	33	38	96	53	45	46	41	28	12
13	88	66	49	66	37	35	40	94	55	47	47	42	30	13
14	92	68	51	68	39	37	42	92	58	48	48	44	31	14
15	96	70	53	70	41	39	44	90	60	49	49	46	32	15
16		72	56	72	43	42	46	88	62	51	50	48	33	16
17		75	58	75	45	44	48	86	64	52	51	50	35	17
18		77	60	77	47	46	51	84	66	53	53	52	36	18
19		79	62	79	49	48	53	82	68	55	54	54	37	19
20		82	64	81	52	50	55	79	71	56	55	55	39	20
21		84	67	84	54	52	57	77	73	58	56	57	40	21
22		86	69	86	56	54	59	75	75	59	57	59	41	22
23		89	71	88	58	56	61	73	77	60	58	61	42	23
24		91	73	90	60	58	63	71	79	62	59	63	44	24
25		93	75	93	62	60	65	69	82	63	60	65	45	25
26		95	77	95	65	62	67	67	84	64	61	67	46	26
27		98	80	97	67	64	69	65	86	66	62	69	48	27
28		100	82	99	69	66	71	63	88	67	63	70	49	28
29		102	84	102	71	68	74	61	90	68	64	72	50	29
30		104	86	104	73	70	76	59	93	70	65	74	52	30
31		107		106	75	72	78	57	95	71	66	76	53	31
32		109		108	78	74	80	55	97	72	68	78	54	32
33		111		110	80	76	82	53	99	74	69	80	55	33
34		114			82	79	84	51	101	75	70	82	57	34
35		116			84	81	86	49	103	76	71	83	58	35
36		118			86	83	88	47	106	78	72	85	59	36
37		120			88	85	90	45	108	79	73	87	61	37
38		123			90	87	92	42	110	80	74	89	62	38
39		125			93	89	95	40	112	82	75	91	63	39
40		127			95	91	97	38	114	83	76	93	64	40
41		130			97	93	99	36		85	77	95	66	41
42		132			99	95	101	34		86	78	96	67	42
43		134			101	97	103	32		87	79	98	68	43
44		136			103	99	105	30		89	80	100	70	44
45		139			106	101	107	28		90	82	102	71	45
46		141			108	103	109	26		91	83	104	72	46
47		143			110	105	111	24		93	84		73	47
48		146			112	107	113	22		94	85		75	48
49		148			114	109	115	20			86		76	49
50		150			116	111	118	18			87		77	50
51		152			119	113		16			88		79	51
52		155			121	115		14			89		80	52
53		157			123	118		12			90		81	53
54		159			125	120		10			91		82	54
55		162			127	122		8			92		84	55
56		164			129	124		6			93		85	56
57		166			131	126		3			94		86	57
58		168			134	128		1			95		88	58
59		171			136	130		-1			97		89	59
60		173			138	132		-3			98		90	60
61		175									99		92	61
62		178									100		93	62
63		180									101		94	63
64		182									102		95	64
65											103		97	65
66											104		98	66
67											105		99	67
68											106		101	68
69											107		102	69
70											108		103	70
71											109			71
72											110			72
73											112			73
74											113			74
75											114			75
76											115			76
77											116			77
78											117			78

Table 16. *T-Score Conversions without K Corrections for Adolescent Females Age 16*

Raw Score	L	F	K	1	2	3	4	5	6	7	8	9	0	Raw Score
0	29	35	22	35	8	10	11	127	21	27	32	12	10	0
1	34	37	24	37	10	12	14	125	24	29	33	14	12	1
2	38	39	26	40	12	14	16	122	27	30	34	17	13	2
3	42	41	28	42	14	16	18	120	29	32	35	19	15	3
4	47	44	30	44	16	18	20	118	32	33	36	21	16	4
5	51	46	33	47	18	20	23	116	35	34	38	23	17	5
6	56	48	35	49	20	22	25	113	37	36	39	26	18	6
7	60	50	37	51	22	24	27	111	40	37	40	28	20	7
8	64	53	39	54	24	26	29	109	42	38	41	30	21	8
9	69	55	41	56	26	28	31	106	45	40	42	32	22	9
10	73	57	44	58	28	30	33	104	48	41	43	35	23	10
11	78	59	46	61	30	32	36	102	50	42	44	37	24	11
12	82	62	48	63	32	34	38	100	53	44	45	39	26	12
13	86	64	50	65	34	36	40	98	55	45	46	41	27	13
14	91	66	52	67	36	38	42	96	58	46	47	44	28	14
15	95	68	55	70	38	40	44	94	61	48	48	46	29	15
16		71	57	72	40	42	47	91	63	49	49	48	31	16
17		73	59	74	43	44	49	89	66	50	50	50	32	17
18		75	61	77	45	46	51	87	68	52	51	53	33	18
19		77	63	79	47	48	53	84	71	53	52	55	34	19
20		80	66	81	49	50	55	82	74	54	53	57	36	20
21		82	68	84	51	52	57	80	76	56	54	59	37	21
22		84	70	86	53	54	60	77	79	57	55	62	38	22
23		86	72	88	55	56	62	75	81	58	56	64	39	23
24		89	74	91	57	57	64	73	84	60	58	66	41	24
25		91	77	93	59	59	66	70	87	61	59	68	42	25
26		93	79	95	61	61	68	68	89	62	60	71	43	26
27		95	81	98	63	63	71	66	92	64	61	73	44	27
28		98	83	100	65	65	73	64	94	65	62	75	46	28
29		100	85	102	67	67	75	61	97	66	63	77	47	29
30		102	88	105	69	69	77	59	99	67	64	80	48	30
31		104		107	71	71	79	57	102	69	65	82	49	31
32		107		109	73	73	82	54	105	70	66	84	51	32
33		109		112	75	75	84	52	107	71	67	86	52	33
34		111			77	77	86	50	110	73	68	89	53	34
35		113			79	79	88	47	112	74	69	91	54	35
36		116			81	81	90	45	115	75	70	93	55	36
37		118			83	83	92	43	118	77	71	95	57	37
38		120			85	85	95	40	120	78	72	98	58	38
39		122			87	87	97	38	123	79	73	100	59	39
40		125			89	89	99	36	125	81	74	102	60	40
41		127			92	91	101	34		82	75	104	62	41
42		129			94	93	103	31		83	77	106	63	42
43		131			96	95	106	29		85	78	109	64	43
44		134			98	97	108	27		86	79	111	65	44
45		136			100	99	110	24		87	80	113	67	45
46		138			102	101	112	22		89	81	115	68	46
47		140			104	103	114	20		90	82		69	47
48		143			106	105	116	17		91	83		70	48
49		145			108	107	119	15			84		72	49
50		147			110	109	121	13			85		73	50
51		149			112	111		10			86		74	51
52		152			114	113		8			87		75	52
53		154			116	115		6			88		77	53
54		156			118	117		4			89		78	54
55		158			120	119		1			90		79	55
56		161			122	121		-1			91		80	56
57		163			124	123		-3			92		82	57
58		165			126	124		-6			93		83	58
59		167			128	126		-8			94		84	59
60		170			130	128		-10			95		85	60
61		172									97		86	61
62		174									98		88	62
63		176									99		89	63
64		179									100		90	64
65											101		91	65
66											102		93	66
67											103		94	67
68											104		95	68
69											105		96	69
70											106		98	70
71											107			71
72											108			72
73											109			73
74											110			74
75											111			75
76											112			76
77											113			77
78											114			78

Table 17. *T-Score Conversions without K Corrections for Adolescent Females Ages 17 and 18*

Raw Score	L	F	K	1	2	3	4	5	6	7	8	9	0	Raw Score
0	28	32	18	31	5	7	7	125	21	25	29	15	7	0
1	33	35	21	34	7	9	10	122	24	27	31	17	9	1
2	37	37	23	36	9	11	12	120	27	28	32	19	10	2
3	41	40	26	38	11	13	14	117	30	30	33	22	11	3
4	45	42	28	41	13	15	17	115	33	31	35	24	13	4
5	49	45	31	43	15	17	19	113	35	33	36	26	14	5
6	54	47	33	45	17	19	21	111	38	34	37	28	15	6
7	58	49	36	48	20	21	24	108	41	36	38	30	17	7
8	62	52	38	50	22	23	26	106	44	37	39	32	18	8
9	66	54	41	52	24	25	28	104	47	39	40	34	19	9
10	70	57	44	55	26	27	31	102	50	40	41	37	21	10
11	74	59	46	57	28	29	33	100	53	42	43	39	22	11
12	79	62	49	59	30	31	35	98	56	43	44	41	23	12
13	83	64	51	61	32	33	37	96	59	44	45	43	25	13
14	87	67	54	64	35	35	40	94	61	46	46	45	26	14
15	91	69	56	66	37	37	42	92	64	47	47	47	27	15
16		72	59	68	39	39	44	89	67	49	48	50	29	16
17		74	61	71	41	41	47	87	70	50	49	52	30	17
18		77	64	73	43	43	49	85	73	52	50	54	31	18
19		79	66	75	45	45	51	83	76	53	52	56	33	19
20		81	69	77	47	47	54	81	79	55	53	58	34	20
21		84	71	80	50	49	56	78	82	56	54	60	35	21
22		86	74	82	52	51	58	76	84	58	55	63	37	22
23		89	76	84	54	53	61	74	87	59	56	65	38	23
24		91	79	87	56	55	63	71	90	60	57	67	39	24
25		94	81	89	58	57	65	69	93	62	58	69	41	25
26		96	84	91	60	59	67	67	96	63	60	71	42	26
27		99	86	93	62	61	70	65	99	65	61	73	43	27
28		101	89	96	65	63	72	62	102	66	62	76	45	28
29		104	91	98	67	65	74	60	105	68	63	78	46	29
30		106	94	100	69	67	77	58	108	69	64	80	47	30
31		109		103	71	69	79	56	110	71	65	82	49	31
32		111		105	73	71	81	53	113	72	66	84	50	32
33		113		107	75	73	84	51	116	74	68	86	51	33
34		116			78	75	86	49	119	75	69	89	53	34
35		118			80	77	88	47	122	77	70	91	54	35
36		121			82	79	91	44	125	78	71	93	55	36
37		123			84	81	93	42	128	79	72	95	57	37
38		126			86	83	95	40	131	81	73	97	58	38
39		128			88	85	98	38	134	82	74	99	59	39
40		131			90	87	100	36	136	84	76	101	61	40
41		133			92	89	102	33		85	77	104	62	41
42		136			95	91	104	31		87	78	106	63	42
43		138			97	93	107	29		88	79	108	65	43
44		141			99	95	109	27		90	80	110	66	44
45		143			101	97	111	24		91	81	112	67	45
46		145			103	99	114	22		93	82	114	69	46
47		148			105	101	116	20		94	84		70	47
48		150			108	103	118	18		95	85		71	48
49		153			110	105	121	15			86		73	49
50		155			112	107	123	13			87		74	50
51		158			114	109		11			88		75	51
52		160			116	111		9			89		77	52
53		163			118	113		6			90		78	53
54		165			120	115		4			92		79	54
55		168			123	117		2			93		81	55
56		170			125	119					94		82	56
57		173			127	121		-3			95		83	57
58		175			129	123		-5			96		85	58
59		177			131	125		-7			97		86	59
60		180			133	127		-9			98		87	60
61		182									100		89	61
62		185									101		90	62
63		187									102		91	63
64		190									103		93	64
65											104		94	65
66											105		95	66
67											106		97	67
68											108		98	68
69											109		99	69
70											110		101	70
71											111			71
72											112			72
73											113			73
74											114			74
75											116			75
76											117			76
77											118			77
78											119			78

scale F corresponds to a T-score of 56, and a raw score of 8 on scale K corresponds to a T-score of 38. Converting the remaining raw scores to T-scores shows:

Scale	1	2	3	4	5	6	7	8	9	0
Raw Score	23	36	35	20	37	18	27	32	13	42
T-Score	94	87	84	57	46	67	67	71	43	67

The coded clinical scale scores, disregarding elevation symbols, now become 1238670459.

The next step, which would usually require plotting the profile, is not essential to using the adolescent descriptive data. However, in the event the user wishes to plot the profile, and perhaps compare its shape to profiles in the Mean Profile Index, then certain precautionary measures should be carried out. First, the sex of the patient should correspond to that indicated on the profile sheet; that is, male profiles should be plotted on the side of the sheet indicated for men and female profiles on the side of the sheet indicated for women (although even this is not essential, since the sexes have separate T-score conversions). A check should next be made to make certain that the T-scores plotted in the body of the profile correspond to those printed in the extreme left and right T-score columns. That is, the T-scores obtained from raw-score conversions should *not* be plotted on the raw-scores which typically appear in the body of the standard (adult) profile. An error of this sort, like an error arising from failure to use the adolescent conversion tables or from erroneously including the K "corrections," will invariably result in a misclassification of the profile. We mentioned in Chapter 1 an instance in which a profile was misclassified 6-8, when it should have been 8-6, a change of trivial consequence since the two codes share the same actuarial description. Not all profile changes are so innocuous, however, and Figure 3 illustrates a code change which does have considerable psychological consequences. The profile based on the appropriate adolescent norms without K (coded 4-1) would, in this case, entail an actuarial description quite different from either that of the profile based on the adolescent norms with K (coded 4-7) or the profile based on the adult norms printed on the standard profile sheet (coded 8-9).

In the event that a scale F T-score exceeds 80, the user is advised to read the discussion of scale F in Chapter 1 before proceeding further.[12] Next, the user should make sure that the first two digits in the code correspond, in fact, to the order of elevation and arrangement of the corresponding scales. That is, if a profile has been coded 1-2, then scale 1 should be highest or equal to scale 2; if a profile is coded 4-3, then scale 4 should be higher than scale 3. Whenever ties between high scales occur, the profile should be coded on the basis of the scale

---

[12] We recommend this simply as a precaution. The adolescent code types themselves were actually derived without regard to F-scale elevation.

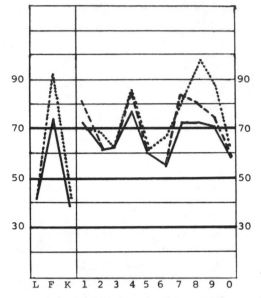

Fig. 3. Differences in code type and profile patterns between T-scores based on adolescent norms without K (*solid line*), adolescent norms with K (*broken line*), and adult norms with K (*dotted line*) for a 15 year-old hospitalized male.

with the smallest numeric value. For example, if scales, 4, 8, and 9 are high points with identical T-scores, the profile should be coded 4-8. Similarly, if scale 8 is the high point and scales 4 and 9 are tied for second, the profile should be coded 8-4. Once the profile has been coded by two points, the user may wish to refer to the Mean Profile Index or he may opt to go directly to Table 18 in order to classify the profile.

Table 18 lists the 90 possible two-point permutations for 10 scales paired two at a time and their corresponding code-type designations. The user should locate, in the "Profile Two-point" columns, the code which corresponds to that of the individual patient's profile. If the patient's code fits one of the given types, then its code-type classification will appear to the right of the code. If the patient's code does not fit one of the types, then an "S" will appear, indicating that the profile should be recoded and that classification should proceed with reference to the substitute two-point code. Recoding involves disregarding the second highest scale and in its place substituting the third. Again, in the event that two or more scales are tied, the scale having the smallest numeric designation should be used.

If the profile is then classifiable, all descriptive data for the substitute code type may be read as equally applicable to the individual patient. If a second attempt fails to classify a profile, then the profile is rendered unclassifiable and the interpretive data should not be used.

Table 18. *Code Type Classification of Individual Adolescent Profiles*

Profile Two-point	Code-Type Class	Profile Two-point	Code-Type Class	Profile Two-point	Code-Type Class
1-2	1-2/2-1	4-5	4-5/5-4	7-8	7-8/8-7
1-3	1-3/3-1	4-6	4-6/6-4	7-9	7-9/9-7
1-4	1-4/4-1	4-7	4-7/7-4	7-0	7-0/0-7
1-5	1-5/5-1	4-8	4-8/8-4	8-1	1-8/8-1
1-6	1-6/6-1	4-9	4-9/9-4	8-2	2-8/8-2
1-7	S	4-0	4-0/0-4	8-3	S
1-8	1-8/8-1	5-1	1-5/5-1	8-4	4-8/8-4
1-9	S	5-2	2-5/5-2	8-5	S
1-0	S	5-3	3-5/5-3	8-6	6-8/8-6
2-1	1-2/2-1	5-4	4-5/5-4	8-7	7-8/8-7
2-3	2-3/3-2	5-6	5-6/6-5	8-9	8-9/9-8
2-4	2-4/4-2	5-7	S	8-0	S
2-5	2-5/5-2	5-8	S	9-1	S
2-6	S	5-9	5-9/9-5	9-2	S
2-7	2-7/7-2	5-0	5-0/0-5	9-3	S
2-8	2-8/8-2	6-1	1-6/6-1	9-4	1-6/6-1
2-9	S	6-2	S	9-5	5-9/9-5
2-0	2-0/0-2	6-3	3-6/6-3	9-6	S
3-1	1-3/3-1	6-4	4-6/6-4	9-7	7-9/9-7
3-2	2-3/3-2	6-5	5-6/6-5	9-8	8-9/9-8
3-4	3-4/4-3	6-7	S	9-0	S
3-5	3-5/5-3	6-8	6-8/8-6	0-1	S
3-6	3-6/6-3	6-9	S	0-2	2-0/0-2
3-7	S	6-0	S	0-3	S
3-8	S	7-1	S	0-4	4-0/0-4
3-9	S	7-2	2-7/7-2	0-5	5-0/0-5
3-0	S	7-3	S	0-6	S
4-1	1-4/4-1	7-4	4-7/7-4	0-7	7-0/0-7
4-2	2-4/4-2	7-5	S	0-8	S
4-3	3-4/4-3	7-6	S	0-9	S

S Unclassifiable two-point code. Recode the profile by dropping the second high point and substituting the third. Classification should proceed with the substitute two-point code. If the profile is still unclassifiable, it should not be interpreted by this system.

The procedure for preparing and classifying an individual adolescent MMPI profile may be summarized as follows:

1. Convert raw scores, without K-corrections, to T-scores using the appropriate tables for age and sex (Tables 10 through 17).

2. If the F scale T-score exceeds 80, consult the discussion of that scale in Chapter 1.

3. Code the T-scores following the procedure given in Chapter 1. The first 2 digits of the code should be recorded in order of descending magnitude.

4. If the T-scores are to be plotted on the standard profile sheet, care should be exercised to plot the scores for boys on the side of the profile sheet indicated for "Males," and for girls on the side indicated for "Females."

5. The T-score plottings should be checked to make certain that their elevations correspond to the T-values listed to the left and right of the profile and *not* to the raw-score values which appear in the body of the profile.

6. The individual profile may now be compared to the code-type profiles in the Mean Profile Index.

7. Compare the first two digits of the code with the two-point listings given in Table 18; if the two points are classifiable by type, refer to Chapter 6 for the appropriate personality description.

8. If the two points are not classifiable, drop the second high point and substitute the third. If the profile is now classifiable, refer to Chapter 6 for the corresponding personality description.

9. If the profile is still unclassifiable, the actuarial interpretive system should not be used. In this case, the reader may wish to refer to the discussion of scales in Chapter 1, and to references on other interpretive material given at the end of Chapter 5.

It is hoped that the preceeding discussion and illustrations will clarify the procedures involved in classifying an individual adolescent MMPI profile. Again, it cannot be emphasized too strongly that the best way to become familiar with these procedures is through continued practice and use.

REFERENCES

BALL, J. C. *Social deviancy and adolescent personality*. Lexington, Ky.: University of Kentucky Press, 1962.

BARRINGTON, B. L. A list of words descriptive of affective reactions, *J. Clin. Psychol. 19*, 259-262, 1963.

BERRY, D. F. A comparison of multivariate procedures for grouping MMPI profile data. Doctoral dissertation, The Ohio State University, 1971.

BERRY, D. F., AND MARKS, P. A. Comparison of multivariate procedures for grouping MMPI profile data. *Proceedings, 80th Annual Convention, American Psychological Association*, p. 387-388, 1972.

BLOCK, J. On the number of significant findings to be expected by chance. *Psychometrika. 25*, 369-380, 1960.

BRIGGS, P. F. M-B history record (a) Female form, (b) Male form. Mimeographed material. Author, 1963, Copyright, 1957.

BELL, H. M. *Youth tell their story*. Washington, D.C.: American Council on Education, 1938.

BUSS, A. H., AND GERJUOY, H. The scaling of terms used to describe personality. *J. Consult. Psychol. 21*, 361-369, 1957.

CAMPBELL, D. T., AND FISKE, D. W. Convergent and discriminant validation by the multitrait-multimethod matrix. *Psychol. Bull. 56*, 81-105, 1959.

COYLE, F. A., FOWLER, R. D., AND MARKS, P. A. A methodological aide in correlating personality descriptions using the Marks Q sort. *Psychol. Rep. 21*, 563-564, 1967.

DAHLSTROM, W. G. An exploration of mental status syndromes by factor analytic techniques. Doctoral dissertation, University of Minnesota, 1949.

DAHLSTROM, W. G. *Personality systematics and the problem of types*. Morristown, N.J.: General Learning Press, p. 1-27, 1972.

DAHLSTROM, W. G., WELSH, G. S., AND DAHLSTROM, L. E. *An MMPI handbook. Volume I: Clinical interpretation*. Minneapolis: University of Minnesota Press, 1972.

GILBERSTADT, H., AND DUKER, J. *A handbook for clinical and actuarial MMPI interpretation*. Philadelphia: W. B. Saunders, 1965.

GILBERT, H. H. High-school students' opinions on reasons for failure in high-school subjects. *J. Ed. Res. 23*, 46-49, 1931.

GOLDBERG, L. R. Some recent trends in personality assessment. *J. Personal. Assess. 36*, 547-560, 1972.

GOUGH, H. G. The adjective check list as a personality assessment research technique. *Psychol. Rep. 6*, 107-122, 1960.

GYNTHER, M. D. White norms and black MMPI's: A prescription for discrimination? *Psychol. Bull. 78*, 386-402, 1972.

GYNTHER, M. D. A new replicated actuarial program for interpreting MMPI's of state hospital patients. In J. N. Butcher (Chm.) MMPI symposium. Presented at the Seventh Annual Symposium on Recent Developments in the Use of the MMPI, Mexico City, February, 1972.

GYNTHER, M. D., ALTMAN, H., AND SLETTEN, I. W. Development of an empirical interpretive system for the MMPI: Some after-the-fact observations. *J. Clin. Psychol. 29*, 232-234, 1973.

GYNTHER, M. D., ALTMAN, H., AND SLETTEN, I. W. Replicated correlates of MMPI two-point code types: The Missouri actuarial system. *J. Clin. Psychol. 29*, 263-289, 1973.

HATHAWAY, S. R., AND MCKINLEY, J. C. *The Minnesota multiphasic personality inventory manual*, revised. New York: The Psychological Corporation, 1967.

HATHAWAY, S. R., AND MONACHESI, E. D. *Analyzing and predicting juvenile delinquency with the MMPI*. Minneapolis: University of Minnesota Press, 1953.

HATHAWAY, S. R., AND MONACHESI, E. D. *An Atlas of juvenile MMPI profiles*. Minneapolis: University of Minnesota Press, 1961.

HATHAWAY, S. R., AND MONACHESI, E. D. *Adolescent personality and behavior*. Minneapolis: University of Minnesota Press, 1963.

HILDRETH, C. Adolescent interests and abilities. *J. Gen. Psychol. 43*, 65-93, 1933.

JACKSON, P. W., AND GETZEL, J. W. Psychological health and classroom functioning: A study of dissatisfaction with school among adolescents. *J. Abnorm. Soc. Psychol. 50*, 295-300, 1959.

LEWANDOWSKI, D., AND GRAHAM, J. R. Empirical correlates of frequently occurring two-point MMPI code types: A replicated study. *J. Consult. Clin. Psychol. 39*, 467-472, 1972.

LEWINSOHN, P. M., NICHOLS, R. C., PULOS, L., LOMONT, J., NICKEL, H., AND SISKIND, G. The reliability and validity of quantified judgments from psychological tests. Mimeographed material. Authors, 1964.

MARKS, P. A. The validity of the diagnostic process in a child guidance setting: A multidisciplinary approach. Doctoral dissertation, University of Minnesota, 1959.

MARKS, P. A. An assessment of the diagnostic process in a child guidance setting. *Psychol. Monogr. 75*, No. 3 (Whole No. 507), p. 41, 1961.

MARKS, P. A. Progress on a cookbook of personality descriptions of emotionally disturbed youth. In J. N. Butcher (Chm.) Recent developments in the use of the MMPI. Symposium presented at the University of Minnesota, Minneapolis, 1967.

MARKS, P. A. 4-9 = $\sqrt{49}$: The illicit minor. In J. N. Butcher (Chm.) Recent developments in the use of the MMPI. Symposium presented at the University of Minnesota, Minneapolis, 1971.

MARKS, P. A., AND SEEMAN, W. Addendum to an assessment of the diagnostic process in a child guidance setting. *J. Consult. Psychol. 26*, 485, 1962a.

MARKS, P. A., AND SEEMAN, W. On the Barnum effect. *Psychol. Rec. 12*, 203-208, 1962b.

MARKS, P. A., AND SEEMAN, W. The heterogeneity of some common psychiatric stereotypes. *J. Clin. Psychol. 18*, 266-270, 1962c.

MARKS, P. A., AND SEEMAN, W. A study of change in stereotype conceptions of psychological disorders. *J. Clin. Psychol. 18*, 507-510, 1962d.

MARKS, P. A., AND SEEMAN, W. *The actuarial description of abnormal personality: An Atlas for use with the MMPI.* Baltimore: Williams & Wilkins Co., 1963.

MARKS, P. A., AND SINES, J. O. Methodological problems of cookbook construction. In. J. N. Butcher (Ed.) *MMPI: Research developments and clinical applications.* New York: McGraw-Hill, 1969.

MATHER, W. G. The courtship ideals of high school youth. *Sociol. Soc. Res. 19*, 166-172, 1934.

MAYFIELD, P. N., AND STRUPP, H. H. Items from "Section D" of a study of psychotherapist values. Mimeographed material. Authors, 1961.

MCNAIR, D. M., AND LORR, M. Three kinds of psychotherapy goals. *J. Clin. Psychol. 20*, 390-393, 1964.

MEEHL, P. E. An investigation of a general normality or control factor in personality testing. *Psychol. Monogr. 59*, No. 4 (Whole No. 274), p. 62, 1945.

MEEHL, P. E. The cognitive activity of the clinician. *Amer. Psychol. 15*, 19-27, 1960.

MEEHL, P. E. Reactions, reflections, projections. In J. N. Butcher (Ed.) *Objective Personality Assessment.* New York: Academic Press, p. 131-189, 1972.

MILES, H. H. W., BARRABEE, E., AND FINESINGER, J. E. Evaluation of psychotherapy. *Psychosom. Med. 13*, 82-105, 1951.

MOONEY, R. L. *Mooney problem check list.* New York: The Psychological Corporation, 1950.

PATTERSON, G. R. An empirical approach to the classification of disturbed children. *J. Clin. Psychol. 20*, 326-337, 1964.

PERSONS, R. W., AND MARKS, P. A. Self-disclosure with recidivists: A study of interviewer-interviewee matching. *J. Abnorm. Psychol. 76*, 387-391, 1970.

PERSONS, R. W., AND MARKS, P. A. The violent 4-3 MMPI personality type. *J. Consult. Clin. Psychol. 36*, 189-196, 1971.

PETERSON, D. R. Behavior problems of middle childhood. *J. Consult. Psychol. 25*, 205-209, 1961.

RAMSEY, G. V. The sex information of younger boys. *Amer. J. Orthopsychiat. 13*, 347-352, 1943.

ROEBER, E., AND GARFIELD, S. Study of the occupational interests of high school students in terms of grade placement. *J. Ed. Psychol. 34*, 355-362, 1943.

SCHOFIELD, W., HATHAWAY, S. R., HASTINGS, D. W., AND BELL, D. M. Prognostic factors in schizophrenia. *J. Consult. Psychol. 18*, 155-166, 1954.

SYMONDS, P. M. Sex differences in the life problems and interests of adolescents. *School Soc. 43*, 751-752, 1936.

WALSH, G. S., AND DAHLSTROM, W. G. *Basic readings on the MMPI in psychology and medicine.* Minneapolis: University of Minnesota Press, 1956.

WILSON, A. B. Residential segregation of social classes and aspirations of high school boys. *Amer. Sociol. Rev. 24*, 836-845, 1959.

WIRT, R. D. Interview followup of Minneapolis school students: History record and definition of variables. Mimeographed materials. Author, 1964.

WIRT, R. D., AND BRIGGS, P. F. Personality and environmental factors in the development of delinquency. *Psychol. Monogr. 73*, No. 15 (Whole No. 485), p. 47, 1959.

WOODWARD, C. A. Combining methods of description in personality assessment. Doctoral dissertation, The Ohio State University, 1968.

6

Characteristics of Adolescent Codes

Adolescent Mean Profile Index

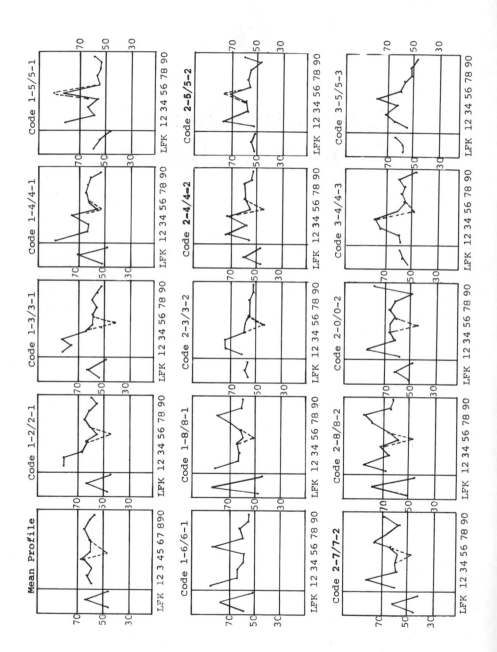

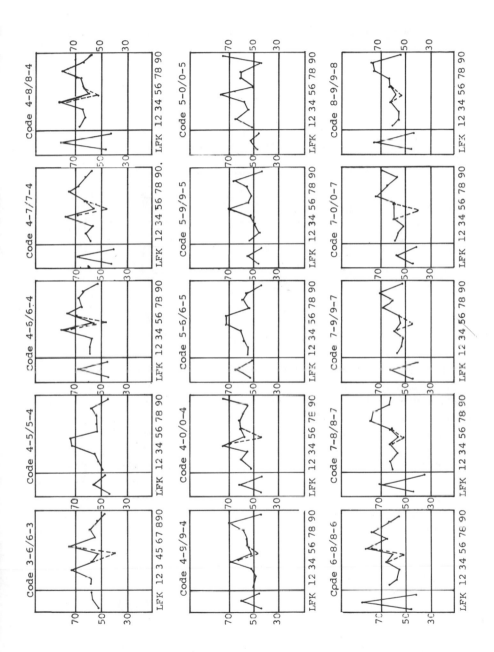

AVERAGE ADOLESCENT PATIENT[1]

Mean Profile[2]

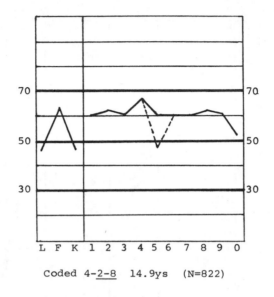

Coded 4-2-8   14.9ys   (N=822)

Personality Description

The average emotionally disturbed adolescent comes from a community of 100,000 or more. He is protestant, enrolled in and attending public school, and living with his natural parents. The source of referral is, most often, the court followed by the parents. Reasons for referral include aggressiveness, disobedience, defiance, excessive lying, immaturity, impulsiveness, stealing, running away, temper tantrums, restlessness, truancy, emotionally inappropriate behavior, and underachievement at school. He is described as dreamy, has difficulty concentrating, is anxious, tense, negativistic, and depressed. His parent, peer, and sib relations are all described as poor. He is difficult to control, demands attention, is provocative, mischievious, and frequently gets into trouble with the law. All of these behaviors seem to manifest themselves in the home;

[1] In reference to the "average patient", as indicated in Chapter 4, we do not wish to suggest that there exists an individual or group of adolescents who "fit" a set of descriptive statements. Rather, we are suggesting that it may be useful to present a stereotype which incorporates the base rate facts of all our adolescent patients. Such a stereotype may be referred to in order to supplement the unique discriminating information reported for each of the profile types. The relevant data (*i.e.,* the base rates), together with their associated frequencies appear under the "Total" and "BR" columns of Appendix D.

[2] The mean profiles throughout this chapter are based on adolescent norms, plotted without K additions. It is therefore necessary to convert raw scores to appropriate T-scores using the tables in Chapter 5. This should be done *before* classifying the profile and referring to the personality descriptions in this section. The T-scores for boys and girls are combined for all scales except scale 5 (Mf), where separate scores for boys (*solid lines*) and girls (*broken lines*) are reported.

other areas greatly affected are the school and interpersonal adult and peer relations. His personality, of course, is also a chief locus affected by his disorder.

Throughout most of his life, this adolescent has lived in his natural home. During childhood, he was rarely, if ever, included in his parents' activities. When it came to deciding things, mother made most of the decisions—at least the important ones. She was interested in the things that he did, was affectionate, and overprotective. The father, however, did not show much interest in the child's activities and his relationship with the patient was described as ambivalent, dominating, indifferent, and neglecting. Both parents have high school educations. The father, now in his early 40's is a skilled worker and supports his family. His income has been generally steady throughout the years. The mother, also in her early 40's, sees herself as a homemaker. Rarely is either parent out of the home for any extended period of time, the use of alcohol has been minimal, and there is no criminal history for either.

The average adolescent patient was a first born. Development was normal, the child was as active as others and fairly healthy. He was not described as particularly fearful or temperamental. School achievement was average or perhaps a little below, although nonacademically, things came easily. His attitude toward school was not one of enthusiasm and his behavior frequently placed him in trouble. Although he had a few problems with other students, he was usually able to settle them himself and his relations outside of school followed a similar pattern. In general, the average patient had friends, usually his own age. His main activities were sports, hobbies, television, movies, music, and bicycle riding.

Frequent conflicts between the patient and his parents centered around the average adolescent's behavior. He did not feel free to discuss problems with them and rarely felt that he could disagree with them. The average patient was closer to his mother, despite the fact that she was the disciplinarian. Punishment usually consisted of threatening, verbal scolding, or prohibiting him from doing something he wanted to do.

During later childhood and adolescence, his grades have dropped further and his attitude toward school has deteriorated to the point where he dislikes almost all aspects of it. Frequently, he is in trouble at school and, on occasion, he has been expelled. There is very little, if any, recognition of achievement for him and there are, likewise, few extracurricular activities in which he participates.

Leisure time activities as a teen-ager include watching television, listening to records, attending movies, riding around in cars, "hanging around" downtown, parties, sporting events, indoor and outdoor hobbies, reading, and working on cars. Most of the time, these activities involve others. Dating began about age 13 with the parents' general approval. The strongest personal values of the average patient during adolescence have been friends, entertainment, social success, and family life; nevertheless, he has little or no association with his brothers and sisters and there is actual fear of the father.

The focal concern of the average patient is himself. Although he acknowledges that he has problems and that he needs help, he insists on limiting the scope of his troubles to a specific area (*e.g.*, getting along with his parents). It is not surprising then to find that his therapist views denial as one of his chief mechanisms of defense; acting-out, rationalization, projection, and depression are other frequently employed defenses. Less often, fantasy, repression, regression, suppression, displacement, intellectualization, and compulsion are in evidence. The feelings verbally expressed by the average patient are those of inadequacy, inferiority, doubt, shame, guilt, and isolation.

The symptom pattern is, in general, one of immaturity and narcissism; the degree of disturbance is seen as moderate to severe; and the motivation for treatment is judged to be mild to moderate. Intellectual functioning and memory (past and present) are intact, although there is minor distortion apparent in reality testing and judgment is somewhat impaired. Typically, only the patient is involved in the actual treatment process although the parents are also interviewed. Both individual and group therapy are employed techniques. At the time of this study, the average patient had been in therapy for 3 to 6 months, had been interviewed on a weekly basis, and the goal of personality reconstruction had been given only a fair chance of success.

The therapist, who is seen as one of the most influential figures in this adolescent's life, describes the average patient as defensive, immature, impatient, impulsive, moody, nervous, anxious, confused, rebellious, pleasure-seeking, self-centered, dissatisfied, and queer. Other adjectives applied to the average patient include alert, active, adventurous, aggressive, changeable, demanding, resentful, stubborn, restless, and temperamental. He is also seen as suspicious, distrustful, evasive, and sensitive. He is generally friendly, good-looking, and intelligent, but has narrow interests and is dependent.

The average emotionally disturbed adolescent is a basically narcissistic and insecure individual who possesses a great need for attention. At the same time, he is afraid of emotional involvement with others and has inner conflicts about dependency, self-assertion, and sexuality. He resents authority figures and has impulses to derogate them. These impulses are often undercontrolled and he "acts-out," verbally or otherwise, without sufficient deliberation. Sensitive to anything that might be construed to be a demand, he makes use of projection as well as rationalization.

· The average adolescent patient, in characterizing his parents during childhood, describes them as encouraging, active, close, and warm. Father was also seen as punishing and mother as tense. While in the company of his parents, the patient says he felt proud and secure. He believed that he could tell in advance what kind of moral judgements they would make, what kind of disciplinary actions they would take, and what kind of emotional reactions they would have in various situations. As a teen-ager, the patient now sees his father as strong and his mother as lenient and rewarding.

Nail biting, nervousness, specific fears (e.g., of the dark, of heights), being teased, not being taken seriously, making and keeping friends, school subjects, lying, disobedience, and "being a difficult child" were the most troublesome problems reported by this adolescent. He now complains of not having the opportunity to do the things he wants to do, of being afraid of making mistakes, of taking things too seriously, of people finding fault with him, nobody's understanding him, of getting into trouble, of losing his temper, of family quarrels, and of getting low grades in school; the most frequently cited reasons for school failure are laziness, lack of interest, and dislike of the subject.

Leisure time activities are indoor and outdoor hobbies, listening to records, going to movies, watching television, reading, attending parties and concerts, riding around in cars, and "hanging around" downtown. The average patient says that he smokes and dates, but doesn't drink very often. He feels that the most desirable traits to look for in a person of the opposite sex are good looks, honesty, maturity, cheerfulness, cleanliness, thoughtfulness, good health, and being admired by others.

The average adolescent patient is not sure what he would like to do following high school, but his main goal in life is to "make money" and have fun. Lack of education and training, laziness, lack of money and lack of "pull with the right people" are considered by the patient as the main obstacles which he needs to overcome.

This adolescent describes himself as active, adventurous, having wide interests, cheerful, easy-going, curious, alert, good-natured, friendly, forgiving, honest, healthy, kind, intelligent, soft-hearted, and warm. On the other hand, he also says that he is anxious, emotional, dissatisfied, confused, lazy, nervous, restless, serious, worrying, and stubborn. The second picture conforms more to how his therapist sees him.

When he experiences depression, the average adolescent patient reports difficulty in concentrating, difficulty going to sleep, emptiness inside, loss of interest, tiredness, loss of appetite, boredom, and restlessness. When he experiences anxiety, the same symptoms are prevalent. Guilt feelings, however, elicit fear and wishes of death. When angry, he is likely to shout, swear, and go off by himself.

ADOLESCENT CODE 1-2/2-1

Mean Profiles

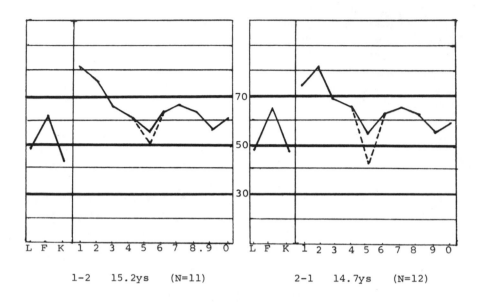

1-2   15.2ys   (N=11)   2-1   14.7ys   (N=12)

Personality Description

Many of the 1-2/2-1 emotionally disturbed adolescents involved in this study were referred for treatment because they were shy, overly sensitive, and obsessed with specific topics. This problem of personal isolation is reflected in the fact that 55% of the 1-2s had few friends of any kind as a child while the 2-1s merely had no *close* friends.

There is very little which is distinctive to the childhood of the 1-2/2-1 adolescents except that they tended to discuss problems with their parents more frequently than the "average patient" and that 67% had dominating mothers. These teen-agers describe their mothers as having been lenient and their fathers as passive. As adolescents, they now describe their fathers as warm and sympathetic. During early childhood, being teased was a problem for the 1-2/2-1s. They say that now, they are afraid of making mistakes. These young people do not smoke or drink and they report that their main source of sex information was through conversation (92%) as opposed to actual experience or printed material.

Therapists describe the 1-2/2-1 adolescents as quiet and moderately disturbed—yet often grossly depressed. Their rate of speech is retarded. Complaints of weakness and easy fatigability are common and they report that they feel tired when they experience guilt. These 1-2/2-1 adolescents are basically insecure and possess a great need for attention*. They are serious, achievement oriented young people who tend to anticipate problems and difficulties. They see lack of education and training as the biggest obstacle in life. Often ruminative, obsessional, overideational, and perfectionistic, these teen-agers report difficulty in thinking and concentrating. They see themselves as good-natured yet sulky.

The 1-2/2-1s are generally fearful and phobias are likely to be present. Accordingly, they tend to delay action and have difficulty committing themselves to any definite course. They are suggestable and overly responsive to others' evaluations rather than to their own. The 1-2s, more than the 2-1s, evidence impaired judgment. They are more anxious, reflective, and preoccupied. The 1-2s are also more ambitious and achievement oriented. They react to frustration by punishing themselves, exhibit manifest sad mood, and have inner conflicts about their sexuality. The 2-1s, on the other hand, appear more self-assured and socially at ease. They have more of a capacity for forming close interpersonal relationships, are more narcissistic, and are more demanding of sympathy.

The 1-2/2-1 adolescents do *not* utilize acting-out as a defense mechanism nearly to the degree of the "average patient" or to that of some of the other code types. In keeping with this finding, they are *not* typically resentful or demanding. It is not surprising that instead, obsession and compulsion are the mechanisms of defense employed by the 1-2/2-1s.

Only 2 of 12 1-2/2-1 adolescents in the 1970-73 sample reported any involvement with drugs whatsoever; both of these teenagers attempted suicide by ingestion of Valium. They also experimented with amphetamines, alcohol, and gasoline. Two others made suicide attempts, one with a gun and the other by slashing of wrists. Three-fourths of these 1-2/2-1s came from homes where the parents were either separated or divorced. They were quite slow academically with truancy, grade failures, and placement in "slow learner" classes frequent. Several were diagnosed "school phobia."

ADOLESCENT CODE 1-3/3-1

Mean Profiles

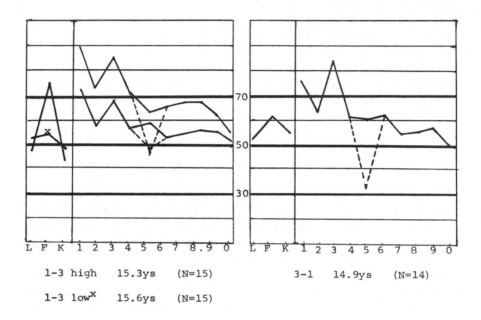

1-3 high   15.3ys   (N=15)

1-3 low^x 15.6ys   (N=15)

3-1   14.9ys   (N=14)

Personality Description

Adolescents with the 1-3/3-1 profile are often referred for treatment by the school (40%). The main reasons for their referral are attention seeking behavior and somatic concern. Accordingly, the mechanisms of defense most characteristic of them are displacement and somatization.

Therapists state that 1-3/3-1s possess "diagnostic" insight into the descriptive features of their behavior. They show ability to talk about conflicts and are not evasive. In sum, these young people have good verbal-cognitive awareness of their own personality structures. This is even more the case for the 3-1s than it is for the 1-3s. Interestingly, 52% of the 1-3/3-1s were seen by psychoanalysts for treatment.

The 1-3/3-1 adolescents typically present themselves as physically and organically sick. That is, they manifest hypochondriacal tendencies by allowing psychic conflicts to be represented in somatic symptoms. These young people also possess a basic insecurity and need for attention* and are conflicted about emotional dependency and sexuality. They are *not* grandiose* nor delusional*.

The 1-3/3-1 adolescents are, in general, *not* worriers. Neither are they particularly irritable, demanding, or defensive about admitting psychological difficulties. The adjectives which therapists deem most distinctive to 1-3/3-1s are fault-finding, prejudiced, and loud. Those adolescents with high 1-3 profiles are described as more self-accepting and nonjudgmental than are those with low 1-3 profiles; low 1-3s, on the other hand, are less afraid of committing themselves to any definite course of action. While 3-1s tend to be more nervous and anxious than 1-3s, 1-3s are more apt to be irritable, self-indulgent, and flippant. In addition, the 1-3s are more likely to rationalize and project blame on others. They are seen as hostile.

The 1-3/3-1 teen-agers lived in their natural home until between the ages of 10 and 15 years. During their early childhood, the 1-3s had fathers whom they viewed as relaxed and noncritical; they experienced feelings of closeness, pride, and warmth when in their fathers' company. The 3-1s, in contrast, felt insecure when with their fathers as children. The 1-3s, more than the 3-1s, were liked by most students at school; presently, they report having many friends and a few close friends.

The 1-3/3-1 emotionally disturbed adolescents have definite intellectual interests (41%), and those with elevated 1-3 profiles view lack of ability as their biggest obstacle in life. The concerns of the 1-3/3-1s now include feelings that nobody likes them and not knowing how to make a date. In addition, the 1-3s are afraid of getting poor grades (57%) and, in fact, 44% are a full year behind in school. Interestingly, low 1-3s are more afraid of school failure than are high 1-3s.

When these 1-3/3-1 adolescents describe themselves, they say that they are dignified, resourceful, tactful, outgoing and unselfish, and that they are *not* fussy, lazy, or particularly healthy. The 1-3s see themselves as more peaceable than the 3-1s. While low 1-3s use the adjectives adaptable, and foresighted to describe themselves, high 1-3s say they are noisy, yet submissive and sulky.

The 1-3/3-1 adolescent is typically *not* a drug user. Of the 20 patients (25% of whom were black) who comprised the 1970-73 sample, over two-thirds had no known involvement with drugs. Two of the 6 "users" were attempted suicides. The other 4 with drug histories had used marijuana, LSD, "uppers," sopors, gasoline, and glue. In concurrence with our earlier findings, these young people had multiple somatic concerns such as abdominal pain, dizziness, headaches, insomnia, nausea, blurred vision, "spells," seizures, and anorexia. They were nearly all seen as depressed and described themselves as such.

ADOLESCENT CODE 1-4/4-1

Mean Profiles

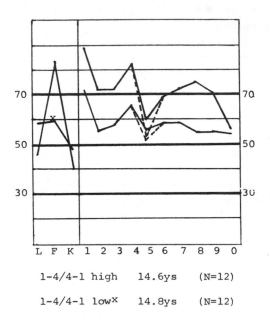

1-4/4-1 high   14.6ys   (N=12)

1-4/4-1 lowˣ   14.8ys   (N=12)

Personality Description

Adolescents with 1-4/4-1 profiles were referred for treatment because they are defiant, disobedient, impulsive, mischieveous, and provocative; over 90% of those with elevated profiles are referred by the court system.[3] Low 1-4/4-1s are, in addition, often hyperactive. Their complaints are characterological in nature and develop slowly over a long period of time. Although scale 1 would suggest the presence of somatic complaints, there is absolutely *no* physical system involvement reported by any of the low 1-4/4-1s.

High 1-4/4-1s come from homes where there is frequently a history of mental disturbance—46% of the mothers of these adolescents being mentally ill. Their mothers typically were ambivalent towards them as children, while their fathers were rejecting. These 1-4/4-1 adolescents describe their mothers as having been inactive and say that they were unable to discuss personal problems with them as children; at the same time, they admit to *not* feeling secure when with their fathers. As adolescents, they now describe their mothers as cool, unrewarding, and not very close. Their fathers are *not* seen as encouraging. About one-half of the low 1-4/4-1s felt indifferent toward their siblings as children while *none* of the high 1-4/4-1s had this attitude. Surprisingly, "family life" is considered an

---

[3] As compared to Hathaway and Monachesi (1953) who found a 33% delinquency rate among those adolescents with both high points from among scales 4, 8, or 9.

important personal value in the lives of these patients. The high 1-4/4-1s now date more than twice a week.

Some of the problems characteristic of the "average patient" during early childhood, were *not* characteristic of the 1-4/4-1s. Specifically, they did not bite their nails and they had no difficulty making friends. In general, they were liked by some students and disliked by others. It is interesing to note, that these young people attended three or more schools where about 58% of the high 1-4/4-1s were enrolled in special programs.

Adolescents with the 1-4/4-1 profile are constantly in trouble with their parents due to their excessive misbehavior. They say that it bothers them that they are not taken more seriously by their parents. In addition, high 1-4/4-1s lose their tempers, get into fights, and are afraid of failing in school. They also frequently get into trouble with the law, and when this occurs, they blame themselves. Unlike the "average patient," 1-4/4-1s say they do *not* experience boredom when depressed. High 1-4/4-1s do experience dry mouths when they feel guilty and surprisingly, *none* of the low 1-4/4-1s say that they get angry when they feel guilty.

The 1-4/4-1 teen-agers are *not* of average weight. They are negativistic, defensive, and *not* easy to talk with. Their rapport with their psychotherapists is only superficial. In reality testing, these adolescents are found to be somewhat loose and their judgment is often moderately impaired. Low 1-4/4-1s have mild intellectual impairment and make minor errors in memory, while high 1-4/4-1s have fairly accurate memories. In general, the expression of affect by the 1-4/4-1 patients is *not* appropriate—for the high 1-4/4-1s, it is mildly inappropriate. The symptom pattern for the 1-4/4-1s is one of impulsivity and hyperactivity. The degree of disturbance is seen by their therapists as mild to moderate for 67% of the low 1-4/4-1s. At the time of this study, over 70% of the 1-4/4-1 young people had been in treatment from 3 to 6 months.

The 1-4/4-1 adolescents use acting-out as their chief defense mechanism. They resent authority figures and have impulses to derogate them. They undercontrol their impulses*, and act without sufficient deliberation. They are provocative, and socially extroverted. Those with low profiles are sensitive to anything that can be construed as a demand; they are critical, skeptical, and not easily impressed. They also tend to judge others in terms of their material worth. Those with elevated profiles are more likely to show hysteroid trends. They somatize, complain of weakness and easy fatigability, are excitable and overanxious about minor matters—reacting to them as if they were emergencies. The 1-4/4-1s, in contrast to other profile types, spend a good deal of time in personal fantasy and daydreaming; at times they are delusional and adolescents with low profiles occasionally have ideas of grandeur.

Therapists describe 1-4/4-1 adolescents as aggressive, boastful, outspoken, resentful, hasty, cynical, headstrong, and self-centered. Those with elevated profiles are also seen as stubborn and moody. According to their therapists, these youth are basically insecure*. They experience conflict over emotional dependency*, are fearful of emotional involvement with others*, and demand attention. They are *not* worriers; they do *not* obsess and they are *not* compulsive. They also are *not* shy, or inhibited. Neither are they self-accusatory, self-condemning, or guilt ridden. Nevertheless, they do *not* function well in the world—probably because of their socially inappropriate behavior. They would *not* be original or adaptive in an emergency situation*.

Youth with the 1-4/4-1 profile, see themselves as wholesome; 67% of the low 1-4s describe themselves with this term. In addition, they say that they are warm and insightful. High 1-4/4-1s, on the other hand, see themselves as anxious, self-punishing, lazy, attractive, and patient. Adjectives which 1-4/4-1s do *not* attribute to themselves include gentle, conservative, and curious.

From the 1970-73 sample of 11, we found that adolescents with the 1-4/4-1 code type are typically *not* drug abusers; in fact, the only drug-related incidents that these young people were involved in were suicide attempts. One girl overdosed on phenobarbital and 1 boy on aspirin. Three other teenagers in this group tried to take their lives by ingesting "unknown" pharmacological agents; 1 of whom also slashed her wrists. There was only 1 case of drug use which was not specifically identified as suicidal—it also was with an unknown agent. Thus while 5 of these adolescents attempted to take their lives, 6 had no history whatsoever of drug use or abuse. Other findings from the case summaries indicated a high rate of school truancy, sexual promiscuity, pregnancy, having illegitimate children, and heavy drinking or alcoholic fathers.

ADOLESCENT CODE 1-5/5-1
Mean Profiles

14.7ys   (N=15)

Personality Description

Adolescents with the 1-5/5-1 profile are referred for treatment by either their parents or the school. Their hyperactivity (47%) is one of the chief reasons for referral. They differ from other disturbed adolescents in that their symptoms are *not* manifested in the area of interpersonal relations—either peer or adult. In 80% of the cases, there are no symptoms prior to the onset of the disorder.

Typically, the 1-5/5-1 young people come from small communities of 5,000 to 25,000 population. As children, their fathers who drank rarely, if ever, were indifferent to them (58%). They say that as disciplinarians, they were neither strict nor lenient and that their tempers were neither mild nor strong. Their mothers were characterized as nonaffectionate. The parents did quarrel openly on occasion.

These young people also differ from other disturbed adolescents in that they did *not*, as children, enjoy bicycle riding and they do *not*, as adolescents, like to attend parties or concerts. Fewer than half of them consider cleanliness a desirable trait to look for in members of the opposite sex. Sex is *not* a personal value for them. Only occasionally will they disagree with their parents.

The 1-5/5-1s often express feelings of unreality. Their ideation is somewhat deviant (80% of cases), they exhibit intellectual impairment (67%), and they make minor errors in memory (67%). Their affect is seen as mildly inappropriate by their therapists with whom they establish only superficial rapport. The symptom pattern of these adolescents is one of impulsivity and hyperactivity. Compulsion is the defense mechanism most distinctive to this group (60%). The outlook for future adjustment is considered fair (80%). Interestingly, 60% of these teen-agers were seen in therapy by orthodox Freudians who interviewed the parents as well as the adolescents.

As is expected with scale 1 elevation, these adolescents have hypochondriacal tendencies and frequently present themselves as physically or organically sick. They were, in fact, seriously ill on several occasions as children; as adolescents, only one-third are in generally good health although there have been only a few serious illnesses. They have difficulty going to sleep. They are manneristic, ruminative, obsessional, and overideational. They are also narcissistic and occasionally express delusions of grandeur. When depressed, they say that they do *not* experience fatigue, but rather shortness of breath. When anxious, they report heart palpatations, and when guilty they experience "butterflies" in the stomach as well as a pounding heart.

Their psychotherapists describe the 1-5/5-1s as enterprising, artistic, and effeminate. They are *not* viewed as careless, pessimistic, or moody. Nor are they particularly friendly; in fact, their therapists find them difficult to talk to. They are unable to talk about areas of conflict, they are *not* frank about discussing their problems, and they are *not* reliable informants. They also lack the capacity to form close personal relationships. They are nonaccepting and judgmental and tend *not* to arouse liking in others.

When the 1-5/5-1 adolescents describe themselves, they say that they are enthusiastic, industrious, insightful, witty, tolerant, dignified, pleasant, and zany. They also see themselves as precise, reflective and thorough. They are *not* hard-headed or mischievous.

ADOLESCENT CODE 1-6/6-1
Mean Profiles

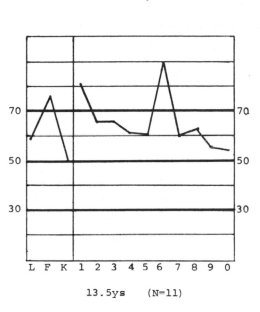

13.5ys   (N=11)

Personality Description

The case data for the 1-6/6-1 adolescent indicate emotional overcontrol as the referral reason in almost 50% of the cases—a figure well in excess of that for the "average disturbed adolescent." Disruption of the family, in one way or another, is an extraordinarily frequent event in the lives of these adolescents. Indeed, more than half of them live with their mothers only. When there is a father present in the home, his attitude toward the child is reported to be one of rejection.

Therapists consistently characterize the 1-6/6-1 adolescents as defensive* and evasive. Insecurity and strong needs for attention* are also indicated as is fear of emotional involvement with others*. These teen-agers are seen as egocentric, self-centered, and selfish*; they emphasize oral pleasures*; they are self-indulgent and are given to rationalization*. A theoretically curious fact about this code lies in the *low* frequency of reported physical complaints; that is, these adolescents do *not* present themselves as physically, organically sick*; they likewise exhibit few hysteroid personality traits* or hypochondriacal tendencies*. They are *not* likely to capitalize on secondary gains*. Complaints of weakness and easy fatigability are infrequent*. It would appear that scale 1 operates in some unusual and obscure fashion for this adolescent group and thus bears further study.

These young people also do *not* consciously express guilt feelings*. They are *not* self-condemning, or self-accusatory*. Consistent derogation of the opposite sex is perceived by their therapists as *infrequent,* as are grandiose ideas*.

Although more than 70% of these adolescents characterize themselves as affectionate, very few see themselves as friendly. The majority state that a lack of money is the greatest obstacle they have to overcome in life, and yet being happy and respected for their work is *not* a frequently cited goal. There may be some intuitive consistency in the fact that over 50% of the 1-6/6-1s rate themselves as hasty and none rate themselves as cautious.

The data obtained from the 10 additional 1-6/6-1 adolescents seen between 1970-73 indicate some drug usage, although not widespread involvement. Five of these teenagers had *no* known drug histories. Five did have drug histories which were, however, related to suicide attempts. One individual overdosed on barbiturates (he also "threw" himself in front of a police car in a suicide attempt), another on Sominex, a third on aspirin, and 2 on "unknown" agents. Other pertinent findings were not only rebelliousness, but actually violent physical outbursts and even threats to kill! The anger they expressed was almost without exception directed toward their parents.

ADOLESCENT CODE 1-8/8-1

Mean Profiles

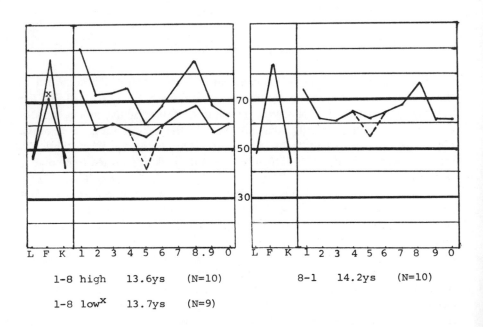

1-8 high	13.6ys	(N=10)
8-1	14.2ys	(N=10)
1-8 low^x	13.7ys	(N=9)

Personality Description

As is to be expected with scale 1 elevated, these adolescents manifest hypochondriacal tendencies and present themselves as physically, organically sick. As children, they were seriously ill physically on several occasions and only about half of them were in generally good health. Young people with 1-8/8-1 profiles were closer to their mothers than to other family members. They say that they were "very successful" as mothers and describe them as having been strong, relaxed, and rewarding. As children, their discipline was described as average and consisted mainly of spankings. Surprisingly, then, 1-8s were at times afraid of their mothers! The fathers of 1-8/8-1s, who were characterized as bossy, typically were *not* skilled tradesmen, salesmen, or office workers (4%). The 8-1s felt that their fathers were more sympathetic than did the 1-8s. They also tended to have better relationships with their brothers and sisters. Those with high 1-8s felt that they could tell in advance, almost always, what kind of moral judgment or emotional reaction their fathers would have in various situations but they were not always sure what actions their mothers would take.

The problems that troubled the 1-8/8-1s during early childhood were being teased, difficulty with school subjects, and difficulty reading. Nevertheless, they say that their teachers were of superior ability and they do *not* hold unfavorable attitudes toward them. There was never any recognition of achievement for any of these youths and, in fact, 1-8s were often in serious trouble with the other students at school. Interestingly, 67% of the high 1-8s attended private or parochial schools. Outside of school, most things were difficult for these adolescents and occasionally, there were complete failures. They did *not* have many friends and those that they did have were generally not the same age.

As teen-agers, the 1-8/8-8-1s now say that they are afraid of failing in school, that they dislike being a grade behind others (47%), and that they wish they had regular allowances. High 1-8s are afraid to speak up in class and are frequently teased. The 1-8/8-1s describe themselves as affected, distractable, forgetful, shy, quick, hasty, hurried, noisy, conscientious, simple, understanding, forceful, strong, warm, wise, helpful, shiftless, and having narrow interests. The 1-8s, who claim they were "difficult children," say they are resentful but that they are also appreciative. High 1-8s use the adjectives clever, daring, and dull to describe themselves; they also say that they are *not* very confident. When they are sad or depressed, 1-8/8-1s sweat easily; high 1-8s also report loss of appetite. When they feel anxious and tense, 1-8/8-1s say they become tired and it is difficult for them to get out of bed in the morning. When they feel guilty, they shake and their hearts palpatate. And when they are angry, they are likely to hit something— high 1-8s also shout when provoked.

Psychotherapists describe these teen-agers as basically insecure*, impunitive, unambitious, and in constant demand of attention. Their tempo is slow and they seem to have little need to achieve. They are sexually conflicted* and frequently act-out*. Their other defenses (specifically somatization for the 1-8s and regression for the high 1-8s) seem to function fairly well in providing them relief from psychological distress. Adolescents with the 1-8/8-1 profile are sometimes delusional and spend a good deal of time in personal fantasy and daydreaming. They also have difficulty thinking and concentrating. High 1-8s are complaining, irritable, self-centered, egocentric, selfish, and narcissistic; their focal concern (100%) is themselves. Low 1-8s are more cheerful and accepting, less judgmental, and more socially appropriate. They also exhibit better heterosexual adjustment.

Although they handle their anxieties by refusing to recognize their presence, they have better insight into their own personality structures than do the high 1-8s. In about one-third of the cases, there is intellectual impairment among adolescents with low 1-8 profiles.

The 8-1s, in contrast to the 1-8s, describe themselves as more civilized, easy-going, pleasant, mannerly, conventional, and cheerful. Nevertheless, they are also more likely to exhibit manifest depression. Where the 1-8s overreact to danger and even make emergency responses in its absence, are obsessional, nervous, tense, sweat, and show other signs of anxiety—the 8-1s are more organized and adaptive under stress, fear loss of control, and cannot "let go" even when it would be appropriate for them to do so. They in general get along better in the world as it is.

The 1-8/8-1s are, in contrast to other adolescents with scale 1 in the defining code, quite likely to be involved with drugs; less than half (8 of 20) of the 1970-73 sample have no reported drug history. There was no evidence of narcotic or inhalent use, however. The drugs used came from the hypnotic, tranquilizer, and hallucinogenic classes and included marijuana, LSD, mescaline, barbiturates, alcohol, Librium, Valium, Stelazine, "unknown" and "other." The "other" involved aspirin and turpentine, as well as wrist cutting, in three suicide attempts. In addition, 10 other 1-8/8-1s attempted suicide with pharmacological agents. This appears to be a high suicide risk group with as many as 65% attempting to take their lives! It is interesting that two-thirds of these adolescents had divorced parents while for several others their parents were deceased. One was born illegitimate while another lived alone with a grandmother (with both parents diagnosed psychotic). Thus, only 3 of the 20 (15%) were living within their nuclear families! Fighting and arguing with parents or guardians was invariably characteristic of the 1-8/8-1s. Six had 1 or both alcoholic parents and 4 had 1 or both parents who were mentally ill. Conflict with family and peers appeared to be the pattern, with their problems manifesting themselves both at home and at school. Twenty-five per cent of this sample were black.

ADOLESCENT CODE 2-3/3-2

Mean Profiles

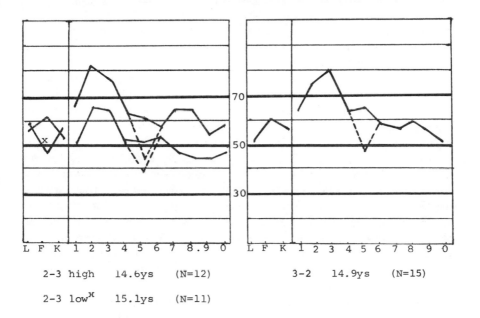

| 2-3 high | 14.6ys | (N=12) |
| 2-3 low^x | 15.1ys | (N=11) |

3-2   14.9ys   (N=15)

Personality Description

Adolescents who present the 2-3/3-2 profile are rather lonely people who have long histories of personal isolation. They are referred for treatment because of the poor relationships that they have with their peers. At school, they are liked by few students and outside of school, they have few friends of any kind. Their activities are almost always engaged in alone.

Seventy per cent of these young people have known cases of mental disturbance in their families. Their fathers, who are neither bossy nor authoritarian, are also *not* responsible for making any major decisions in the family. About one-half of the 3-2s have fathers who are either professional men or top executives. The 2-3s say that rarely can they tell in advance what kind of moral judgement their fathers will pass on their behavior—interestingly, most of the conflict 2-3/3-2s have with their parents revolves around *normal* adolescent behavior as opposed to misbehavior. While their fathers' discipline is seen as lenient, their mothers' discipline is described as average. The 2-3/3-2 patients feel secure when with their mothers. These parents, more than those of the "average patient" tend to include their children in their own activities.

During childhood, the 2-3/3-2 adolescents report that they were not disobedient and that they did not lie. Now, they say that they do not get into trouble or select the wrong kind of friends and that their parents are not critical of what few friends they may have. The 3-2s do not particularly enjoy going to parties. Instead of wanting to get a job after they finish high school (3%), 2-3/3-2 adolescents prefer to go directly to a 4-year college. About one-third of the 2-3s enjoy music and play in the school band. The 2-3s are afraid of failing in school, but any reasons given for such failure do *not* include dislike of the subjects being taught or lack of interest, as the base rates would suggest. The majority of these teen-agers do *not* smoke, and they see religion as a moderately important factor in their upbringing. In addition, sex is definitely *not* an important personal value for these adolescents.

Psychotherapists, less than one-third of whom profess an eclectic orientation, report that their 2-3/3-2 patients speak slowly and show psychomotor retardation. The rapport established with 2-3s is distant; these adolescents express feelings of inferiority (83%), and have conflicts about emotional dependency*. However, their thinking is basically intact and they are neither grandiose* nor delusional*. Their therapists also say that 2-3/3-2 adolescents tend to avoid situations where their own performance may be inferior to that of others. They tend toward over control of their impulses. They are *not* headstrong or persevering in nature—2-3/3-2s are *not* psychopathic. Neither are they resentful, unpredictable, or changeable in behavior or attitudes. They do *not* show paranoid trends or use projection as a defense. It is interesting that many of the correlates of scale 3 for adults are *not* correlates of that scale for adolescents; that is, these young people are *not* seen as immature, infantile, egocentric, or narcissistic.

Although 3-2s are more aggressive and tactless than are 2-3s, neither group rates particularly high on either of these traits. The 3-2s tend to avoid or delay action; they fear committing themselves to any definite course (also characteristic of adults with scale 3 elevation). They are shy, anxious, inhibited, and have difficulty asserting themselves. The 2-3s complain of difficulty in going to sleep.

In describing themselves, 2-3/3-2 adolescents say that they are commonplace, discreet, and dependable. They do *not* see themselves as strong, loud, or reckless. The 2-3s, in addition say that they are shy, quiet, timid, deliberate, and stern.

Drug usage among these adolescents is not at all prevalent. Out of the 1970-73 sample of 25, 19 (76%) reported *no* drug use, although several had attempted suicide by alternative means (with a knife or in a car). Of those who did report drug involvement, 1 used morphine, 1 marijuana, and 1 paint thinner. The 3 other teenagers with drug histories were all suicide attempts—overdoses of amphetamines, phenobarbital, and some "unknown." Additionally, these young people manifested somatic and/or hysterical symptoms of all sorts. These ranged from "black-out spells," "spells of rapid breathing," dizziness, constipation, headache, flushing, coldness, chest and stomach pain, to amnesia and "vague malaise." More than a few were severely phobic (of men and of school) and nauseous much of the time. Not one of these 25 adolescents failed to experience some sort of somatic or "hysterical" crises with regularity. Another interesting finding was that several of the 2-3/3-2s had been either raped or molested by a relative or person of the same sex.

ADOLESCENT CODE 2-4/4-2

Mean Profiles

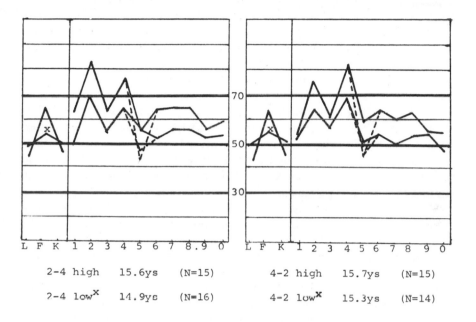

2-4 high	15.6ys	(N=15)
2-4 low^X	14.9ys	(N=16)

4-2 high	15.7ys	(N=15)
4-2 low^X	15.3ys	(N=14)

Personality Description

Sixty per cent of the 2-4/4-2 adolescents involved in this study were referred for treatment because they had difficulty concentrating. Of those with low 2-4 profiles, about one-half were seen in child guidance clinics by therapists whose main orientation was general psychoanalytic. There is *no* physical system involvement in 90% of the cases; this statement is in accord with that made by the therapists—that these teen-agers do *not* present themselves as physically or organically sick*.

The fathers of 2-4/4-2 patients are characterized as inconsistent and cool. One-third of the low 2-4s view their fathers as punishing. The mothers of 2-4/4-2 adolescents, who are often skilled workers, are also seen as inconsistent; they were further described as critical and distant. These young people do *not* see their mothers as warm, they are *not* proud to be with them, and they do *not* feel close to them. Indeed, neither their mothers nor their fathers were *ever* characterized as affectionate. Sixty-two per cent of these adolescents say that they have no one in the family with whom to discuss their personal problems. The parents of 2-4/4-2s share equally in any disciplinary actions that are taken, but their children express occasional fear of only their mothers. These parents were interviewed by the therapists along with their children.

As do other adolescents with an elevated 4 scale, 2-4/4-2 patients resent authority figures and typically have impulses to derogate them. They are argumentative, but they are also vulnerable to threat—both real and imagined. They have inner conflicts about emotional dependency* and are afraid of involvement with others*. The 2-4/4-2 group as a whole appears mildly depressed; their affect level is described as shallow. The mechanism of defense most characteristic of them is displacement. When describing themselves, they say that they are *not* shiftless or easy-going and that they are also *not* strong, wise, warm, or progressive. The 2-4/4-2s do *not* experience dry mouth and do *not* sweat when they are sad or depressed. They also do *not* experience fear, dry mouth, or heart palpitations when they feel guilty. The therapists' goals for outcome of therapy for this group are *not* simply situational adjustment.

The 2-4s, in contrast to the 4-2s, express feelings of perplexity (61%). They are more likely to have somatic concern, manifest hypochondriacal tendencies, report difficulty in thinking and concentrating, and to experience inner conflicts about sexuality. They see themselves as clever. The 4-2s are more cheerful and yet more flippant in word and gesture. They are self-centered and judge others in terms of their material possessions.

The high 2-4s date frequently and enjoy going to parties and concerts. They claim they are irritable, complicated, provocative, and yet shy; they complain about not having any place to entertain their friends. About one-half of them have either been on probation or held in detention.[4] The defense mechanism most characteristic of them is, not surprisingly, acting-out. They see themselves as frank, mischievous, and rebellious. Their therapists see them as demanding; they take the attitude that the world "owes them a living." High 2-4s have difficulty going to sleep when they are depressed or sad. They experience fear as well as headaches when they feel guilty.

Low 2-4s see social success as one of their main personal values. They also complain about getting low grades in school. Their defenses are fairly adequate in relieving their psychological distress. Their behavior is generally socially appropriate. In addition, they overcontrol their impulses and fear loss of control; it is difficult for them to "let go." They do considerable daydreaming and fantasizing. When they are depressed, tense, or anxious, they say that they sweat.

High 4-2s are occasionally foolhardy about their use of money; by their own admission, they are *not* thrifty. They tend to *undercontrol* their impulses and act without sufficient thinking or deliberation. They are concerned about their sex behavior. Often they are tearful and cry openly. They appear to get considerable seondary gain from their symptoms. They are also more ambitious than are low 4-2s. Their therapists see them as helpful and impulsive. When they are tense and anxious, they report difficulty in going to sleep and when they feel guilty, they experience fear and headaches. Both high and low 4-2s, additionally, experience boredom when they feel guilty.

Low 4-2s are very demanding and have only moderate ego strength. As children they had difficulty in school, as adolescents they have inner conflicts

---

[4] As compared to Hathaway and Monachesi (1953) who found a 17% delinquency rate if one high point was among scales 2, 5, or 0.

about self-assertion. They are seen by their therapists as somewhat psychopathic, stereotypic and unoriginal in their approaches to problem solving. They handle their anxieties by refusing to recognize their presence. They also value wealth and material possessions and tend to judge others in terms of them.

Adolescents with the 2-4/4-2 profile report a wide variety of drug usage with the exception of narcotics. From the 1970-73 sample of 22, there were 9 who used marijuana, 6 LSD, 2 MDA, and 1 mescaline. Other agents of abuse beyond these hallucinogens were amphetamines, barbiturates, Sopors, Valium, deoderant, glue (with aspirin and rat or insect poison), and "unknown." Several of the users of this spectrum of chemicals reported not only regular use but actual addiction. In all, there were 11 suicide attempts (50%) among these youth! The 2-4/4-2s were especially interesting in view of their inclination "to escape" from what appeared to them as an intolerable home situation. They turned to drugs; the girls got pregnant and the boys impregnated their girlfriends; they ran away from home, were truant from school, and frequently went AWOL from the hospital. Needless to say, they were constantly an elopement risk! There were typically reports of an extremely chaotic family life with 9 having alcoholic or drug-addicted parents and 12 having parents who were either separated or divorced.

ADOLESCENT CODE 2-5/5-2

Mean Profiles

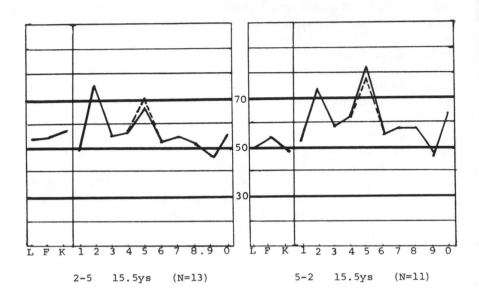

2-5   15.5ys   (N=13)   5-2   15.5ys   (N=11)

Personality Description

Sixty-three per cent of the adolescents with 2-5/5-2 profiles are first-borns. A major reason for referral for treatment is their poor relationships with their siblings; they especially have little to do with their brothers. Other reasons for referral are their indecisiveness and extreme negativism as well as their shyness, hypersensitivity, and suspiciousness.

Both parents of the 2-5/5-2 adolescents are described as warm (79%) and "fairly successful" as parents. Their mothers are said to be sympathetic (71%) and lenient (68%); their tempers are characterized as mild. Within the family, both parents are equally responsible for making decisions. The 2-5/5-2 patients now say that their mothers are warm, sympathetic, and consistent. They say that their fathers are active and critical; the 5-2s say that they also are consistent. As children, the 2-5/5-2s were *not* punished by being forbidden to do something that they were looking forward to. In school, 2-5s were in trouble about as frequently as others; outside of school, 2-5/5-2s had a few troubles with others, but were usually able to settle them by themselves.

Interestingly, about 17% of these young people are extremely tall for their age. Their general attitude is one of suspicion; their therapists agree that their genotype has paranoid features. They are vulnerable to both real and imagined threat*. At the extreme, delusions of grandeur are sometimes exhibited. The 2-5/5-2 adolescents are worriers*; they are consciously guilt-ridden, self-condemning, and self-accusatory. They describe themselves as cautious and their therapists agree—they tend to avoid or delay action, they fear committing themselves to any definite course, and they have inner conflicts about self-assertion. Consistent with this, these adolescents do *not* see themselves as courageous or daring. Many of the correlates of depression expected with scale 2 elevated are also present. These adolescents are sad, apathetic, and *not* cheerful; they express feelings of hopelessness as well. The genotype further has obsessive-compulsive features. In fact, obsession is one of the major defenses of these adolescents; the 5-2s are compulsive as well. The 2-5/5-2s are perfectionistic and meticulous. They are ruminative, obsessional, and overideational. They also place high value on intellectual and cognitive skills, activities, and attitudes. "Lack of pull" with the right people is viewed by them as their main obstacle in life. It is not surprising that one of their main mechanisms of defense is intellectualization. The intellectual functioning of the 2-5/5-2s is *not* average; their school subjects were of moderate interest to them, and yet 55% are not now in school.

Therapists say that the 2-5/5-2s are *not* socially extroverted and they describe themselves as *not* being outgoing. They are *not* poised, self-assured, or socially at ease*. They also do *not* experience conflict over emotional dependency. Their heterosexual adjustment is *not* good, and these patients generally do not date at all until around the age of 15. Among 88% their information about sex comes from conversation as opposed to actual experience, observation, or printed matter.

The 2-5/5-2 teen-agers are *not* psychopathic in nature, flippant, or resentful, and their personal tempo is *not* particularly fast*. They also do *not* rationalize their misfortunes. They say that they do *not* lose their tempers, pick the wrong kind of friends, or feel that they are treated like children. They do *not* see themselves as loud, jolly, or sly, but rather as timid and cautious. The 5-2s say that they are also stable and peaceable. When angry, these adolescents are *not* likely to throw anything or to hit people or objects. When they are tense and nervous, 5-2s do experience heart palpitations.

The 2-5/5-2 adolescent code is *not* a "drug type." Eleven of the 15 cases (all male) in the 1970-73 sample had no known drug history. The 4 who reported using drugs had tried marijuana, LSD, mescaline, amphetamines, barbiturates, Sopors, Valium (in a suicidal gesture), gasoline, glue, and lighter fluid; but only 2 individuals actually accounted for 83% of this abuse! One-third of these adolescents were teased in school even though they were considered bright intellectually and did well academically. The 2-5/5-2s were *not* athletic, and did poorly in sports. They were frequently described as *not* masculine and they rarely dated. Rather, they were seen as passive, shy, and ridden with guilt. Surprisingly, however, they were often involved in such antisocial activities as breaking and entering, stealing, and vandalism. Further, bizarre behaviors were noted for nearly half of these teenagers with mutism, regression, and "urges to attack male genitals" among the examples.

ADOLESCENT CODE 2-7/7-2

Mean Profiles

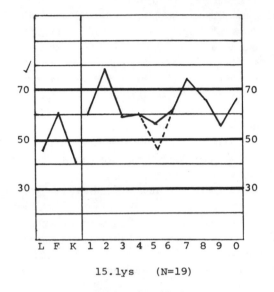

15.lys   (N=19)

Personality Description

There are multiple reasons for referral of the 2-7/7-2 adolescents for both psychological diagnosis and for psychotherapy; tearfulness, restlessness, nervousness, anxiety, worry, being among the leading factors cited by their therapists. Somewhat less frequently, excessive fantasy is noted, as is dreaminess. Almost 40% of the 2-7/7-2 adolescents are indicated as expressing suicidal thoughts. In contrast, school truancy is a *low* frequency reason for referral (10%).

Nearly 70% of these 2-7/7-2 adolescents are first-borns and in nearly 60% of the cases the father is recorded as "interested in most things the patient did." In 60% of the cases the 2-7/7-2s are characterized as being "rarely in trouble" with their parents. Nearly 50% comment on the close relationship between brothers and sisters within the family.

Verbal expression is characterized as impoverished in slightly more than 50% of these adolescents. Nearly 70% are characterized as exhibiting minor reality distortions and mild affective inappropriateness. *Severe* depression is noted in almost one-fourth of this group.

On vigorous adjectives (active, aggressive, assertive) the 2-7/7-2s rank notoriously *low*. None are characterized as assertive or as boastful, whereas nearly 80% are described as dependent and 70% as suggestible. They are also characteristically perceived by therapists as self-punishing and withdrawn.

Given the referral problems already cited, it is not surprising to find that psychotherapists see the 2-7/7-2s as spending a good deal of time in personal fantasy and in daydreams. Depressive mood is a major affective feature and open tearfulness occurs with some frequency. Feelings of hopelessness are openly expressed. Anxiety, also, is a major feature of the 2-7/7-2 adolescents; it is noted by therapists that these young people overreact to danger or make emergency responses in the absence of any situations which one would ordinarily interpret as dangerous or threatening. Minor irritants are responded to as "federal cases." They are also described as exhibiting multiple neurotic symptoms such as being unable to "let go," apparently fearing loss of control. They are described as fearfully phobic. Strong tendencies toward self-punishment are noted when these adolescents face frustrating circumstances. Self-blame rather than blaming others is the characteristic response mode. Thus, it is hardly surprising to find that therapists report conscious expressions of guilt, of self-condemnation, of self-accusation in this adolescent group. The 2-7/7-2s are also described as self-defeating and consistent in their tendencies to place themselves in a bad light.

Behavior orientation with respect to other persons is described as essentially passive and unassertive. The 2-7/7-2 adolescents are unusually suggestible and are perceived as overly responsive to other people's evaluations, tending to disparage their own evaluations. The shaky self-concept which this adolescent group shares is reflected in some of their self-evaluations. Over 60% express fear of making mistakes and over half are afraid of what the future holds for them. Only 15% describe themselves as capable. Most tend to see themselves as unplanful (the endorsement for planful being zero!) and only 10% call themselves reliable. The adjectives silent and shy are highly endorsed in the self-descriptions. Not a single adolescent in the 2-7/7-2 group is willing to embrace the adjective wholesome!

ADOLESCENT CODE 2-8/8-2

Mean Profiles

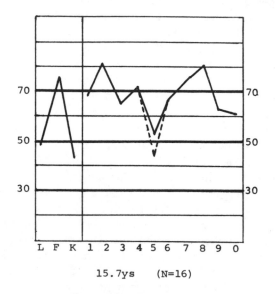

15.7ys   (N=16)

Personality Description

Considering the elevation of scale 8 for this group of adolescents, it is not surprising that the chief reason for referral for over 60% was "emotionally inappropriate." They were also described on referral as nervous and anxious. Their early childhood was characterized by quarrels between parent and child (70%). This adolescent group is not very well-liked by other students, nor are their friendships outside of school plentiful. Only a small percentage (6%) seem to claim peers as influential factors in their lives. The 2-8/8-2 adolescents seem unable to elicit liking and acceptance in either their peers or other people.

Nearly half of the 2-8/8-2s are described by their therapists as timid. The central fact about the emotional orientation of these adolescents vis-a-vis others, is the emotional distance they maintain. They appear fearful of emotional involvement and are perceived as consistently avoiding situations where their own performance may be inferior to the performance of others. They also have inner conflicts about sexuality* and emotional dependency*. Isolation and repression are assigned by therapists in almost equal proportions as the major mechanisms of defense (about 70%).

Basic insecurity and needs for attention are distinctive characteristics of this adolescent group as reflected in their therapists' descriptions. Their behavior is seen as highly emotional and they are characterized as being unable to modulate, steady, or "tone it down." Not surprisingly, they are rated *low* in social appropriateness of their behavior. The ambitions and aspirations of this group are extremely low or modest. They are characterized, too, as lacking in insight. Therapists see this 2-8/8-2 group as generally unempathic.

The timidity commented on by their therapists is paralleled in the adolescent self-descriptions; over 75% describe themselves as afraid of making mistakes and over half as afraid to speak up in class. They attribute the word awkward to themselves rather frequently and the word capable rather infrequently. Nearly 70% see themselves as quiet and 75% as silent. None see themselves as realistic. Over half claim tiredness as the way they express anxiety. Although less than half say thumb sucking was a childhood problem, the 2-8/8-2s did exceed the base rate in the frequency of this behavior. Well over one-third describe themselves as fearful and/or cold when in the presence of their fathers.

Among the 2-8/8-2s there was some evidence of drug abuse, although almost without exception, it was associated with suicide attempts. That is, in every instance of drug abuse, there was an overdose! From the 1970-73 sample of 16, 56% had no drug involvement. The 2-8/8-2 code was rather a "suicide profile." Forty-four percent of these teenagers attempted to take their lives either by overdosing on drugs or by slashing their wrists—1 adolescent also walked in front of a truck and contemplated using a shotgun but later "chickened out." The overdoses were from Dexedrine, tranquilizers, aspirin (in conjunction with hanging), penicillin, and some "unknown." Aside from these incidents, there was 1 adolescent who used alcohol and commented "I want to get off dope." These teenagers frequently were truant—both from home and from school. Their school difficulties were both social, as mentioned above, and academic, although as many as 94% stated that they were "A" students before the onset of their present symptoms! As a group, the 2-8/8-2s engaged in some unusual and low-frequency behaviors. Some hallucinated voices telling them to kill or mutilate themselves or others—for example—to jump out of windows or burn themselves in the fireplace. One was preoccupied with mystic and religious concerns, 1 was involved in sexual relations with her father, while another was accused of making sexual advances toward his sister. Also of note was the finding that over one-fourth of these young people had vague and non-localized "organic deficits," "minimal brain damage," seizure disorders, epilepsy as children, etc. The fathers of the 2-8/8-2s were often reported to be very abusive.

ADOLESCENT CODE 2-0/0-2

Mean Profiles

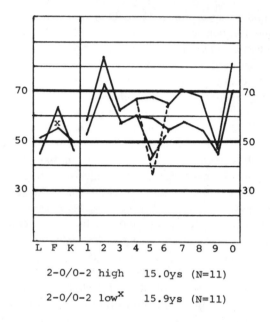

2-0/0-2 high   15.0ys (N=11)

2-0/0-2 low^x   15.9ys (N=11)

Personality Description

The 2-0/0-2 adolescent involved in this study are unique individuals. They are *not* referred for treatment because they lie, are defiant, disobedient, attention demanding, impulsive, mischievous, provocative, or difficult to control, but rather because they are nervous and anxious (82%), listless, apathetic, shy, and overly sensitive (64%). As children, they were passive, inactive, and generally fearful; none of them were known as "roughnecks." They did *not* dislike class subjects, but showed very little interest in other aspects of school. Outside of school, they had few friends of any kind (62%). They say that making friends was their chief problem during early childhood (64%). As adolescents, they are interested *only* in class subjects, which they say are of about average interest. Their attitude toward their teachers is neutral and nearly 70% remain essentially friendless at school. Their leisure time activities include service club membership, art, science projects, and chess—all of which are very *atypical* for other profile types. These activities are always, or almost always, engaged in alone.

The 2-0/0-2 teen-agers do *not* enjoy parties or concerts, do *not* like riding around in cars, and are very *unlikely* to "hang around" downtown. There is *no* conflict with their parents because they conform to parental standards. Low 2-0/0-2s have a rather easy-going relationships with their brothers and sisters. They do *not* drink alcohol (82%), they do *not* smoke (73%), and they see religion as a moderately important factor in their upbringing. They are totally undecided about what they would like to do in life after school, but the high 2-0/0-2s believe that "lack of pull" with the right people will be their biggest obstacle.

Eighty-seven per cent of the 2-0/0-2s express feelings of inferiority to their therapists. They say that they are *not* good-looking, that they do *not* like being picked on, that they are afraid to speak up in class, and that they feel awkward when they meet people or try to make a date (64%—and 91% of high 2-0/0-2s). They also say that they feel that no one likes them, that they wish others would like them better, and that they are slow in making friends. High 2-0/0-2s are, in addition, afraid of making mistakes and dislike being criticised by their parents; they see themselves as bitter and emotional. The 2-0/0-2 adolescents describe themselves as awkward, dull, gloomy, cowardly, shy, silent, quiet, and meek. They say that they are *not* energetic, enthusiastic (0%), daring, loud, out-going, friendly, good-natured, frank, independent, self-confident, sexy (0%), or good-looking (0%). When they are angry, they brood and when they feel guilty, all of the high 2-0/0-2s report becoming frightened.

Their therapists see the 2-0/0-2s as anxious, fearful, cautious, conservative, shy, timid, withdrawn, inhibited, submissive, mild, meek, quiet, and self-controlled. They are depressed, and very vulnerable to threat, consciously guilt-ridden, self-condemning, and self-accusatory; they continually place themselves in a bad light and thus are self-defeating. They react to frustration by punishing themselves. High 2-0/0-2s are described as self-denying, while low 2-0/0-2s are seen as more cooperative. The 2-0/0-2 adolescents are over-controlled; they cannot let go, even when it would be appropriate for them to do so. They do *not* overreact to danger*, or judge others in terms of material possessions*. They handle anxiety by refusing to recognize its presence. Nevertheless, they are tense in manner, sweat, tremble, and show other signs of manifest anxiety. They are also afraid of emotional involvement with others and, in fact, seem to have little need for such affiliation.

These adolescents are viewed by their psychotherapists as schizoid; they think and associate in unusual ways and spend a good deal of time in personal fantasy and daydreaming. They are serious young people who tend to anticipate problems and difficulties. Indeed, they are prone toward obsessional thinking and are compulsively meticulous. They also tend to avoid situations where their own performance is likely to be inferior to that of others. Therapists of the 2-0/0-2s, further state that they do *not* act-out or resent authority figures; they are *not* demanding, argumentative, boastful, out-spoken, assertive, provocative, daring, excitable, restless, rebellious, impulsive, or hasty. Neither are they deceitful (they are actually fairly reliable informants), unpredictable, change-able, irresponsible, talkative, sociable, adventurous, pleasure seeking or reckless.

The 2-0/0-2s, almost without exception, are not a drug-using group. In fact, of the 17 adolescents who comprised the 1970-73 sample, only 1 reported using drugs for pleasure (LSD, marijuana, and mescaline), although 3 had attempted suicide with other agents—an "assortment of pills," aspirin, and pencillin. These teenagers were a motley group, with their most cohesive characteristics being poor social interaction, unpopularity, and few significant friendships. Individual symptoms varied from running away, truancy, burglary, and breaking and entering to bed wetting, autistic rocking and headshaking, intensive fear of germs and poisons, seizures, homicidal ideation, and hallucinations. One boy was arrested innumerable times for exposure, attempted rape, sodomy, and "grabbing" girls in drugstores. A tendency for at least the girls in the group was to dress "old fashioned" and inappropiately for their age. That is, they made many attempts at looking younger with several even shaving their pubic hair!

ADOLESCENT CODE 3-4/4-3

Mean Profiles

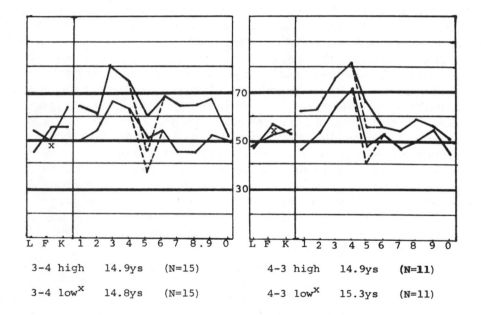

3-4 high	14.9ys	(N=15)
3-4 low^x	14.8ys	(N=15)

4-3 high	14.9ys	(N=11)
4-3 low^x	15.3ys	(N=11)

Personality Description

One of the main reasons for referral of the 3-4/4-3 adolescents is sleep difficulties. In addition, 54% of those with elevated 3-4 profiles have suicidal thoughts. Low 4-3s are referred because they fight excessively; their symptom pattern is one of hostility and aggression. About half of these patients are involved in family therapy; this is possibly related to the fact that the 3-4/4-3s, in general, resent their sisters bitterly.

As children, the 3-4/4-3s showed interest in all aspects of school. Their grades were mainly B's and C's. Their therapists report that they got along very well with the other students although 45% were known as "roughnecks" and all of the high 3-4s manifested their symptoms at school. Outside of school, the 3-4/4-3s were not without friends. Nonacademically, most things came easily for them although some things were more difficult than others.

The focal concern of the 3-4/4-3 teen-agers is their parents. The low 3-4s, especially, were *not* close to either parent as children and yet they described their fathers as close and "fairly successful" and their mothers as warm and sympathetic. The 3-4/4-3 group as a whole considered their mothers to be discouraging and not very affectionate and the high 3-4s felt insecure when in the presence of their fathers. Perhaps surprisingly, then, they tended *not* to have "poor" relationships with their parents and only about 8% report quarreling constantly with them.

The childhood problems of the 3-4/4-3s did *not* include keeping friends or reading difficulty (6%). The fact that they had little difficulty in school is reflected in their description of their classmates as "just bright enough." As adolescents, school activities occupy a good part of their leisure time. They report no difficulty in making friends, picking the wrong kind of friends, or being picked on. They are *not* concerned about proper sex behavior, but then only 8% have gained their knowledge of sex from actual experience. Although the genotype has definite psychopathic features, many of the traits associated with scale 4 are *atypical* for these adolescents. That is, they do *not* like to ride around in cars and they do *not* particularly enjoy going to parties. The low 4-3s, however, *do* report getting into trouble.

Therapists describe these patients as depressed. At the same time, they exhibit fairly good ego strength. These adolescents see themselves as adaptable, energetic, friendly, original, sociable, unselfish, and independent. They say that they are not cruel, greedy, loud, sly, or suspicious. When they are tense or anxious, the 3-4/4-3s say that they have difficulty in going to sleep (67%).

The 3-4s, as opposed to the 4-3s, are seen as more intropunitive, self-condemning, and self-accusatory. They tend to have difficulty in expressing their emotions in any adaptable way. Their therapists view them as suspicious. The treatment goal for these youth is one of reconstruction of the personality (63%). The prognosis is judged to be fair (50%). The 4-3s, on the other hand, have a more resilient ego defense system. They seem more poised, self-assured, and socially at ease. Their heterosexual adjustment is judged to be better than that of the 3-4s. When angry, these adolescents are more likely to speak out. The 3-4 adolescents also tend to be more flippant in word and gesture.

The high 3-4s are generally easy to talk with in the therapeutic situation and they tend to arouse liking and acceptance of others. Although they complain about others finding fault with them, they have more of a capacity for forming close interpersonal relationships than do the low 3-4s. The high 3-4s manifest hypochondriacal tendencies and complain about weakness and easy fatigability. They say that when sad or depressed, they experience loss of appetite along with loss of interest. When they feel guilty, they experience headaches and feel empty inside (this is true for both high and low 3-4s). Their therapists view them as complicated and say that compulsion is their main defense. These young people describe themselves as logical and peaceable. The low 3-4s are viewed by their therapists as unrealistic. They demand sympathy from others, are passively resistant, and overly critical. They are generally skeptical and not easily impressed as well as distrustful of people in general. Often they question the motivations of others. In addition, they manifest narcissism and fear emotional dependency. The rapport established with the low 3-4s is only superficial.

High 4-3s are especially well-groomed. They tend to be perfectionistic and compulsively meticulous. In keeping with this, they see themselves as conscientious. The low 4-3s, in contrast, are disorderly. They are also seen as hostile and self-indulgent. They handle their anxieties by refusing to recognize their presence. Like the high 3-4s, they manifest hypochondriacal tendencies. They view themselves as shrewd.

The 3-4/4-3 is a "heavy" drug-user profile. While the 1970-73 sample was large (N=38), only 14 (37%) of these adolescents had *no* recorded drug history. Those who used drugs tried everyone on our roster! From among the hallucinogenics, marijuana, LSD, psilocybin, and mescaline were all used. Stimulants reported included two unspecified "uppers," cocaine, and two types of amphetamines (one in a suicide attempt). "Downers" were also popular with this code type: 9 of these teenagers used unspecified hypnotics and 5, specifically, barbiturates. Three 3-4/4-3s were addicted to drugs and 5 made suicide attempts. Additionally, Sopors use was common for a number of these young people. It is of some moment that another 10 individuals were involved with "unknown" drug agents, and that 4 of these also made suicide attempts. Glue, gasoline, deodorant, Darvon, aspirin, and various phenothiazines were all experimented with at one time or another. Altogether, there were 13 youngsters who made suicide attempts; apparently over one-third of these adolescents believed that they would be better off dead! The 3-4/4-3s typically came from broken homes with 61% having their parents either separated or divorced. Fifty-eight per cent were either the oldest child or the only child in their family. They, like the 2-4/4-2s, often ran away from home, were truant from school, and went AWOL from the hospital. Promiscuity was extremely common among this group with 80% of the girls having premarital sexual experiences. Stealing was also a significant occurrence, and ranged from taking money and items from lockers to stealing payroll checks and cars. Over 30% had recorded histories of theft. Only 1 of the 38 3-4/4-3s was a black adolescent!

ADOLESCENT CODE 3-5/5-3

Mean Profiles

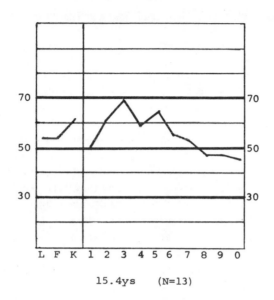

15.4ys   (N=13)

Personality Description

Fifty-four per cent of the 3-5/5-3 adolescents involved in this study were referred for therapy by their parents and none (0%) were referred by the court;[5] both of these figures differ significantly from the base rates. The *reasons* given for referral are not distinctive, though the area of manifestation of symptoms is clearly the personality (80%) (*e.g.*, as opposed to the school or interpersonal-relations). The symptom pattern is one of withdrawal and inhibition. Most often, both parents are involved in the treatment process as well as the referred adolescent.

The 3-5/5-3s come from homes where the religious atmosphere is moderate but firm (*i.e.*, strict church attendance is required or dietary rules are enforced). The mothers of these adolescents, who describe themselves as "homemakers," frequently have educations beyond the high school level. Their children view their moral judgments of behavior as highly predictable. They are these adolescents' closest confidants (80%)—and this is an all male code type! Their fathers, on the other hand, are seen as neglecting. Ninety-three per cent of the 3-5/5-3s had no brothers living at the time of their birth, and 68% had specific fears (*e.g.*, dark, heights) during their early childhood.

The objective mood of the 3-5/5-3s is seen by their therapists as moderately depressed; perhaps surprisingly, some see themselves as *extremely* elated. Their

---

[5] As compared to Hathaway and Monachesi (1953) who found a 17% delinquency rate if one high-point was among scales 2, 5, or 0.

general attidude is one of reticence and their affect level is described as shallow. Often, their rate of speech is rapid. Psychotherapists say that these adolescents are neither active (they, in fact, see themselves as lazy—86%) nor aggressive. Despite the elevation of scale 3, they do *not* present themselves as physically or organically ill (though this may be an expression of denial!). Rather, they are seen as queer, yet sincere and idealistic. They are basically insecure and have strong needs for attention*. At the same time, they are shy, anxious, inhibited, and *not* extroverted. Their friends are usually younger. This genotype definitely has obsessive-compulsive features; 3-5/5-3s are ruminative, obsessional, and overideational. They are vulnerable to real or imagined threat and are characterized as worriers. There are also schizoid components to their personalities; these adolescents spend a good deal of time in personal fantasy and daydreaming. Although they are *not* characteristically delusional, they some-times express gradiose ideas, the extreme being delusions of grandeur. They do *not* employ acting-out as a defense. In fact, they tend toward *overcontrol* of impulses. They are *not* provocative or excitable. They, in addition, say that they are *not* argumentative. They do project and rationalize to a greater extent than does the "average adolescent patient." In general, their defenses are *inadequate* in relieving psychological distress.

The majority of 3-5/5-3 adolescents in the 1970-73 sample did *not* use drugs. Those who did, however, experimented with a wide variety of pharmacological agents. Of the 14 who comprised this group, 5 were involved regularly with marijuana, amphetamines, and Sopors. Four used alcohol. Other drugs of abuse included heroin, codeine, barbiturates, gasoline and various "uppers" and "downers." Interestingly, the suicidal gestures by these young people were made with saline solution (5 liters ingested in the hospital) and cold tablets! When they "got into drugs" it was serious, but their suicide attempts, while dramatic, were generally quite harmless. Forty-three per cent of the 3-5/5-3s had serious weight problems. One adolescent had gained over 100 pounds, another was described as "extremely obese," another as moderately so; 4 were anorexic, while 1 merely didn't eat regularly or well. These teenagers, like the 2-0/0-2s, had a varied list of presenting symptoms—some of which were rather bizarre. One girl cropped her hair, clipped her eyelashes, shaved her eyebrows, poured dirt, flour, and sugar in her hair, smeared mucous on her face, and asked others to call her "Freddie Flintstone." A boy ran for a butcher knife every time he was upset. Another was "on a mission for Christ." Considering the nature of scales 3 and 5, it appeared that the adolescents who obtained this profile, were more pathological than would have been expected.

ADOLESCENT CODE 3-6/6-3

Mean Profiles

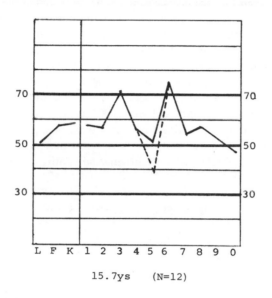

15.7ys   (N=12)

Personality Description

There are only a few descriptors uniquely characteristic of 3-6/6-3 adolescents. The domain most affected by their disorder is the personality, and yet their focal concern is the self in only 50% of the cases—significantly less than for the other adolescents. The only distinctive referral reason is suicide attempts; about one-third of these adolescents are seen for therapy following such attempts. Frequently they are seen for treatment as often as twice a week.

The 3-6/6-3 adolescents come from homes where the income is often *very* irregular throughout the years. Psychotherapists see the father's relationships with these adolescents as ambivalent, although curiously, the 3-6/6-3s view their fathers as warm and rewarding though weak; they say that they feel calm when in their presence. They admit to being closer to their mothers (75%) than to any other family member. Two-thirds of the 3-6/6-3s exhibit ill feelings toward their sibs and maintain generally poor relationships with them. In reflecting on their past, these adolescents typically report difficulty in keeping friends. They also have trouble speaking in front of others. Over half state that their goal in life is to become prominent and respected members of the community and about half fear this goal will be subverted by their lack of ability. These adolescents see themselves as wary, indifferent, prejudiced, yet natural.

Quite understandably, in view of scale 6 elevation, psychotherapists view their attitude as generally suspicious and further characterize them as paranoid.

Additionally, they are obsessional and most reluctant to acknowledge the presence of psychological conflict. They are resentful*, though *not* particularly touchy, and make generous use of rationalization*. Nevertheless, the 3-6/6-3s are more likely than the "average patient" to be calm, and clear-thinking.

Of the 10 3-6/6-3 adolescents in the 1970-73 sample, half were involved with drugs but only 1 made a suicide attempt—this a girl who overdosed with methaqualone. Another girl had tried mescaline once, but denied any further use. The remaining 2 "users" had sampled a variety of drugs with the exception of narcotics—rather, marijuana, LSD, mescaline, "uppers," "downers," and tranquilizers. Even from this small sample, it became obvious that this was an intelligent subgroup. Forty per cent were "A" students and 1 had skipped two grades. They, in addition, tended to come from upper-middle class homes. A rather interesting finding was that the marriages of these adolescents' parents all appeared to be good; rarely was there any marital conflict reported.

ADOLESCENT CODE 4-5/5-4

Mean Profiles

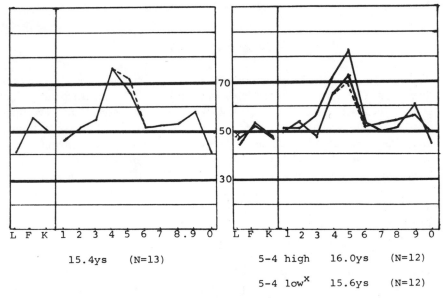

15.4ys   (N=13)

5-4 high   16.0ys   (N=12)

5-4 low^x   15.6ys   (N=12)

Personality Description

Although there are no reasons for referral uniquely characteristic of the 4-5/5-4 adolescents, these youth tend *not* to be referred because they are emotionally inappropriate or because they have poor relationships with their peers. In fact, they typically do not manifest *any* of their symptoms in the area of interpersonal-peer relations. They get along exceptionally well with the other students at school (although they mention being called "roughnecks" as one of their childhood problems), have neutral attitudes toward their teachers, and are liked by most others outside of school. In general, they have many friends—for the 4-5s, these are generally older—and a few close friends. It is not surprising to find that friends are the main personal value of over 80% of these adolescents and that peers are viewed as the most influential figures in their lives (60%). Nor is it surprising, in light of their apparent need for affiliation with others, to learn that these patients almost never engage in any activities alone.

On the other hand, family life is *not* a personal value of these adolescents. This is perhaps odd since the 5-4s discussed their personal problems with their parents and nearly half of the 4-5s (and 67% of the low 5-4s) report that as children they were closer to their fathers than to any other family member. Although the low 5-4s were included in the discussion of family problems, they did *not* feel free to disagree with their parents. The 4-5/5-4 patients say that they felt calm in the presence of their fathers and the low 5-4s, in addition, say that they felt secure (75%). Interestingly too, these fathers drank moderately but were rarely, if ever, out of the home for longer than a day. As adolescents, the 4-5/5-4s report that they feel calm when with their fathers. They describe them as sympathetic, while their therapists describe the relationship between these fathers and their children as one of general indifference. Their mothers are seen as critical, yet encouraging; they are *not* ambivalent. These parents were interviewed in only about one-fourth of the cases—less often than were the parents of other teen-agers involved in the study.

The 4-5/5-4 adolescents are generally *not* short. About 92% of 5-4s (more so than the 4-5s) were described as well-groomed. The rapport established with their therapist is friendly, though with the 5-4s, it is more likely to be superficial. These adolescents show no impairment of judgment, their affect level is normal, as is the amount of their verbal expression. The 4-5s, however, tend to speak more rapidly than do the 5-4s.

Psychotherapists view these adolescents as being in "better shape" than many of the other young people involved in this study. That is, they say that 4-5/5-4s have a resilient ego system (*i.e.*, a safe margin of integration and good control). They also say that the defenses of these adolescents are fairly adequate in relieving psychological distress. More than the "average patient," these 4-5/5-4s would be adaptive and organized when under stress or trauma. This genotype has psychopathic features and patients with this profile utilize acting-out as a defense; they also tend toward rationalization. Defenses *atypical* of them are isolation and regression. At the same time, therapists describe the 4-5/5-4s as argumentative, impulsive, and rather distrustful of people in general. These patients are *not* hypochondriacal in nature; they do *not* present themselves as physically ill. Neither are they shy, anxious, inhibited, or conflicted about emotional dependency. These teen-agers are also *not* defensive about admitting psychological conflicts, they do *not* experience feelings of hopelessness, and they do *not* cry openly.

When the 4-5/5-4 adolescents describe themselves, they say that they like to ride around in cars (71%). They are *not* interested in church activities, however (0%). Over 80% of these adolescents date, a figure much higher than the base rate. They apparently do *not* have trouble with being teased or being picked on. They do *not* endorse as self-descriptive adjectives determined, peculiar, or rattlebrained.

The 4-5s have more difficulty concentrating than do the 5-4s. One-third of these adolescents, however, say that their school subjects are very interesting and challenging. In contrast, the 5-4s say that the other students in school are "just bright enough," which perhaps is the reason for some of their apparent boredom. The 4-5s also have more difficulty controlling their tempers than do the 5-4s. They describe themselves as argumentative, cautious, quick, defensive, opinionated, sly, steady, and unselfish. The prognosis for the 4-5s is seen as good in over 50% of the cases. Therapists describe the 5-4s as clear-thinking when compared with the 4-5s. They say that the 5-4s are more likely to avoid situations where their performance may be inferior to that of others.

Those youth with elevated 5-4 profiles are more irritable and hysteroid than those with low profiles. While those with low profiles are seen as wary and basically insecure, they describe themselves as more healthy and rebellious.

This is a "heavy" drug use profile with all but 4 of the 14 adolescents (72%) in the 1970-73 sample evidencing some form of drug abuse. There was not a single drug class on our roster that went uninvestigated by these youth. They experimented with heroin, codeine, Darvon, marijuana, hashish, cocaine, LSD, mescaline, psilocybin, MDA, Seconal, Etraphon, Doriden, Sopors, alcohol, Librium, Valium, thorazine, paint thinner, gasoline, glue, and several "unknowns." Although there were 2 cases of overdoses reported (both with Darvon), there were no serious suicide attempts among this group. As they used a vast array of drugs, they were also involved in all kinds of trouble. They shoplifted, stole automobiles, lied, vandalized, were involved in breaking and entering, concealed stolen property, and frequently sold drugs. They were highly emotionally reactive; they evidenced tantrums, violent temper outbursts (1 girl stabbed another, while 1 boy threatened his mother with a butcher knife), and physically fought with parents, teachers, peers, and sibs alike. They also had serious difficulty in school, being truant, suspended, expelled, or merely failing class subjects. About one-third of these young people had been declared incorrigible by the court. Again, there was a large incidence of disrupted family life, with divorce, alcoholism, and physically abusive parents being a frequent occurrence.

ADOLESCENT CODE 4-6/6-4

Mean Profiles

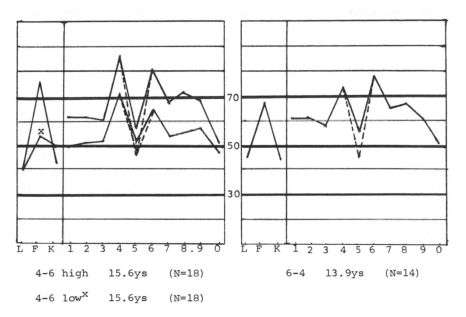

4-6 high	15.6ys	(N=18)
4-6 low^x	15.6ys	(N=18)

6-4   13.9ys   (N=14)

Personality Description

Adolescents who present the 4-6/6-4 profile are referred for treatment because they are defiant, disobedient, tense, restless, and negativistic; half of the time, the court is the referral source. The relationships that these teen-agers have with their parents are almost without exception, poor and most of their symptoms are manifested in this area of interpersonal-adult relations. In addition, the 6-4 adolescents are likely to be phobic, shy, and overly sensitive. In general, there is no somatic system involvement in their disorder and the primary symptoms are over a year in developing.

During early childhood, the 4-6/6-4s were neither passive, inactive, nor fearful. Their mothers drank alcohol, moderately if not to excess, and their relationship with their children can best be described as dependent. These young people describe their mothers, in turn, as having been critical and not very warm and say that their fathers were inconsistent; 4-6s, in addition, report that their fathers were strong-tempered.

The 4-6/6-4 teen-agers did *not* like class subjects, but liked most other aspects of school. They report that cheating was a problem for them during early childhood. As adolescents, their attitude toward school has deteriorated to the point where they dislike nearly all aspects of it; and they are now frequently in trouble with others as far as school relationships are concerned. They believe that the other students are just "too bright" to keep up with. The friends of 4-6/6-4s are typically older.

The 4-6/6-4 adolescents date frequently (41% of the high 4-6s date more than once a week) and their parents are *not* wholly approving. They like to spend their leisure time "hanging around" downtown. Fewer 4-6s than 6-4s admit to using alcohol, although 72% say that they do drink liquor.

When 4-6/6-4s are asked what problems are troubling them now, they invariably reply that they get into trouble (66%—and 89% of 4-6s). High 4-6s say that they do not have the chance to do the things they want to do (78%), that they feel that nobody likes them, that they wish others would like them better, that they have no place to entertain their friends, and that they are afraid of getting bad grades and failing in school.

The 4-6/6-4 adolescents are constantly in trouble with their parents due to excessive misbehavior. When they get into trouble with the law, they blame others—elevated 4-6s do so more than low 4-6s. When angry, they will typically go off by themselves or throw things. These young people remain unusually distant from their sisters, deny that religion is of any importance in their lives, and discount being happy and respected as important goals in life.

Psychotherapists say that 4-6/6-4s have a need to think of themselves as unusually self-sufficient; that they are extroverted, unpredictable, and changeable. Their genotype has definite psychopathic features—these patients undercontrol their impulses, act without sufficient deliberation, and are flippant in both word and gesture. They resent authority figures and typically derogate them whenever possible. They are demanding and believe that the "world owes them a living." They are *not* particularly fearful, have *no* difficulty in getting to sleep, have *no* physical complaints, are rarely tired or feel weak, tense, or nervous. They report *no* difficulty in thinking or in concentrating, experience *no* delusions, and are rarely hesitant to commit themselves to a definite course of action. The 4-6 adolescents are, in addition, self-dramatizing and histrionic. They demand sympathy from others, are argumentative, emphasize oral pleasures, and are narcissistic and self-centered.

Therapists see these 4-6/6-4 adolescents as provocative. They are talkative and appear mildly elated. However, there tends to be mild intellectual impairment among those with high 4-6 profiles and poor judgment characterizes those with 6-4 profiles. The symptom pattern of 4-6/6-4s is *not* one of fear or anxiety, and acting-out (90%) and projection (82%) are their main mechanisms of defense. These patients are *not* obsessional and they do *not* isolate themselves from others. Rather, their therapists say they are active, quick, clever, informal, loud, mischievous, opportunistic, out-spoken, pleasure-seeking, sharp-witted, and shrewd. They are also said to be aggressive, bitter, deceitful, hostile, irresponsible, quarrelsome, and reckless. They get considerable "secondary gain" from their symptoms. They are *not* self-denying, submissive, quiet, worrying, withdrawn, timid, inhibited, rigid, or infantile. The 4-6s demand attention, and are further described as disorderly, impulsive, hasty, rebellious, restless, and stubborn. High 4-6s are more cautious, impatient, and moody than low 4-6s. The picture that these 4-6/6-4 teen-agers have of themselves differs considerably from that of their therapists. They view themselves as attractive, daring, confident, spunky, jolly, and loud. They also admit to being defensive and undependable. The 4-6s believe that they are disorderly and the 6-4s actually say that they are pleasant! High 4-6s have an apparent willingness to say socially undesirable things about themselves; they claim they are cold, cruel, hard-headed, headstrong, fussy, deceitful, lazy, quitting, rattlebrained, restless, reckless, and sharp-witted. Low 4-6s say only that they are clear-thinking and sophisticated. Adjectives that 4-6/6-4 adolescents think are unfitting to them are quiet, cowardly, and forgetful.

About half (9 of 20) of the 4-6/6-4 adolescents in the 1970-73 sample were involved with drugs. Consistent with earlier findings for 4-6/6-4s, the most frequently abused drug was alcohol with 5 of 9 "users" drinking heavily and regularly. Narcotics, on the other hand, were not part of this code type's drug-use pattern. They experimented with marijuana, amphetamines, barbiturates, Sopors, Valium, cleaning fluid, and such "others" as "nerve pills," aspirin, and phenobarbital. A striking aspect of this profile type was the consistent and very intense struggles that these young people had with their parents, especially the girls with their mothers. Case after case reported tension, arguments, fights, and altercations with mothers (or less frequently, fathers). Other case summaries reported, and quite emphatically, that there was severe conflict in the home. One-half of this sample had been beaten with a strap. There was also a high incidence of physical disorders among the 4-6/6-4s with unconsciousness and aphasia (following head trauma), congenital birth defects, brain damage, epilepsy, encephalitis, seizures, and insomnia all experienced by these adolescents.

ADOLESCENT CODE 4-7/7-4

Mean Profiles

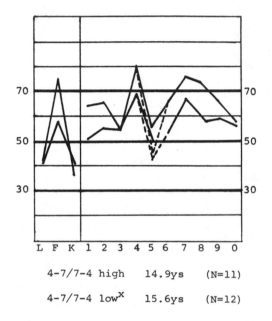

```
4-7/7-4 high      14.9ys     (N=11)

4-7/7-4 low^X     15.6ys     (N=12)
```

Personality Description

This profile type is especially interesting because there are nearly as many descriptors which distinguish the high 4-7/7-4s from the low 4-7/7-4s as there are descriptors which distinguish the combined 4-7/7-4s from all other adolescents. There is little in the personal histories of the 4-7/7-4s which is uniquely characteristic of them. About one-third have two brothers and one-fourth have fathers who have been in trouble with the law for either major or minor offenses. The 4-7/7-4s say that during early childhood, their mothers were *very* strict. They now see them as distant and punishing; their disciplinary actions are quite often anticipated. Their fathers, in contrast, are described as weak.

As is typical of persons with scale 4 elevation, these adolescents employ acting-out as a defense; they do *not* manifest regression. They undercontrol their impulses, act without sufficient thinking and deliberation, are provocative*, resentful*, and flippant in both word and gesture. Their therapists see them as aggressive, careless, irresponsible, and undependable. They are anything but timid! At the same time, they are basically insecure* and have an inordinate need for attention*. They are further conflicted about emotional dependency* and sexuality*. Although they are less cooperative than other adolescents involved in this study, their therapists judge that their outlook for future adjustment is at least fair (80%), if not good. The 4-7/7-4s do *not* see themselves as sociable. Nevertheless, they typically have many friends and a few close friends. They do say that picking the right kind of friends (64%) and their parents not liking their friends (60%) are two of the main problems that are troubling them now. Over half of these adolescents see themselves as self-punishing.

In addition, high 4-7/7-4s frequently express feelings of guilt (82%) and shame (64%). They are seen, by their therapists, as consciously guilt-ridden, self-condemning, and self-accusatory. All of them (100%) are described as confused. They are unpredictable and changeable in behavior and describe themselves as fussy. These adolescents tend to be liked by some students and disliked by others. The rapport they establish with their therapists is generally friendly in nature.

As children, the low 4-7/7-4s enjoyed watching sporting events. To their therapists, they appear more normal, healthy, and symptom-free than do the high 4-7/7-4s. Their defenses are operating fairly adequately and thus provide at least some relief from their psychological distress; they may even appear mildly elated. They would be more likely, than the high 4-7/7-4s, to be organized and adaptive under stress or trauma. Reaction-formation is the main defense (73%) attributed to them. In sum, these adolescents are in "better shape." They get along well in the world as it is and are more socially appropriate than are the high 4-7/7-4s. Low 4-7/7-4s see themselves as modest.

ADOLESCENT CODE 4-8/8-4

Mean Profiles

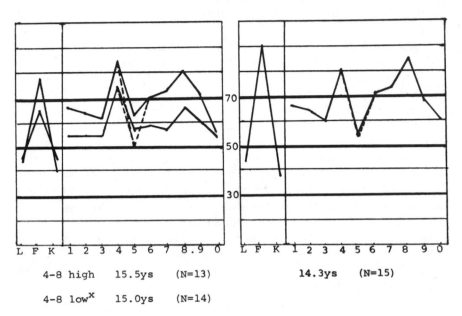

4-8 high   15.5ys   (N=13)

14.3ys   (N=15)

4-8 low^x   15.0ys   (N=14)

Personality Description

Nearly half of the 4-8/8-4 adolescents involved in this study were seen for treatment in child guidance clinics. Their symptom pattern is unmistakably one of immaturity coupled with extreme narcissism. They have only minimal motivation for treatment and thus only about 16% show any definite improvement during the course of therapy. Needless to say, the outlook for future adjustment for these adolescents is not good (9%).

As is characteristic of persons with elevations on scale 4, these adolescents employ acting-out as a defense; they also frequently use projection. They are provocative, argumentative, irritable, resentful, and flippant in both word and gesture. They undercontrol their impulses and act without sufficient thinking or deliberation. They are constantly in trouble with their parents because of excessive misbehavior. In addition, they do *not* have a resilient ego-defense system. They are self-defeating and continuously place themselves in a bad light. They experience feelings of hopelessness, are tearful and cry openly, and demand sympathy from others. At the same time, they are not open and frank about discussing their problems and show little ability to talk about conflict areas. Rather, they are evasive and attempt to handle their problems by refusing to recognize their presence. They are stereotyped and unoriginal in their approaches to problem solving as well. These 4-8/8-4 adolescents are *not* ambitious, and *not* achievement oriented; they place little or no value on intellectual or cognitive interests, activities, or skills. Not surprisingly, their grades are poor—consisting mainly of D's and F's. Their therapists use the adjectives mischievous, bossy, demanding, hostile, and selfish to describe them.

Their self-defeating attitude is also exemplified in the adjectives which they attribute to themselves. They readily admit that they are thankless, shiftless, noisy, loud, rude, nagging, fussy, and mischievous. They do *not* see themselves as adaptable. When they feel guilty, the 4-8/8-4s say they cry and experience headaches (high 4-8s do this to an even greater extent); and when they are anxious or tense, they become bored and apathetic.

As children, about one-fourth of the 4-8/8-4s felt that they were too short. As adolescents, they acknowledge that their greatest difficulties are getting into trouble, getting into fights, and losing their tempers. They also dislike being criticized by their parents and having their parents not like their friends. They start smoking at an early age (12 years) and say that their knowledge of sex comes mainly from actual experience as opposed to written material or conversation. Nearly all of the activities of the 4-8/8-4s are done with others. They especially enjoy hanging around downtown. Sixty per cent of them do *not* attend church.

The mothers of the 4-8/8-4 adolescents were *not* encouraging and, in fact, showed little interest in anything that their children did; they were strict, but by no means overprotective! Their fathers were described as cold and unfeeling; they tended to spend more time out of the home than did the fathers of other adolescents involved in this study.

In comparing the 4-8s with the 8-4s and the high 4-8s with the low 4-8s, it becomes apparent that there are some definite differences in these subgroups—with the 4-8s, perhaps, being more deviant than the 8-4s. Although the 4-8s were liked by most other students (as compared with the 8-4s who had few friends of any kind) their therapists say that their attitude is negativistic (as opposed to cooperative for the 8-4s) and that their rapport is only superficial (as opposed to friendly). Though the 8-4s tend to have more difficulty with nonacademic activities, and, perhaps, reflecting the influence of scale 8 appear more regressed (67%) than the 4-8s, the degree of disturbance for the 4-8s is judged severe in 68% of the cases. Also, while the 8-4s ideation is mainly conventional, that of the 4-8s is seen as deviant; the 4-8s think and associate in unusual ways, are unpredictable, changeable, and sometimes delusional. Their genotype, besides having obvious psychopathic features, also has schizoid, paranoid, and obsessive-compulsive ones. These people resent authority (43% have been on probation or held in detention or both).[6] They describe themselves as defensive yet understanding and, interestingly, they view laziness as their biggest obstacle in life! Therapists describe them as aloof, dissatisfied, and distrustful. The 8-4s,

---

[6] As compared to Hathaway and Monachesi (1953) who found a 33% delinquency rate among those adolescents with both high-points from among scales 4, 8, or 9.

in contrast, are easier to talk to and to get along with, are more reliable informants, and have more of a capacity for forming close interpersonal relationships. They also tend to use identification as a defense. They present a more favorable prognosis. They complain about not having a regular allowance, about being picked on, and about feeling that no one likes them; they wish others would like them better. The 8-4 adolescents see themselves as enthusiastic, yet dull.

Adolescents with low 4-8 profiles were referred for treatment because they lied excessively and because they were mischievous and provocative. They come from homes where their mothers are the disciplinarians and where the income has been *very* irregular throughout the years. Their attitude toward their sibs is one of indifference. Psychotherapists describe these adolescents as bossy, irritable, egotistical, selfish and self-centered, while they see themselves as adventurous, cooperative, and organized. When they feel guilty, they say they experience heart palpatations as well as headaches; when they get angry, they shout. The high 4-8s, in comparison, come from homes where the fathers, who are seen as critical and tense, make all the major decisions. The high 4-8s say that they are also genuinely fond of their brothers and sisters. They see being treated like a child as their main problem. These anxious, mildly depressed adolescents report difficulty in going to sleep. They are often seen in therapy as often as three times a week. They attribute the adjectives hard-headed, foolish, and prejudiced as well as loud, noisy, and rude, to themselves.

The 4-8/8-4s do *not* appear to be a "heavy" drug using group. Of the 15 adolescents who comprised the 1970-73 sample, 8 had taken *no* drugs either for pleasure or in suicide attempts. The 7 who had tried them were not chronic users, nor had they experimented widely. Four of the "users" also admitted to drinking alcohol and 2 to smoking marijuana. One had tried LSD once and 1 had taken phenobarbital once. There was one instance of an overdose, this with Darvon. The only other pharmacological agents mentioned in the case summaries of the 4-8/8-4 teenagers were Sominex, vitamins, and a single "unknown"—all were overdoses taken in suicide attempts. These adolescents had problems of all sorts. Their family lives were chaotic. The parents typically drank heavily, argued incessantly, fought openly, deserted or eventually divorced. The children acted-out violently and "explosively," getting into fights at school which led to expulsion, stealing, and running away. They often cried, reported tenseness, insomnia, and were anorexic. Other less frequent symptoms included encopresis, enuresis, hyperkineses, Hodgkin's disease, hyperventilation, and phobias. Many of these teenagers "hated" school; several were borderline retarded, had "minimal brain dysfunction," various learning disabilities, and were enrolled in special classes. This appeared to be one of the most "miserable" and unhappy groups of adolescents we studied.

ADOLESCENT CODE 4-9/9-4

Mean Profiles

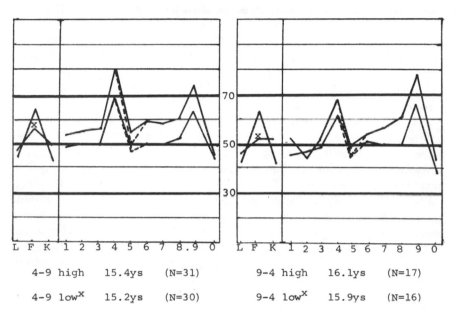

4-9 high	15.4ys	(N=31)	
4-9 low[x]	15.2ys	(N=30)	
9-4 high	16.1ys	(N=17)	
9-4 low[x]	15.9ys	(N=16)	

Personality Description

Invariably, the 4-9/9-4 adolescent is referred for treatment because he is defiant, disobedient, impulsive, provocative, mischievous, and truant from school. The 4-9 (but not the 9-4) is also likely to be a run-away, to lie, and to be difficult to control. There is, in most cases, constant conflict with the parents over misbehavior. Rarely, if ever, is there any physical system involvement in adolescents with this profile; when there is somatic concern expressed, it is more likely to come from the 9-4 than the 4-9. While adolescents with highly elevated 4-9 profiles tend to be negativistic, those with lower profiles are seen as more dreamy and more likely to fantasize excessively.

Fewer of the 4-9/9-4s than other adolescents were raised in their natural homes; 17% say they grew up in foster or adoptive homes and 20% do not now reside with their parents. Their mothers were frequently neglecting and drank more than the mothers of other adolescents involved in the study. Although their fathers were generally the disciplinarians, these patients tended to show little fear of them. As children, few 4-9/9-4s were passive or inactive; often, they were known as "roughnecks." In school, they had many friends and were well-liked. Outside of school, they seemed to succeed in just about everything they did. They were involved in outdoor hobbies and extracurricular activities. The 4-9s liked parties and movies as well.

As adolescents, riding around in cars has become one of the major activities of the 4-9/9-4s. A fourth of them have remained active in school activities. Most often, they do things with others and rarely do they do anything alone. They date at an early age and frequently. It is apparent that their main personal values include friends and sex. About one-half of these teen-agers have been in trouble with the law and have either been put on probation or placed in detention.[7] Although they will acknowledge their troubles by blaming themselves, they deviate from other disturbed adolescents in that they do *not* typically express feelings of inferiority or inadequacy. They do *not* manifest any anxiety in any discernable way. Their memories are intact, their intellectual functioning is *not* impaired, and their emotional tone is *not* depressed.

It is not surprising, then, to find that their chief mechanism of defense is acting-out (93%). The 9-4s will rationalize more than 4-9s and neither type will evidence compulsive behavior, regression or repression. The 4-9s are often seen in therapy twice a week and both 4-9s and 9-4s are likely to become involved in treatment with their families.

Psychotherapists agree that the most descriptive adjectives that can be applied to 4-9/9-4 adolescents are assertive, daring, bossy, energetic, hard-headed, hasty, impatient, impulsive, good-natured, pleasure-seeking, self-seeking, and reckless; they undercontrol their impulses and act without sufficient deliberation. The 4-9s are also described as argumentative, quarrelsome, boastful, deceitful, demanding, enterprising, irresponsible, mischievous, noisy, opportunistic, and shrewd. High 4-9s are wittier than low 4-9s; those with lower profiles are seen as more affected. Adolescents with low 9-4 profiles, are viewed as curious.

Therapists believe that 4-9/9-4s are basically insecure*, resent authority figures, and have impulses to derogate them. They are socially extroverted and excitable, and have a fast personal tempo. They emphasize oral pleasures, are narcissistic, egocentric, self-centered, selfish, and demanding. They have exaggerated needs for affection and value wealth and material possessions—judging others in terms of these things. The 4-9s, in contrast to the 9-4s, are more vulnerable to threat and more likely *to appear* depressed. The 9-4s, on the other hand, need to think of themselves as unusually self-sufficient and have greater achievement needs. Those youth with elevated 4-9 profiles tend to arouse liking in others, are cheerful, poised, socially at ease, and get along well in the world as it is. Low 4-9s are more likely to be delusional and to show hysteroid trends. The elevated 9-4s are more unpredictable, changeable, refuse to recognize the presence of conflicts, complain of weakness and easy fatigability, have feelings of hopelessness, and have difficulty going to sleep; those with low 9-4 profiles are more likely to appear symptom-free and healthy and to make better use of their defenses.

When 4-9/9-4 adolescents describe themselves, they say basically the same things that their therapists do. That is, that they are active, adventurous, alert, ambitious, argumentative, daring, energetic, enthusiastic, good-natured, hard-

---

[7] As compared to Hathaway and Monachesi (1953) who found a 33% delinquency rate among those adolescents with both high-points from among scales 4, 8, or 9.

headed, healthy, humorous, jolly, logical, realistic, sociable, steady, and warm. It is the 9-4s who are most likely to be ambitious; they are also likely to be more friendly than the 4-9s. It is the 4-9s who are more rebellious, reckless, enthusiastic, and, by their own admission, lazy.

During their early childhood, the 4-9/9-4s say that excessive lying was their worst problem. The 4-9s say that they were "difficult children." They were *not* bothered by many of the problems that seemed to trouble other children; that is, they had no difficulty with being teased or making and keeping friends. Those with low 9-4 profiles describe their parents as warm and say that they felt calm while in their presence. Those with low 4-9 profiles, felt secure with their mothers.

As adolescents, the 4-9/9-4s say that they enjoy going to parties and concerts and riding around in cars. Typically, they do not enjoy school; reasons for failure include lack of interest and dislike of the subjects being taught. Eighty per cent of the adolescents with this profile smoke and about 60% also claim to drink alcoholic beverages. Over one-third of these patients report that they gained their knowledge of sex first hand; that is, from actual experience as opposed to printed matter or conversation. Many 4-9/9-4s want to get a job immediately after they finish high school and only about 7% think that they might like to go to a 4-year college. They consider "lack of pull" with the right people the greatest obstacle they need to overcome in life.

When asked what problems are troubling them now, the 4-9/9-4s reply that their parents do not like their friends. When they feel sad, they say that they experience boredom. They do *not* experience psychophysiological distress (*e.g.,* dry mouth, pounding heart, shortness of breath). There does not appear to be any particular symptom that these adolescents develop when they feel tense, anxious, or guilty, although high 4-9s experience "loss of interest" when they feel guilty. When they are angry, however, adolescents with this profile admit to speaking out and arguing verbally.

As expected, these adolescents were prolific drug users, although they were somewhat selective about what they ingested! Of the 18 4-9/9-4s in the 1970-73 sample, only 7 (39%) had *no* known drug history. The only drugs used, however, were marijuana, amphetamines, and Sopors. Nine of the 11 "users" smoked marijuana. The same 9 had used "speed" and had tried Sopors. There was an isolated instance of barbiturate use. It should also be noted that 9 of these teenagers used some "other" (unspecified) drug at one time or another. Only one instance of ingestion might possibly have been a suicide attempt—these young people apparently wanted to live! Eighty-three per cent of the 4-9/9-4s were chronically truant from school, had run away from home, and eventually went AWOL from the hospital—frequently they did all three. They were "problem children" who had long histories of lying, stealing, extortion, breaking and entering, and sexually acting-out. They were raped, molested by fathers or step-fathers, and often described as provocative, seductive, and handsome. They were the "disobedient beauties!"

ADOLESCENT CODE 4-0/0-4

Mean Profiles

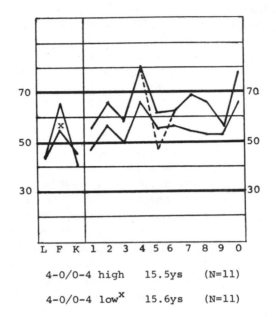

4-0/0-4 high   15.5ys   (N=11)

4-0/0-4 low^x   15.6ys   (N=11)

Personality Description

Interestingly, many of the descriptors of the 4-0/0-4 adolescents seem more related to scale 6 than to either scale 4 or scale 0. That is, 4-0/0-4s are suspicious (64%); their therapists describe them as questioning of the motivations of others and distrustful of people in general. High 4-0/0-4s frequently express grandiose ideas, the extreme being delusions of grandeur. The main defense of the 4-0/0-4s is projection (86%). It seems quite likely that scale 0 is operating here as a subtle indicator of paranoid tendencies!

In keeping with their scale 4 elevations, these adolescents are prone toward acting out*. They are resentful*, argumentative, and typically have impulses to derogate authority figures*. They see themselves as irresponsible. They do *not* see themselves as cheerful, friendly, kind, warm, patient, rational, or responsible. They say that they experience boredom when they feel sad or depressed.

In accord with the scale 0 elevation is their self-acclaimed shyness. The 4-0/0-4s say that they are neither friendly nor sociable. Their therapists add that they are *not* very talkative, are passively resistant, and tend *not* to become involved in many activities. Although those with elevated profiles seem to have more of a need to affiliate with others, their therapists feel that none of the 4-0/0-4s have exaggerated needs for affection. At the same time, however, these adolescents claim that one of the things that troubles them most is their slowness in making friends. They tend to have only a few rather close friends. Nevertheless, they see peers as the most influential figures in their lives (64%). The low 4-0/0-4s, in addition, describe their therapists as influential.

As children, the 4-0/0-4s were often afraid of their fathers whom they describe as critical and *not* relaxed. Their mothers were seen as bossy. Interestingly, all of low 4-0/0-4s live with their natural mothers, 64% of whom have high school educations. The high 4-0/0-4s were not particularly close to either parent. Typically, the 4-0/0-4 adolescents had little association with their sisters. They do *not* enjoy school activities and give "lack of interest" as their excuse for failure.

One hundred per cent of the low 4-0/0-4s express feelings of doubt to their therapists. They are more perfectionistic and meticulous than are the high 4-0/0-4s and they appear to have greater achievement needs. They also tend to be more serious and to anticipate problems and difficulties to a greater extent. They see themselves as gentle. They say that they get tired when they feel guilty. Though the low 4-0/0-4s present a more favorable prognosis, it is the high 4-0/0-4s who are judged to have moderate ego strength. They tend to be overanxious and to react to minor matters as though they were actual emergencies.

ADOLESCENT CODE 5-6/6-5

Mean Profile

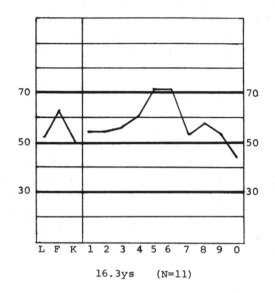

16.3ys   (N=11)

Personality Description

There is nothing distinctive in the symptomatology which leads the 5-6/6-5 adolescents to be referred for treatment. Rarely, if ever, do they present themselves as physically, organically ill. As compared with the average patient, fewer of the 5-6/6-5s lived with their natural parents, though this is not to misread that the majority of them lived outside of the home. They preferred indoor hobbies and activities. They described their fathers as strong-tempered but say that they knew in advance, almost always, what kind of disciplinary action they would take. As adolescents, they now describe their fathers' tempers as very strong. Their mothers, on the other hand, are seen as weak. The 5-6/6-5 adolescents typically have friends who are older. They date about once a week, smoke a pack of cigarettes a day, (they see this as one of their main problems), and deny that religion has had any influence at all in their upbringing (50%). They also claim to have intellectual interests to a far greater degree than do the other adolescents involved in this study.

Therapists say that the 5-6/6-5 adolescents experience *less* of a sense of isolation than does the average patient. In addition, their affect is seldom seen as shallow. Youth with this profile are inclined to acknowledge their psychological problems but hesitate to establish "deep" (or at least frequent) contacts with their therapists. The 5-6/6-5s are also seen as fearful of emotional involvement with others*. Nevertheless, these young people are easy to talk with in the therapy situation. About 36% are given a poor prognosis as compared with 12% for the entire patient sample.

The 5-6/6-5 adolescents are also judged by their therapists to value wealth and material possessions and to judge others in terms of these. Irritability is frequently noted in these teen-agers. They undercontrol their impulses and act without sufficient thinking or deliberation. Indeed, their major defense is acting-out*. They are also described as resentful*, insecure*, and having strong needs for attention*. Quite *uncharacteristic* of these patients is the occurrence of phobias. Nor are they perceived as being especially responsive to the evaluations of others. They do *not* anticipate problems and difficulties. Their therapists are not inclined to view them as apathetic, stereotyped, or their thinking as unoriginal or delusional.

The 5-6/6-5 adolescents characterize themselves as self-controlled, self-denying, reasonable, alert and uninsightful.

The 5-6/6-5 adolescents who did use drugs, used almost every one on our list. While 4 of the 10 teenagers in the 1970-73 sample had no known drug history, the 6 who did had used a variety of agents. Drugs in the narcotic category included heroin, morphine, codeine, and one "unknown." Among the hallucinogens, mescaline, psilocybin, LSD, hashish, and marijuana were all used. Amphetamines, cocaine, barbiturates, alcohol, and Sopors were the "uppers" and "downers" listed in the case summaries. Tranquilizers were also employed—specifically, Librium, Valium, Miltown, and Equinal. Finally, glue and gasoline were the inhalants of choice. There was one specified "other." This further appeared to be a very violent personality type. Young people with the 5-6/6-5 code were arrested for such offenses as assault and battery and assault with a deadly weapon. There was some preoccupation with knives, several adolescents threatening to stab their parents and several actually stabbing themselves. Death, murder, and brutality were predominant themes. These teenagers were sometimes suicidal and seemingly, sometimes homicidal! The majority had been in trouble with the law and were not in school, either because they had been suspended, expelled, or had dropped out. Not one of the 5-6/6-5s was black.

ADOLESCENT CODE 5-9/9-5

Mean Profiles

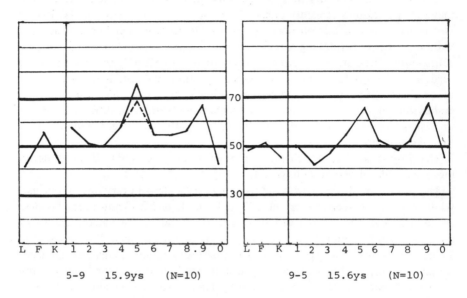

5-9   15.9ys   (N=10)   9-5   15.6ys   (N=10)

Personality Description

The 5-9/9-5 adolescents are generally peaceable, rational, and ambitious. They value wealth and material possessions and judge others in these terms. Their therapists see them as serious young people who tend to anticipate problems and difficulties. They are *not* particularly unpredictable or changeable, nor do they avoid situations where their own performance is likely to be inferior to that of others. Further, they do *not* present themselves as physically or organically sick*, they are not hypochondriacal, and rarely are they delusional*. In sum, they get along fairly well in the world as it is, at least more so than the other adolescents involved in this study, and their degree of disturbance is judged to be only mild to moderate.

The 5-9 adolescents tend to be nervous and tense in manner; they tremble, sweat, and show other signs of anxiety. Their essential defense is rationalization. The 9-5s, on the other hand, handle anxiety by refusing to recognize its presence. They fear loss of control and cannot "let go," even when it would be appropriate for them to do so. In addition, they are stereotyped and unoriginal in their approaches to solving problems.

When the 5-9/9-5 teen-agers describe themselves, they say that they are fair-minded, good-natured, and interested in many different things. They all (100%) indicate that parties and concerts are two of their favorite leisure time activities. The 9-5s believe that they are quick and mannerly while the 5-9s view themselves as talkative (80%) and intelligent (90%). The 5-9/9-5s do *not* see themselves as either restless or self-seeking. They do *not* complain of weakness or fatigue, nor do they report difficulty in going to sleep.

Psychotherapists indicate emotional dependency and self-assertion* as areas of conflict for adolescents presenting the 5-9/9-5 profile. About one-third of these young people report that during their childhood they lived alone with their mothers. And the 9-5s further report that they formed quite close relationships with their parents. Although, in the judgment of their therapists most things came easily for both 5-9 and 9-5 adolescents as children, those with 9-5 profiles had more difficulty outside of school.

Out of the 16 5-9/9-5s who made up the 1970-73 sample, only 7 (44%) were *not* involved with drugs. The most frequently used agent was cannabis—marijuana and hashish—with 9 of the 11 "users" reporting that they smoked "dope." Five also had alcohol histories and 4 reported experimentation with LSD. Other drugs which appeared in the case summaries were opium, unidentified hallucinogens, amphetamines, cocaine, Sopors, "downers," Valium, unidentified tranquilizers, postoperative medications, No-Doz, "pain pills," and aspirin. There were 2 instances of overdose—both with tranquilizers. The adolescents who presented this profile were indeed unique. Unlike almost all other disturbed teenagers, they did well in school! Of the 16 in the group, 9 stated that they got "A's" and "B's" or that they could if they applied themselves. None of them had been suspended or expelled and only 1 had dropped out of school, although several reported being truant. This appeared to be a high-aspiration and aesthetic-interest group. Several were interested in music, one drew extensively and hoped to become an architect, another was an Eagle Scout who was active in service clubs. The 5-9/9-5s reported that they got along well with their peers and had many friends. Nevertheless, they were characterized by their parents as unmanagable and rebellious. They exhibited such undesirable behaviors as lying, stealing, breaking and entering, vandalism, receiving stolen goods, traffic violations, "dealing" in drugs, and running away from home. Only 2 of these teenagers had parents who were divorced.

ADOLESCENT CODE 5-0/0-5

Mean Profile

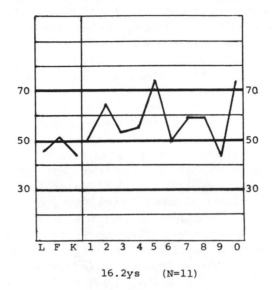

16.2ys   (N=11)

Personality Description

There are no uniquely characteristic referral reasons for the 5-0/0-5 adolescents; however, they tend *not* to be referred because they are runaways or because they are defiant or disobedient. Also, the court typically is *not* a referral source.[8] The 5-0/0-5s describe their fathers as warm and passive; they characterize their tempers as mild. Their mothers, who are seen as sympathetic, consistent, and affectionate, tend to be older (45 to 49) than the mothers of other adolescents involved in this study. Seemingly, the 5-0/0-5s come from homes where they are equally close to both parents and where, at least occasionally, they discuss their personal problems with them.

The 5-0/0-5 adolescents' attitudes toward school are mixed. They do *not* like class subjects, but do enjoy other aspects of school. Yet, at the same time, psychotherapists perceive them as having intellectual interests. Over one-third of the 5-0/0-5s, in addition, say that their teachers are of superior ability. Thirty-six per cent are involved in special programs, such as treatment schools for emotionally disturbed children, or schools attached to institutions where they are receiving residential treatment.

Nearly three-quarters of the 5-0/0-5s report having had difficulty keeping

---

[8] As compared to Hathaway and Monachesi (1953) who found a 17% delinquency rate if one high-point was among scales 2, 5, or 0.

friends as children. They now see their awkwardness in meeting people (64%) and their slowness in making friends (82%) as their main problems. Perhaps strangely, then, they do not view friends as an important personal value. In describing themselves, they say that they are awkward, shy, timid, inhibited, cautious, submissive, obliging, and moderate. They also attribute the adjectives opinionated, logical, idealistic, boastful, sulky, and pessimistic to themselves.

Psychotherapists feel that their 5-0/0-5 teen-agers manifest severe anxiety. Nevertheless, they are generally optimistic about prognosis. They view these adolescents as serious people who tend to anticipate problems and difficulties and describe them as cautious, conservative, conventional, dependable, and *not* irresponsible. They are also considered to be reliable informants. In addition, the 5-0/0-5s have considerable diagnostic insight into the descriptive features of their own behavior; they do *not* use denial as a defense. Being shy, anxious, and inhibited, they are afraid of emotional involvement with others*, while at the same time they exhibit great needs for attention*. They are also conflicted about sexuality* and about asserting themselves aggressively. Unlike many of the other adolescents involved in this study, the 5-0/0-5s do *not* act-out. They are *not* provocative, flippant, unpredictable, or changeable in behavior or attitudes. Neither are they excitable, impulsive or histrionic, but rather quiet and civilized. They do *not* have a particularly fast personal tempo. The 5-0/0-5s do tend toward overcontrol of their impulses. They are ruminative, overideational (like yon Cassius, they think too much!), perfectionistic, and compulsively meticulous. Their memories are intact. Finally, the 5-0/0-5s do tend to think and associate in unusual ways; that is, they have unconventional thought processes. They also tend to spend more time than the average adolescent patient in personal fantasy and in daydreaming.

ADOLESCENT CODE 6-8/8-6

Mean Profiles

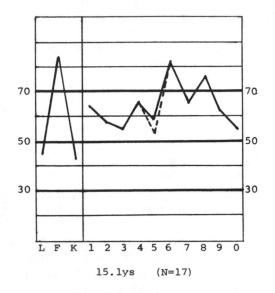

15.1ys   (N=17)

Personality Description

Given the elevations on scales 6 and 8, it is hardly surprising that one of the main reasons for referral of these adolescents is bizarre behavior. Excessive fantasy is another frequently encountered referral reason for the 6-8/8-6s. The family environment of these youngsters is characteristically poor. Though 40% say that they enjoy church activities in their leisure time, there is typically *no* religion whatsoever in the home. As a form of discipline, the 6-8/8-6s were spanked and nearly half were severely thrashed. In addition, the parents quarrelled at least once a week. Sixty per cent of their fathers had been in trouble with the law for either major or minor offenses. Despite this adversity, these adolescents describe their fathers as active and their mothers as relaxed. The 6-8/8-6s were also moved from school to school; it is no wonder that their attitudes toward teachers were not favorable—30% report attending five or more schools in the first six grades!

The 6-8/8-6 adolescents, who are known as "roughnecks," often have violent tempers. They are liked by few students and, in fact, have few friends of any kind; any friends they might have are older. They report that even during childhood, they had difficulty in making friends—other problems were cheating and nail biting (75%). As adolescents, they say that they have difficulty studying at home. They are also afraid of failure and with apparent reason; nonacademically, most things are very difficult for these adolescents and, occasionally, there is complete failure. They are afraid of making mistakes and of picking the wrong kind of friends. They do not like being teased, picked on, or having others find fault with them. They see lack of ability as their greatest obstacle in life. They feel that no one likes them and they wish others would like them better. They also admit to losing their tempers and getting into fights. In sum, they seem to be very dissatisfied and inadequate young people who are preoccupied with their physical appearance.

When they are sad or depressed, the 6-8/8-6s report experiencing dry mouths. When anxious or tense, they become tired, they sweat, and they have difficulty getting out of bed in the morning. When they feel guilty, they experience anger (71%) along with loss of interest, loss of appetite, tiredness, shakiness, and dry mouths. And, when angry, these adolescents are quite likely to hit something (65%), throw something (59%)—or they may try to forget the whole thing. The 6-8/8-6s see themselves as weak, simple, commonplace, clear-thinking, fair-minded, enterprising, healthy, polished, loyal, responsible, trusting, and mannerly. However, they also admit to being affected, bitter, assertive, rude, nagging, cruel, foolish, restless, gloomy, reckless, disorderly, rattlebrained, quitting, selfish, superstitious, self-punishing, prejudiced, stern, and thankless. They also feel that their interests are narrow.

Psychotherapists consider these adolescents to be of below average appearance. They are generally *not* well-groomed and, in fact, are described as awkward and disorderly. They are by no means poised, self-assured, or socially at ease. Their objective mood is one of moderate depression. They are not clever and, in fact, they evidence intellectual impairment. They also exhibit poor heterosexual adjustment. The feelings most often expressed by the 6-8/8-6s are guilt (76%) and shame (53%). The goal of treatment is frequently seen as situational adjustment—that is, improving the current life situations. Unlike the average patient, the 6-8/8-6 adolescents are typically *not* seen for treatment on a once a week basis.

The 6-8/8-6 adolescents are frequently delusional; they have grandiose ideas (the extreme being delusions of grandeur) and are generally dreamy. Fears and phobias are also manifested. These young people are tearful and cry openly. They do *not* fear loss of control—in fact, they use acting-out as a defense*. In addition, they are changeable and unpredictable as well as distractable and confused. Though they are, according to their therapists, typically forgiving and obliging, they have no apparent need to see themselves as particularly self sufficient.

Adolescents who present the 6-8/8-6 profile do use drugs, many times in connection with suicide attempts. Ten of the 19 in the 1970-73 sample (of whom as many as 8 were black!) had drug histories—five had overdosed with intent to take their lives. These attempts were made with barbiturates, Valium, phenothiazines, and two "unknowns." Drugs used for pleasure by the 6-8/8-6 group included marijuana, LSD, "uppers," Sopors, alcohol, gasoline, glue, and two unidentified substances. These teenagers were described as "paranoid" and, for the most part, were blatantly psychotic. They evidenced delusions of grandeur, feelings of persecution, hallucinations, and outbursts of hostility and violence. They were reported to stare and exhibited incoherent speech, bizarre rocking, thrashing, and head shaking. Additionally, these young people were said to be very dull intellectually; they typically were borderline retarded or "slow learners" who could "not survive" academically. Many had histories of head trauma and subsequent brain damage along with a variety of somatic complaints. These adolescents, who tended to be neither only nor oldest children, were said to have had absolutely no insight into their problems.

ADOLESCENT CODE 7-8/8-7

Mean Profiles

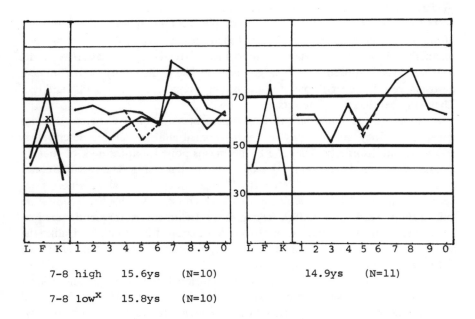

7-8 high	15.6ys	(N=10)
7-8 low^x	15.8ys	(N=10)

14.9ys	(N=11)

Personality Description

Ninety-five per cent of the 7-8/8-7 adolescents involved in this study reside with one or both natural parents. They view their mothers as warm, consistent, strong, yet lenient, and their moral judgements in regard to behavior are frequently anticipated by their children. Three-fourths of the 7-8/8-7s say that they feel secure when they are with their mothers and all of the low 7-8s, in addition, say that they feel warm. The 8-7s, more than the 7-8s, claim to be closer to their mothers than to any other family member. Their fathers are older (50-59) and the 7-8/8-7s typically have one sister. Religion is viewed as having some importance in the upbringing of these adolescents.

As children, the 7-8/8-7s report having had difficulty in making friends. They also say that they were both liars and cheaters. The low 7-8s were, in addition, bedwetters. As adolescents, the 7-8/8-7s admit that they are careless and that they pick the wrong kind of friends. They appear afraid of failure in school and, in fact, half of them are at least one grade behind. The 8-7s blame their difficulty on the family situation, saying that it is impossible to study in the home. The 7-8s (highs and lows) are afraid of the future and what it may hold in store for them. The low 7-8s are worried about their not being good-looking. All 7-8s are, in general, liked by some students and disliked by others; and friends are the main personal value of 100% of the high 7-8s.

When the 7-8/8-7 adolescents feel tense or anxious, they report difficulty in getting out of bed in the morning. When they feel guilty, they have difficulty concentrating and experience dry mouths. When they are angry, they say they speak out, although the low 7-8s say that they become silent. And when they are sad or depressed, the 7-8s also report having difficulty in concentrating. The 7-8/8-7 teen-agers describe themselves as careless, opportunistic, simple, and gentle. The 7-8s, in addition, see themselves as more confident and daring than do the 8-7s. And the low 7-8s view themselves as more hard-headed, yet friendly, than the high 7-8s.

Psychotherapists see the affect of these 7-8/8-7 adolescents as generally inappropriate. They are worriers—vulnerable to both real and imagined threat. Being generally fearful, none are described as daring although a few are seen as sly. They are overanxious about minor matters and react to them as if they were actual emergencies. They would tend *not* to be organized or adaptive when under even minimal stress or trauma. They exhibit depression (the high 7-8s are seen as moderately depressed), are shy, anxious, and inhibited. They are conflicted about emotional dependency* and are afraid of emotional involvement with others. Despite the elevation on scale 7, these young people do not differ significantly from the base rate on obsessive-compulsive features. The 7-8/8-7 genotype also lacks psychopathic features. These adolescents are *not* flippant in word and gesture although they do tend to undercontrol their impulses*. They do *not* have a resilient ego-defense system. They are *not* self-assured, poised, or socially at ease. Neither are they mannerly (0%). Rather, they are basically insecure, have great needs for attention*, and yet seem incapable of expressing their emotions in any adaptive or modulated way. None of these youth are seen as either capable or pleasant. They use rationalization as a defense.

When comparing the 7-8s to the 8-7s, it becomes evident that those adolescents with 7-8 profiles are more critical and skeptical. They are not easily impressed and, in fact, take any opportunity to resist or derogate authority figures. At the same time, psychotherapists see them as more serious young people who tend to anticipate problems and difficulties. The goal of therapy for the 7-8 adolescents is one of finding insights and effecting personality change. Improvement is generally slight. The 8-7 adolescents, on the other hand, are more hysteroid and hypochondriacal in nature. They appear to get appreciable secondary gain from their symptoms. They use regression as a defense, are frequently tearful and cry openly. However, they are more helpful and cooperative as well as more pleasant, mannerly and forgiving than the 7-8s.

Those 7-8 adolescents with elevated profiles react to frustration by punishing themselves. At the same time, they exhibit evidence of narcissism. They are more serious and overanxious about minor matters and tend to anticipate troubles to a greater degree than do the low 7-8s. They are also more critical, evasive, and report more difficulty concentrating.

Ten of the 1970-73 sample of 17 7-8/8-7 adolescents were non-drug users. Those who did have drug histories had tried a variety of agents. Opium, Talwin, cannabis, LSD, mescaline, amphetamines, barbiturates, alcohol, Sopors, Librium, Valium, gasoline, aspirin, and several "unknowns" were all mentioned. For 3 youngsters their encounter with drugs resulted in overdoses which were considered suicide attempts. For adults, scale 7 is sometimes believed to be a suppressor of scale 8; that is, the more similar the elevations of these two scales, the more "intact" the individual—even though in acute subjective distress. This does *not* appear to be the case with adolescents. Many of the teenagers in this 7-8/8-7 group evidenced very deviant thought and behavior. Forty-seven per cent experienced auditory and/or visual hallucinations. Several were quite violent, stabbing other students at school. Their anger was sometimes turned inward, with several stabbing themselves or driving their car over a cliff or into a tree. The 7-8/8-7s were plagued with nightmares, preoccupied with death, and enamoured by religion, witches, and demons. Many reported headaches, dizzy spells, black outs, etc. Four were diagnosed "catatonic," being withdrawn, uncommunicative, and exhibiting "autistic" rocking. Nine of these young people had family members who either were mentally ill or had been under extensive psychiatric care.

ADOLESCENT CODE 7-9/9-7

Mean Profiles

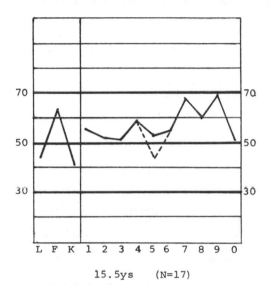

15.5ys   (N=17)

Personality Description

The 7-9/9-7 adolescent code type is enigmatic in that there are few nontest correlates uniquely distinctive to it. For example, there are no characteristic referral reasons for these adolescents. The 7-9/9-7s have affectionate relationships with their fathers and only about 5% see their fathers as the person in their families to whom they are *least* close. Even as children, these fathers were seen as *very* affectionate. They are further described as weak and *not* tense. Although openly expressed resentment toward brothers is reported in only 30% of the cases, this figure significantly exceeds the base rate. Typically, the 7-9/9-7s were punished by being told not to do something again. Fifty-three per cent of these teen-agers are a grade behind in school; they say that the reason for their failure is that they are disliked by their teachers. They enjoy "hanging around" downtown in their leisure time (65%). Unlike many of the other adolescents involved in this study, the 7-9/9-7s do *not* complain about their appearance.

When tense or anxious, the 7-9/9-7s say that they become tired and when they are angry, they say that they speak out (in contrast to the 7-0/0-7s who withdraw when they are angry). They characterize themselves as alert, clever, efficient, easy-going, wholesome, and out-going. They also say that they are sophisticated and moderate as well as cautious and dependent.

Psychotherapists describe only about 12% of the 7-9/9-7 adolescents as mildly elated; this is somewhat surprising in view of the scale 9 elevation. The 7-9/9-7 adolescents are characterized by their therapists as worrying (77%), and vulnerable to threat—either real or imagined*. They are basically insecure and express strong needs for attention*. At the same time, they are conflicted over emotional dependency. However, they are *not* seen as having exaggerated needs for affection. These young people fear loss of control; they have difficulty "letting go"—even when it would be appropriate for them to do so. They are sensitive to anything that may be construed to be a demand* and are defensive about admitting psychological problems. Although this genotype does have psychopathic features, the 7-9/9-7 adolescents are no more resentful than is the average patient. They do *not* undervalue or derogate members of the opposite sex. But they do rationalize. They are generally *not* tearful and do not cry openly. Their therapists see them as conventional.

ADOLESCENT CODE 7-0/0-7

Mean Profiles

15.4ys   (N=11)

Personality Description

Two reasons for referral for treatment characteristic of the 7-0/0-7 adolescents are their shyness and their extreme sensitivity. They are also referred for unique reasons ranging from hallucinations, thumb-sucking, and auto theft to kidnapping! Although 65% are referred because they are defiant and disobedient, this figure is significantly less than the base rate for all adolescents involved in the study. Over one-third of the 7-0/0-7s are seen for therapy in community mental health centers.

There are known cases of mental disturbance in 44% of these adolescents' families. In describing their parents, the 7-0/0-7s say only that their mothers were strict disciplinarians. During childhood, they did not seem to have much difficulty in accomplishing the things they set out to do. As teen-agers, they have some difficulty, though occasional failures occur in only about 44% of the group. Therapists claim that these adolescents have intellectual interests; they appear interested in their class subjects, but show little interest or involvement in other aspects of school. Their behavior at school is about average, they get into trouble no more frequently than do the other students.

When the 7-0/0-7s describe themselves, they say that they are practical, obliging, yet awkward. They also say that they wander off by themselves when they become angry (82%).

Psychotherapists like these 7-0/0-7s more than the average adolescent; they say that they tend to arouse feelings of liking and acceptance in others as well. They believe that these adolescents have considerable "diagnostic" awareness into the descriptive features of their behavior. They say that they have good cognitive-verbal insight into their own personality structures. Though seen as moderately depressed, these adolescents, nevertheless, exhibit appropriate affect. Their ego strength is described as moderate. They are reliable informants with at least moderate motivation for treatment and, consequently, the prognosis is good.

It makes theoretical sense, given the nature of scale 7, that reaction-formation is a defense attributed to the 7-0/0-7s by their therapists. Seventy-three per cent also employ isolation as a defense. They tend to be intropunitive in their reactions to frustration—they share a proclivity for blaming and punishing themselves rather than others. They also tend toward overcontrol. It is very difficult for them to "let go" even when it would be appropriate for them to do so. They are, in general, serious young people who are given to anticipating problems and difficulties (they cross bridges before there are bridges to cross). In addition, they have a need to strive to do something as well as they possibly can. The 7-0/0-7s have high achievement needs.

The 7-0/0-7 adolescents are basically insecure and have great needs for attention*. At the same time, they are conflicted about emotional dependency* and about self-assertion. They are described by their therapists as adaptable, cooperative, obliging, sincere, peaceable, thoughtful, clear-minded, fair-minded, and rational. They are also viewed as slow, dependent, easy-going, self-controlled, and inhibited.

ADOLESCENT CODE 8-9/9-8

Mean Profiles

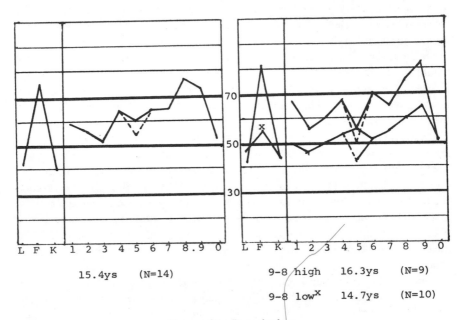

15.4ys   (N=14)

9-8 high   16.3ys   (N=9)

9-8 low^x   14.7ys   (N=10)

Personality Description

Though there are no uniquely characteristic referral reasons for the 8-9/9-8 adolescent type, there are some *unlikely* referral reasons. That is, these adolescents are *not* seen for treatment because they have poor peer or sib relations or because they have difficulty concentrating. The 9-8s, more than the 8-9s, are referred because of their impulsiveness and the high 9-8s, more than the low 9-8s, are referred because they are worried.

Few of these teen-agers describe their mothers as critical. In fact, the 8-9/9-8s say that they are closer to their mothers than to any other family member. Their fathers are *not* indifferent to them, although they are characterized as lenient. The low 9-8s, more than the high 9-8s, view their fathers as encouraging. While the fathers of the 8-9s appeared interested in almost everything that their children did, those of the high 9-8s paid little attention to anything their children were involved in. The fathers of the 9-8s were, in addition, very unpredictable in their moral judgements. In the families of the 9-8 adolescents, the father was responsible for the major decisions and the children felt free to disagree with their parents. Now, the 8-9s tend to get along well with their parents and are rarely in trouble with them (64%); also, their brothers are among their closest associates. These young people, too, seem more interested in school than do the 9-8s—who dislike nearly all aspects of school. Any school failure is attributed to lack of interest. Only 67% of the 8-9/9-8s see acquiring knowledge as their main goal in life.

The 8-9/9-8 adolescents claim many friends. As children, these were often older boys. For 63% of the 9-8s, friends remained older throughout adolescence. It is not surprising to find that friends are an important personal value of these young people.

The 9-8s view disobedience as having been their main problem during early childhood. As teen-agers, the only difficulties characteristic of the 8-9/9-8 group are being afraid of making mistakes (for the high 9-8s) and not being good looking (for the 8-9s). These adolescents consider themselves to be hasty, reckless, hurried, loud, and sly. The high 9-8s, in contrast to the low 9-8s, see themselves as strong, unselfish, and self-punishing. The 8-9/9-8s experience boredom when they are tense, anxious, or when they feel guilty. When angry, they are likely to shout or to hit something.

Psychotherapists say that the 8-9/9-8 adolescents act-out*. They resent authority figures and typically have impulses to resist or derogate them (9-8s more than 8-9s). They also exhibit a great need for affiliation with others. They are *not* depressed and have *no* difficulty in going to sleep. Neither do they spend much time in personal fantasy and daydreaming. They also have little capacity for forming close personal relationships.

The 8-9s are tearful and cry openly. More than the 9-8s, these young people are shy and inhibited. They sweat, tremble, and show other manifest signs of anxiety. Their judgement is impaired. They are also self-defeating and continuously place themselves in a bad light. They are further vulnerable to threat either real or imagined. Characteristically, they are worriers. The 9-8s, on the other hand, are more demanding; they take the attitude that the world owes them a living. They judge others in terms of material possessions. They need to think of themselves as unusually self-sufficient. Their therapists describe them as clever, opportunistic, sharp-witted, resentful, reckless, and tolerant. At the same time, they appear more poised, self-assured, and socially at ease than do the 8-9s. These adolescents use intellectualization as their major defense. Interestingly, 61% of these adolescents are seen as above average in appearance.

In comparing the high 9-8s with the low 9-8s, it becomes apparent that those youth with more elevated profiles are tense, nervous, and jumpy. They are seen as anxious (89%), argumentative (89%), foolish, immature, nagging, out-spoken, high-strung, and pleasure seeking. They have a rapid personal tempo—think, talk, and move at a fast pace. They are self-dramatizing and histrionic, tending to overreact to minor matters as though they were actual emergencies. They undercontrol their impulses and act without sufficient thinking or deliberation. In addition, they have exaggerated needs for affection. The high 9-8s, more than the low 9-8s, are likely to be delusional; at times they express grandiose ideas (the extreme being delusions of grandeur). The low 9-8s, on the other hand, tend to keep a "better rein" on their impulses. Their memories are intact. Though they have a few difficulties in getting along with others, they are usually able to settle them themselves. They are passively resistant and tend *not* to become involved in many things. They avoid situations where their own performance is likely to be inferior to that of others. The low 9-8s do have difficulty in asserting themselves and are conflicted about becoming emotionally dependent. Yet, their defenses are fairly adequate in relieving their psychological distress. These adolescents tend to be involved in individual therapy more often than those with elevated 9-8 profiles.

Eight of the 13 8-9/9-8 adolescents who comprised the 1970-73 sample had *no* record of drug use. The five who had used drugs had ingested an assortment, including Valium, heroin, marijuana, LSD, mescaline, amphetamines, cocaine, barbiturates, alcohol, and Sopors. Some had also inhaled glue, paint thinner, lighter fluid, typewriter fluid, and other "unknown" substances. Six of these teenagers exhibited some type of seizure disorder, hyperkinesis, dizziness, or hyperventilation symptoms. Six had fathers whom they had never seen, who had deserted the family, committed suicide, or who were chronic alcoholics. Eight of the 13 had school difficulties. The 8-9/9-8 adolescents were more likely than the other emotionally disturbed adolescents, to hallucinate, evidence visual disturbances, and be characterized as "paranoid" and "schizoid."

REFERENCE

Hathaway, S. R., and Monachesi, E. D. *Analyzing and predicting juvenile delinquency with the MMPI*. Minneapolis: University of Minnesota Press, 1953.

PART

FOUR

APPENDIXES

Appendix A. Glossary of Abbreviations and Symbols

ACL — Adjective Check List
ATA — against therapist advice
BR — base rate
Brn — brain syndrome
CDS — Case Data Schedule
C_H — correction for hypochondriasis
C — Rorschach color response
CQ — Shipley conceptual quotient
D — MMPI depression scale
ds — days
ECT — electroconvulsive therapy
F — MMPI frequency scale
Fe — female
FS — WAIS full scale
Hs — MMPI hypochondriasis scale
Hy — MMPI hysteria scale
Ip — inpatient
IQ — intelligence quotient
K — MMPI correction scale
K+ — "normal" profile code, adult psychiatric inpatients only
KUMC — Kansas University Medical Center
L — MMPI lie scale
M — Rorschach human movement response
Ma — MMPI hypomania scale
M, Me — male
Mf — MMPI masculinity-femininity scale
N — number of cases
Op — outpatient
Pa — MMPI paranoia scale
Pd — MMPI psychopathic deviate scale
PD — personality disorder
PDS — Personal Data Schedule
Per — personality disorder
PS — WAIS performance scale
Psn — psychoneurotic
Pso — psychotic
Pt — MMPI psychasthenia scale

? — MMPI cannot scale
Q — Q distribution, item, sort, or statement
Q_1 — first quartile
Q_2 — second quartile
Q_3 — third quartile
Q_4 — fourth quartile
Sc — MMPI schizophrenia scale
SES — socioeconomic status
Si — MMPI social introversion-extroversion scale
T — T score or standard score
TAT — Thematic Apperception Test
Ts — T score or standard score
VS — WAIS verbal scale
WAIS — Wechsler Adult Intelligence Scale
WISC — Wechsler Intelligence Scale for Children
ys — years
1 — MMPI hypochondriasis scale
2 — MMPI depression scale
3 — MMPI hysteria scale
4 — MMPI psychopathic deviate scale
5 — MMPI masculinity-femininity scale
6 — MMPI paranoia scale
7 — MMPI psychasthenia scale
8 — MMPI schizophrenia scale
9 — MMPI hypomania scale
0 — MMPI social introversion-extroversion scale
16PF — Sixteen Personality Factor Test
+ — fourth quarter scores, scores above the third quartile
++ — fourth quarter scores twice the BR minus Q_3 difference
+++ — fourth quarter scores three times the BR minus Q_3 difference
− — first quarter scores, scores

below the first quartile

—— — first quarter scores half the BR minus Q_1 difference

——— — first quarter scores one-third the BR minus Q_1 difference

x^2 — chi square

r — Pearson product-moment co-efficient of correlation

Σ — summation of the expression which follows

$>$ — is greater than

$\geqslant$ — is greater than or (at least) equal to

$<$ — is less than

$\leqslant$ — is less than or (at most) equal to

* — Designates "least" and "most" descriptive (though not significant) Q items.

Appendix B. Conceptual Scheme for Personality Description

There are many conceptual schemes under which personality data may be classified. Our high-point codes represent one. Another scheme we have found helpful in organizing and clarifying such data can be illustrated with the Q statements which comprise one aspect of the adult and adolescent personality descriptions. At the same time, no attempt has been made to establish the statistical reliability of descriptor membership for the various categories. (The numbers preceding the items indicate their numeric arrangement in the standard list. See Appendix D.)

I. Attitudes toward self:
- 4. Has a need to think of self as an unusually self-sufficient person
- 18. Is consciously guilt-ridden; self-condemning; self-accusatory
- 23. Judges self and others in conventional terms like "popularity," etc.
- 55. Has feeling of hopelessness
- 62. Exhibits evidence of narcissism (latent or manifest)
- 80. Emphasizes oral pleasures; is self-indulgent
- 92. Is self-defeating; places self in an obviously bad light
- 98. Is egocentric; self-centered; selfish

II. Attitudes towards others:
- 2. Demands sympathy from others
- 22. Resents authority figures and typically has impulses to resist or derogate them
- 43. Undervalues and consistently derogates the opposite sex
- 44. Is distrustful of people in general; questions their motivations
- 67. Is able to sense other person's feelings; is an intuitive, empathic person
- 68. Keeps people at a distance; avoids close interpersonal relationships
- 72. Is demanding; tends to take the attitude "the world owes me a living"
- 83. Is argumentative
- 84. Is critical; not easily impressed; skeptical
- 87. Is afraid of emotional involvement with others
- 95. Accepts others as they are; is not judgmental
- 97. Is sensitive to anything that can be construed as a demand

III. Motivational needs:
- 3. Values wealth or material possessions and judges others in terms of them
- 5. Possesses a basic insecurity and need for attention

245

6. Places value on intellectual and cognitive activities, skills, and attitudes
31. Has a high aspiration level for self; is ambitious; wants to get ahead
35. Has a need to achieve; to strive to do something as well as possible
50. Has a need to affiliate with others
65. Has an exaggerated need for affection
82. Gets appreciable "secondary gain" from symptoms

IV. Areas of conflict:
60. Has inner conflicts about self-assertion
75. Has inner conflicts about emotional dependency
85. Has inner conflicts about sexuality

V.   Mechanisms of defense:
7. Psychic conflicts are represented in somatic symptoms
12. Tends not to become involved in things; is passively resistant
14. Utilizes acting-out as a defense mechanism
17. Utilizes projection as a defense mechanism
47. Handles anxieties and conflicts by refusing to recognize their presence
64. Expresses impulses by verbal acting-out
70. Utilizes rationalization as a defense mechanism
74. Utilizes regression as a defense mechanism
76. Avoids situations where own performance will be inferior to that of others
101. Utilizes intellectualization as a defense mechanism

VI. Types of control:
A.   *Undercontrol:*
8. Overacts to danger or makes emergency responses in the absence of danger
14. Utilizes acting-out as a defense mechanism
16. Is overanxious about minor matters and reacts to them as if they were real emergencies
34. Undercontrols own impulses; acts with insufficient thinking and deliberation
64. Expresses impulses by verbal acting-out
73. Is excitable
77. Is tearful and/or cries openly
78. Is irritable
79. Is resentful
89. Is provocative

B.   *Overcontrol:*
26. Reacts to frustration intropunitively (*i.e.* punishes self)
29. Tends to avoid or delay action; fears committing self to any definite course
48. Fears loss of control; cannot "let go," even when appropriate

86. Is shy, anxious, and inhibited
91. Tends toward overcontrol of needs and impulses

C. *Inadequate control:*
1. Is vulnerable to real or fancied threat; generally fearful; is a worrier
10. Fears or phobias present
21. Has multiple neurotic manifestations
46. Is nervous; tense in manner; trembles, sweats, or shows other signs of anxiety
57. Seems unable to express own emotions in any modulated, adaptive way

D. *Tenuous control:*
24. Spends a good deal of time in personal fantasy and daydreams
45. Thinks and associates in unusual ways; has unconventional thought processes
103. Reports difficulty in thinking; cannot concentrate
104. Delusional thinking is present
106. Has grandiose ideas (extreme is delusions of grandeur)

VII. Character traits:
12. Tends not to become involved in things; is passively resistant
36. Has a rapid personal tempo; thinks, talks, moves at a fast rate
38. Is suggestable; overly responsive to other people's evaluations rather than own
39. Genotype has psychopathic features
40. Genotype has schizoid features
52. Is self-dramatizing; histrionic
59. Is socially extroverted (outgoing)
71. Genotype has obsessive-compulsive features
81. Is perfectionistic; is compulsively meticulous
88. Is readily dominated by others; is submissive
96. Genotype has paranoid features
102. Genotype has hysteroid features

VIII. Ego strengths:
25. Presents a favorable prognosis
37. Defenses are fairly adequate in relieving psychological distress
42. Is "normal," healthy, symptom-free
49. Appears to be poised, self-assured, socially at ease
51. Exhibits good heterosexual adjustment
63. Has a resilient ego-defense system; has a safe margin of integration
69. Gets along well in the world as it is; is socially appropriate in own behavior
107. Would be organized and adaptive when under stress or trauma
108. Has the capacity for forming close interpersonal relationships

IX. Accessibility:
27. Has shown ability to talk about conflicts in most areas
28. Is evasive
30. Has "diagnostic" insight; awareness of the descriptive features of own behavior
33. Is a reliable informant
41. Has good verbal-cognitive insight into own personality structure and dynamics
53. Is open and frank in discussing problems
54. Is defensive about admitting psychological conflicts

Appendix C. Adult Section

Relative Frequency of Characteristics Across Code Types*

Codes	Total	2-3-1	λ-7	2-7-4	2-7-8	2-8	3-1	3-2-1	4-6	4-6-2	4-8-2	4-9	8-3	8-6	8-9	9-6	K+
DESCRIPTIVE DATA																	
Age	N 320	N 20	N 20	N 20	N 20	N 20	N 20	N 20	N 20	N 20	N 20	N 20	N 20	N 20	N 20	N 20	N 20
Mean age (years)	39.7	45.5	48.3	33.5	41.2	41.1	47.2	45.9	36.5	37.9	32.8	27.6	38.8	42.2	33.8	34.1	43.1
Range	19:79	30:69	22:69	19:59	19:61	23:59	22:60	26:75	24:45	21:55	20:55	19:37	19:71	20:79	19:56	19:55	19:76
Type of Contact	N 300																
Inpatient	58.7†	60.0	85.0	40.0	65.0	40.0	35.0	80.0	60.0	50.0	50.0	40.0	55.0	65.0	85.0	70.0	100.0
Outpatient	41.3†	40.0	15.0	50.0	35.0	60.0	65.0	20.0	40.0	50.0	50.0	60.0	45.0	35.0	15.0	30.0	0.0
Type of Disorder	N 350	N 24	N 25	N 21	N 24	N 20	N 22	N 23	N 20	N 20	N 24	N 20	N 21	N 22	N 23	N 20	N 21
Brain	6.3	16.7	4.0		4.2	15.0	4.5	8.7						13.6	8.7		23.8
Chronic	4.0	16.7	4.0			5.0		8.7						9.1			19.0
Acute	2.3				4.2	10.0	4.5							4.5	8.7		4.8
Psychotic	45.7	29.2	36.0	19.2	58.4	70.0	13.6	34.7	55.0	10.0	70.9	15.0	47.6	68.1	69.5	85.0	47.7
Involutional	8.6	16.7	20.0	4.5	16.7	15.0	9.1	17.4	5.0	5.0	8.3		14.3	13.6	4.3	10.0	9.5
Affective	5.4	8.3	12.0	4.5	4.2	5.0		4.3					14.3		4.3	10.0	4.8
Manic	3.4		8.0	4.5	4.2						8.3						4.8
Depressive	2.0	8.3	4.0			5.0			5.0								
Schizophrenic	30.8	4.2	4.0	9.3	37.5	50.0	4.5	13.0	45.0	5.0	62.6	15.0	33.3	54.5	65.2	60.0	33.4
Paranoid	11.4	4.2							35.0		25.0	5.0	14.3	36.4	17.4	45.0	14.3
Chronic undif	8.6		4.0	4.3	33.3	20.0		4.3			16.7		19.0	9.1	21.7	10.0	9.5
Affective	6.0			4.3	4.2	25.0	4.5	8.7	10.0		4.2	5.0			8.7	5.0	
Acute undif	2.3								10.0		4.2			4.5	8.7		4.8
Catatonic	1.1										4.2						
Simple	0.9					5.0											
Hebephrenic	0.6										8.3			4.5			4.8
Paranoid State	0.9															15.0	
Psychophysiologic	0.8	20.8	56.0	9.5		10.0	27.3	21.7		10.0			9.5			5.0	
Psychoneurotic	21.2	33.3	32.0	33.3	33.3	5.0	49.9	17.3		20.0	8.4		33.3		4.3	5.0	14.3
Depressive	9.7	33.3		23.8	12.5		4.5	8.7		10.0			9.5				
Conversion	4.3		24.0	9.5		5.0	40.9	4.3					9.5			5.0	4.8
Anxiety	4.0				8.3					5.0	4.2		4.8				
Obsessive comp	2.0				12.5					5.0	4.2						
Dissociative	0.9							4.3					9.5				9.5
Phobic	0.3						4.5										

	N 5	N 5	N 5	N 5	N 5	N 5	N 5	N 5	N 5	N 5	N 5	N 5	N 5	N 5	N 6	N 81	N 5
Personality	14.4	5.0		18.1	9.5	80.0	20.8	60.0	45.0	17.3	4.5	5.0	4.2	33.3	4.0	19.3	
Pattern	4.8			13.6	9.5	5.0	4.2		15.0			5.0	4.2			3.7	
Schizoid				13.6	0.5		4.2		10.0			5.0	4.2			2.0	
Paranoid									5.0							1.1	
Cyclothymic																0.3	
Inadequate	4.8					5.0										0.3	
Trait	4.8			4.5		30.0		60.0	20.0	13.0	4.5			33.3	4.0	10.9	
Aggressive						15.0	8.3	50.0	15.0	13.0				23.8		7.4	
Unstable	4.8			4.5		15.0	8.3	10.0								2.0	
Compulsive									5.0		4.5			9.5		0.9	
Dependent		5.0														0.6	
Sociopathic	4.8					45.0									4.0	4.6	
Situational			4.3			5.0	8.3		10.0	4.3				4.8		0.9	
Q ITEM DATA																	
Mean placements‡	N 5	N 5	N 5	N 5	N 5	N 5	N 5	N 5	N 5	N 5	N 5	N 5	N 5	N 5	N 6	N 81	N 5
1	7.2	7.0	5.6	6.4	8.0	4.8	6.6	5.4	5.2	7.6	7.6	6.6	8.8	8.2	8.0	6.95	8.0
2	4.0	5.0	3.6	3.8	5.4	6.2	4.8	7.4	7.4	6.0	7.6	5.8	5.2	6.0	4.5	5.62	7.4
3	5.8	4.4	4.4	4.8	3.4	5.6	4.8	5.2	6.0	4.6	5.2	2.6	3.0	4.8	4.7	4.59	4.2
4	4.2	2.2	3.0	2.8	3.8	5.2	4.0	3.0	4.8	2.2	3.6	3.4	2.0	4.2	4.7	3.70	6.0
5	6.6	6.8	6.4	5.8	7.4	8.0	7.4	7.2	7.0	6.4	7.4	6.8	6.8	7.4	6.7	6.94	7.0
6	3.8	5.6	3.4	4.4	4.2	5.2	5.0	4.0	5.6	3.4	3.8	3.0	4.4	3.0	6.7	4.44	5.2
7	5.4	3.6	2.4	5.0	4.4	3.8	2.4	4.0	1.2	7.6	8.6	8.2	5.6	7.4	8.0	5.43	8.8
8	5.6	8.4	6.6	4.2	6.0	6.4	5.6	5.8	6.0	6.6	7.2	5.2	8.0	6.8	5.0	6.11	4.6
9	5.0	3.6	2.2	3.8	2.2	3.4	2.2	2.6	1.2	6.0	8.4	7.0	4.2	6.0	5.3	4.48	8.4
10	6.0	6.8	6.0	7.8	5.8	3.4	6.2	3.2	4.2	5.8	6.6	5.4	8.4	8.2	8.5	6.13	5.4
11	2.8	1.0	3.0	1.8	1.4	3.2	1.4	2.4	2.8	1.0	2.8	1.4	1.0	1.6	2.3	2.00	2.0
12	7.6	4.6	5.4	6.6	7.0	4.8	5.8	3.0	7.8	6.6	5.2	7.6	6.2	4.4	5.3	5.85	5.8
13	5.2	3.6	3.4	3.2	4.0	4.4	4.6	5.2	3.8	6.0	6.8	4.2	3.4	4.6	5.8	4.48	5.2
14	2.0	3.4	7.6	5.4	5.2	8.4	7.2	8.6	4.6	5.0	3.4	5.0	4.0	7.0	3.2	5.26	4.6
15	4.0	3.8	3.6	1.6	5.0	4.4	4.0	4.2	3.4	4.0	6.4	4.6	3.2	4.2	5.3	4.22	5.6
16	6.0	7.6	6.4	5.0	7.0	5.0	5.0	4.6	7.0	6.4	5.8	6.2	8.0	8.0	6.8	6.30	5.8
17	6.4	7.4	7.8	8.0	6.4	5.6	8.4	8.0	7.2	5.8	4.2	4.8	5.0	6.0	4.3	6.26	5.2
18	5.8	5.8	5.0	6.0	6.2	5.0	6.8	5.0	5.4	6.6	5.8	4.8	7.4	4.8	6.8	5.73	4.2
19	5.0	4.6	8.2	7.6	5.0	6.2	7.4	4.8	5.0	3.0	3.0	6.0	5.2	6.6	3.2	5.38	5.8
20	6.4	6.8	6.0	4.8	8.0	7.4	3.8	5.0	2.8	8.2	7.8	8.0	8.2	7.8	9.0	6.76	7.8

* Female patient data only.
† Normal K+ code excluded.
‡ Criterion descriptions only.

Q ITEM DATA *Continued*

Codes	Total	2-3-1	2-7	2-7-4	2-7-8	2-8	3-1	3-2-1	4-6	4-6-2	4-8-2	4-9	8-3	8-6	8-9	9-6	K+
21	5.37	7.4	8.0	6.8	8.6	6.4	4.0	7.0	1.4	3.2	2.8	6.0	3.6	5.6	3.4	6.6	4.6
22	5.06	5.2	2.2	5.4	4.4	5.8	3.6	5.4	7.4	7.0	6.4	7.4	3.4	6.2	5.2	4.0	2.6
23	4.52	4.6	4.0	3.6	2.6	4.2	5.0	3.4	5.4	4.4	5.2	4.4	4.2	6.0	4.6	5.6	5.2
24	5.22	3.6	4.2	2.2	6.0	4.0	2.4	5.8	4.4	3.8	6.4	3.8	6.6	8.2	8.8	6.6	7.0
25	3.47	4.8	6.8	3.8	2.4	4.2	8.2	2.0	2.6	3.8	2.8	2.6	2.8	2.0	1.6	2.4	2.0
26	6.61	7.0	8.3	5.6	6.4	6.2	4.4	7.8	5.2	3.4	7.4	5.4	7.4	5.4	6.0	6.4	6.8
27	3.85	5.4	5.5	3.0	4.4	3.4	3.4	4.0	1.4	5.2	4.0	4.6	5.0	2.0	3.8	4.0	2.2
28	5.69	5.2	3.5	6.2	4.2	6.0	4.8	4.6	9.0	5.4	5.6	5.8	7.0	6.6	6.4	5.8	5.4
29	5.47	6.2	6.2	6.8	7.2	5.6	5.6	6.6	5.0	1.4	3.8	2.4	6.4	6.8	6.2	5.0	6.2
30	3.34	5.4	6.0	2.6	4.4	3.8	3.8	2.8	2.4	2.0	2.4	3.0	3.8	1.2	2.0	2.6	4.8
31	3.96	4.0	6.3	2.2	3.0	2.2	3.8	3.0	4.2	3.0	4.2	4.8	3.8	4.2	4.4	4.6	5.2
32	6.10	4.8	7.5	7.6	6.8	7.2	5.6	6.0	5.0	5.8	3.4	6.4	5.8	5.4	6.4	8.4	5.2
33	4.91	5.6	6.7	4.6	5.2	5.4	6.8	5.0	4.2	4.8	4.4	3.6	4.4	4.0	3.6	4.6	5.4
34	5.21	5.0	3.3	7.6	4.4	4.4	4.4	4.0	6.6	8.6	5.2	8.8	3.6	3.6	5.4	5.2	3.6
35	3.90	4.0	4.8	3.4	3.2	2.4	4.2	3.6	3.4	4.0	4.2	4.2	4.0	4.6	4.8	3.6	3.8
36	3.70	2.4	2.0	3.0	3.0	1.8	3.4	3.4	4.4	3.8	3.6	7.4	2.2	4.4	5.8	3.4	5.8
37	2.37	2.6	2.8	1.8	1.4	3.0	2.6	3.2	4.6	2.8	2.2	2.4	1.0	2.0	1.4	1.4	2.6
38	4.84	6.6	4.8	3.0	4.0	4.0	5.4	5.6	4.6	4.0	3.4	5.4	5.0	3.4	6.0	5.0	7.2
39	3.32	2.0	1.5	5.8	2.2	1.4	1.2	3.2	4.8	7.6	5.2	8.0	1.2	1.6	3.2	3.4	1.2
40	5.32	2.0	3.7	4.0	7.4	2.6	1.2	7.2	4.8	3.2	7.6	2.2	7.8	7.8	9.0	6.8	8.2
41	2.69	3.0	5.0	2.4	3.2	2.2	3.8	2.4	1.6	2.6	2.0	2.0	2.6	1.8	1.6	3.6	2.8
42	1.44	1.0	1.0	1.6	1.0	1.4	1.2	1.0	2.8	2.4	1.0	1.8	1.0	1.2	1.0	1.8	2.0
43	4.51	2.6	2.8	3.0	5.0	4.2	2.6	4.6	6.0	6.4	5.8	4.8	6.2	5.6	5.6	4.0	3.2
44	6.16	3.0	4.7	4.2	7.0	7.6	3.2	6.4	6.4	7.6	8.6	5.2	6.2	7.2	8.4	7.4	6.2
45	4.81	6.2	2.2	3.2	5.8	4.4	1.0	5.8	2.8	3.0	5.8	2.4	8.6	8.8	8.2	6.0	6.6
46	6.23	6.2	7.7	8.2	8.4	6.4	5.0	6.2	5.2	6.0	4.8	5.6	5.8	5.0	5.6	7.4	6.0
47	5.27	4.8	2.7	7.6	3.8	6.6	4.2	6.0	8.4	5.0	4.8	5.6	4.4	4.8	4.2	4.6	6.0
48	4.80	3.6	6.5	5.6	5.8	7.0	4.6	4.4	3.6	3.0	4.2	2.8	5.8	4.8	4.6	5.0	6.0
49	2.46	6.6	2.3	1.8	1.4	2.6	4.6	1.8	4.0	1.2	1.6	3.0	1.8	2.6	2.4	2.0	2.6
50	3.84	6.6	4.8	4.8	3.0	1.6	4.8	3.8	3.4	5.2	2.8	5.2	4.2	2.0	2.8	3.6	2.6
51	2.79	4.6	4.5	2.0	2.2	2.8	5.0	3.6	1.6	2.0	1.8	2.0	2.2	1.8	2.4	2.6	3.2
52	5.75	6.8	3.5	6.8	4.6	5.2	6.4	3.2	6.2	8.0	6.2	8.0	6.0	5.6	4.8	6.8	4.4
53	3.94	3.8	6.0	2.2	4.2	3.8	5.0	4.6	2.0	5.2	4.0	3.2	5.0	3.0	3.4	3.4	3.8

	1	2	3	4	5	6	7	8	9	10	11	12	13	14	15	16	Mean
54	8.4	5.6	5.0	6.0	4.2	6.0	5.6	6.6	8.8	4.6	4.8	7.2	3.4	5.8	4.2	6.4	5.76
55	4.8	6.8	3.8	6.4	7.2	4.6	7.2	5.6	5.8	7.4	6.2	6.4	8.2	6.4	8.7	5.8	6.36
56	5.8	4.2	5.2	4.4	6.0	4.6	7.8	3.4	4.0	7.6	8.8	7.6	8.0	7.6	7.8	7.0	6.26
57	7.0	8.6	8.6	8.2	8.2	7.0	7.2	6.8	6.8	7.4	7.0	5.6	7.2	8.2	4.5	5.2	7.06
58	6.2	7.4	8.8	8.6	7.8	4.2	7.0	3.6	4.2	6.4	4.4	7.4	7.4	7.8	6.5	4.8	6.41
59	2.0	2.0	2.8	1.8	1.4	6.2	2.2	4.2	4.0	1.6	5.0	1.4	1.6	2.8	3.2	4.4	2.91
60	6.6	5.6	6.2	4.8	5.2	5.2	4.6	6.8	4.6	5.2	6.8	7.0	6.0	6.6	7.2	7.2	5.99
61	2.4	2.8	4.8	3.0	2.2	8.0	4.8	4.8	2.8	2.8	2.8	2.6	2.2	3.2	1.5	2.6	3.31
62	4.0	5.4	7.4	7.0	4.6	7.6	6.0	6.2	7.6	4.4	6.2	5.0	4.4	6.8	4.0	6.2	5.78
63	3.4	1.2	1.2	2.0	1.4	1.2	2.2	1.2	3.4	1.6	2.4	2.8	1.4	2.0	3.3	3.0	2.12
64	3.0	2.4	5.0	6.0	5.0	8.0	6.6	7.8	5.2	4.8	3.8	3.6	3.8	4.8	1.7	3.6	4.73
65	5.8	7.6	6.0	5.6	7.6	7.8	7.0	8.0	7.6	5.8	7.8	6.0	6.0	7.0	6.7	7.0	6.83
66	6.4	6.6	5.2	5.0	6.4	3.2	6.2	4.4	4.6	6.8	6.4	6.2	7.0	5.0	7.0	3.0	5.85
67	3.2	2.6	2.8	1.4	2.8	2.8	2.4	2.0	1.8	2.6	4.2	3.0	2.8	3.0	4.7	4.4	2.92
68	7.8	5.2	8.2	7.6	5.4	8.2	8.6	6.4	6.6	7.8	3.8	8.8	7.8	6.2	4.7	3.6	6.64
69	4.6	2.8	2.8	3.2	2.8	1.8	4.2	2.2	4.4	3.6	7.2	3.2	1.6	4.0	5.5	5.6	3.73
70	5.4	5.4	6.0	5.4	5.4	7.8	8.4	7.8	8.0	4.6	6.2	6.0	3.8	6.8	5.5	5.4	6.12
71	5.8	4.4	4.6	6.6	5.6	2.6	4.4	4.0	4.2	5.2	4.2	7.0	7.4	6.2	6.7	5.4	5.31
72	4.6	3.6	3.4	4.0	5.2	6.2	4.4	7.6	6.4	4.6	6.2	5.4	3.4	3.2	2.7	3.0	4.47
73	5.6	6.6	6.8	6.8	5.8	7.4	4.8	7.8	4.8	4.2	5.4	4.8	5.4	7.0	4.8	5.4	5.83
74	6.2	6.0	8.8	6.0	7.0	4.6	5.8	6.0	5.2	5.8	4.2	4.0	6.2	5.0	5.3	5.8	5.74
75	7.2	6.2	6.0	5.6	6.2	8.0	7.0	8.2	6.8	6.8	8.4	7.0	7.2	7.6	5.7	7.0	6.91
76	7.0	4.6	3.6	4.8	4.8	3.8	6.4	5.6	5.4	4.8	5.0	3.8	4.6	4.2	5.2	3.0	4.79
77	6.0	7.4	4.4	4.6	6.4	3.8	4.2	5.2	6.2	6.0	4.8	7.2	5.2	7.6	5.8	6.4	5.83
78	6.0	7.2	6.4	7.8	5.4	7.2	6.8	7.8	7.8	6.4	6.6	7.4	6.2	7.0	5.8	5.4	6.69
79	4.2	5.4	6.4	7.8	7.8	7.4	7.6	8.6	7.8	5.4	5.8	7.8	5.4	4.8	4.5	5.6	6.37
80	5.0	5.2	6.0	4.4	4.0	8.0	5.6	7.0	7.0	3.8	5.8	5.4	3.8	6.2	2.8	3.6	5.20
81	6.6	3.8	4.6	6.2	4.2	3.4	3.0	4.2	3.4	5.2	5.2	5.2	7.2	4.4	7.5	5.2	4.99
82	3.2	4.4	4.8	5.6	5.0	6.2	3.8	5.8	5.4	4.2	7.6	7.8	4.8	7.8	3.3	7.6	5.42
83	4.2	3.0	5.6	6.6	5.6	6.6	7.6	7.8	7.2	4.8	4.8	5.4	4.4	7.2	3.0	3.6	5.44
84	2.8	3.0	3.6	5.6	3.0	4.6	6.2	8.0	6.0	5.6	5.8	5.2	4.8	4.6	3.8	4.8	4.80
85	5.6	7.8	7.8	7.8	7.6	6.6	8.2	6.8	4.6	7.2	5.6	7.8	7.2	7.0	4.5	6.2	6.91
86	8.6	5.2	6.4	7.8	4.4	2.0	6.0	2.2	6.8	6.6	5.0	5.6	7.4	3.0	6.7	5.2	5.40
87	8.0	8.0	8.0	6.6	6.0	6.6	8.4	5.8	4.6	6.2	3.8	4.8	7.4	5.9	6.2	4.8	6.68
88	7.2	6.2	6.0	5.8	6.4	3.8	4.0	3.4	5.6	5.6	5.0	7.4	5.0	3.0	5.8	5.8	5.30
89	2.0	2.8	5.4	3.8	1.8	7.2	6.0	8.0	5.4	3.2	6.4	6.8	2.0	3.8	1.7	3.6	4.10
90	5.4	5.6	3.6	5.6	7.4	3.2	5.6	2.8	5.4	6.2	6.4	8.6	5.8	3.0	5.8	5.2	5.14

Codes	Total	2-3-1	2-7	2-7-4	2-7-8	2-8	3-1	3-2-1	4-6	4-6-2	4-8-2	4-9	8-3	8-6	8-9	9-6	K+
Q ITEM DATA *Continued*																	
91	4.74	5.0	6.3	4.0	5.4	6.2	7.2	4.4	4.0	1.2	3.8	1.2	5.4	5.4	3.6	5.4	7.0
92	5.27	4.4	6.3	4.4	6.2	3.6	5.4	7.2	5.4	6.2	5.2	6.2	5.6	4.2	3.6	4.4	5.8
93	7.15	8.2	9.0	8.0	7.6	7.6	6.6	8.8	5.6	7.2	6.2	7.6	7.8	6.0	5.2	7.6	5.0
94	4.83	4.6	4.7	4.6	5.6	5.8	5.2	3.8	4.4	4.6	3.2	4.8	5.6	4.0	5.8	5.6	5.0
95	3.25	3.0	5.8	3.2	2.6	3.8	4.4	3.6	2.2	1.8	1.8	3.0	3.8	2.0	2.6	3.8	4.0
96	5.78	2.0	2.3	4.4	6.4	4.6	2.2	7.2	5.6	7.0	8.4	3.8	5.8	8.6	8.6	8.4	7.8
97	6.20	3.8	4.5	3.6	5.6	6.4	6.4	6.8	7.6	7.8	7.6	8.0	5.8	7.6	4.0	6.8	7.2
98	5.63	5.0	3.0	6.8	4.4	6.2	6.4	5.0	8.2	8.4	5.8	8.2	3.6	5.6	4.6	4.6	4.8
99	6.02	6.0	5.2	5.8	5.0	7.6	4.0	6.6	6.2	6.0	5.8	5.2	7.2	5.6	8.0	6.2	6.2
100	6.22	5.2	7.2	7.4	7.8	7.8	4.2	7.0	5.4	4.4	5.0	2.8	6.8	8.0	7.0	7.2	6.2
101	4.43	3.0	3.8	3.0	4.4	5.2	3.8	3.6	5.0	4.8	5.4	5.2	5.2	4.8	3.0	6.4	4.4
102	5.43	8.2	4.0	6.8	4.4	4.4	7.6	7.6	6.6	5.2	5.6	5.6	4.6	2.8	4.6	4.6	4.6
103	5.78	4.8	6.7	2.4	8.2	4.5	1.8	8.0	4.4	4.0	4.4	5.8	8.8	7.2	7.8	7.8	5.4
104	4.75	1.8	3.2	2.2	6.6	2.3	2.0	5.4	4.0	4.2	6.0	1.8	8.4	8.8	9.0	8.6	3.4
105	5.25	9.0	7.0	6.6	4.8	7.4	7.6	7.0	3.4	2.4	2.6	4.8	5.6	5.2	1.6	4.4	4.2
106	3.44	1.8	1.5	2.4	4.0	1.3	1.6	2.0	3.8	3.2	4.8	2.6	3.6	7.0	7.6	5.0	3.2
107	1.98	2.2	2.7	2.0	1.0	2.2	1.8	1.2	3.6	2.0	1.4	2.4	3.8	1.6	1.2	1.0	1.4
108	3.02	5.2	4.8	3.4	2.0	1.2	5.8	2.8	2.0	3.8	1.4	3.2	3.4	1.8	1.0	3.0	3.2
CASE HISTORY DATA																	
Presenting Illness																	
Areas of Manifestation	N 515	N 20	N 20	N 20	N 20	N 20	N 20	N 20	N 20	N 19	N 20	N 18	N 20	N 20	N 20	N 20	N 18
Personality	84.7	80.0	100.0	70.0	100.0	90.0	55.0	75.0	85.0	57.8	85.0	100.0	85.0	100.0	95.0	95.0	83.3
Home	33.9	25.0	25.0	30.0	30.0	5.0	15.0	20.0	45.0	36.8	35.0	77.8	60.0	45.0	30.0	55.0	16.7
Marital	28.8	5.0	10.0	35.0	15.0	20.0	10.0	10.0	60.0	47.4	82.4	66.7	50.0	25.0	20.0	25.0	22.2
Social	28.5	25.0	15.0	10.0	25.0	15.0	10.0	20.0	20.0	15.8	60.0	33.3	30.0	45.0	65.0	45.0	22.2
Sexual	17.7		5.0	5.0	20.0	10.0	5.0	25.0	25.0	31.6	20.0	72.2	20.0		20.0	10.0	22.2
Occupational	14.9	5.0	25.0	10.0	5.0	10.0	5.0	10.0	25.0	15.8	25.0	22.2	10.0	15.0	10.0	30.0	22.2
Educational	4.4		5.0				5.0	5.0	5.0	5.3	10.0	5.5	5.0	5.0	5.0	5.0	5.5
Religious	1.6	5.0			10.0					5.3							
System Involvement																	
Musculoskeletal	30.7	50.0	10.0	40.0	30.0	20.0	60.0	55.0	30.0	15.8	20.0	16.7	60.0	30.0	15.0	15.0	11.1
Gastrointestinal	22.5	45.0	30.0	5.0	35.0	10.0	65.0	45.0	15.0	15.8	5.0	5.5	10.0	5.0	15.0	30.0	22.2

Cardiorespiratory	11.6	25.0	10.0	20.0	15.0	20.0	15.0	40.0	20.0	10.5	5.0	11.1	15.0	10.0	5.0	15.0	16.7
Genitourinary	11.1	5.0	5.0	5.0			10.0	20.0	10.0	10.5	15.0		25.0	20.0	20.0		5.5
Age of Onset																	
N	239	15	20	16	15	12	20	14	14	14	14	14	14	14	16	12	17
Mean age (years)	36.4	40.7	49.0	29.9	41.6	37.0	43.9	41.6	32.7	33.4	28.6	22.6	31.4	41.6	30.7	26.1	44.0
Range	13:76	16:64	22:69	16:58	22:60	19:58	18:58	19:74	18:50	13:54	15:54	16:31	17:48	16:74	18:53	16:35	20:76
Length of Onset																	
N	311	20	20	20	20	20	19	20	20	18	20	16	20	20	20	20	18
Less than a week	10.9	5.0	10.0	0.0	5.0	0.0	10.5	0.0	15.0	5.5	10.0	0.0	20.0	30.0	25.0	25.0	11.1
A week to a month	19.9	15.0	35.0	30.0	10.0	15.0	21.0	15.0	25.0	5.5	10.0	0.0	20.0	25.0	40.0	30.0	16.7
A month to a year	38.5	50.0	45.0	30.0	45.0	50.0	31.6	60.0	25.0	50.0	35.0	31.2	30.0	15.0	30.0	25.0	66.7
Over a year	30.5	30.0	10.0	40.0	40.0	35.0	36.8	25.0	35.0	30.9	45.0	68.7	30.0	30.0	5.0	20.0	5.5
Duration of Illness																	
Less than a week	0.6	0.0	0.0	0.0	0.0	0.0	0.0	0.0	0.0	0.0	0.0	0.0	0.0	0.0	10.0	0.0	0.0
A week to a month	11.2	5.0	20.0	15.0	5.0	0.0	5.3	10.0	10.0	5.5	10.0	0.0	15.0	25.0	25.0	25.0	0.0
A month to a year	33.7	30.0	55.0	25.0	35.0	35.0	31.6	35.0	25.0	33.3	25.0	18.7	40.0	30.0	30.0	30.0	61.1
Over a year	54.3	65.0	25.0	60.0	60.0	65.0	63.1	55.0	65.0	61.1	65.0	81.2	45.0	45.0	35.0	45.0	38.9
Previous Episodes																	
N	297	20	20	20	20	20	20	16	14	18	20	16	20	15	20	20	18
None	48.8	45.0	70.0	60.0	35.0	60.0	75.0	37.5	50.0	27.8	55.0	43.7	50.0	53.3	40.0	30.0	44.4
Similar	34.3	50.0	20.0	30.0	45.0	20.0	20.0	50.0	42.8	50.0	30.0	50.0	40.0	40.0	35.0	30.0	22.2
Other	16.8	5.0	10.0	10.0	20.0	20.0	5.0	12.5	7.1	22.2	15.0	6.2	10.0	6.7	25.0	40.0	33.3
Personal History																	
Birth (N)	314	20	20	20	20	20	20	20	20	18	20	18	20	20	20	20	18
Abnormal	2.5							5.0		5.3	5.0	5.5			5.0	5.0	
Illegitimate	3.1	5.0		5.0	5.0	5.0			5.0		10.0	11.1	5.0	5.0	5.0		
Sibling Status																	
N	271	20	20	18	20	13	20	15	16	16	15	15	19	17	17	17	18
Only child	13.6	15.0	5.0	5.5	25.0	7.7	13.3	20.0	12.5	12.5	20.0	13.3	15.8	23.5	11.8	11.8	5.5
Youngest	28.2	20.0	35.0	44.4	30.0	23.1	33.3	6.7	25.0	37.5	33.3	20.0	38.8	35.3	23.5	29.4	11.1
Middle	34.6	40.0	25.0	16.7	25.0	38.4	33.3	66.7	37.5	31.2	20.0	40.0	42.1	23.5	41.2	47.0	33.3
Oldest	23.6	25.0	35.0	33.3	20.0	30.8	20.0	6.7	25.0	18.7	26.7	26.7	5.3	17.6	23.5	11.8	50.0
Childhood Health																	
N	317	20	20	20	20	20	20	20	20	18	20	18	20	20	20	20	18
Behavior problem	22.3	20.0	5.0	30.0	10.0		10.0	15.0	45.0	26.3	35.0	61.1	25.0	30.0	40.0	30.0	16.7
Physical illness	13.8	10.0	10.0		25.0		30.0	10.0	20.0	21.0	5.0	16.7	5.0	5.0	10.0	20.0	5.5

Codes	Total	2-3-1	2-7	2-7-4	2-7-8	2-8	3-1	3-2-1	4-6	4-6-2	4-8-2	4-9	8-3	8-6	8-9	9-6	K+
CASE HISTORY DATA *Continued*																	
School Achievement	N 287	N 20	N 18	N 20	N 19	N 16	N 15	N 16	N 18	N 19	N 20	N 15	N 19	N 20	N 17	N 18	N 17
Above average	22.6	12.5	50.0	20.0	15.8	12.5	13.3	50.0	16.7	15.8	10.0	20.0	47.4	10.0	23.5	16.7	35.3
Average	59.5	85.0	50.0	60.0	57.9	75.0	73.3	25.0	61.1	68.4	50.0	44.4	47.4	60.0	52.9	72.2	58.8
Below average	17.7	5.0	0.0	20.0	26.3	12.5	13.3	25.0	22.2	15.8	40.0	26.7	5.3	30.0	23.5	11.1	5.9
Social	N 261	N 20	N 16	N 20	N 20	N 12	N 14	N 14	N 20	N 18	N 20	N 11	N 14	N 17	N 15	N 16	N 14
Withdrawal	57.1	40.0	56.2	65.0	80.0	41.7	78.6	64.3	20.0	61.1	65.0	18.2	57.1	76.4	66.7	43.7	71.4
Participation	42.9	60.0	43.8	35.0	20.0	58.3	21.4	35.7	80.0	38.9	35.0	81.8	42.8	23.5	33.3	56.2	28.6
Menarchal Age	N 145	N 8	N 15	N 7	N 10	N 5	N 8	N 10	N 8	N 10	N 10	N 10	N 15	N 7	N 9	N 6	N 7
Mean age (years)	12.7	13.6	12.8	12.7	12.3	13.4	12.6	13.0	12.5	12.9	12.3	12.3	12.3	12.6	12.6	12.7	12.4
Range	9:17	12:17	12:14	11:16	11:14	12:15	10:14	12:13	10:14	11:16	9:16	11:14	11:14	11:16	11:14	12:15	10:15
Sex Instruction																	
Family	18.6	15.0	35.0	15.0	20.0	10.0	15.0	20.0	15.0	15.8	45.0	27.8	10.0	10.0	10.0	20.0	16.7
Dating	N 233	N 15	N 12	N 16	N 15	N 20	N 10	N 14	N 20	N 16	N 14	N 14	N 14	N 14	N 17	N 15	N 12
Often or steady	67.6	73.3	83.3	37.5	53.3	75.0	60.0	64.3	75.0	68.7	57.1	92.8	71.4	78.5	58.9	60.0	75.0
Rarely or never	32.3	26.7	16.7	62.5	46.7	25.0	40.0	35.7	25.0	31.2	42.9	7.2	28.5	21.4	41.1	40.0	25.0
Delinquency																	
Sexual	19.0	15.0		15.0	15.0	15.0		30.0	30.0	31.6	30.0	55.5	15.0	5.0	20.0	20.0	11.1
Other	5.3				5.0				10.0	10.5	10.0	33.3		10.0	5.0	5.0	
Criminal Record	2.8								10.0	5.3	5.0	16.7		5.0			
Education	N 282	N 20	N 18	N 20	N 20	N 16	N 15	N 17	N 14	N 19	N 20	N 14	N 19	N 18	N 17	N 17	N 18
Grade school	23.4	30.0	16.7	30.0	30.0	31.2	23.7	17.6	28.6	21.0	35.0	14.3	10.5	16.7	23.5	23.5	16.7
High school	43.6	40.0	44.4	35.0	50.0	62.5	63.0	47.0	42.8	36.8	35.0	50.0	47.4	50.0	35.3	47.0	22.2
Junior college	15.6	20.0	11.1	20.0	10.0	0.0	3.7	23.5	14.3	10.5	20.0	14.3	21.0	11.1	17.6	17.6	27.8
College	17.3	10.0	27.8	15.0	10.0	6.2	3.7	11.8	14.3	31.6	10.0	21.4	21.0	22.2	23.5	11.8	33.3
Marital Status	N 306	N 20	N 18	N 20	N 18	N 20	N 20	N 18	N 20	N 19	N 18	N 17	N 20	N 20	N 20	N 20	N 18
Married	65.3	70.0	77.8	80.0	61.1	70.0	80.0	72.2	60.0	84.2	50.0	47.0	70.0	45.0	55.0	55.0	66.7
Single	16.3	5.0	11.1	5.0	22.2	10.0	10.0	11.1	10.0	10.5	33.3	17.6	10.0	35.0	25.0	30.0	16.7
Divorced	8.1	10.0	0.0	15.0	5.5	5.0	0.0	5.5	20.0	5.3	11.1	17.6	0.0	15.0	5.0	5.0	11.1
Widowed	5.5	10.0	11.1	0.0	11.1	5.0	5.0	11.1	5.0	0.0	0.0	0.0	5.0	5.0	10.0	5.0	5.5
Separated	4.5	5.0	0.0	0.0	0.0	10.0	5.0	0.0	5.0	0.0	5.6	17.6	15.0	0.0	5.0	5.0	0.0

	Total																
Length of Courtship	N 210	N 15	N 15	N 14	N 13	N 9	N 10	N 12	N 17	N 14	N 14	N 12	N 18	N 12	N 13	N 11	N 11
Less than a week	19.1	26.7	20.0	28.6	30.8	44.4	0.0	16.7	11.8	28.6	14.3	0.0	16.7	16.7	30.8	9.1	9.1
A week to a month	28.2	33.3	40.0	28.6	30.8	44.4	20.0	25.0	17.6	35.7	14.3	16.7	16.7	41.7	30.8	45.4	18.2
A month to a year	26.1	20.0	13.3	42.8	7.7	11.1	40.0	16.7	35.3	28.6	14.3	33.3	33.3	25.0	23.1	18.2	54.5
Over a year	26.6	20.0	26.7	0.0	30.8	0.0	40.0	41.7	35.3	7.1	57.1	50.0	33.3	16.7	15.4	27.3	18.2
Marital Age	N 231	N 18	N 15	N 18	N 14	N 16	N 14	N 16	N 14	N 17	N 11	N 11	N 14	N 13	N 14	N 13	N 13
Mean age (years)	20.5	22.2	22.8	19.8	19.0	18.9	19.6	21.0	19.3	19.6	19.1	19.8	20.6	21.3	21.8	19.7	22.1
Range	14:33	16:30	19:30	14:25	14:23	16:22	15:26	15:33	15:23	16:25	17:25	16:26	16:30	14:32	16:33	15:28	18:33
Parental Consent	60.6	75.0	75.0	57.8	71.4	50.0	50.0	45.0	25.0	52.9	10.0	28.5	25.0	61.5	80.0	78.5	46.7
Number of Children	N 236	N 18	N 15	N 19	N 14	N 16	N 15	N 15	N 15	N 16	N 10	N 14	N 16	N 13	N 14	N 13	N 13
Mean number	2.1	2.0	1.9	2.3	2.4	2.1	2.0	2.8	2.5	2.4	2.4	1.7	2.5	1.6	2.1	1.5	1.5
Range	0:9	0:4	0:4	1:4	1:6	0:6	0:5	0:9	0:5	0:5	1:5	0:6	0:7	0:4	0:5	0:4	0:4
Illegitimate Births	8.4	5.0			7.1	5.0	5.0	10.0	15.0	5.9	10.0		5.0		10.0	10.0	13.3
Extramarital Relations	22.8	10.0		10.5	50.0	15.0	5.0	20.0	25.0	41.2	25.0	33.3	16.7	7.7		21.4	13.3
Marital Adjustment	N 242	N 19	N 15	N 18	N 14	N 17	N 15	N 15	N 16	N 17	N 13	N 12	N 18	N 12	N 14	N 13	N 14
Poor	52.4	45.0	13.3	38.9	42.8	41.2	20.0	53.3	75.0	82.3	69.2	100.0	50.0	66.7	35.7	30.7	35.7
Good	47.5	55.0	86.7	61.1	57.1	58.8	80.0	46.7	25.0	17.6	30.8	0.0	50.0	33.3	64.3	69.2	64.3
Gynecology																	
Abortions	11.4	5.0	10.0	10.0	15.0	10.0	5.0	20.0	30.0	15.8	10.0	22.2	5.0	10.0	20.0	10.0	
Hysterectomy	11.4	15.0	10.0		15.0		25.0	60.0	15.0	5.3		5.5	5.0	5.0	5.0	5.0	11.1
Parental Home	N 315	N 20	N 20	N 20	N 20	N 20	N 20	N 20	N 20	N 20	N 19	N 20	N 18	N 20	N 20	N 20	N 18
Poverty	6.3	5.0				5.0	5.0	5.0	5.0	10.5		11.1	5.0	10.0	5.0	5.0	16.7
Disruption	49.8	60.0	55.0	55.0		60.0	45.0	40.0	55.0	42.1	35.0	50.0	35.0	55.0	55.0	55.0	16.7
Alcoholism	12.0	5.0	5.0	10.0		15.0	5.0	10.0	20.0	21.0	15.0	16.7	30.0	15.0	15.0	15.0	55.5
Father	10.7	5.0	5.0	10.0		10.0	5.0	10.0	20.0	15.8	15.0	16.7	25.0	15.0	15.0	15.0	5.5
Mother	2.2					5.0				5.2		5.5	5.0				5.5
Physical illness	14.9	5.0	10.0	15.0	30.0		30.0	20.0	5.0		10.0	38.9	5.0	25.0	10.0	10.0	11.1
Father	4.7			10.0	15.0			10.0			10.0	5.5	5.0	15.0	5.0	5.0	11.1
Mother	10.4	5.0	10.0	5.0	20.0	15.0	30.0	10.0	5.0	5.0		33.3	15.0	10.0	5.0	5.0	
Mental illness	8.8	10.0	5.0	5.0		10.0		10.0	20.0	15.8	10.0		15.0		5.0	10.0	11.1
Father	6.0	5.0	5.0			5.0		5.0	15.0	15.8	10.0		15.0		5.0	5.0	5.5
Mother	2.8	5.0				5.0		5.0	5.0				5.0			5.0	5.5
Death	31.7	55.0	35.0	35.0	45.0	35.0	60.0	15.0	35.0	26.3	10.0	16.7	25.0	35.0	35.0	30.0	38.9
Father	20.6	35.0	25.0	25.0	15.0	20.0	40.0	10.0	20.0	15.8	10.0	11.1	20.0	15.0	25.0	25.0	33.3
Mother	16.1	35.0	20.0	10.0	35.0	20.0	35.0	20.0	15.0	10.5	5.0	5.5	10.0	35.0	20.0	5.0	11.1

Codes	Total	2-3-1	2-7	2-7-4	2-7-8	2-8	3-1	3-2-1	4-6	4-6-2	4-8-2	4-9	8-3	8-6	8-9	9-6	K+
CASE HISTORY DATA																	
Continued																	
Paternal Relations	N 243	N 15	N 12	N 15	N 18	N 10	N 17	N 16	N 14	N 15	N 16	N 15	N 19	N 14	N 15	N 17	N 15
Indifference	27.5	46.7	25.0	6.7	27.8	30.0	23.5	18.7	35.7	20.0	43.8	53.3	15.8	21.4	26.7	29.4	20.0
Rejection	14.4	26.7	8.3	26.7	22.2	30.0	0.0	12.5	14.3	13.3	12.5	6.7	15.8	21.4	20.0	11.8	0.0
Affection	45.2	13.3	66.7	46.7	38.9	30.0	76.5	37.5	35.7	60.0	37.5	26.7	42.1	50.0	40.0	47.0	73.3
Domination	10.0	3.7	0.0	20.0	5.5	20.0	0.0	25.0	14.3	6.7	6.2	13.3	26.3	7.1	6.7	5.9	0.0
Overprotection	2.0	6.7	0.0	6.7	5.5	0.0	0.0	6.2	0.0	0.0	0.0	0.0	0.0	0.0	6.7	5.9	0.0
Neglect	0.8	0.0	0.0	0.0	0.0	0.0	0.0	0.0	0.0	0.0	0.0	0.0	0.0	0.0	0.0		6.7
Discipline																	
Strict	25.5	46.7	16.7	40.0	15.0	15.0	10.0	43.7	14.3	13.3	15.0	20.0	25.0	42.8	26.7	23.5	6.7
Permissive	38.2	20.0	33.3	40.0	30.0	10.0	25.0	25.0	57.1	53.3	30.0	73.3	25.0	35.7	40.0	64.7	26.7
Maternal Relations	N 255	N 15	N 14	N 16	N 16	N 13	N 15	N 16	N 16	N 15	N 17	N 16	N 20	N 19	N 15	N 18	N 16
Indifference	11.3	20.0	0.0	6.2	6.2	15.4	13.3	13.3	31.2	26.6	17.6	12.5	10.0	0.0	0.0	5.5	6.2
Rejection	21.0	6.7	21.4	18.7	18.7	23.1	20.0	13.3	31.2	40.0	47.0	12.5	25.0	31.6	20.0	0.0	6.2
Affection	26.5	40.0	21.4	18.7	12.5	38.5	13.3	46.7	6.2	20.0	0.0	12.5	20.0	42.1	60.0	44.4	31.2
Domination	31.2	20.0	28.6	50.0	43.7	7.6	43.7	26.7	31.2	6.7	29.4	56.2	40.0	21.0	20.0	22.2	43.7
Overprotection	9.7	13.3	28.6	25.0	18.7	15.4	3.7	0.0	0.0	6.7	0.0	6.2	5.0	5.3	0.0	22.2	6.2
Neglect	1.1	0.0	0.0	0.0	0.0	0.0	0.0	0.0	0.0	0.0	6.0	0.0	0.0	0.0	0.0	5.5	6.2
Discipline																	
Strict	38.6	26.7	42.9	50.0	45.0	15.0	30.0	53.3	26.6	26.6	45.0	43.7	20.0	21.0	20.0	50.0	31.2
Permissive	17.9	33.3		25.0				6.7	40.0	40.0		37.5	25.0	26.3	46.7	22.2	12.5
MENTAL STATUS DATA																	
Attitude/Behavior	N 280	N 20	N 16	N 18	N 16	N 12	N 16	N 16	N 20	N 16	N 20	N 15	N 20	N 20	N 20	N 20	N 15
Agitated	52.1	50.0	50.0	44.4	43.7	33.3	62.5	50.0	80.0	68.7	25.0	26.6	35.0	75.0	70.0	65.0	40.0
Tearful/crying	36.4	45.0	37.5	55.5	50.0	50.0	18.7	68.7	35.0	62.5	20.0	6.6	20.0	45.0	10.0	40.0	26.6
Dishevelled	20.0	40.0	6.2	16.6	6.2	8.3	18.7	6.2	10.0	18.7	15.0	40.0	35.0	10.0	30.0	25.0	26.6
Apathetic	27.1	35.0	25.0	27.7	37.5	16.6	12.5	6.2	20.0	18.7	30.0	13.3	5.0	45.0	30.0	30.0	13.3
Poor cooperation	31.2	15.0	25.0	33.3	6.2	25.0	25.0	18.7	35.0	25.0	10.0	26.6	30.0	40.0	45.0	40.0	53.3
Gestures	12.1	10.0	6.2	5.5	6.2	8.3		31.2	15.0		5.0	20.0	55.0	20.0	35.0	15.0	6.6
Stream of Thought	N 284	N 20	N 16	N 18	N 16	N 12	N 16	N 15	N 20	N 16	N 20	N 15	N 20	N 20	N 20	N 20	N 15
Irrelevant	31.3	10.0	12.5	27.8	18.7	25.0	25.0	6.2	35.0	12.5	35.0	26.6	60.0	50.0	60.0	70.0	33.3
Retarded	15.1	10.0	12.5	22.2	18.7	25.0		12.5	15.0		10.0	6.6	15.0	15.0	40.0	20.0	13.3
Incoherent	14.0	5.0		11.1					10.0		10.0	6.6	35.0	25.0	35.0	35.0	26.6

Emotional Tone

	N 291	N 20	N 20	N 17	N 19	N 19	N 17	N 18	N 17	N 17	N 20	N 15	N 20	N 20	N 20	N 17	N 20	N 15
Anxious	63.2	60.0	65.0	82.3	89.4	84.2	82.3	94.4	70.5	64.7	40.0	33.3	40.0	25.0	40.0	64.7	40.0	86.6
Depressed	69.7	95.0	90.0	94.1	84.2	78.9	88.2	72.2	47.0	82.3	80.0	20.0	60.0	85.0	60.0	35.2	45.0	40.0
Irritable	14.0	10.0		5.8	5.2		5.8	5.5	35.2	17.6	15.0	33.3	15.0	15.0	20.0	29.4	20.0	13.3
Labile	16.1		10.0	23.5	15.7		11.7	22.2	29.4	17.6	30.0	13.3	30.0	15.0	5.0	29.4	20.0	20.0
Disoriented	5.8		5.0		10.5				5.8		5.0			5.0	15.0	29.4	10.0	6.6
Poor Judgment	34.0	5.0	20.0	47.0	10.5	21.0	11.7	16.6	64.7	17.6	40.0	60.0	40.0	60.0	30.0	47.0	65.0	33.3
Poor Memory	15.1	10.0	25.0	5.8	10.5	21.0	5.8	22.2	5.8		15.0	20.0	15.0	5.0	25.0	23.5	20.0	26.6

Feelings

	N 286	N 20	N 20	N 17	N 19	N 19	N 17	N 18	N 17	N 16	N 20	N 15	N 20	N 20	N 20	N 16	N 20	N 15
Inferiority	39.5	45.0	50.0	70.5	93.7	36.8	18.7	70.5	17.6	31.2	40.0	60.0	55.0	65.0	55.0	31.2	5.0	13.3
Doubt	21.6	35.0	27.7	5.8	81.2	15.7	25.0	11.7	11.7	31.2	10.0	6.6	30.0	15.0	30.0	31.2	30.0	6.6
Guilt	19.5	25.0	44.4	29.4	25.0	31.5	6.2	5.8	11.7	18.7	30.0	13.3	15.0	30.0	45.0	18.7	15.0	53.3
Perplexity	38.4	20.0	11.1	17.6	43.7	36.8	62.5	52.9	35.2	25.0	15.0	20.0	25.0	45.0	40.0	25.0	60.0	53.3
Unreality	19.9	5.0		11.7	37.5	36.8		11.7	5.8	18.7	30.0		30.0	40.0	50.0	18.7	35.0	13.3

Symptoms/Complaints

	N 313	N 20	N 20	N 17	N 19	N 19	N 17	N 18	N 17	N 19	N 20	N 18	N 20	N 20	N 20	N 19	N 20	N 18
Alcoholism	7.6	15.0	5.0	10.0	5.0	5.0	5.0	5.0	16.6		10.0	22.2	10.0	5.0	5.0		10.0	5.5
Amnesia	2.8				5.0				5.5			5.5						
Amorality	4.4				5.0				5.5		15.0	38.8			5.0			
Anorexia	18.2	30.0	50.0	5.0	20.0	15.0	15.0	40.0	11.1	5.2	10.0	27.7	15.0	15.0	25.0	5.2	15.0	11.1
Anxious	71.2	75.0	75.0	80.0	90.0	75.0	75.0	85.0	77.7	73.6	75.0		55.0	50.0	65.0	73.6	60.0	77.7
Autistic	13.0		15.0	15.0	10.0	25.0	25.0	5.0	11.1		60.0		60.0	20.0	40.0		15.0	16.6
Back pain	4.7		5.0		5.0	15.0		20.0				5.5	5.0	5.0				5.5
Blackout spells	7.6	5.0	5.0	5.0	10.0	5.0	10.0	10.0	33.3	5.2	10.0	6.6	10.0	5.0	10.0	5.2		
Blurred vision	3.5	20.0		5.0	5.0	5.0		5.0	5.5		30.0		30.0	5.0	5.0		5.0	
Cardiac comp	3.5	15.0	5.0	10.0	5.0	5.0		5.0	11.1		5.0		5.0	5.0				
Chest pain	5.4	10.0	10.0	10.0	5.0	5.0	5.0	25.0	5.5		10.0	5.5	5.0	30.0	5.0		5.0	5.5
Compulsive	14.0		25.0		35.0		5.0	35.0	5.5	21.0	5.0		30.0	10.0	15.0		5.0	16.6
Constipation	9.2		20.0		25.0		10.0	5.0	5.5		15.0		10.0	10.0	15.0		5.0	11.1
Convulsions	3.8	5.0				5.0	5.0	5.0	5.5		5.0	11.1	5.0	5.0	15.0		10.0	5.5
Delusions	22.3	10.0	5.0	10.0	15.0	5.0	5.0	5.0	38.8	10.5	30.0	16.6	45.0	45.0	55.0	10.5	55.0	22.2
Dependent	27.4	15.0	15.0	25.0	20.0	30.0	10.0	30.0	44.4	42.1	15.0	66.6	5.0	5.0	20.0	42.1	30.0	11.1
Depression	73.4	100.0	90.0	95.0	90.0	80.0	70.0	70.0	66.6	73.6	80.0	22.2	85.0	85.0	60.0	73.6	45.0	61.1
Diarrhea	2.2		5.0					10.0	6.5		10.0	5.5				6.5		11.1

MENTAL STATUS DATA

Continued

Codes	Total	2-3-1	2-7	2-7-4	2-7-8	2-8	3-1	3-2-1	4-6	4-6-2	4-8-2	4-9	8-3	8-6	8-9	9-6	K+
Difficulty concentrating	22.3	10.0	25.0	20.0	55.0	15.0	5.0	15.0	5.5	10.5	25.0	16.6	35.0	30.0	40.0	40.0	5.5
Disturbance thought	21.7	5.0	5.0	10.0	25.0	20.0	5.0	5.0	22.2	10.5	35.0	11.1	50.0	30.0	35.0	45.0	33.3
Dizziness	5.4		10.0		5.0	20.0	20.0		5.5		5.0		10.0	5.0	5.0	5.0	
Drug usage	5.4			15.0	10.0		5.0		27.7		5.0		5.0		10.0		
Emotional inapprop	19.1	5.0	10.0		5.0	5.0	15.0		16.6	21.0	40.0	22.2	65.0	35.0	70.0	30.0	5.5
Excitability	15.9	15.0	5.0		5.0	5.0	5.0	5.0	16.6		20.0	5.5	15.0	15.0	25.0	60.0	5.5
Eye complaints	3.1								6.5		5.0	33.3	10.0	5.0	5.0		11.1
Fatigue	22.3	35.0	35.0	35.0	15.0	15.0	45.0	30.0		21.0	25.0	5.5	5.0	25.0	5.0	20.0	16.6
Forgetful	5.1	10.0		5.0		20.0	20.0				5.0		5.0	5.0	5.0		
Genital pain	7.3	10.0			10.0	10.0	15.0	25.0	5.5		5.0		15.0	5.0	5.0		
Hallucinations	14.0		15.0		10.0	10.0	5.0		16.6	10.5	25.0	11.1	30.0	20.0	55.0	30.0	11.1
Headache	18.5	40.0		20.0	20.0	15.0	25.0	5.0	27.7	15.7	10.0	5.5	45.0	20.0	20.0	5.0	5.5
Homicidal	4.1		5.0		5.0				5.5		15.0	16.6	15.0			10.0	
Homosexual	1.5		5.0									11.1		5.0		5.0	
Hostile	44.0	30.0	5.0	25.0	5.0		15.0	40.0	94.4	47.3	65.0	83.3	50.0	55.0	65.0	80.0	44.4
Hypertension	2.5	5.0					5.0	10.0		5.2				5.0			5.5
Ideas of reference	23.0				35.0	5.0	5.0	5.0	55.5	26.3	40.0	55.5	25.0	35.0	35.0	50.0	22.2
Immaturity	19.1	5.0		10.0	10.0	15.0	5.0	15.0	27.7	21.0	20.0	44.4	50.0	30.0	15.0	20.0	16.6
Impulsivity	15.3			10.0	5.0	5.0			38.8	26.3	20.0	38.8	15.0	15.0	30.0	35.0	11.1
Indecisive	13.4	20.0	5.0		15.0			15.0	22.2	36.8	15.0	22.2	30.0	10.0	25.0	15.0	
Insomnia	34.5	40.0	75.0	10.0	40.0	20.0	50.0	55.0	11.1	47.3	20.0	27.7	25.0	35.0	45.0	35.0	27.7
Irritability	30.9	25.0	10.0	10.0	5.0	10.0	20.0	35.0	77.7	21.0	70.0	50.0	30.0	20.0	40.0	50.0	11.1
Loss of consciousness	0.9											5.5			5.0		5.5
Loss of interest	21.4	35.0	30.0	15.0	50.0	10.0	10.0	30.0	5.5	5.2	20.0	5.5	5.0	30.0	5.0	10.0	11.1
Manipulative	11.3	10.0		5.0	5.0	10.0			38.8		20.0	38.8	10.0	20.0	5.0	15.0	
Meticulous	9.2	10.0	20.0	5.0	25.0	5.0	20.0	10.0		15.7		11.1		10.0	5.0	5.0	22.2
Moodiness	15.3	5.0	5.0	5.0	15.0	10.0	10.0	20.0	11.1	5.2	40.0	5.5	5.0	25.0	20.0	35.0	11.1
Nausea/vomiting	10.5	30.0	15.0		10.0	20.0	25.0	25.0	5.5	5.2		5.5	5.0	10.0	10.0	5.0	11.1
Negativism	4.7		5.0	5.0	5.0			5.0		15.7	5.0		15.0	5.0	20.0		5.5
Numbness	5.4	5.0	40.0	5.0		5.0	25.0	20.0	5.5	5.2			15.0	10.0		5.0	5.5
Neurasthenia	9.5	5.0	20.0	15.0	5.0	15.0	30.0	5.0	16.6	5.2	5.0	5.5	10.0	5.0	25.0	10.0	11.1
Obsessional	15.0	10.0	10.0	5.0	40.0	5.0	25.0	5.0	6.5	21.0	25.0	38.8	10.0	20.0	25.0	5.0	49.9
Paranoid	24.2	10.0	10.0	5.0	15.0	5.0	5.0	5.0	44.4	5.2			10.0	60.0	40.0	65.0	11.1
Parasthesia	4.1	10.0		5.0		5.0	15.0	10.0					10.0				11.1
Passivity	9.9	5.0	5.0	5.0	5.0	15.0		15.0	22.2	5.2	20.0	33.3	5.0	5.0		15.0	5.5

	1	2	3	4	5	6	7	8	9	10	11	12	13	14	15	16	17
Perfectionist	11.1	15.0	30.0	10.0	20.0	10.0	5.0	20.0	22.2	21.0			15.0	15.0	15.0		38.8
Perspiration	3.1	5.0		5.0	10.0	5.0	5.0	5.0	16.6		5.0	16.6					
Phobic/fearful	21.4	10.0	25.0	20.0	60.0	10.0	15.0	10.0	5.5	15.7	25.0	11.1	30.0	15.0	30.0	10.0	5.5
Religious	11.8	5.0	40.0	5.0	15.0	5.0	5.0	10.0		5.2	15.0	11.1	5.0	5.0	20.0	25.0	
Restless	12.4	15.0	5.0	5.0	10.0	15.0	15.0	15.0	5.5	10.5		27.7		15.0	30.0	20.0	5.5
Rigid	4.1	15.0	20.0	5.0					27.7	5.2		11.1		10.0		5.0	
Ruminative	17.2	20.0	30.0	15.0	35.0	20.0	5.0	5.0	11.1	10.5			35.0	20.0	30.0	5.0	
Schizoid	8.9		5.0	10.0	10.0	10.0		5.0			10.0		20.0	30.0	15.0	5.0	
Secondary gain	7.0	5.0		5.0			10.0	30.0	16.6	10.5	25.0		15.0				
Sensitive	7.9	10.0	5.0						11.1	5.2	10.0	11.1	20.0	30.0		15.0	
Sexual difficulty	31.6	25.0	20.0	20.0	30.0	35.0	20.0	40.0	27.7	47.3	5.0	27.7	35.0	5.0	30.0	15.0	33.3
Shut-in	1.5				5.0			5.0			40.0	88.8	5.0	5.0			
Somatic complaints	36.7	60.0	45.0	20.0	30.0	30.0	90.0	70.0	22.2	26.3	5.0		60.0	10.0	5.0	20.0	49.9
Stiffness	2.8	5.0		5.0			5.0	5.0	5.5		30.0	16.6			10.0		5.5
Suicidal attempts	16.9	5.0	10.0	20.0	5.0	20.0	20.0	10.0	38.8	26.3	5.0		5.0	15.0	10.0	20.0	5.5
Suicidal ruminations	23.0	20.0	20.0	10.0	65.0	50.0	5.0	10.0	16.6	31.5	45.0	16.6	20.0	35.0	25.0		5.5
Suicidal threats	4.7				10.0	15.0		15.0	5.5	15.7	35.0	11.1	5.0	5.0			
Suspicious	36.1	15.0	5.0	25.0	30.0	15.0	10.0	15.0	61.1	5.2	10.0	5.5	15.0	75.0	80.0	5.0	72.2
Talkative	8.9	5.0	5.0				15.0	15.0	16.6	10.5	55.0	50.0	5.0	10.0	20.0	55.0	5.5
Tense/nervous	69.3	90.0	75.0	70.0	100.0	55.0	65.0	75.0	83.3	73.6	5.0	22.2	60.0	70.0	60.0	55.0	38.8
Tremor/trembling	7.6	15.0	5.0	15.0	10.0	10.0	15.0	15.0		5.2	75.0	61.1	10.0		5.0		11.1
Ulcer	5.1	10.0	5.0	5.0	10.0	5.0	20.0	5.0		5.2	5.0		5.0	5.0			
Weakness	7.0	15.0	5.0	10.0	5.0	10.0	35.0			5.2		5.5	10.0	5.0			
Weight loss	13.7	25.0	40.0	15.0	20.0	15.0	25.0	30.0	5.5	10.5	10.0	11.1	45.0	35.0	45.0	10.0	5.5
Withdrawn	30.0	35.0	25.0	15.0	40.0	35.0	5.0	20.0	22.2	26.3	50.0	16.6	10.0	20.0	5.0	20.0	44.4
Worrisome	16.6	10.0	35.0	45.0	30.0	10.0	15.0	5.0	5.5	15.7	25.0					10.0	22.2

TREATMENT DATA

Length of Treatment

	1	2	3	4	5	6	7	8	9	10	11	12	13	14	15	16	17
	N 170	N 11	N 13	N 8	N 10	N 5	N 11	N 12	N 10	N 9	N 8	N 10	N 13	N 12	N 13	N 13	N 12
Mean days	54.3	57.6	61.9	36.1	67.5	56.4	39.9	50.6	46.7	58.7	60.5	36.4	62.6	46.7	55.5	63.3	61.8
Range	8:225	8:133	9:82	33:191	30:92	12:75	12:75	5:93	10:151	17:122	7:178	7:88	10:225	13:100	23:93	10:148	26:138

Type of Treatment

	1	2	3	4	5	6	7	8	9	10	11	12	13	14	15	16	17
	N 297	N 20	N 20	N 16	N 18	N 17	N 20	N 20	N 20	N 19	N 17	N 15	N 20	N 20	N 20	N 18	N 17
Psychotherapy only	55.9	45.0	40.0	75.0	44.4	52.9	75.0	50.0	70.0	63.1	70.6	80.0	50.0	60.0	25.0	38.8	64.7
Plus tranquilizers	27.3	20.0	20.0	18.7	44.4	23.5	5.0	30.0	20.0	21.0	23.6	20.0	40.0	25.0	60.0	44.4	17.6
Plus energizers	7.7	25.0	20.0	0.0	5.5	17.6	10.0	5.0	10.0	5.2	5.8	0.0	5.0	5.0	5.0	0.0	0.0
Plus ECT	9.1	10.0	20.0	6.2	5.5	5.8	5.0	15.0	0.0	10.5	0.0	0.0	5.0	10.0	10.0	16.6	17.6

TREATMENT DATA
Continued

Codes	Total	2-3-1	2-7	2-7-4	2-7-8	2-8	3-1	3-2-1	4-6	4-6-2	4-8-2	4-9	8-3	8-6	8-9	9-5	K+
Response to Treatment (N)	N 249	N 14	N 19	N 13	N 16	N 13	N 16	N 17	N 14	N 14	N 18	N 15	N 17	N 13	N 18	N 16	N 16
No change	29.3	7.1	15.7	30.7	25.0	30.7	25.0	29.4	42.8	28.5	22.2	80.0	35.2	15.3	27.7	31.2	25.0
Small improvement	43.8	64.3	42.1	38.4	25.0	53.8	62.5	41.1	35.7	57.1	38.8	20.0	52.9	38.4	38.8	37.5	56.2
Decided improvement	26.9	28.6	42.1	30.7	50.0	15.3	12.5	29.4	21.4	14.2	38.8	0.0	11.7	46.1	33.3	31.2	18.7
Prognosis (N)	N 243	N 14	N 15	N 13	N 14	N 17	N 14	N 18	N 14	N 16	N 16	N 14	N 15	N 14	N 17	N 15	N 17
Good	23.4	21.4	53.3	30.7	28.5	23.5	21.4	33.3	28.5	25.0	18.7	0.0	20.0	7.1	29.4	6.6	23.5
Fair	33.3	50.0	20.0	30.7	28.5	17.6	42.8	38.8	7.1	37.5	50.0	35.7	33.3	42.8	23.5	33.3	41.1
Poor	43.2	28.6	26.6	38.4	42.8	58.8	35.7	27.7	64.2	37.5	31.2	64.2	46.6	50.0	47.0	60.0	35.2
Disposition (N)	N 267	N 17	N 16	N 15	N 16	N 12	N 11	M 17	N 18	N 18	N 20	N 16	N 20	N 16	N 20	N 18	N 17
Referred outpatient	50.5	64.7	50.0	26.6	50.0	66.6	54.5	64.7	55.5	66.6	30.0	31.2	50.0	62.5	45.0	50.0	47.0
Referred inpatient	13.1	0.0	6.2	20.0	18.7	8.3	18.1	17.6	0.0	11.1	15.0	12.5	15.0	25.0	25.0	0.0	17.6
Terminated	16.8	17.6	37.5	26.6	25.0	16.6	27.2	5.8	0.0	5.5	25.0	18.7	15.0	6.2	5.0	16.6	29.4
Terminated ATA	12.7	17.6	6.2	20.0	6.2	0.0	0.0	11.7	27.7	16.6	0.0	37.5	15.0	0.0	10.0	22.2	5.8
Committed	6.7	0.0	0.0	6.6	0.0	8.3	0.0	0.0	16.6	0.0	30.0	0.0	5.0	6.2	15.0	11.1	0.0

PSYCHOMETRIC DATA

Codes	Total	2-3-1	2-7	2-7-4	2-7-8	2-8	3-1	3-2-1	4-6	4-6-2	4-8-2	4-9	8-3	8-6	8-9	9-5	K+
Shipley IQ (N)	N 307	N 12	N 18	N 18	N 21	N 24	N 14	N 13	N 24	N 20	N 21	N 27	N 21	N 18	N 18	N 26	N 12
Mean scores	110.4	113.0	113.5	112.0	112.0	108.0	110.0	115.0	114.5	112.0	113.0	111.5	109.0	101.0	103.5	108.0	115.0
Range	85:131	95:126	103:122	100:128	97:124	91:117	103:125	101:126	88:124	101:129	85:131	97:122	96:130	94:122	90:119	96:117	97:125
Shipley CQ (N)	N 310	N 12	N 18	N 18	N 21	N 16	N 14	N 13	N 24	N 20	N 21	N 27	N 21	N 21	N 18	N 26	N 12
Mean scores	82.8	66.0	85.5	84.5	70.0	91.5	75.0	81.0	92.0	84.0	93.5	86.5	80.0	80.0	70.5	76.0	98.5
Range	50:125	56:93	56:102	62:106	59:125	56:115	53:106	56:113	50:100	60:118	67:118	59:118	50:107	56:102	50:97	50:97	73:115
WAIS FS (N)	N 231	N 15	N 18	N 9	N 15	N 9	N 9	N 12	N 15	N 15	N 15	N 18	N 18	N 9	N 21	N 15	N 18
Mean scores	106.8	114.0	119.0	108.3	110.0	112.3	112.0	105.0	87.8	108.0	111.2	118.0	103.5	102.3	92.0	106.4	112.0
Range	65:136	96:128	99:132	71:133	97:115	101:125	105:134	87:117	68:116	89:136	96:128	103:125	72:130	69:122	65:127	81:126	94:127

	N 219	N 15	N 18	N 9	N 15	N 9	N 9	N 12	N 15	N 15	N 12	N 15	N 18	N 9	N 18	N 12	N 18
WAIS VS																	
Mean scores	108.1	110.0	122.5	114.3	109.0	112.0	116.3	98.5	90.6	111.0	105.7	119.0	105.0	101.3	84.0	105.5	114.5
Range	61:138	95:123	104:134	80:135	98:117	102:124	107:129	89:123	68:129	101:138	95:122	107:130	74:127	70:121	61:136	80:130	99:130
Information	10.4	12	12	11	10	10	10	8	6	12	10	13	10	11	7	9	12
Comprehension	11.9	13	16	18	11	13	12	10	8	13	13	15	10	11	9	9	12
Arithmetic	9.6	9	16		7	11	12		8	11	9	13	9	8	10	10	9
Similarities	11.0	11	12	15	10	11	11	10	10	12	11	12	11	11	9	10	12
Digit span	10.0	7	13	14	11	10	10	10	7	11	10	10	10	7	6	10	11
Vocabulary	11.6	13	13	15	11	12	13	9	8	14	11	15	12	9	9	11	14
WAIS PS																	
Mean scores	103.3	116.0	112.5	101.0	109.0	110.7	106.3	108.0	86.4	103.0	108.0	112.0	101.3	103.3	84.0	102.2	105.0
Range	66:131	93:131	93:129	66:127	94:110	100:122	102:114	87:114	72:98	77:127	96:130	103:125	74:131	71:121	76:113	85:121	88:119
Digit symbol	9.6	11	10	9	8	11	9	11	6	9	12	11	9	10	8	9	11
Picture completion	9.1	12	10	6	9	10	8	8	8	10	11	10	8	10	6	10	9
Picture arrangement	9.2	7	10		7	14	8	11	7	8	12	10	8	9	9	9	9
Block design	9.8	9	10	14		8	9	11	7	9	10	14	10	9	8	9	10
Object assembly	10.2	14	12	10	10	7	11	12	8	9	11	15	11	9	8	7	13
Admission MMPI	N 300	N 20	N 20	N 20	N 20	N 20	N 20	N 20	N 20	N 20	N 20	N 20	N 20	N 20	N 20	N 20	N 20
L	4.6†	4.6	5.3	4.1	4.7	4.5	6.9	4.7	5.3	3.5	3.9	3.5	5.7	3.8	3.8	4.2	7.2
F	9.8†	5.0	6.3	8.5	10.6	11.5	4.2	7.5	10.5	9.4	11.8	8.5	10.6	19.6	15.1	8.5	1.9
K	13.8†	13.2	14.5	15.4	13.9	10.7	21.7	14.5	14.4	12.4	13.5	13.9	17.0	9.5	11.1	11.7	20.3
1 (Hs)	68.3†	79	72	59	70	76	82	82	60	66	66	52	80	67	63	50	52
2 (D)	76.9†	92	90	82	93	88	67	86	65	84	79	56	73	83	62	51	53
3 (Hy)	72.9†	82	76	67	74	75	84	91	67	76	72	61	83	68	63	53	56
4 (Pd)	73.6†	64	62	78	72	68	66	70	85	85	85	82	72	81	67	65	56
5 (Mf)	47.6†	44	42	46	49	51	52	48	44	41	45	48	52	50	52	48	51
6 (Pa)	71.2†	65	66	79	73	70	62	68	84	85	69	59	68	93	69	74	54
7 (Pt)	73.5†	70	85	64	91	75	61	77	66	81	77	58	72	80	74	55	51
8 (Sc)	76.1†	65	69	68	88	86	63	71	73	76	86	65	85	98	87	61	54
9 (Ma)	60.3†	48	47	53	55	54	54	54	60	53	62	75	64	66	81	77	50
0 (Si)	62.5†	65	69	69	76	70	51	61	57	68	64	48	58	71	59	53	48

PSYCHOMETRIC DATA
Continued

Codes	Total	2-3-1	2-7	2-7-4	2-7-8	2-8	3-1	3-2-1	4-6	4-6-2	4-8-2	4-9	8-3	8-6	8-9	9-6	K+
Projected Discharge MMPI																	
N	N 258	N 22	N 22	N 10	N 18	N 12	N 10	N 22	N 22	N 22	N 10	N 22	N 20	N 14	N 18	N 16	N 16
Mean days	8.0	17.0	8.0	5.0	3.0	7.7	5.0	13.0	5.0	7.0	6.0	8.0	8.0	8.0	12.0	9.0	8.0
Range	2:39	3:25	2:30	3:30	2:33	2:18	2:30	2:34	2:31	3:28	4:30	2:39	4:31	2:14	7:19	5:31	3:37
T ≥ 70 Scales (%)	45.7†	36.3	18.2	40.0	44.4	33.3	80.0	18.2	50.0	54.5	60.0	72.7	50.0	42.8	66.7	37.5	12.5
T ≥ 70 Codes (%)	14.7†	0.0	8.2	0.0	11.1	16.7	40.0	0.0	30.0	0.0	20.0	36.4	20.0	0.0	11.1	37.5	
L	6.8†	7.9	7.1	7.0	7.4	8.7	9.4	7.1	6.0	7.8	9.0	4.2	5.4	7.0	4.0	8.6	7.6
F	4.6†	3.4	4.0	4.8	3.8	6.3	4.0	2.7	6.5	3.0	5.6	4.3	4.5	7.0	8.2	3.5	2.1
K	19.3†	19.2	18.4	21.0	20.0	19.5	19.2	21.6	18.5	20.4	22.0	20.9	20.1	16.6	15.4	18.9	21.7
1 (Hs)	53.7†	52	54	52	52	52	63	54	52	50	52	50	52	48	54	47	52
2 (D)	52.5†	51	59	55	47	50	67	46	49	51	55	47	47	49	46	43	55
3 (Hy)	57.8†	59	52	56	57	53	72	56	62	59	59	57	59	55	52	49	56
4 (Pd)	61.3†	57	55	57	69	58	64	60	61	60	71	70	66	60	64	53	57
5 (Mf)	52.1†	51	53	45	59	57	59	53	53	47	56	51	54	51	49	52	48
6 (Pa)	57.8†	50	59	56	56	55	47	56	63	59	56	53	59	62	50	56	53
7 (Pt)	54.5†	53	56	56	51	51	53	51	58	53	55	55	57	53	55	46	50
8 (Sc)	59.4†	54	58	60	58	55	55	55	62	55	64	58	62	58	61	52	55
9 (Ma)	58.2†	53	50	58	55	55	53	53	54	53	68	70	60	65	63	62	55
0 (Si)	49.1†	51	56	55	46	50	50	42	52	44	47	44	46	51	48	43	47
Final Discharge MMPI																	
N	N 320	N 24	N 24	N 12	N 22	N 18	N 18	N 28	N 14	N 26	N 20	N 18	N 24	N 30	N 24	N 18	N 20
Mean days	63.6	35.0	58.5	22.0	54.0	40.5	62.0	53.5	68.0	56.5	*48.0	77.0	80.0	31.4	32.5	34.0	33.0
Range	4:289	20:176	21:240	9:31	13:242	19:147	27:149	28:120	23:240	7:247	4:172	17:110	8:289	10:183	18:72	6:172	5:151
T ≥ 70 Scales (%)	62.5†	66.7	41.7	50.0	54.5	88.9	33.3	57.2	57.1	76.9	90.0	88.9	66.7	66.7	50.0	44.4	10.0
T ≥ 70 Codes (%)	26.9†	25.0	16.7	16.7	36.4	66.7	33.3	14.3	14.3	23.1	40.0	33.3	25.0	20.0	25.0	22.2	
L	5.4†	5.3	6.7	4.8	5.6	4.3	8.4	5.6	7.4	3.7	5.2	4.7	5.6	4.2	4.8	6.2	5.8
F	5.9†	4.0	2.5	5.2	6.3	8.5	3.5	5.3	8.6	6.2	9.2	5.3	4.6	8.5	7.6	2.8	2.7
K	16.7†	13.4	20.4	18.5	16.1	11.4	20.2	17.3	20.4	14.8	14.8	17.0	18.7	12.2	16.3	18.4	21.1

1 (Hs)	58.9†	62	55	52	50	72	60	55	58	62	52	50	59	52	55	50	52
2 (D)	64.2†	71	64	61	69	84	59	59	55	72	73	56	60	63	54	47	51
3 (Hy)	63.9†	64	63	60	63	70	66	65	63	68	67	59	63	56	61	55	60
4 (Pd)	65.8†	60	57	70	60	69	57	61	67	73	77	73	67	61	67	53	59
5 (Mf)	48.6†	47	49	43	51	55	55	48	49	43	49	42	46	51	55	51	52
6 (Pa)	61.9†	59	58	60	62	62	53	56	62	62	64	59	64	67	58	56	56
7 (Pt)	62.2†	63	63	61	63	71	51	54	58	66	65	56	62	60	57	55	51
8 (Sc)	64.6†	58	55	60	61	80	54	58	64	64	73	64	68	66	65	54	57
9 (Ma)	56.3†	50	48	56	48	58	53	52	50	60	60	68	55	55	67	50	56
0 (Si)	56.8†	62	55	55	73	70	50	53	53	54	59	44	56	70	49	51	48

Appendix C.

Rules for Profile Discrimination*

These rules for discriminating psychotic from neurotic profiles were developed by Meehl and Dahlstrom (1959) for research purposes and are not for routine clinical use.

MEEHL-DAHLSTROM PROCEDURE

The following restrictions and warnings should be noted. If $L \geq 70$, $F \geq 80$, or $? \geq 60$,† these rules do not apply. The rules assume the diagnostic issue is between neurosis and psychosis. The digits 0 and 5 should either be deleted in recording the codes or ignored in applying the rules; for example, a 58'4 curve falls under Rule 9. "P" and "N" should be taken to mean *curve types*, not as mechanically diagnosing the *patient*. Cutting scores are based on equal base rates and will be increasingly nonoptimal for greater asymmetries in the population split. The calculations use K-corrected T scores, derived on males only.

The basic calculations should be recorded on the profile sheet for use. There are four computations:

1. Band Location: $(Pt + Sc) - (Hs + D) = Beta$

Band No.	Beta Value
1	−31 and less
2	−30 through −11
3	−10 through +6
4	+7 through +25
5	+26 and above

(It may be useful to circle the band number on the profile sheet so that it is not confused with other numbers.)

2. Delta $= (Pd + Pa) - (Hs + Hy)$
3. Hathaway Code
4. Welsh Index (compute only if the profile has no score ≥ 70):

$$IR = \frac{Hs + D + Pt}{Hy + Pd + Ma}$$

---

* Goldberg (1965) has raised serious questions about the efficacy of configural rules as compared with simple linear ones. Using a cutting score based on the T-score values of (L+Pa+Sc)-(Hy+Pt) he was able to classify profiles as "neurotic" and "psychotic" more efficiently than did the Meehl-Dahlstrom rules (scores <45=neurotic). Moreover, in uncontaminated (MMPI) samples the simple unweighted *rank* sum of (D+Hy+Pt) correctly classified 67 per cent of the sample, also outperforming the configural rules (if Σ ranks <12, call neurotic; if Σ ranks >12, call psychotic). The clinician is advised to compute both indices for purpose of comparison.

† Experience suggests that profiles with $? \geq 60$ can be handled by calling them "P" if they appear so under Rule 4 or by the usual application of the subsequent rules; otherwise call them "I" (*i.e.*, "N" should not be diagnosed from such profiles).

(Round off the numerator and denominator sums to two digits before dividing. If the third digit is 5, round downward.)

Apply the rules consecutively until the classification is reached. Classification is either "psychotic curve," "neurotic curve," or "indeterminate." "Indeterminate" is considered a classification; if a rule so classifies a profile, do *not* proceed to subsequent rules. Since most rules will not apply to a given profile, proceed in order until one is reached that does. If a rule applies but does not classify the curve as either "N," "P," or "I," it will instruct "Proceed," which means go on to the next rule which applies and so continue until a decision is made.

Rules for Males Only

1. Elevation Rule: If 7 of the 8 clinical scores ≥ 80 and 5 of them ≥ 90, then call P, unless delta ≤ -15, then call I.
2. Manic Rule: Apply only if the code begins with 9 or 9̲ (9̲ must be *first* if underlined!).
   A. Ma > (Hs and D and Hy) by 15 points or more, call P, unless one of the following conditions holds, in which case proceed:
      (1) D + Pt $\geq$ 115 *or*
      (2) Hs, D, Hy all ≥ 50.
   B. Ma not > all three of the neurotic triad by 15 points, proceed.
3. "Normal Profile" Rule: Apply only if none of the 8 clinical scores ≥ 70.
   A. All scores ≤ 55, call I
   B. IR $\leq$ 0.90
      (1) Delta $\leq$ 0, call I.
      (2) Otherwise, call P.
   C. IR > 0.90
      (1) Delta ≤ -10, call N, unless code 4, 6, or 8; then call I.
      (2) Delta > -10
         (a) Both D and Hy $\geq$ (highest among Pd, Pa, Ma), call N.
         (b) Either D or Hy $\geq$ (highest among Pd, Pa, Ma), call I.
         (c) Neither D nor Hy $\geq$ (highest among Pd, Pa, Ma), call P.
4. "Fake Good" Rule: Apply if L $\geq$ 60.
   A. Band 3, 4, or 5, call P.
   B. Band 2, call I.
   C. Band 1, call N.
5. Psychotic Code Rule: Apply to primed codes only. If the first three digits of the code are among the four digits 4, 6, 8, and 9, and at least one is primed, call P.
6. Slope Rule: If each of the three scores Pa, Pt, and Sc is $\geq$ all of the three scores Hs, D, and Hy; and Pa or Sc or both ≥ 70, call P.
7. 4′ Rule: Apply if the code is 4′ or 4″ (or 4...′ or 4...″).
   A. Band 4 or 5 and delta $\geq$ 0, call P.
   B. Band 1 or 2 and delta negative, call N.
   C. Otherwise, call I.
8. 6′ Rule: Apply if code is 6′ or 6″ (or 6...′ or 6...″).
   A. Code 6″ or 6...″ call P.
   B. Code 6′ or 6...′ call P, unless
      (1) Band 1, call I, *or*
      (2) Delta $\leq$ +20 and (Pa − Pt) $\leq$ +10, call I.

9. 8'4 Rule: Apply if code 8'4 or 84' or higher.
   A. Sc > Pt by 10 points or more, call P.
   B. Otherwise, proceed.
10. (Sc − Pt) Rule: Apply only if Sc ≥ 80.
    A. Sc > Pt by 10 or more points, unless delta ≤ −60, call P, *or*
    B. Pt ≤ both Pa and Sc, and Pa ≥ 70, call P.
    C. Otherwise, proceed.
11. (Pa − Pt) Rule: Apply if Pa ≥ Pt and Pa ≥ 70. Pa ≥ 70 and (Pa − Pt) ≥ 10 call P, unless Band 1, in which case proceed.
12. Band 1 Rule: Curve in Band 1. Call N, unless one of the following hold, in which case call I:
    A. F, Pd both ≥70, *or*
    B. Pd ≥ 65 and Pa ≤ 45, *or*
    C. Delta ≥ 0, *or*
    D. D ≥ 100 and (D − Ma) ≥ 60.
13. Band 2 Rule: Curve in Band 2. Call N, unless one of the following hold, in which case call I:
    A. D ≥ 100 and (D − Ma) ≥ 60, *or*
    B. Pa ≥ 75.
14. Band 3 Rule: Curve in Band 3.
    A. D ≥ 85
       (1) Pd > Hs by 10 points and Pd or Pa ≥ 70, call P.
       (2) 27 or 72 code, no other score ≥80, both Pd and Pa ≤ 70, call N.
       (3) Otherwise, call I.
    B. D < 85
       (1) F ≥ 70, call I.
       (2) Code 4, 6, 8, or 9, call I.
       (3) Delta ≥ −10, call I.
       (4) Otherwise, call N.
15. Band 4 Rule: Curve in Band 4.
    A. All three signs below present, call P:
       (1) (Sc ≥ Pt) *and*
       (2) Code 9 or 8 *and*
       (3) Sc *or* Pd ≥ D.
    B. None of three present, call N.
    C. Otherwise, call I.
16. Band 5 Rule: Curve in Band 5.
    A. D ≥ 75. Both signs below present, call P; otherwise, call I:
       (1) Pd ≥ 75 and ≥Hy *and*
       (2) Sc ≥ Pt.
    B. D < 75. All three signs below present, call N; otherwise, call I:
       (1) Pt > Sc by ten points *and*
       (2) Sc ≤ 80 *and*
       (3) Pa ≤ 70.

The following rules, developed by Henrichs (1964, 1966), provide psychotic, neurotic and character-disorder (Pd type) determinations. Separate rules are given for men and women.

HENDRICKS PROCEDURE

These rules are derived from alterations and additions to the Meehl-Dahlstrom Neurotic-Psychotic Rules for the MMPI. If $L \geq 70$, $F \geq 80$, or $? \geq 60$, these rules do not apply. Digit 5 should be deleted in recording the codes, but recorded separately as it is employed under certain rules. "P," "N," and "Pd" should be taken to mean *curve types*, not *diagnoses*. The calculations employ K-corrected T scores. The four basic calculations should be recorded on the profile sheet.

1. Band Location: $(Pt + Sc) - (Hs + D) = Beta$

Band No.	Beta Value
1	−31 and less
2	−30 through −11
3	−10 through +6
4	+7 through +25
5	+26 and above

2. Delta = $(Pd + Pa) - (Hs + Hy)$
3. Welsh Code
4. Welsh Index (compute only if the profile has no score ≥ 70):

$$IR = \frac{Hs + D + Pt}{Hy + Pd + Ma}$$

(Round off the numerator and denominator sums to two digits before dividing. If the third digit is 5, round downward.)

Apply the rules consecutively until the classification is reached. Classification is either "P," "N," "Pd," or "I." Indeterminate (I) is a classification; if a rule so classifies a profile, do not proceed to subsequent rules. Since most rules will not apply to a given profile, proceed in order until one is reached that does. If a rule applies but does not classify the curve as either N, P, Pd, or I, it will instruct "Proceed," which means go on to the next rule which applies and continue until a decision is made.

Rules for Males

1. Elevation Rule: If 7 of the 8 clinical scores ≥ 80 and 5 of them ≥ 90, then call P, unless delta ≤ -15, then call I.
2. Manic Rule: Apply only if the code begins with 9 or $\underline{9}$ ($\underline{9}$ must be first if underlined!).
   A. Ma > (Hs and D and Hy) by 15 points or more, call P, unless one of the following conditions holds, in which case proceed:
      (1) $D + Pt \geq 115$, *or*
      (2) Hs, D, Hy all ≥ 50, *or*
      (3) $Mf \geq 65$.
   B. If the following conditions hold call Pd:
      (1) (a) Curve in Band 3 and delta < 0, and
          (b) Ma and Pd among first three scales, and
          (c) Ma greater than next scale by 7 points; *or*
      (2) Curve in Band 4 and delta ≥ 0.
   C. Otherwise, proceed.
3. "Normal Profile" Rule: Apply only if none of the 8 clinical scores ≥ 70.
   A. All scores ≤ 55, call I.
   B. IR $\leq .90$
      (1) Delta ≤ 0, call I.
      (2) If code 9, or 4 and 9 among first 3 scales, and delta > 0, call Pd.
      (3) Otherwise, call P.
   C. IR $> .90$
      (1) If code 0, call Pd.
      (2) Delta $\leq .10$, call N, unless code 4, 6, or 8; then call I.
      (3) Delta > -10
          (a) Both D and Hy $\geq$ (highest among Pd, Pa, Ma), call N.
          (b) Either D or Hy $\geq$ (highest among Pd, Pa, Ma), call I.
          (c) Neither D nor Hy $\geq$ (highest among Pd, Pa, Ma), call P.

4. "Fake Good" Rule: Apply if L ≥ 60.
   A. Band 3, 4, or 5, call P, unless curve in Band 3 or 4, delta ≥ 0 and 4' code, in which case proceed.
   B. Band 2, proceed.
   C. Band 1, call N.
5. Psychotic Code Rule: Apply to primed codes only. If the first three digits of the code are among the four digits 4, 6, 8, and 9, and at least one is primed, call P.
6. Slope Rule: If each of the three scores Pa, Pt, and Sc is ≥ all of the three scores Hs, D, and Hy; and Pa or Sc or both ≥ 70, call P.
7. 4' Rule: Apply if the code is 4' or 4" (or 4 . . .', or 4 . . .").
   A. Band 4 or 5 and delta ≥ 0, call P, unless Band 4 and either Mf > Hy, or Hy ≥ 60, call Pd.
   B. Band 1 or 2 and delta negative, call N.
   C. Band 2 or 3 and delta ≥ 0, call Pd.
   D. Otherwise, call I.
8. 6' Rule: Apply if code is 6' or 6" (or 6 . . .' or 6 . . .").
   A. Code 6" or 6 . . .", call P.
   B. Code 6' or 6 . . .', call P, unless
      (1) Band 1, call I.
      (2) Delta ≤ +20 and (Pa − Pt) ≤ +10, call I.
9. 8'4 Rule: Apply if code 8'4 or 84' or higher.
   A. Sc > Pt by 10 points or more, call P.
   B. Otherwise, proceed.
10. (Sc − Pt) Rule: Apply only if Sc ≥ 80.
    A. Sc > Pt by 10 or more points, unless delta ≤ −60, call P, *or*
    B. Pt ≤ both Pa and Sc, and Pa ≥ 70, call P.
    C. Otherwise, proceed.
11. (Pa − Pt) Rule: Apply if Pa ≥ Pt and Pa ≥ 70. Pa ≥ 70 and (Pa − Pt) ≥ 10, call P, unless Band 1, in which case proceed.
12. Band 1 Rule: Curve in Band 1. Call N, unless one of the following hold, in which case call I:
    A. F, Pd both ≥ 70, *or*
    B. Pd ≥ 65 and Pa ≤ 45, *or*
    C. Delta ≥ 0, *or*
    D. D ≥ 100 and (D − Ma) ≥ 60.
13. Band 2 Rule: Curve in Band 2. Call N, unless one of the following hold, in which case call I:
    A. D ≥ 100 and (D − Ma) ≥ 60, *or*
    B. Pa ≥ 75.
14. Band 3 Rule: Curve in Band 3.
    A. D ≥ 85
       (1) Pd > Hs by 10 points and Pd or Pa ≥ 70, call P.
       (2) 27 or 72 code, no other score ≥ 80, both Pd and Pa ≤ 70, call N.
       (3) Otherwise, call I.
    B. D < 85
       (1) F ≥ 70, call I.
       (2) Code 4, 6, 8, or 9, call I.
       (3) Delta ≥ −10, call I.
       (4) Otherwise, call N.
15. Band 4 Rule: Curve in Band 4.
    A. All three signs below present, call P:
       (1) Sc ≥ Pt, *and*
       (2) Code 9 or 8, *and*
       (3) Sc *or* Pd ≥ D.
    B. None of three present, call N.
    C. Otherwise, call I.

16. Band 5 Rule: Curve in Band 5.
   A. $D \geq 75$. Both signs below present, call P; otherwise, call I:
      (1) $Pd \geq 75$ and $\geq Hy$ *and*
      (2) $Sc \geq Pt$
   B. $D < 75$. All three signs below present, call N; otherwise, call I:
      (1) $Pt > Sc$ by ten points, *and*
      (2) $Sc \leq 80$, *and*
      (3) $Pa \leq 70$.

Rules for Females

1. Elevation Rule: If 7 of the 8 clinical scores ≥ 80 and 5 of them ≥ 90, then call P, unless delta ≤ -5, then call I.
2. Manic Rule: Apply only if the code begins with 9 or 9 (9 must be first if underlined!).
   A. $Ma > (Hs$ and D and $Hy)$ by 15 points or more, call P, unless one of the following conditions holds, in which case proceed:
      (1) $D + Pt \geq 115$, *or*
      (2) Hs, D, Hy all ≥ 50, *or*
      (3) $Mf \geq 65$.
   B. If the following conditions hold, call Pd:
      (1) (a) Curve in Band 3 and delta $< +10$, *and*
          (b) Ma and Pd among first three scales; *or*
      (2) Curve in Band 4 and delta $\geq +10$.
   C. Otherwise, proceed.
3. "Normal Profile" Rule: Apply only if none of the 8 clinical scores ≥ 70.
   A. All scores ≤ 55, call I.
   B. $IR \leq .90$
      (1) Delta $< +10$, call I.
      (2) If code 4 or code 9, or 4 and 9 among first three scales, and delta $\geq +10$, call Pd.
      (3) Otherwise, call P.
   C. $IR > .90$
      (1) If code 0, call Pd.
      (2) Delta ≤ 0, call N, unless code 4, 6, or 8; then call I.
      (3) Delta > 0
          (a) Both D and Hy $\geq$ (highest among Pd, Pa, Ma), call N.
          (b) Either D or Hy $\geq$ (highest among Pd, Pa, Ma), call I.
          (c) Neither D nor Hy $\geq$ (highest among Pd, Pa, Ma), call P.
4. "Fake Good" Rule: Apply if $L \geq 60$.
   A. Band 3, 4, or 5, call P, unless curve in Band 3 or 4, delta $\geq +5$ and 4' code, in which case proceed.
   B. Band 2, proceed.
   C. Band 1, call N.
5. Psychotic Code Rule: Apply to primed codes only. If the first three digits of the code are among the four digits 4, 6, 8, and 9, and at least one is primed, call P.
6. Slope Rule: If each of the three scores Pa, Pt, and Sc is $\geq$ all of the three scores Hs, D, and Hy; and Pa or Sc or both ≥ 70, call P.
7. 4' Rule: Apply if the code is 4' or 4" (or 4 . . .' or 4 . . .").
   A. Band 4 or 5 and delta $\geq +10$, call P, unless Band 4 and either $Mf > Hy$, or $Hy \geq 60$, call Pd.
   B. Band 1 or 2 and delta negative, call N.
   C. Band 2 or 3 and delta $\geq +5$, call Pd.
   D. Otherwise, call I.

8. 6' Rule: Apply if code is 6' or 6" (or 6 . . .' or 6 . . .").
   A. Code 6" or 6 . . .", call P.
   B. Code 6' or 6 . . .', call P, unless
      (1) Band 1, call I.
      (2) Delta ≤ +30 and (Pa − Pt) ≤ +10, call I.
9. 8'4 Rule: Apply if code 8'4 or 84' or higher.
   A. Sc > Pt by 10 points or more, call P.
   B. Otherwise, proceed.
10. (Sc − Pt) Rule: Apply only if Sc ≥ 80.
   A. Sc > Pt by 10 or more points, unless delta ≤ −50, call P, or
   B. Pt ≤ both Pa and Sc, and Pa ≥ 70, call P.
   C. Otherwise, proceed.
11. (Pa − Pt) Rule: Apply if Pa ≥ Pt and Pa ≥ 70. Pa ≥ 70 and (Pa − Pt) ≥ 10, call P, unless Band 1, in which case proceed.
12. Band 1 Rule: Curve in Band 1. Call N, unless one of the following hold, in which case call I:
   A. F, Pd both ≥ 70, or
   B. Pd ≥ 65 and Pa ≤ 45, or
   C. Delta ≥ +10, or
   D. D ≥ 100 and (D − Ma) ≥ 60.
13. Band 2 Rule: Curve in Band 2. Call N, unless one of the following hold, in which case call I:
   A. D ≥ 100 and (D − Ma) ≥ 60, or
   B. Pa ≥ 75.
14. Band 3 Rule: Curve in Band 3.
   A. D ≥ 85
      (1) Pd > Hs by 10 points and Pd or Pa ≥ 70, call P.
      (2) 27 or 72 code, no other score ≥ 80, both Pd and Pa ≤ 70, call N.
      (3) Otherwise, call I.
   B. D < 85
      (1) F ≥ 70, call I.
      (2) Code 4, 6, 8, or 9, call I.
      (3) Delta ≥ 0, call I.
      (4) Otherwise, call N.
15. Band 4 Rule: Curve in Band 4.
   A. All three signs below present, call P:
      (1) Sc ≥ Pt, and
      (2) Code 9 or 8, and
      (3) Sc or Pd ≥ D.
   B. None of three present, call N, unless code O or O among first three scales and ≥ 70, then call I.
   C. Otherwise, call I.
16. Band 5 Rule: Curve in Band 5.
   A. D ≥ 75. Both signs below present, call P; otherwise, call I:
      (1) Pd ≥ 75 and ≥ Hy and
      (2) Sc ≥ Pt.
   B. D < 75. All three signs below present, call N; otherwise, call I:
      (1) Pt > Sc by ten points, and
      (2) Sc ≤ 80, and
      (3) Pa ≤ 70.

Appendix D. Adolescent Section

INSTRUCTIONS TO PARTICIPANTS

The research in which you are participating is designed to provide an extensive library of personality descriptions of emotionally disturbed adolescents for whom the descriptions have been empirically derived. The specific aims are (a) to assemble a nationally representative sample of Minnesota Multiphasic Personality Inventory (MMPI) profiles of emotionally disturbed youth; (b) to identify common and statistically stable personality patterns from among these profiles; (c) to derive objective criteria for specifying each homogeneous test pattern; and (d) to compile for each test pattern a corresponding set of nontest personal, social, and psychiatric data.

I. Rating Materials
   A complete set of rating materials consists of the following:
   A. One (1) box of reusable Q-sort cards with sorting directions.
   B. One (1) folder of rating forms (for each subject), consisting of
      1. Instructions to participants
      2. MMPI profile sheet
      3. Personal data schedule
      4. Adjective check list
      5. Case data schedule
      6. Q-item list
      7. Return-addressed envelope

II. Selection of Cases
   Subjects (patients or clients) are suitable for rating who have taken or can take the MMPI and who meet these additional criteria:
   A. Either sex, ages 12-18 inclusive
   B. Caucasian
   C. Emotionally disturbed (i.e., youth having some adjustment problem--objective or subjective--who are either seeking professional help or have been referred for it by others)
   D. Not mentally deficient or retarded
   E. Not organically brain damaged

III. Participation of Subjects
   Each subject is required to complete the MMPI and Personal Data Schedule. MMPI testing, completion of the PDS, and therapist ratings should not be more than one

month apart.
   A. Identification of subjects
      1. Each case should be identified either by name or number, with an entry made on every form.
      2. If a number is used, then the same number should be written on your permanent file or record folder.
   B. MMPI instructions
      1. Either box (individual) or booklet (group) form may be used.
      2. Subjects should be encouraged to answer every question; you may eliminate the "cannot say"category from the testing instructions.
      3. Subjects leaving 50 or more questions blank (or answering both "true" and "false") should be retested or excluded.
      4. Consider only vision, cooperativeness, and freedom from gross confusion as affecting valid results. Subjects should be retested (or excluded) if in your judgment any one of these apply.
      5. Record scores for all scales appearing on the standard profile sheet.
   C. PDS instructions
      1. Subjects should be encouraged to answer every question (average working time is 30 minutes). All answers should be recorded directly on the self-administered form.
      2. In Parts I and II, "father", "mother," "parents" and "family" should be read as the adult(s) with whom the subject lived the longest during the specified period of time (e.g., before age 12).

IV. Participation of Therapists

There are three forms for each case which require approximately one and one-half hours to complete. Before making your first rating, it is strongly recommended that you read over the forms at one sitting. This will serve both to familiarize you with their content and give you their over-all flavor.

A. General instructions

1. For each subject, you should complete in order: one (1) Adjective Check List, one (1) Case Data Schedule, and one (1) Q-sort description

2. All ratings should be made following a minimum of 10 diagnostic and/or therapeutic interviews of 45-60 minutes duration; interview frequency should not be less than one session every two weeks.

3. Your ratings should be based on all evidence available, including informant reports, interview notes, chart notes, case history, psychological test reports, etc. However, it is imperative that ALL RATINGS BE UNINFLUENCED BY THE MMPI, either directly or indirectly.

Please Note

a. If you regularly obtain the MMPI on patients, it will be necessary either to withhold this until after you have made your ratings, or to wait for a new patient who fulfills the criteria but has not as yet taken the MMPI.

b. If you do not regularly obtain the MMPI on patients, you should schedule the test just prior to the time when you plan to make your ratings.

4. MMPI testing, completion of the PDS, and therapist ratings should not be more than one month apart. If changes have occurred since the date of MMPI testing, and if retesting is not feasible, then you should rate the patient as he was at the time he completed the MMPI.

B. ACL instructions

1. Follow the modified instructions that are stamped on the form.

2. You will note that the same adjectives appear as Part III of the PDS to be completed by the patient. You should avoid being influenced by this; rate the patient as he appears to you, independent of his own rating of himself. Refer to the patient's self-rating, if you wish, only after your own rating has been made.

C. CDS instructions

1. Read over the schedule prior to the interview after which you will make your rating. This will enable you to secure any factual information that may not be readily available.

2. You should check or record the information requested for every item, avoiding the "other" category when at all possible.

3. In Part II, "father," "mother," "parents," and "family" should be read as the adult(s) with whom the subject lived during the specified period of time (e.g., before age 12).

4. Also in Part II, if the patient lived with more than one family (father, mother, or adults), your ratings should be based, first, on the family that had the greatest influence on the patient; or, second, on the family with whom the patient spent the longest period of time.

5. In Part V, the patient should be rated as he appeared at the time he completed the MMPI.

D. Q-sort instructions

A Q sort is a systematic procedure for obtaining and recording clinical judgments. The Q-item deck you will use in this study consists of 108 genotypic (dynamic) and phenotypic (descriptive) statements of personality structure and function. The object is to sort the statements into levels which are ranked in order of how descriptive they are of the patient.

1. Read over the Q-item list before making your first sort.

2. Remove all cards from the box and arrange the orange cards (numbered 1 through 9) in numerical order from left to right (see Q-sort direction card).

3. Go through the Q deck and sort the 108 items into three piles. In pile 3 to your right, place those items which are most descriptive of the patient; in pile 2, those items which are only middlingly descriptive, or items about which you can make no confident judgment; in pile 1 to your left, place those items which are least descriptive of the patient. The next step is to sort the three piles into nine levels.

4. Set aside piles 1 and 2. Go through pile 3 (the most descriptive items) and sort the items in this pile into three piles in the same way you sorted originally (i.e., most, middlingly, and least). Now, go through pile 1 (the least descriptive items) and sort this pile into three piles as above. Then, go through pile 2 and repeat the same procedure. You should now have nine piles (levels) of indeterminate size.

5. Now, beginning with the extreme most descriptive pile (level 9), pick out 12 items which characterize the most salient features of the patient's personality. You must have 12 items

in this pile (see direction card). If you have more than 12 items in pile 9, place the surplus in pile 8 (after deciding on the 12 most salient). If you have fewer than 12 items in pile 9, go through pile 8 and select the number of items you need. Now, return to the extreme least descriptive pile (level 1) and repeat the same procedure. Then return to the next most descriptive pile (level 8), then back to the next least descriptive pile (level 2), and so forth. Each time return to the opposite end of the continuum and sort toward the middle. When you have finished count each pile and make certain you have 12 items at each level.

6. You should now refer to the (orange) Q-sort recording sheet for recording instructions.

V. Processing Ratings

You are asked to return the MMPI profile sheet, personal data schedule, adjective check list, case data schedule, Q-sort recording sheet, and folder in the preaddressed envelope immediately after completing each patient rating. The reusable deck of Q cards should be returned only after you have made your final set of ratings. If there is someone coordinating your participation in this project, please keep him informed as to the number of cases you have rated and the number you are planning to rate. If you have any questions concerning the selection of subjects or rating procedures, please write the project director.

BASE RATE CHARACTERISTICS OF THE SAMPLE
CASE DATA SCHEDULE
(Therapist Form Revised)

PART I: IDENTIFYING DATA

(BR)[1]

1. Patient's name (or case code)_____

2. Sex
	(BR)[1]
( ) male N=509	63
( ) female N=325	37

3. Age to nearest year
( ) 12	3
( ) 13	12
( ) 14	17
( ) 15	24
( ) 16	18
( ) 17	18
( ) 18	8

4. Grade in school
( ) 5th	1
( ) 6th	3
( ) 7th	15 6
( ) 8th	16
( ) 9th	18
( ) 10th	23
( ) 11th	16
( ) 12th	7
( ) graduated from high school	3

5. Status in school
( ) enrolled and attending	68
( ) enrolled but not attending	8
( ) dropped-out	7
( ) graduated	2
( ) other_____	21 10

6. School system
(XX) public	89
( ) private-parochial	3
( ) private-other	7

7. Religious denomination
(XX) Catholic	22
( ) Jewish	7
(XX) Protestant	60
(XX) none or non-participating	10

8. Adults with whom the patient now lives
(XX) natural parent(s)	70
( ) step-parent(s)	6
( ) foster parent(s)	3
( ) adoptive parent(s)	5
(XX) other(s)_____	21

(BR)[1]

9. Community size
(XX) 100, 000 or more	46
(XX) 25, 000-100, 000	19
(XX) 5, 000-25, 000	22
( ) 500-5, 000	9
( ) 500 or less	3

10. Treatment setting
(XX) child guidance clinic	24
( ) university clinic	2
( ) medical center	6
(XX) mental health center	12
(XX) private practice	11
( ) private agency	5
(XX) other_____	44

11. Type of service
( ) outpatient	42 57
(XX) inpatient	56
( ) day hospital	5

12. Number of interview hours prior to rating   24[*]   29[*]
(Minimum of 10)_____

13. Date of rating_____

14. Collating code (Leave blank)_____

PART II: REFERRAL DATA

15. Source of referral
( ) self	5
(XX) parent(s)	26
( ) relative(s)	1
(XX) school	16
(XX) court	35
( ) physician	10 22
( ) other(s)	19 11

16. Reasons for referral: Presenting symptoms and/or complaints (Check primary
in column A and secondary in column B)[2]
Check all that apply

	A	B	
( ) ( ) aggressive			45 32
(XX) ( ) bizarre behavior			19
( ) ( ) compulsive acts			25 17
(XX) ( ) defiant, disobedient			65
(XX) ( ) demands attention			36
( ) ( ) destructive			30 13
(XX) ( ) dreamy, day dreams			31
(XX) ( ) difficult to control			61

* Mean hours
[1] Base rate in percent. Male, left column; female, right column. See page 310.
[2] Columns A and B combined for this analysis.

16. Reasons for referral continued
  A B
  (X) ( ) difficulty concentrating   44
  ( ) ( ) eating difficulties   8
  ( ) ( ) enuretic, soiling   4
  (X) ( ) emotionally inappropriate   26
  (X) ( ) emotionally overcontrolled   11
  (X) ( ) excessive fantasy   20
  ( ) ( ) excessive fatigue   9
  (X)(X) excessive fighting   19
  (X) ( ) excessive lying   29
  (X) ( ) fearful, phobic   20
  (X) ( ) hyperactive   18
  (X) ( ) immature   48
  (X) ( ) impulsive   49
  (X) ( ) indecisive   18
  (X) ( ) listless, apathetic   16
  (X) ( ) mischievous, provocative   29
  (X) ( ) negativistic   30
  (X) ( ) nervous, anxious   47
  (X) ( ) obsessed with specific topics   17
  ( ) ( ) passive, overly conforming   7
  ( ) ( ) perfectionistic   9
  ( ) ( ) physically handicapped   2
  (X) ( ) poor parent relations   69
  (X) ( ) poor peer relations   40
  (X) ( ) poor sib relations   27
  (X) ( ) runs away   39
  ( ) ( ) sad, depressed   35 50
  ( ) ( ) sex difficulties   20 37
  (X) ( ) shy, overly sensitive   23
  (X) ( ) sleep difficulties   13
  (X) ( ) somatic concern   15
  ( ) ( ) speech difficulties   4
  ( ) ( ) stealing   39 15
  (X) ( ) suicidal attempts   6 21
  (X) ( ) suicidal thoughts   11 22
  (X) ( ) suicidal threats   8
  (X) ( ) suspicious   20
  (X) ( ) temper tantrums   26
  (X) ( ) tense, restless   38
  ( ) ( ) tics, mannerisms   10   2
  ( ) ( ) tearful, cries easily   14 27
  ( ) ( ) trouble with the law   47 27
  (X) ( ) truant from school   35
  ( ) ( ) under-achieves in school   59 44
  (X) ( ) worried   28
  (X) ( ) other(s)_____   10

17. Areas of manifestation of symptoms
      Check one or more
    (X) home   87
    (X) school   80
    ( ) work   4
    (X) personality   44
    (X) interpersonal-adult   54
    (X) interpersonal-peer   42
    ( ) other(s)_____   2
18. Somatic system involvement
      Check one or more
    (X) none   71
    ( ) cardiorespiratory   4
    (X) gastrointestinal   11
    ( ) genitourinary   33
    ( ) musculoskeletal   4
    (X) nervous system   12
19. Age at onset of primary symptom(s)
    ( ) birth to a year   1
    ( ) 1-5 years   7
    ( ) 6-7 years   10   5
    ( ) 8-9 years   8
    (X) 10-11 years   17
    (X) 12-13 years   33
    ( ) 14-15 years   15 28
    ( ) 16-17 years   6
20. Development of primary symptom(s)
    ( ) less than a week   2
    ( ) a week to a month   5
    (X) a month to a year   30
    (X) over a year   62
21. Previous symptoms or complaints
    (X) none known   41
    (X) some similar to present   54
    ( ) other(s)_____   5

PART III: FAMILY HISTORY

A. General

22. Throughout most of his or her life, the
    patient was raised in
    (X) his or her natural family   82
    ( ) a single family but not as a member
        (e.g., foster home)   3
    ( ) a number of different households 6
    ( ) an institution   1
    ( ) other_____   9

23. Both of the patient's natural parents lived in the home until the patient was
    ( ) less than a year old   6
    (X) 1-5 years old   17
    ( ) 6-9 years old   9
    (X) 10-15 years old   35
    (X) 16 years old or older   26
    ( ) never lived in the home   6
24. The home was first disrupted when the patient's
    ( ) parents separated   12 20
    (X) parents were divorced   17
    ( ) mother died   2
    ( ) father died   6
    ( ) mother deserted   2
    ( ) father deserted   5
    (X) home was never disrupted   52

Throughout most of the patient's childhood (before the age of 12)
25. the adults with whom the patient lived
    (X) usually included the patient in on discussions of family problems   16
    (X) occasionally included the patient   29
    (X) rarely if ever included the patient   55
26. the adults with whom the patient lived
    (X) did not depend upon each other for happiness   38
    (X) depended upon each other about as much as others do for happiness   41
    (X) were very dependent upon each other for happiness   20
27. when it came to deciding things in the family
    (X) the father took responsibility for making all major decisions   22
    (X) the father decided the most import-ant things, but mother took respon-sibility for her own affairs   20
    ( ) neither parent was especially re-sponsible for making decisions   14   23
    (X) the mother made most of the im-portant decisions, though father decided about his own affairs   25
    (X) the mother took responsibility for making all major decisions   16

28. the earned income of the family was for the most part
    (X) steady over the years   55
    (X) regular with a few bad times   27
    (X) very irregular   16
    ( ) almost totally absent   2
29. the money supporting the family came chiefly from
    (X) husband's earnings   66
    ( ) wife's earnings   9
    (X) husband's and wife's earnings   21
    ( ) social agencies   9
    ( ) relatives   1
    ( ) other_____   2
30. the religious atmosphere of the home was
    ( ) strict, with religious bans on most activities   10
    (X) moderate but firm (dietary laws, regular church attendance, etc.)   31
    (X) rather easy-going   43
    (X) no religion in home   15
    ( ) religion was openly rejected in home   1
31. the center of family activities was
    (X) mainly in the home to the detriment of outside contacts   33
    (X) balanced with both home and out-side activities   37
    (X) mainly outside of the home   30
32. Cases of mental or emotional disturbance in the family
    Check one or more
    (X) none known   56
    (X) mother   23
    (X) father   17
    (X) brother(s) or sister(s)   11
    ( ) aunt(s), uncle(s) or their families   8
    ( ) other(s)_____   5

B. Father

33. Relationship of father with whom patient spent most of his of her childhood years (before age 12)
    ( ) natural father   80 71
    ( ) step-father   10
    ( ) foster father   2
    ( ) adoptive father   6
    ( ) other_____   6

34. This father's present age
    ( ) 25-29 years   0
    ( ) 30-34 years   3
    (XX) 35-39 years   17
    (XX) 40-44 years   30
    (XX) 45-49 years   23
    (XX) 50-59 years   19
    ( ) 60 years or older   4
35. This father's education
    ( ) 0-6 years   7
    (XX) 7-9 years   20
    (XX) 10-11 years   13
    (XX) 12 years   23
    ( ) 12 years + trade school   7
    (XX) 13-15 years   12
    ( ) 16 years   7
    ( ) 16 years +   10
36. This father's occupation
    (XX) professional man, scientific expert,   15
        or corporation executive-I
    (XX) small business owner or teacher-II   11
    (XX) skilled tradesman, office worker,   29
        or salesman-III
    ( ) farmer-IV   3
    (XX) skilled laborer or minor clerical   22
        worker-V
    (XX) unskilled laborer-VI, VII   17
    ( ) chronically unemployed   4
37. Time spent by this father outside of home
    during patient's childhood
    (XX) rarely if ever longer than a day   55
    (XX) occasionally away for a week's   23
        time
    (XX) occasionally away for a month's   10
        time
    ( ) a year   2
    ( ) 1-5 years   3
    ( ) more than 5 years   5
38. This father's interest in the activities of
    patient during patient's childhood
    (XX) was interested in most things the   32
        patient did (in school, at play, etc.)
    (XX) showed interest in only a few things   37
        the patient did
    (XX) was interested in little if anything   31
        the patient did

39. Quality of this father's relation with pat-
    ient during patient's childhood
    Check one or more
    (XX) affectionate   36
    (XX) ambivalent   30
    ( ) dependent   6
    (XX) dominating   30
    (XX) indifferent   27
    (XX) neglecting   21
    (XX) overprotecting   12
    (XX) rejecting   21
40. Quality of this father's relation with pat-
    ient now
    Check one or more
    (XX) affectionate   30
    (XX) ambivalent   34
    ( ) dependent   5
    (XX) dominating   21
    (XX) indifferent   22
    (XX) neglecting   15
    (XX) overprotecting   10
    (XX) rejecting   24
41. This father's use of alcohol
    (XX) almost daily and usually to excess   12
    ( ) almost daily though moderately   7
    (XX) to excess but only now and then   13
    (XX) moderately now and then   26
    (XX) rarely if ever   27
    (XX) unknown   14
42. Trouble with law on part of this father
    (XX) none known   75
    (XX) one or two minor offenses such as   12
        traffic
    ( ) a number of minor offenses   4
    ( ) one or two more serious offenses   5
    ( ) some major offense for which con-   2
        victed and imprisoned

C. Mother

43. Relationship of mother with whom patient
    spent most of his or her childhood years
    (before age 12)
    (XX) natural mother   87
    ( ) step-mother   2
    ( ) foster mother   2
    ( ) adoptive mother   6
    ( ) other_____   3

44. This mother's present age
( ) 25-29 years — 1
( ) 30-34 years — 9
(X) 35-39 years — 27
(X) 40-44 years — 31
(X) 45-49 years — 18
( ) 50-59 years — 10
( ) 60 years or older — 2

45. This mother's education
( ) 0-6 years — 7
(X) 7-9 years — 19
(X) 10-11 years — 14
(X) 12 years — 31
( ) 12 years + business school — 7
(X) 13-15 years — 11
( ) 16 years — 6
( ) 16 years + — 3

46. This mother's occupation
( ) professional woman (such as nurse, teacher, etc.) — 8
(X) skilled worker (secretary, dressmaker, etc.) — 11
( ) semi-skilled worker (saleswoman, office clerk, etc.) — 9
(X) unskilled worker (cashier, waitress, etc.) — 18
(X) homemaker — 54
( ) other_____ — 3

47. Time spent by this mother outside of home during patient's childhood
(X) rarely if ever longer than a day — 65
(X) daily part-time — 13
(X) daily full-time — 13
( ) occasionally away for a week's time — 6
( ) a year — 0
( ) 1-5 years — 1
( ) more than 5 years — 1

48. This mother's interest in the activities of patient during patient's childhood
(X) was interested in most things the patient did (in school, at play, etc.) — 63
(X) showed interest in only a few things the patient did — 25
(X) was interested in little if anything the patient did — 12

49. Quality of this mother's relation with patient during patient's childhood
Check one or more
( ) affectionate — 56   44
(X) ambivalent — 33
(X) dependent — 15
(X) dominating — 32
( ) indifferent — 10
(X) neglecting — 13
(X) overprotecting — 42
( ) rejecting — 14   24

50. Quality of this mother's relation with patient now
Check one or more
(X) affectionate — 44
(X) ambivalent — 39
( ) dependent — 10   17
(X) dominating — 25
(X) indifferent — 12
( ) neglecting — 10
(X) overprotecting — 30
( ) rejecting — 15   25

51. This mother's use of alcohol
( ) almost daily and usually to excess — 4
( ) almost daily though moderately — 2
( ) to excess but only now and then — 6
(X) moderately now and then — 20
(X) rarely if ever — 50
(X) unknown — 18

52. Trouble with law on part of this mother
(X) none known — 89
( ) one or two minor offenses such as traffic — 5
( ) a number of minor offenses — 3
( ) one or two more serious offenses — 2
( ) some major offense for which convicted and imprisoned — 0

PART IV: PERSONAL HISTORY

A. Birth and Pre-School (0-5 years)

53. Patient's ordinal position among sibs at birth
(X) first — 37
(X) middle — 30
(X) last — 11
( ) only child — 6

54. Number of brothers or half-brothers at
    time of the patient's birth
    ( ) none   56
    ( ) 1   28
    ( ) 2   9
    ( ) 3 or more   7
55. Number of sisters or half-sisters at time
    of the patient's birth
    ( ) none   79
    ( ) 1   28
    ( ) 2   9
    ( ) 3 or more   6
56. Patient's physical status at birth
    ( ) normal   94
    ( ) minor physical defect (such as dis-   4
        figurement)
    ( ) major physical defect (such as de-   1
        formity with handicap)

During his or her pre-school years
57. the patient
    ( ) was often seriously ill   5
    ( ) was seriously ill only once or   25
        twice
    ( ) was seldom if ever seriously ill   70
58. the patient
    ( ) was slow in development (walking,   8
        talking, etc.)
    ( ) developed as rapidly as other child-   88
        ren
    ( ) developed more rapidly than others   14
59. the patient
    ( ) was a passive and inactive child   13
    ( ) was about as active as other child-
        ren   60 71
    ( ) was an extremely active child   22
60. the patient
    ( ) was a fearful child   32
    ( ) was no more fearful than other   59
        children
    ( ) appeared to have no fear at all   8
61. the patient
    ( ) had a violent temper   23
    ( ) had a temper no worse than other   57
        children
    ( ) had very little temper at all   19

62. the patient
    ( ) was particularly close to his or her
        mother (or other female adult)   53 36
    ( ) was particularly close to his or her
        father (or other male adult)   8 17
    ( ) was equally close to both parents   13
    ( ) was not particularly close to either
        parent   24 36

B. Childhood (6-11 years)

63. Muscular limitations
    ( ) none—patient could do about any-   89
        thing he or she wished
    ( ) slight—patient could do most things   9
    ( ) marked—patient could do only a   1
        very few things
64. General health
    ( ) was often seriously ill   3
    ( ) was seriously ill only once or   24
        twice
    ( ) was seldom if ever seriously ill   73
65. Number of schools attended (grades 1-6)
    ( ) 1 or 2   64
    ( ) 3   16
    ( ) 4   7
    ( ) 5 or more   12
66. Grades in school
    ( ) mainly A's   4
    ( ) A's and B's   13 21
    ( ) mainly B's   9
    ( ) B's and C's   26
    ( ) mainly C's   19
    ( ) C's and D's   26 13
    ( ) D's and F's   6
67. Non-academic performance in school
    ( ) seemed to succeed at whatever he   12
        or she did
    ( ) most work came easily though   49
        there was some that was difficult
    ( ) most things were difficult with an   33
        occasional complete failure
68. Involvement in special programs
    ( ) none known   90
    ( ) special class placement   2
    ( ) remedial reading   4
    ( ) developmental reading   1
    ( ) other_____   4

59. Attitude toward school
   - (X) seemed interested in all aspects of school — 34
   - (X) was interested in only class subjects — 11
   - (X) did not really like class subjects but liked other aspects of school — 25
   - (X) disliked most things about school — 27

70. Attitude toward teachers
   - (X) held a generally unfavorable attitude toward teachers — 19
   - (X) held a favorable attitude toward some teachers and an unfavorable attitude toward others — 53
   - (X) neutral — 16
   - (X) remembers teachers with favor — 12

71. Behavior in school
   - ( ) was well behaved — 33   47
   - (X) got into trouble about as often as others did — 30
   - ( ) was frequently in trouble — 28   18
   - ( ) was expelled at least once — 10   2

72. Relations with other students in school
   - (X) got along very well with others — 23
   - (X) had a few problems in getting along but was usually able to settle them — 56
   - ( ) was often in serious trouble with others — 22   12
   - ( ) had to change schools because of trouble with others — 2

73. Relations of others with patient
   - (X) was liked by most students — 26
   - (X) was liked by some students and disliked by others — 46
   - (X) was liked by few students — 27

74. Type of friendships outside of school
   - (X) had many friends and a few close friends — 23
   - (X) had a few close friends only — 31
   - (X) had many friends but no very close friends — 17
   - (X) had few friends of any kind — 29

75. Age of friends
   - (X) often older than the patient — 23
   - (X) usually about the patient's age — 65
   - ( ) often younger than the patient — 15   6

76. Leisure time activities
   Check all that apply
   - (X) indoor hobbies — 41
   - (X) outdoor hobbies — 39
   - ( ) sporting events – participant — 41   27
   - (X) sporting events — spectator — 27
   - (X) bicycle riding — 41
   - ( ) scouting — 23   14
   - (X) movies — 55
   - (X) television — 73
   - ( ) reading — 26   41
   - ( ) music, records — 32   54
   - (X) parties — 22
   - ( ) model building — 32   1
   - (X) other(s)_____ — 11
   - ( ) no constructive activities — 5

During his or her childhood (6-11 years)
77. the patient
   - (X) got along well and was rarely in trouble with his or her parents — 34
   - (X) got along well most of the time but was frequently in trouble with his or her parents — 42
   - (X) got along poorly and was constantly quarrelling with his or her parents — 23

78. the patient
   - (X) usually talked over his or her personal problems with one or both parents — 10
   - (X) occasionally talked over personal problems with one or both parents — 22
   - (X) rarely talked over personal problems with either parent — 68

79. the patient
   - (X) rarely felt free to disagree with his or her parents — 38
   - (X) would occasionally disagree with his or her parents — 33
   - (X) would often openly disagree with his or her parents — 30

80. the patient
   - (X) was often afraid of his or her mother — 17
   - (X) was at times afraid of his or her mother — 35
   - (X) was seldom if ever afraid of his or her mother — 47

During his or her childhood (6-11 years)
81. the patient
    (X) was often afraid of his or her   37
       father
    (X) was at times afraid of his or her 34
       father
    (X) was seldom if ever afraid of his or 26
       her father
82. the patient
    ( ) was particularly close to his or her 46   34
       mother (or other female adult)
    ( ) was particularly close to his or her
       father (or other male adult)   8   14
    ( ) was equally close to both parents 16   7
    (X) was not particularly close to either 34
       parent
83. the patient
    (X) was disciplined primarily by his or 29
       her father
    (X) was disciplined primarily by his or 44
       her mother
    (X) was disciplined about equally by 22
       both parents
    ( ) was disciplined by neither parent 5
84. the patient
    Check one or more
    (X) was punished by being told not to do 43
       something again
    (X) was punished by being kept from do- 53
       ing something he or she wanted to do
    (X) was threatened   46
    (X) was severely scolded   47
    (X) was spanked   28
    (X) was severely thrashed   19
    ( ) was told to leave home   6
    ( ) was seldom if ever punished   9
85. the patient
    (X) had violent quarrels with his or her 16
       sib(s) and a very poor relationship
    (X) had ill feelings toward sib(s) and a 28
       generally poor relationship
    (X) felt rather indifferent toward sib(s) 21
       and had an easy-going relationship
    (X) was fond of sib(s) and had a good 29
       relationship
    ( ) had no sib(s)   6

86. the patient
    ( ) was known as a "sissy"   21   2
    (X) was known as a "rough-neck"   23
    ( ) was neither a "sissy" nor "rough-
       neck"   56   74
87. the patient
    ( ) had no known trouble with the law 65   82
    (X) was in trouble once or twice   14
    ( ) was in trouble a number of times 8   2
    ( ) was placed on probation at least 4
       once
    ( ) was placed in a correctional insti- 6
       tution at least once
88. the patient
    ( ) had no known trouble with the law 61   78
    ( ) had trouble but denies it   2
    ( ) admits to some trouble   25   14
    ( ) considers self to be (or have been) 10
       delinquent

C. Puberty and Adolescence (12-18 years)

89. Menarchal age (age at puberty)
    ( ) 9 years   0
    ( ) 10 years   1
    ( ) 11 years   6   19
    ( ) 12 years   22   37
    (X) 13 years   31
    ( ) 14 years   15   6
    ( ) 15 years   2
    ( ) 16 years   0
    ( ) other   4
90. Muscular limitations
    (X) none—patient can do about anything 88
       he or she wishes
    (X) slight—patient can do most things 11
    ( ) marked—patient can do only a very 7
       few things
91. General health
    ( ) is often seriously ill   4
    (X) is seriously ill no more than other 22
       adolescents
    (X) is seldom if ever seriously ill   74
92. Number of schools attended (grades 7-12)
    (X) 1 or 2   66
    (X) 3   15
    ( ) 4   7
    ( ) 5 or more   10

During adolescence (12-18 years)

93. Grades in school
- ( ) mainly A's — 3
- ( ) A's and B's — 8
- ( ) mainly B's — 6
- (X) B's and C's — 21
- (X) mainly C's — 14
- ( ) C's and D's — 40 27
- (X) D's and F's — 15

94. Non-academic performance in school
- (X) seems to succeed at whatever he or she does — 12
- (X) most things come easily though there are some that are difficult — 43
- (X) most things are difficult with an occasional complete failure — 44

95. Involvement in special programs
- (X) none — 79
- ( ) special class placement — 5
- ( ) part-time work — 5
- ( ) vocational school — 1
- (X) other _____ — 11

96. Attitude toward school
- ( ) seems interested in all aspects of school — 15 27
- (X) is interested in only class subjects in school — 12
- (X) does not really like class subjects but likes other aspects of school — 28
- (X) dislikes most things about school — 40

97. Attitude toward teachers
- (X) holds a generally unfavorable attitude toward teachers — 25
- (X) holds favorable attitude toward some teachers and an unfavorable attitude toward others — 50
- (X) neutral — 16
- ( ) mentions teachers with favor — 9

98. Behavior in school
- ( ) is very well behaved — 18 34
- (X) gets into trouble about as often as others do — 32
- (X) is frequently in trouble — 25
- ( ) is in trouble most of the time and has been suspended or expelled at least once — 23 11

99. Relations with other students in school
- (X) gets along very well with others — 20
- (X) has a few problems in getting along but is usually able to settle them — 52
- (X) is often in serious trouble with others — 23
- ( ) has had to change schools because of trouble with others — 4

100. Relations of others with patient
- (X) is liked by most students — 20
- (X) is liked by some students and disliked by others — 48
- (X) is liked by few students — 31

101. Type of friendships outside of school
- (X) has many friends and a few close friends — 23
- (X) has a few close friends only — 27
- (X) has many friends but no very close friends — 16
- (X) has few friends of any kind — 33

102. Age of friends
- (X) often older than patient — 32
- (X) usually about the patient's age — 59
- (X) often younger than patient — 10

103. Recognition for achievement
Check one or more
- (X) none or essentially none — 81
- ( ) high school honor roll — 4 11
- ( ) participation in student government — 3
- ( ) awards (such as science medals, dramatics, debate, scouting, etc.) — 6
- ( ) National Honor Society — 1
- ( ) athletic letters — 6 1
- ( ) scholarships — 0
- ( ) other _____ — 5

104. Extracurricular activities
Check one or more
- (X) none known — 54
- (X) music, band — 14
- ( ) athletics — 22 10
- ( ) scouting — 9
- ( ) drama, debate, etc. — 5 13
- ( ) class politics — 3
- ( ) interest clubs (such as photography, chemistry, biology, etc.) — 6 13
- ( ) service clubs (such as dances, ticket selling, etc.) — 4 14
- ( ) other _____ — 8

During adolescence (12-18 years)
105. Leisure time interests
    Check all that apply
    (X) indoor hobbies   38
    ( ) outdoor hobbies   40 27
    ( ) sporting events – participant   40 23
    (X) sporting events – spectator   34
    ( ) records   50 73
    (X) movies   62
    (X) television   76
    ( ) reading   31 46
    ( ) parties, dances   38 52
    (X) school activities   17
    ( ) church activities   13 22
    ( ) working on car   25 1
    (X) riding around in car   40
    (X) hanging around downtown   35
    (X) other(s)_____   11
106. The above activities
    (X) most often include other people   50
    (X) often are done alone but at times include others   34
    (X) are always or almost always done alone   15
107. Age when dating began
    ( ) before 12 years   5
    ( ) 12 years   7
    (X) 13 years   18
    ( ) 14 years   13 21
    (X) 15 years   12
    ( ) 16 years   5
    ( ) 17 years   1
    ( ) 18 years   0
    ( ) does not yet date   49 25
108. Frequency of dating
    ( ) once or twice a year   8
    (X) about once a month   16
    (X) about once a week   19
    (X) more than once a week   17
    ( ) does not yet date   49 25
109. Attitude of parents toward dating
    ( ) indifferent toward dating   45 28
    ( ) strongly disapprove   12 25
    (X) generally approve of dating   39
    ( ) encourage the patient to date more often   5

110. Primary source of spending money
    ( ) self-earned at home   8
    (X) self-earned outside of home   24
    (X) regular allowance   23
    (X) given by parents as needed   43
    ( ) no source   7
    ( ) other_____   5
111. Age when patient first earned money outside of home
    ( ) before 12 years   17 7
    ( ) 12 years   10
    (X) 13 years   11
    (X) 14 years   11
    ( ) 15 years   7
    ( ) 16-18 years   6
    ( ) has not yet earned own money   36 53
112. Use of money
    ( ) usually spends money wisely   31 44
    (X) occasionally is foolhardy about the use of money   38
    (X) seldom if ever spends wisely by the standards of his or her family   25
113. Church attendance
    ( ) more than once a week   7
    (X) once a week   35
    (X) about once a month   11
    (X) seldom   36
    (X) never   11
114. Attitude toward religion
    ( ) rebels against religion   7
    (X) feels it is unimportant   24
    (X) conventional conformity without strong interest   36
    (X) moderate interest   23
    ( ) strong interest   9
115. Personal values
    Check one or more
    (X) family life   41
    ( ) entertainment   56 45
    ( ) hobbies   14 45
    (X) friends   64
    (X) social success   40
    (X) intellectual interests   25
    ( ) economic interests   32 17
    (X) religious interests   13
    ( ) ethno-cultural interests   6
    (X) sex   29
    ( ) other(s)_____   4

During adolescence (12-18 years)

116. Influential figures in life

Check one or more

(X) parent(s)	69	
(X) brother(s)	26	
(X) sister(s)	25	
(X) relative(s)	17	
(X) peer(s)	40	
( ) teacher(s)	14	23
( ) employer(s)	3	
( ) clergy	8	
(X) therapist	36	
(X) others_____	10	

117. Conflict with parents over adolescent behavior (such as smoking, drinking, late hours, type of friends, etc.)

(X) no conflict because of conformity with parental standards	19
( ) no conflict because of parental permissiveness	10
(X) typical conflict due to parental concern about normal behavior	19
(X) frequent conflict due to parental concern about misbehavior	33
(X) constant conflict due to excessive misbehavior	19

118. Trouble with law on part of patient

( ) none known	42	59
( ) one or two minor offenses such as traffic	7	
( ) a number of minor offenses	8	
( ) some serious offense for which placed on probation	6	
( ) some serious offense for which placed in detention	5	
(X) both probation and detention	25	

119. Way of acknowledging trouble with law

( ) no trouble	39	58
(X) blames others	14	
(X) blames self	24	
( ) denies that he or she has had real trouble	8	
( ) believes the offended part had it coming	5	
( ) believes that he or she did only what others did	9	

120. Number of brothers or half-brothers living with patient now

(X) none	43
(X) 1	31
(X) 2	15
(X) 3 or more	11

121. Relations with brother(s)

( ) brothers are the patients closest associates	7
(X) brothers are among some of the patients closer associates	23
(X) little association with brothers	34
(X) patient resents brothers bitterly	11
(X) no brothers	25

122. Trouble with law on part of brother(s)

(X) none known	78
( ) one or two minor offenses such as traffic	5
( ) a number of minor offenses	3
( ) some serious offense for which placed on probation	3
( ) some serious offense for which placed in detention	2
( ) both probation and detention	6

123. Number of sisters or half-sisters living with patient now

(X) none	46
(X) 1	30
(X) 2	16
( ) 3 or more	8

124. Relations with sister(s)

( ) sisters are the patients closest associates	8
(X) sisters are among some of the patients closer associates	21
(X) little association with sisters	33
(X) patient resents sisters bitterly	12
(X) no sisters	26

125. Trouble with law on part of sister(s)

(X) none known	90
( ) one or two minor offenses such as traffic	1
( ) a number of minor offenses	1
( ) some serious offense for which placed on probation	1
( ) some serious offense for which placed in detention	1
( ) both probation and detention	2

PART V: EXAMINATIONAL DATA

A. Q Sort (see separate instructions)

B. Mental Status

Patient's psychological status at time of your
initial evaluation
126. General physical appearance
    ( ) very attractive
    (X) above average appearance   9
    ( ) average   31
    (X) below average appearance   47 34
    ( ) very unattractive   15
127. Height   2
    ( ) extremely short for age
    (X) short   2
    ( ) medium height   16
    ( ) tall   50 60
    ( ) extremely tall   29 18
128. Weight   3
    ( ) extremely thin for height   1
    (X) thin   25
    (X) medium weight   58
    (X) heavy   12
    ( ) obese   4
129. Grooming
    ( ) unkempt   9
    (X) neglected   22
    (X) well-groomed   69
130. General attitude
    Check one or more
    (X) cooperative   56
    (X) defensive   52
    (X) defiant   17
    (X) negativistic   21
    (X) provocative   23
    (X) resistive   29
    (X) reticent   22
    ( ) subservient   10
    (X) suspicious   36
    ( ) uncooperative   9
131. Manifest anxiety
    ( ) none   10
    (X) mild   32
    (X) moderate   41
    (X) severe   17
    ( ) very severe   1

132. Psychomotor activity
    ( ) grossly retarded   1
    (X) slow   16
    (X) normal   61
    (X) accelerated   19
    ( ) hyperactive   3
133. Rapport
    ( ) close   8
    (X) friendly   43
    (X) superficial   35
    (X) distant   17
134. Rate of speech
    ( ) no speech   0
    (X) slow   18
    (X) normal   65
    (X) rapid   15
135. Amount of verbal expression
    ( ) mute or none   0
    (X) impoverished   21
    (X) normal   41
    (X) talkative   33
    ( ) circumstantial   6
136. Quality of ideation
    ( ) creative   9
    (X) conventional   52
    (X) somewhat deviant   36
    ( ) delusional   2
    ( ) bizarre   2
137. Focal concern
    (X) self   81
    ( ) sibs   7
    (X) parents   28
    (X) peers   14
    (X) school   15
    (X) sex   12
    ( ) other_____   4
138. Feelings expressed
    Check all that apply
    (X) guilt   40
    (X) shame   29
    (X) doubt   56
    ( ) depersonalization   8
    (X) inferiority   56
    (X) inadequacy   62
    (X) perplexity   33
    (X) unreality   13
    ( ) isolation   28
    (X) other(s)_____   11

139. Intellectual functioning
    ( ) borderline   2
    (X) dull normal   15
    (X) average   41
    (X) bright normal   27
    (X) superior   12
    ( ) very superior   2

140. Intellectual impairment
    (X) none   62
    (X) mild   28
    ( ) moderate   7
    ( ) severe   2
    ( ) very severe   0

141. Memory past
    ( ) poor   8
    (X) minor errors only   29
    (X) accurate   33

142. Memory present
    ( ) poor   4
    (X) minor errors only   29
    (X) accurate   67

143. Judgment
    (X) extremely poor   10
    (X) moderately impaired   28
    (X) slightly impaired   30
    (X) intact   31

144. Reality testing
    (X) good   35
    (X) minor distortions   37
    (X) somewhat loose   22
    ( ) very loose   5
    ( ) totally impaired   0

145. Emotional tone
    ( ) stable   6
    (X) anxious   39
    (X) depressed   34
    (X) moody   26
    ( ) irritable   13 21
    ( ) labile   11 24
    ( ) apathetic   4

146. Affective level
    ( ) flat   0
    (X) shallow   43
    (X) normal   34
    (X) somewhat elated   14
    ( ) euphoric   1

147. Affective expression
    ( ) exaggerated   10
    (X) appropriate   43
    (X) mildly inappropriate   37
    ( ) moderately inappropriate   7 15
    ( ) grossly inappropriate   1

148. Subjective mood (self-description)
    ( ) grossly depressed   5
    (X) moderately depressed   20
    (X) mildly depressed   35
    ( ) average   34 22
    ( ) mildly elated   9
    ( ) moderately elated   1
    ( ) extremely elated   0

149. Objective mood (projected expression)
    ( ) grossly depressed   3
    (X) moderately depressed   23
    (X) mildly depressed   40
    (X) average   20
    (X) mildly elated   11
    ( ) moderately elated   3
    ( ) extremely elated   0

150. Level of insight
    (X) does not acknowledge that he or she has any problems   12
    ( ) acknowledges the presence of problems but expresses no need for help   24 16
    (X) acknowledges problems and the need for help, but restricts the nature of the help he or she needs (e.g., once a month rather than weekly, from a psychologist rather than psychiatrist)   15
    ( ) acknowledges problems and the need for help without restrictions, but persists in the view that his or her problems are really organic   3
    ( ) acknowledges all the above, but limits his or her problems to something specific (e.g., dependency, hostility, personal adequacy; or, manifest only at home, away from home, only at school, etc.)   40 51
    ( ) acknowledges all the above without any restrictions (a level of insight rarely achieved)   4

PART VI: DISPOSITIONAL DATA

A. Diagnostic Conclusions

151. Ego strength
    ( ) minimal   10
    (X) slight to moderate   35
    (X) moderate   38
    (X) fairly great   15
    ( ) very great   1
152. Mechanisms of defense (check primary
    in column A and secondary in column B)
    Check all that apply
    A B
    (X) ( ) acting out   75
    (X) ( ) compensation   21
    (X) ( ) compulsion   26
    ( ) ( ) conversion   9 18
    (X) ( ) denial   65
    ( ) ( ) depression   58 66
    (X) ( ) displacement   32
    (X) ( ) fantasy   47
    (X) ( ) identification   16
    (X) ( ) intellectualization 29
    (X) ( ) isolation   37
    (X) ( ) obsession   16
    ( ) ( ) parentification   7
    (X) ( ) projection   62
    ( ) ( ) rationalization   68 51
    (X) ( ) reaction-formation 16
    (X) ( ) regression   28
    (X) ( ) repression   39
    (X) ( ) somatization   20
    ( ) ( ) sublimation   4 11
    (X) ( ) suppression   28
    ( ) ( ) symbolization   5
    ( ) ( ) undoing   9
    ( ) ( ) other(s)_____ 1
153. Symptom pattern
    (X) immature-narcissistic 33
    (X) impulsive-hyperactive 22
    (X) hostile-aggressive   18
    (X) fearful-anxious   22
    (X) withdrawn-inhibited 18
    ( ) other_____   2
154. Formal diagnosis (nosological label)
    ( ) 1 __deferred_____
    ( ) 2_____

155. Degree of disturbance
    ( ) mild   6
    (X) mild to moderate   24
    (X) moderate   30
    (X) moderate to severe   36
    ( ) very severe   4
156. Motivation for treatment
    (X) minimal   20
    (X) slight to moderate   35
    (X) moderate   24
    ( ) fairly great   13 2
    ( ) very great   4

B. Course in Treatment

157. Persons involved in treatment
    (X) patient only   52
    (X) patient + mother   18
    ( ) patient + father   2
    (X) patient + both parents 28
    ( ) other_____   7
158. Type of treatment
    Check one or more
    ( ) individual psychotherapy 65
    (X) group therapy   49
    (X) family therapy   25
    (X) environmental manipulation 26
    ( ) electroshock   1
    (X) tranquilizer (type)_____ 11
    ( ) energizer (type)_____ 0
159. Treatment goals
    (X) reconstructive—effecting personal-
        ity change and finding insights 49
    (X) stabilization—stabilizing current
        personality pattern and preventing
        worsening   23
    (X) situational adjustment—improving
        adjustment to current life situa-
        tions   44
160. Time to date in treatment
    ( ) less than a month   1
    (X) 1-2 months   15
    (X) 3-6 months   44
    (X) 6-12 months   23
    (X) 1-2 years   11
    ( ) 2-3 years   4
    ( ) 3-4 years   1
    ( ) 5 or more years   1

169. Hours per week devoted to therapy____ 18*
170. Years of psychotherapy experience____ 6*
171. Primary theoretical orientation
    ( ) orthodox Freudian   10
    ( ) psychoanalytic general   29
    ( ) Sullivanian   3
    ( ) client-centered   10
    ( ) existential   2
    ( ) Horneyan   0
    ( ) Adlerian   0
    ( ) Jungian   0
    ( ) learning general   9
    ( ) eclectic or mixed   53
    ( ) other_____   1

161. Frequency of interviews
    ( ) twice monthly   9
    ⊗ weekly   58
    ⊗ twice weekly   21
    ⊗ three times weekly   11
    ( ) four times weekly   2
    ( ) five times weekly   2   9

162. Present adjustment (progress to date)
    ( ) worse   1
    ⊗ unimproved   11
    ⊗ slightly improved—slight or variable improvement in symptoms and/or social adjustment   48
    ⊗ improved —definite improvement in symptoms and in one or more areas of social adjustment   31
    ( ) much improved---recovery from symptoms except for a few minor complaints; marked improvement in social adjustment   8
    ( ) apparently recovered--recovery from symptoms and marked improvement in social adjustment with no return of emotional disorder even under severe stress   1

172. Personal liking of this patient
    ( ) dislike   3
    ( ) neutral   14
    ( ) like as much as other patients   57
    ( ) like more than other patients   26

173. Information on which your rating of this patient is based
    Check all that apply
    ( ) interview—patient   99
    ( ) interview--parent(s)   56
    ( ) Rorschach   22
    ( ) TAT   14
    ( ) other_____   45

163. Outlook for future adjustment
    ⊗ poor   12
    ⊗ fair   52
    ⊗ good   27
    ( ) very good   8
    ( ) excellent   2

174. Extent to which your rating may have been influenced by the patient's MMPI
    ( ) not at all—totally independent   90
    ( ) very slight if at all   9
    ( ) some, but not significantly so   1
    ( ) other_____   0

PART VII: PSYCHOTHERAPIST DATA

164. Name_____
165. Age_____   35*
166. Sex
    ( ) male   N=123   71
    ( ) female   N=49   29
167. Highest academic degree_____
168. Major professional identification
    ( ) psychologist   41
    ( ) psychiatrist   27
    ( ) social worker   30
    ( ) psychoanalyst   2
    ( ) other_____   0

   * Mean years or hours

This is the last section. Please feel free to express any comments you may have in the space provided below. We would appreciate your returning this form along with the completed Q sort, patient's MMPI and Personal Data Schedule at your earliest convenience. Thank you.

COMMENTS:

LIST OF Q ITEMS[3]

Therapist Form

(BR)*

1. Is vulnerable to real or fancied threat; generally fearful, is a worrier.   5.9
2. Demands sympathy from others.   5.0
3. Values wealth or material possessions and judges others in terms of them.   5.3
4. Has a need to think of self as an unusually self-sufficient person.   5.2
5. Possesses a basic insecurity and need for attention.   7.3
6. Places value on intellectual and cognitive activities, skills and attitudes.   4.6
7. Psychic conflicts are represented in somatic symptoms.   3.9
8. Overacts to danger or makes emergency responses in the absence of danger.   4.6
9. Presents self as being physically, organically sick.   2.8
10. Fears or phobias present.   4.8
11. Is cheerful.   4.6
12. Tends not to become involved in things; is passively resistant.   5.7
13. Is easy to talk to and get along with in this kind of relationship.   5.7
14. Utilizes acting-out as a defense mechanism.   6.7
15. Tends to arouse liking and acceptance in people.   5.5
16. Is overanxious about minor matters and reacts to them as if they were emergencies.   5.0
17. Utilizes projection as a defense mechanism.   6.1
18. Is consciously guilt-ridden, self-condemning, self-accusatory.   4.5
19. Is unpredictable and changeable in behavior and attitudes.   5.3
20. Complains of difficulty in going to sleep.   4.0
21. Has multiple neurotic manifestations.   5.4
22. Resents authority figures and typically has impulses to resist or derogate them.   6.3
23. Judges self and others in conventional terms like "popularity", "social pressures", etc.   5.2
24. Spends a good deal of time in personal fantasy and daydreams.   5.8
25. Presents a favorable prognosis.   4.8
26. Reacts to frustration intropunitively (i.e., punishes self).   5.2
27. Has shown ability to talk about conflicts in most areas.   4.9
28. Is evasive.   5.8
29. Tends to avoid or delay action; fears committing self to any definite course.   5.3
30. Has "diagnostic" insight; awareness of the descriptive features of own behavior.   4.1
31. Has a high aspiration level for self; is ambitious; wants to get ahead.   4.7
32. Is tense, high-strung and jumpy.   5.7
33. Is a reliable informant.   5.2

---

* Mean placements
[3] See page 310.

Q Items—*Continued*

(BR)

34. Undercontrols own impulses; acts with insufficient thinking and deliberation. 6.1
35. Has a need to achieve; to strive to do something as well as possible. 4.6
36. Has a rapid personal tempo; thinks, talks, moves at a fast rate. 4.4
37. Defenses are fairly adequate in relieving psychological distress. 4.1
38. Is suggestable; overly responsive to other people's evaluations rather than own. 5.3
39. Genotype has psychopathic features. 5.0
40. Genotype has schizoid features. 5.0
41. Has good verbal-cognitive insight into own personality structure and dynamics. 3.6
42. Is "normal", healthy, symptom free. 2.8
43. Undervalues and consistently derogates the opposite sex. 3.6
44. Is distrustful of people in general; questions their motivations. 5.9
45. Thinks and associates in unusual ways; has unconventional thought processes. 4.2
46. Is nervous, tense in manner, trembles, sweats, or shows other signs of anxiety. 5.6
47. Handles anxieties and conflicts by refusing to recognize their presence. 5.7
48. Fears loss of control; cannot "let go" even when appropriate. 4.3
49. Appears to be poised, self-assured, socially at ease. 4.1
50. Has a need to affiliate with others. 5.7
51. Exhibits good heterosexual adjustment. 4.0
52. Is self-dramatizing; histrionic. 4.7
53. Is open and frank in discussing problems. 4.8
54. Is defensive about admitting psychological conflicts. 5.8
55. Has feelings of hopelessness. 5.5
56. Complains of weakness or easy fatiguability. 3.8
57. Seems unable to express own emotions in any modulated adaptive way. 5.8
58. Tends to be ruminative and over-ideational. 4.2
59. Is socially extraverted (outgoing). 4.7
60. Has inner conflicts about self-assertion. 6.2
61. Tends to be flippant both in word and gesture. 4.9
62. Exhibits evidence of narcissism (latent or manifest). 6.4
63. Has a resilient ego-defense system; has a safe margin of integration. 4.1
64. Expresses impulses by verbal acting-out. 6.1
65. Has an exaggerated need for affection. 5.7
66. Is a serious person who tends to anticipate problems and difficulties. 4.1
67. Is able to sense other person's feelings; is an intuitive empathic person. 4.5

Q Items—*Continued*

(BR)

68. Keeps people at a distance; avoids close interpersonal relationships. 5.9
69. Gets along well in the world as it is; is socially appropriate in own behavior. 3.6
70. Utilizes rationalization as a defense mechanism. 6.7
71. Genotype has obsessive-compulsive features. 4.4
72. Is demanding; tends to take the attitude "the world owes me a living. 4.9
73. Is excitable. 5.7
74. Utilizes regression as a defense mechanism. 4.7
75. Has inner conflict about emotional dependency. 6.7
76. Avoids situations where own performance will be inferior to that of others. 5.7
77. Is tearful and/or cries openly. 3.9
78. Is irritable. 5.6
79. Is resentful. 6.4
80. Emphasizes oral pleasures; is self-indulgent. 5.7
81. Is perfectionistic; is compulsively meticulous. 3.7
82. Gets appreciable "secondary gain" from symptoms. 4.9
83. Is argumentative. 5.8
84. Is critical; not easily impressed; skeptical. 5.5
85. Has inner conflicts about sexuality. 6.3
86. Is shy, anxious and inhibited. 4.9
87. Is afraid of emotional involvement with others. 6.3
88. Is readily dominated by others; is submissive. 4.4
89. Is provocative. 5.6
90. Is apathetic. 4.1
91. Tends toward over-control of needs and impulses. 4.1
92. Is self-defeating; places self in an obviously bad light. 5.5
93. Exhibits depression (manifest sad mood). 6.0
94. Exhibits manneristic behavior. 4.0
95. Accepts others as they are; is not judgmental. 4.2
96. Genotype has paranoid features. 4.5
97. Is sensitive to anything that can be construed as a demand. 6.3
98. Is egocentric; self-centered; selfish. 5.9
99. Is sterotyped and unoriginal in approach to problems. 4.9
100. Obsessive thinking is present. 4.4
101. Utilizes intellectualization as a defense mechanism. 4.8
102. Genotype has hysteroid features. 4.5
103. Reports difficulty in thinking; can't concentrate. 5.2
104. Delusional thinking is present. 2.5
105. Manifests hypochondriacal tendencies. 3.5
106. Has grandiose ideas (extreme is delusions of grandeur). 3.0
107. Would be organized and adaptive when under stress or trauma. 3.3
108. Has the capacity for forming close interpersonal relationships. 4.4

ADJECTIVE CHECK LIST [4]
(Therapist Form)

Patient's name (or case code)_____ Age____ Sex____ Date_____

DIRECTIONS: Consider each adjective to describe a relatively stable personality trait or disposition. Check those adjectives which are descriptive (or mostly descriptive) of the patient or
client, and not of a diagnostic stereotype.

	(BR)*				(BR)*	
(X) absent-minded	28			( ) commonplace	10	
(X) active	47			(X) complaining	32	
(X) adaptable	16			(X) complicated	24	
(X) adventurous	39			( ) conceited	13	6
(X) affected	12			( ) confident	8	
( ) affectionate	12	33		(X) confused	57	
(X) aggressive	41			( ) conscientious	14	24
( ) alert	35	45		(X) conservative	12	
(X) aloof	31			( ) considerate	12	22
(X) ambitious	20			(X) contented	30	
(X) anxious	65			(X) conventional	12	
(X) apathetic	17			(X) cool	12	
( ) appreciative	14	24		(X) cooperative	36	
(X) argumentative	43			( ) courageous	5	14
(X) arrogant	17			( ) cowardly	7	
(X) artistic	10			( ) cruel	7	
(X) assertive	26			(X) curious	20	
( ) attractive	26	58		(X) cynical	24	
( ) autocratic	4			(X) daring	21	
(X) awkward	29			(X) deceitful	22	
(X) bitter	27			( ) defensive	65	54
(X) blustery	10			( ) deliberate	12	21
(X) boastful	24			(X) demanding	45	
(X) bossy	19			(X) dependable	12	
(X) calm	10			(X) dependent	44	
(X) capable	28			( ) despondent	19	32
(X) careless	35			(X) determined	19	
(X) cautious	27			( ) dignified	9	
( ) changeable	41	53		( ) discreet	6	
( ) charming	14	2		(X) disorderly	18	
(X) cheerful	18			(X) dissatisfied	52	
(X) civilized	18			(X) distractible	33	
(X) clear-thinking	11			(X) distrustful	45	
(X) clever	22			( ) dominant	6	
( ) coarse	7			(X) dreamy	33	
( ) cold	9			( ) dull	8	

* Base rate in percent. Male, left column; female, right column.
[4] See page 310.

( ) easy going	17	
( ) effeminate	12	
( ) efficient	5	13
( ) egotistical	21	
( ) emotional	26	58
( ) energetic	24	
( ) enterprising	13	
( ) enthusiastic	8	25
( ) evasive	44	
( ) excitable	28	44
( ) fair-minded	16	
( ) fault-finding	32	
( ) fearful	32	
( ) feminine	6	52
( ) fickle	4	17
( ) flirtatious	5	45
( ) foolish	18	
( ) forceful	7	
( ) foresighted	4	
( ) forgetful	31	18
( ) forgiving	14	
( ) formal	5	
( ) frank	16	29
( ) friendly	45	
( ) frivolous	6	18
( ) fussy	10	
( ) generous	12	
( ) gentle	12	22
( ) gloomy	21	
( ) good-looking	43	
( ) good-natured	19	
( ) greedy	8	
( ) handsome	16	1
( ) hard-headed	19	
( ) hard-hearted	3	
( ) hasty	32	
( ) headstrong	37	
( ) healthy	37	
( ) helpful	14	
( ) high-strung	32	
( ) honest	17	32
( ) hostile	30	
( ) humorous	11	21
( ) hurried	15	
( ) idealistic	13	
( ) imaginative	20	
( ) immature	70	

( ) impatient	52	
( ) impulsive	64	
( ) independent	17	
( ) indifferent	16	
( ) individualistic	21	
( ) industrious	11	
( ) infantile	18	
( ) informal	15	
( ) ingenious	3	
( ) inhibited	32	
( ) initiative	4	11
( ) insightful	9	15
( ) intelligent	39	54
( ) interests narrow	50	
( ) interests wide	22	
( ) intolerant	21	
( ) inventive	7	
( ) irresponsible	32	
( ) irritable	33	
( ) jolly	6	
( ) kind	9	18
( ) lazy	33	19
( ) leisurely	19	9
( ) logical	8	
( ) loud	21	
( ) loyal	9	19
( ) mannerly	21	
( ) masculine	16	6
( ) mature	5	
( ) meek	15	
( ) methodical	9	
( ) mild	15	
( ) mischievous	33	
( ) moderate	5	
( ) modest	8	17
( ) moody	51	
( ) nagging	15	
( ) natural	7	
( ) nervous	52	
( ) noisy	17	
( ) obliging	11	
( ) obnoxious	9	
( ) opinionated	31	17
( ) opportunistic	14	
( ) optimistic	4	
( ) organized	9	
( ) original	7	

( ) outgoing	22 31		(X) self-controlled	11	
(X) outspoken	28		(X) self-denying	10	
( ) painstaking	6		(X) self-pitying	31	
( ) patient	7		(X) self-punishing	35	
(X) peaceable	13		(X) self-seeking	20	
(X) peculiar	15		(X) selfish	22	
( ) persevering	9		( ) sensitive	39 54	
(X) persistent	19		( ) sentimental	10 26	
(X) pessimistic	33		(X) serious	26	
( ) planful	7		( ) severe	3	
(X) pleasant	21		( ) sexy	6 21	
(X) pleasure-seeking	46		(X) shallow	17	
( ) poised	7 17		(X) sharp-witted	14	
( ) polished	4		( ) shiftless	3	
( ) practical	8		( ) show-off	25 13	
( ) praising	2		(X) shrewd	13	
( ) precise	5		(X) shy	30	
(X) prejudiced	13		(X) silent	20	
(X) preoccupied	32		( ) simple	9	
( ) progressive	3		(X) sincere	20	
( ) prudish	7		( ) slipshod	9	
(X) quarrelsome	27		(X) slow	12	
(X) queer	56		(X) sly	14	
(X) quick	18		( ) smug	5	
(X) quiet	24		( ) snobbish	5	
( ) quitting	22 12		(X) sociable	22	
(X) rational	11		( ) soft-hearted	8 24	
(X) rattlebrained	14		( ) sophisticated	3 9	
( ) realistic	5		( ) spendthrift	8	
( ) reasonable	10 18		( ) spineless	5	
(X) rebellious	55		( ) spontaneous	10 25	
(X) reckless	31		( ) spunky	12 24	
(X) reflective	12		( ) stable	5	
( ) relaxed	3		( ) steady	5	
(X) reliable	13		( ) stern	2	
(X) resentful	48		( ) stingy	4	
( ) reserved	31 22		( ) stolid	2	
( ) resourceful	7 14		( ) strong	9	
( ) responsible	9 18		(X) stubborn	41	
(X) restless	48		(X) submissive	21	
( ) retiring	16 9		(X) suggestible	35	
(X) rigid	15		( ) sulky	21 33	
( ) robust	7		( ) superstitious	7	
(X) rude	11		(X) suspicious	43	
(X) sarcastic	18		( ) sympathetic	8 20	
(X) self-centered	53		(X) tactful	11	
( ) self-confident	6		(X) tactless	19	

(X) talkative	38		( ) unfriendly	4		
( ) temperamental	30 42		(X) uninhibited	11		
(X) tense	45		( ) unintelligent	3		
(X) thankless	10		( ) unkind	3		
( ) thorough	5		(X) unrealistic	23		
(X) thoughtful	12		( ) unscrupulous	4		
( ) thrifty	5		( ) unselfish	4		
(X) timid	18		(X) unstable	28		
( ) tolerant	7		(X) vindictive	13		
(X) touchy	40		( ) versatile	5		
( ) tough	9		( ) warm	14 25		
( ) trusting	8		(X) wary	31		
( ) unaffected	9		( ) weak	22 12		
(X) unambitious	16		(X) whiny	12		
(X) unassuming	11		( ) wholesome	3 10		
(X) unconventional	12		( ) wise	4		
(X) undependable	18		(X) withdrawn	30		
( ) understanding	6 15		(X) witty	12		
( ) unemotional	6		(X) worrying	50		
( ) unexcitable	4		( ) zany	5 10		

PERSONAL DATA SCHEDULE
(Self-Administered Form Revised)

Name (please print)_____ Age____Sex_____ Date_____
                     Last   First

DIRECTIONS: This schedule consists of a number of questions about your life, both past and present. Read each question and decide which of the several answers is true or mostly true as applied to you personally. You are to mark your answers directly on the schedule by making a check between the parentheses (✓) opposite the answer you choose. You will note that there are some questions which ask for more than one answer. You are to mark these by checking as many answers as may apply. Unless you are otherwise instructed, however, select only one answer for each question. Only spend enough time on each question to come to the best answer, and move on to the next question. Please answer every question as exactly and truly as you can.

PART I: CHILDHOOD

The following questions apply to your life
BEFORE AGE 12.

1. With what adults did you live throughout
   most of your childhood?   (BR)
   ( ) both natural parents   69   59
   (X) mother only   11
   ( ) father only   2
   ( ) mother and step-father   7   15
   ( ) father and step-mother   2
   (X) foster or adoptive parents   11

2. Which of the following characterized your
   father (the parent checked in question "1"
   above) during your childhood?
   Check as many as apply
   (X) encouraging   44
   (X) discouraging   20
   (X) bossy   29
   (X) lenient   27
   (X) rewarding   30
   (X) punishing   34
   (X) critical   26
   (X) sympathetic   25
   (X) warm   39
   ( ) cold   14   25
   ( ) distant   25   37
   (X) close   35
   (X) active   32
   (X) passive   12
   (X) tense   23
   (X) relaxed   30
   (X) consistent   26
   (X) inconsistent   22

3. Which of the following characterized your
   mother (the parent checked in question "1"
   above) during your childhood?
   Check as many as apply   (BR)
   (X) inconsistent   19
   (X) consistent   29
   ( ) relaxed   35   25
   ( ) tense   34   51
   (X) passive   11
   (X) active   40
   ( ) close   50   45
   ( ) distant   9   25
   ( ) cold   8   18
   (X) warm   58
   (X) sympathetic   45
   (X) critical   23
   (X) punishing   29
   ( ) rewarding   39   25
   (X) lenient   29
   (X) bossy   26
   (X) discouraging   16
   (X) encouraging   53

4. How affectionate was your father during
   your childhood?
   (X) very affectionate   32
   (X) warm   35
   (X) cool   18
   (X) unfeeling   17

5. How affectionate was your mother during
   your childhood?
   ( ) very affectionate   54   41
   (X) warm   38
   ( ) cool   7   14
   ( ) unfeeling   7

5. How successful was your father as a father
   during your childhood?
   - (X) very successful — 23
   - (X) fairly successful — 17
   - (X) about average — 31
   - (X) fairly unsuccessful — 14
   - ( ) very unsuccessful — 10   18

7. How successful was your mother as a mother
   during your childhood?
   - (X) very successful — 31
   - (X) fairly successful — 23
   - (X) about average — 32
   - ( ) fairly unsuccessful — 4   11
   - ( ) very unsuccessful — 8

8. How did you feel while in the company of
   your father as a child?
   Check <u>as many</u> as apply
   - (X) close — 30
   - ( ) distant — 22   32
   - (X) warm — 37
   - (X) cold — 14
   - (X) secure — 45
   - (X) insecure — 26
   - ( ) assertive — 6
   - (X) submissive — 12
   - (X) guilty — 13
   - (X) proud — 40
   - (X) calm — 31
   - ( ) tense — 22   31
   - (X) ashamed — 12
   - ( ) fearful — 22   33

9. How did you feel while in the company of
   your mother as a child?
   Check <u>as many</u> as apply
   - (X) fearful — 11
   - ( ) ashamed — 8
   - ( ) tense — 15   27
   - (X) calm — 46
   - (X) proud — 42
   - ( ) guilty — 9
   - ( ) submissive — 9
   - ( ) assertive — 8
   - ( ) insecure — 13   21
   - (X) secure — 52
   - ( ) cold — 9
   - (X) warm — 52
   - ( ) distant — 11   24
   - ( ) close — 60   48

10. How often as a child did you know what
    moral judgments your father would pass
    on your behavior?
    - (X) almost always — 28
    - (X) usually — 24
    - (X) sometimes — 27
    - (X) rarely — 12
    - ( ) never — 77

11. How often as a child did you know what
    moral judgments your mother would pass
    on your behavior?
    - (X) almost always — 35
    - (X) usually — 28
    - (X) sometimes — 25
    - ( ) rarely — 7
    - ( ) never — 4

12. How often as a child could you tell in ad-
    vance the kind of emotional reaction your
    father would have to various situations?
    - (X) almost always — 27
    - (X) usually — 28
    - (X) sometimes — 23
    - (X) rarely — 13
    - ( ) never — 6

13. How often as a child could you tell in ad-
    vance the kind of emotional reaction your
    mother would have to various situations?
    - (X) almost always — 29
    - (X) usually — 33
    - ( ) sometimes — 29   20
    - ( ) rarely — 8
    - ( ) never — 3

14. How often as a child could you tell in ad-
    vance what disciplinary action your father
    would take?
    - (X) almost always — 32
    - (X) usually — 24
    - (X) sometimes — 25
    - ( ) rarely — 9
    - ( ) never — 8

15. How often as a child could you tell in ad-
    vance what disciplinary action your mother
    would take?
    - (X) almost always — 32
    - (X) usually — 30
    - (X) sometimes — 25
    - ( ) rarely — 8
    - ( ) never — 4

16. How strict was your father's discipline
during your childhood?
    (X) very strict   17
    (X) strict   20
    (X) about average   39
    (X) lenient   15
    ( ) very lenient   8
17. How strict was your mother's discipline
during your childhood?
    (X) very strict   12
    (X) strict   17
    (X) about average   48
    (X) lenient   17
    ( ) very lenient   6
18. How strong was your father's temper during your childhood?
    ( ) very strong   21 34
    (X) strong   23
    (X) about average   27
    (X) mild   17
    ( ) very mild   5
19. How strong was your mother's temper
during your childhood?
    ( ) very strong   11 19
    (X) strong   19
    (X) about average   42
    (X) mild   20
    ( ) very mild   6
20. To whom in your immediate family were
you closest as a child?
    (X) father   20
    ( ) mother   46 36
    ( ) older brother   9
    ( ) older sister   8
    ( ) younger brother   5
    ( ) younger sister   6
    (X) grandparent   11
    ( ) no one   18
21. To whom in your immediate family were
you least close as a child?
    (X) father   31
    ( ) mother   14 22
    ( ) older brother   8
    ( ) older sister   6
    ( ) younger brother   6
    ( ) younger sister   7
    (X) grandparent   10
    ( ) no one   29 19

22. To whom in your family did you talk about
your personal problems as a child?
    Check one or more
    (X) father   16
    (X) mother   40
    (X) older brother   11
    ( ) older sister   9
    ( ) younger brother   3
    ( ) younger sister   3
    ( ) grandparent   8
    (X) no one   37
23. How often did your parents quarrel during your childhood?
    ( ) daily   15 22
    (X) about weekly   19
    (X) occasionally - though not as often as
        once a week   24
    ( ) rarely   30 20
    (X) never   10
24. Who took the responsibility for deciding
things in your family during your childhood?
    ( ) father took responsibility for mak-
        ing all major decisions   29 16
    (X) father decided the most important
        things but mother took responsibil-
        ity for her own affairs   15
    (X) mother made most of the important
        decisions but father decided about
        his own affairs   18
    (X) mother took responsibility for mak-
        ing all major decisions   12
    ( ) neither parent was especially re-
        sponsible   6
    (X) both parents were equally respon-
        sible   27
25. Who of the following were among your
closest friends during childhood?
    Check one or more
    ( ) boys your own age   70 14
    ( ) girls your own age   24 61
    (X) older boys   21
    ( ) older girls   10 23
    ( ) younger boys   11   3
    ( ) younger girls   2   8
    ( ) adult males   9
    (X) adult females   10
    ( ) no one   7

26. Which of the following were problems for you during childhood?

Check <u>as many</u> as apply

(X) allergies (food, asthma, etc.)	12	
(X) bed wetting	18	
(X) nail biting	45	
(X) thumb sucking	16	
( ) eating (feeding)	9	
( ) toilet training	3	
(X) poor eyesight	17	
( ) overweight	14	22
(X) underweight	16	
( ) poor hearing	5	
( ) being too tall	8	
(X) being too short	12	
(X) being teased	42	
( ) being called a "sissy"	18	6
(X) being called a "rough neck"	12	
(X) not being taken seriously	26	
(X) making friends	31	
(X) keeping friends	21	
( ) nervousness	30	47
( ) nightmares	18	30
( ) sleep walking	5	11
( ) sleep talking	11	24
(X) specific fears (dark, height, etc.)	31	
(X) difficulty reading	18	
(X) difficulty speaking	11	
(X) subjects in school	38	
(X) cheating	12	
(X) lying	31	
( ) stealing	29	18
(X) disobedience	27	
(X) being a "difficult" child	25	
( ) trouble with the law	24	11

PART II: ADOLESCENCE

The following questions apply to your life now, SINCE AGE 12.

27. With what adults do you live now?

( ) both natural parents	54	42
(X) mother only	17	
( ) father only	4	
(X) mother and step-father	12	
( ) father and step-mother	4	
(X) foster or adoptive parents	11	
( ) grandparents	3	

28. Which of the following characterize your father (the parent with whom you live) now?

Check <u>as many</u> as apply

( ) warm	49	3
(X) cold	16	
( ) distant	19	3
( ) close	40	2
(X) active	31	
(X) passive	10	
( ) tense	20	3
( ) relaxed	31	2
(X) consistent	25	
(X) inconsistent	13	
(X) strong	45	
(X) weak	11	
(X) encouraging	38	
(X) discouraging	15	
(X) bossy	22	
(X) lenient	24	
(X) rewarding	27	
(X) punishing	22	
(X) critical	24	
(X) sympathetic	22	
(X) no father in home now	18	

29. Which of the following characterize your mother (the parent with whom you live) now?

Check <u>as many</u> as apply

(X) sympathetic	44	
( ) critical	19	3
(X) punishing	25	
(X) rewarding	35	
(X) lenient	32	
(X) bossy	25	
( ) discouraging	12	2
(X) encouraging	49	
(X) strong	36	
(X) weak	16	
(X) inconsistent	16	
(X) consistent	27	
(X) relaxed	28	
( ) tense	36	4
( ) passive	9	
(X) active	33	
(X) close	45	
(X) distant	17	
(X) cold	11	
(X) warm	56	
( ) no mother in home now	5	

30. How affectionate is your father now?
   - (X) very affectionate 22
   - (X) warm 33
   - (X) cool 18
   - (X) unfeeling 12
   - (X) no father in home now 18
31. How affectionate is your mother now?
   - (X) very affectionate 37
   - (X) warm 41
   - (X) cool 13
   - ( ) unfeeling 6
   - ( ) no mother in home now 5
32. How do you feel while in the company of your father now?
   Check as many as apply
   - ( ) close 43 26
   - (X) distant 26
   - (X) warm 34
   - (X) cold 14
   - ( ) secure 42 29
   - ( ) insecure 17 28
   - ( ) assertive 9
   - ( ) submissive 7
   - (X) guilty 15
   - ( ) proud 35 25
   - (X) calm 27
   - (X) tense 25
   - (X) ashamed 12
   - (X) fearful 14
   - (X) no father in home now 18
33. How do you feel while in the company of your mother now?
   Check as many as apply
   - ( ) fearful 10
   - (X) ashamed 11
   - ( ) tense 16 31
   - (X) calm 46
   - ( ) proud 44 34
   - (X) guilty 13
   - ( ) submissive 9
   - ( ) assertive 10?
   - ( ) insecure 11 23
   - (X) secure 44
   - (X) cold 13
   - (X) warm 50
   - ( ) distant 13 25
   - (X) close 46
   - ( ) no mother in home now 5

34. How often now do you know what moral judgments your father will pass on your behavior?
   - (X) almost always 28
   - (X) usually 22
   - (X) sometimes 20
   - ( ) rarely 8
   - ( ) never 4
   - (X) no father in home now 17
35. How often now do you know what moral judgments your mother will pass on your behavior?
   - (X) almost always 32
   - (X) usually 27
   - (X) sometimes 25
   - ( ) rarely 7
   - ( ) never 4
   - ( ) no mother in home now 5
36. How often now can you tell in advance the kind of emotional reaction your father will have to various situations?
   - (X) almost always 23
   - (X) usually 27
   - (X) sometimes 21
   - ( ) rarely 7
   - ( ) never 4
   - (X) no father in home now 17
37. How often now can you tell in advance the kind of emotional reaction your mother will have to various situations?
   - (X) almost always 29
   - (X) usually 30
   - (X) sometimes 24
   - ( ) rarely 7
   - ( ) never 4
   - ( ) no mother in home now 5
38. How strict is your father's discipline now?
   - ( ) very strict 10
   - (X) strict 17
   - (X) about average 36
   - (X) lenient 15
   - ( ) very lenient 4
   - (X) no father in home now 18
39. How strict is your mother's discipline now?
   - ( ) very strict 10
   - (X) strict 17
   - (X) about average 46
   - (X) lenient 17
   - ( ) very lenient 5
   - ( ) no mother in home now 5

40. How often now can you tell in advance what disciplinary action your father will take?
    - (X) almost always   22
    - (X) usually   26
    - (X) sometimes   21
    - ( ) rarely   9
    - ( ) never   5
    - (X) no father in home now 18
41. How often now can you tell in advance what disciplinary action your mother will take?
    - (X) almost always   26
    - (X) usually   30
    - (X) sometimes   25
    - ( ) rarely   9
    - ( ) never   5
    - ( ) no mother in home now   5
42. How would you describe your father's temper now?
    - ( ) very mild   7
    - (X) mild   14
    - (X) about average   29
    - (X) strong   21
    - (X) very strong   12
    - (X) no father in home now 18
43. How would you describe your mother's temper now?
    - (X) very mild   18
    - ( ) mild   25 16
    - (X) about average   38
    - (X) strong   20
    - ( ) very strong   10
    - ( ) no mother in home now   5
44. How often do your parents quarrel now?
    - (X) daily   11
    - (X) about weekly   11
    - (X) occasionally though not as often as once a week   21
    - (X) rarely   29
    - (X) never   22
45. To whom in the family are you closest now?
    - ( ) father   24 11
    - (X) mother   40
    - ( ) older brother   9
    - ( ) older sister   10
    - ( ) younger brother   8
    - ( ) younger sister   8
    - ( ) grandparent   7
    - (X) no one   20

46. To whom in the family are you the least close now?
    - (X) father   31
    - ( ) mother   12 20
    - ( ) older brother   6
    - ( ) older sister   5
    - ( ) younger brother   5
    - ( ) younger sister   6
    - ( ) grandparent   8
    - (X) no one   32
47. To whom in the family do you talk about your personal problems now?
    Check one or more
    - ( ) father   27 12
    - (X) mother   39
    - ( ) older brother   12   6
    - (X) older sister   11
    - ( ) younger brother   5
    - ( ) younger sister   4
    - ( ) grandparent   8
    - ( ) no one   39
48. In what grade are you at school?
    - ( ) 6th   3
    - ( ) 7th   13   6
    - ( ) 8th   18 11
    - (X) 9th   18
    - (X) 10th   20
    - (X) 11th   17
    - ( ) 12th   6 11
    - ( ) not in school   6 12
49. In terms of teaching ability, how would you describe most of your teachers in school?
    - (X) superior   11
    - (X) above average   27
    - (X) average   47
    - ( ) below average   6
    - ( ) inferior   4
    - ( ) not in school   7
50. How interesting and challenging are most of the subjects you are now taking in school?
    - (X) very interesting and challenging   14
    - (X) above average   13
    - (X) about average   36
    - ( ) below average   9
    - (X) dull and routine   21
    - ( ) not in school   9

51. If you have failed any subjects in school, which of the following do you consider to be the major reasons?

Check one or more

( ) laziness	43	29
(X) lack of ability	11	
(X) lack of interest	49	
(X) dislike of subject	45	
(X) disliked by teacher	19	
(X) poor teacher	14	
(X) hard to study at home	26	
( ) sickness	6	
( ) belonging to too many clubs	1	
( ) participating in sports	3	
( ) going to too many parties or shows	10	
( ) too many dates	8	
( ) working part-time	5	
(X) have not failed	23	

52. In terms of intellectual ability, how would you describe most students in your class at school?

(X) too bright—it is difficult to keep up with them	13
(X) just bright enough	62
(X) not bright enough—they do not provide enough stimulation	16
( ) not in school	9

53. Who of the following are among your closest associates at school?

( ) boys your own age	68	13
( ) girls your own age	26	61
(X) older boys	17	
( ) older girls	10	17
( ) younger boys	6	1
( ) younger girls	4	
( ) teachers	9	
( ) no one	8	15

54. Who of the following are among your closest associates away from school?

( ) boys your own age	61	14
( ) girls your own age	24	47
(X) older boys	26	
( ) older girls	12	20
( ) younger boys	9	2
( ) younger girls	5	
(X) adult males	11	
( ) adult females	8	17
( ) no one	9	

55. What do you like to do with your leisure time?

Check as many as apply

(X) indoor hobbies	31	
(X) outdoor hobbies	39	
( ) participate in sports	38	27
( ) watch sports	31	15
( ) listen to records	56	77
(X) go to movies	55	
(X) watch television	62	
( ) read	37	53
(X) attend parties and dances	52	
(X) school activities	17	
(X) church activities	13	
( ) work on car	31	2
(X) ride around in car	49	
( ) sew	1	23
( ) go shopping	10	46
( ) talk on phone	28	52
(X) hang around drive-in	20	
(X) hang around downtown	36	

56. Which one of the following do you plan to do immediately after high school?

( ) enter the military service	20	2
(X) get a job	19	
( ) get married	9	16
( ) go to a technical, trade, or business school	7	
( ) go to a junior college	8	
( ) go first to a junior college and then to a four-year college	8	
(X) go directly to a four-year college	19	
(X) undecided	28	

57. From whom did you first learn about sexual intercourse?

( ) mother	11	29
( ) father	12	4
(X) adults other than parents	11	
( ) brothers	8	
( ) sisters	3	
( ) other boys	55	16
( ) other girls	11	49

58. Which of the following was the main source of your sex information?

(X) conversation	67
( ) observation	5
(X) printed matter	20
(X) actual experience	23

59. How old were you when you started smoking?
    ( ) less than 10   15   3
    ( ) 10   4
    ( ) 11   8
    (XX) 12   12
    (XX) 13   11
    (XX) 14   12
    ( ) 15   6
    ( ) 16   4
    ( ) 17   1
    ( ) 18   0
    (XX) have never started   37
60. How much do you smoke now?
    (XX) a pack or more a day   26
    (XX) three to five packs a week   13
    ( ) a pack or two a week   9
    ( ) about a pack a week   5
    ( ) a couple of packs a month   3
    ( ) less than a pack a month   6
    (XX) do not smoke   39
61. How often do you drink alcohol now?
    ( ) daily   2
    ( ) three to four times a week   3
    ( ) once or twice a week   13   4
    (XX) about once or twice a month   14
    (XX) a couple of times a year   20
    (XX) not at all   52
62. How old were you when you had your first
    date on your own?
    ( ) less than 10   2
    ( ) 10   2
    ( ) 11   4
    (XX) 12   11
    (XX) 13   14
    (XX) 14   19
    ( ) 15   7   15
    ( ) 16   6
    ( ) 17   0
    ( ) 18   0
    ( ) have never dated on own   36   24
63. How often do you date now?
    (XX) several times a week   11
    (XX) about twice a week   12
    (XX) once a week   12
    (XX) about once or twice a month   14
    ( ) several times a year   5
    ( ) once or twice a year   5
    (XX) not at all   42

64. Which of the following traits do you most
    desire in a member of the opposite sex?
    Check as many as apply
    (XX) intelligence   56
    ( ) hard-working   24   47
    (XX) liked by parents   38
    (XX) admired by others   50
    ( ) self-confidence   40   55
    (XX) cleanliness   72
    (XX) cheerfulness   66
    ( ) thoughtfulness   51   72
    ( ) dependability   46   64
    ( ) honesty   64   76
    ( ) maturity   53   69
    (XX) good conversationalist   47
    (XX) good health   52
    ( ) good looks   80   66
    ( ) sexy   40   22
    ( ) sexually pure   31   15
65. To what degree has religion been an influ-
    ence in your upbringing?
    (XX) extremely important   18
    (XX) moderately important   21
    (XX) of some importance   29
    (XX) of little importance   20
    (XX) of no importance at all   13
66. Which of the following come closest to be-
    ing your goals in life?
    Check one or more
    ( ) making money and having fun   52   38
    (XX) acquiring knowledge   28
    (XX) being happy and respected for my work 42
    (XX) being prominent and a respected   23
        member of the community
    (XX) reaching the top of some field of   21
        work and becoming famous
    ( ) living a simple but secure life   29   45
    (XX) serving society and my fellow man   19
67. Which of the following do you consider your
    greatest obstacle to overcome in order to
    reach your goal in life?
    (XX) lack of ability   15
    (XX) lack of training and education   28
    ( ) poor health   4
    (XX) lack of money   26
    (XX) lack of "pull" with the right people 20
    (XX) laziness   28
    (XX) unwillingness to make sacrifices   17

68. Which of the following problems are troubling you now?

Check <u>as many</u> as apply

( ) being an only child	5	
(X) having no regular allowance	13	
( ) not allowed to use the family car	16	7
(X) no chance to do what I want to do	37	
( ) taking things too seriously	21	40
(X) being afraid of making mistakes	39	
( ) too short	9	
( ) too tall	5	
( ) overweight	12	33
( ) underweight	10	
(X) not good looking	25	
(X) being teased	23	
(X) getting into trouble	40	
(X) lacking self-control	15	
(X) being picked on	21	
(X) people finding fault with me	31	
(X) not being taken seriously	25	
( ) having bad dreams	9	21
( ) feeling nobody understands me	34	48
(X) feeling nobody likes me	22	
(X) being careless	13	
(X) smoking	20	
(X) getting in fights	18	
(X) losing my temper	43	
( ) feeling ashamed of something	24	36
(X) afraid of the future	23	
(X) getting low grades in school	41	
(X) being a grade behind in school	22	
(X) afraid of failing in school	27	
(X) afraid to speak up in class	24	
(X) slow in making friends	24	
(X) wishing people liked me better	34	
(X) picking the wrong kind of friends	29	
(X) no place to entertain friends	17	
(X) awkward in meeting people	15	
(X) going out with the opposite sex	17	
(X) not knowing how to make a date	14	
( ) not allowed to have dates	8	
(X) concerned over proper sex behavior	18	
( ) parents not understanding me	28	47
(X) being treated like a child	29	
( ) parents expecting too much of me	20	32
(X) being criticized by my parents	27	
(X) parents not liking my friends	31	
( ) family quarrels	26	47

59. Which of the following do you experience when you feel sad or depressed?

Check <u>as many</u> as apply

(X) tiredness	44	
( ) restlessness	39	53
( ) dizziness	9	19
( ) shakiness	16	37
( ) vomiting	3	
( ) emptiness feeling inside	34	58
(X) sweating	14	
( ) crying	18	65
(X) constipation	31	
(X) diarrhea (loose bowels)	20	
(X) dry mouth	14	
(X) pounding heart	20	
(X) shortness of breath	12	
(X) "butterflies" in stomach	24	
( ) headache	23	42
(X) boredom	39	
(X) loss of appetite	31	
(X) loss of interest	47	
(X) difficulty concentrating	42	
(X) difficulty getting up in the morning	27	
( ) difficulty going to sleep at night	36	48

70. Which of the following do you experience when you feel tense or anxious?

Check <u>as many</u> as apply

( ) difficulty getting up in the morning	14	
( ) restlessness	54	70
( ) headache	22	35
(X) sweating	23	
(X) tiredness	18	
(X) difficulty going to sleep at night	52	
( ) dizziness	7	14
( ) difficulty concentrating	37	50
( ) shakiness	20	38
(X) boredom	18	
( ) vomiting	2	
( ) shortness of breath	7	
( ) crying	5	25
( ) "butterflies" in stomach	26	39
(X) loss of interest	20	
( ) emptiness feeling inside	14	26
( ) constipation	2	
(X) pounding heart	26	
( ) loss of appetite	14	26
( ) diarrhea (loose bowels)	2	
(X) dry mouth	16	

71. Which of the following do you experience
    when you feel guilty?
       Check <u>as many</u> as apply
       (XX) fear   62
       (XX) emptiness feeling inside   33
       (XX) anger   30
       (XX) difficulty getting up   10
       ( ) a wish you were dead   32   49
       ( ) difficulty going to sleep   27   41
       (XX) loss of interest   24
       (XX) tiredness   15
       ( ) restlessness   31   41
       ( ) dizziness   6
       (XX) blushing   15
       (XX) shakiness   31
       ( ) vomiting   2
       (XX) sweating   18
       (XX) crying   19
       ( ) constipation   2
       ( ) diarrhea (loose bowels)   1
       (XX) dry mouth   12
       (XX) pounding heart   25
       ( ) shortness of breath   8
       (XX) "butterflies" in stomach   22
       (XX) headache   18
       (XX) boredom   11
       (XX) loss of appetite   17
       (XX) difficulty concentrating   28
       ( ) never feel guilty   7

72. In which of the following ways do you ex-
    press yourself when you are angry?
       Check <u>as many</u> as apply
       (XX) become silent   36
       (XX) go off by self   44
       (XX) brood   24
       ( ) become tearful   7   30
       ( ) cry   8   45
       (XX) speak out   33
       (XX) shout   40
       (XX) swear   46
       (XX) hit something   37
       (XX) throw something   28
       ( ) hit someone   28   17
       ( ) fight physically   26   9
       (XX) argue verbally   37
       ( ) plunge into activity   8
       (XX) try to forget it   31
       ( ) never get angry   3

PART III: SELF DESCRIPTION

Appearing below is a list of adjectives. You
are to read them quickly and put a check opposite each one you consider descriptive of
yourself as you are now. Do not worry about
duplications, contradictions, and so forth.
Work quickly and do not spend too much time
on any one. Try to be frank and check all adjectives which describe you as you really are,
not as you would like to be.
       Check <u>as many</u> as apply
       (X) absent-minded   31
       (XX) active   52
       (X) adaptable   25
       (XX) adventurous   52
       (XX) affected   15
       ( ) affectionate   32   50
       (XX) aggressive   22
       (XX) alert   48
       ( ) aloof   10   17
       (XX) ambitious   42
       (XX) anxious   55
       ( ) apathetic   7
       ( ) appreciative   26   39
       (XX) argumentative   37
       ( ) arrogant   9
       (XX) artistic   23
       (XX) assertive   10
       (XX) attractive   26
       ( ) autocratic   4
       (XX) awkward   24
       (X) bitter   23
       ( ) blustery   5
       (XX) boastful   14
       ( ) bossy   21   31
       ( ) calm   43   27
       (XX) capable   43
       (XX) careless   35
       (XX) cautious   25
       ( ) changeable   36   55
       (XX) charming   16
       (XX) cheerful   45
       (XX) civilized   40
       (XX) clear-thinking   25
       (XX) clever   33
       ( ) coarse   10
       (XX) cold   15

(X)	commonplace	12		( )	fearful	26 38
( )	complaining	27 40		( )	feminine	3 48
( )	complicated	17 32		( )	fickle	8 21
(X)	conceited	13		( )	flirtatious	16 38
(X)	confident	25		(X)	foolish	33
( )	confused	42 61		(X)	forceful	19
(X)	conscientious	23		(X)	foresighted	12
(X)	conservative	17		(X)	forgetful	40
( )	considerate	29 43		( )	forgiving	44 57
(X)	contented	14		(X)	formal	11
( )	conventional	8		(X)	frank	40
( )	cool	39 27		(X)	friendly	69
(X)	cooperative	38		( )	frivolous	6
(X)	courageous	30		(X)	fussy	28
(X)	cowardly	14		(X)	generous	41
(X)	cruel	16		(X)	gentle	39
(X)	curious	52		(X)	gloomy	20
(X)	cynical	13		(X)	good-looking	35
(X)	daring	44		(X)	good-natured	46
(X)	deceitful	14		(X)	greedy	13
(X)	defensive	39		( )	handsome	27 4
(X)	deliberate	18		(X)	hard-headed	41
(X)	demanding	32		( )	hard-hearted	9
(X)	dependable	43		(X)	hasty	25
(X)	dependent	24		(X)	headstrong	30
(X)	despondent	11		(X)	healthy	61
(X)	determined	41		(X)	helpful	47
(X)	dignified	14		( )	high-strung	23 39
(X)	discreet	10		(X)	honest	50
(X)	disorderly	21		(X)	hostile	18
( )	dissatisfied	35 48		(X)	humorous	42
(X)	distractible	15		(X)	hurried	21
(X)	distrustful	18		(X)	idealistic	17
( )	dominant	7		(X)	imaginative	41
( )	dreamy	27 37		( )	immature	15 22
(X)	dull	20		( )	impatient	37 22
(X)	easy going	47		( )	impulsive	22 35
( )	effeminate	4		(X)	independent	33
(X)	efficient	18		(X)	indifferent	16
( )	egotistical	8		( )	individualistic	23 35
( )	emotional	34 58		(X)	industrious	15
(X)	energetic	28		( )	infantile	5
(X)	enterprising	10		(X)	informal	22
(X)	enthusiastic	26		(X)	ingenious	11
(X)	evasive	15		(X)	inhibited	12
( )	excitable	25 39		( )	initiative	10
(X)	fair-minded	47		(X)	insightful	14
( )	fault-finding	25 34		(X)	intelligent	53

(X) interests narrow	22		(X) practical	37	
(X) interests wide	46		( ) praising	12	19
(X) intolerant	13		(X) precise	13	
(X) inventive	19		(X) prejudiced	14	
(X) irresponsible	19		( ) preoccupied	14	22
( ) irritable	19	31	(X) progressive	19	
(X) jolly	38		( ) prudish	6	
(X) kind	55		(X) quarrelsome	25	
(X) lazy	50		( ) queer	6	15
(X) leisurely	28		(X) quick	36	
(X) logical	26		(X) quiet	36	
(X) loud	33		(X) quitting	14	
(X) loyal	36		(X) rational	17	
(X) mannerly	33		(X) rattlebrained	14	
( ) masculine	32	2	(X) realistic	31	
(X) mature	38		(X) reasonable	40	
(X) meek	14		(X) rebellious	34	
( ) methodical	8		(X) reckless	26	
( ) mild	35	24	(X) reflective	12	
(X) mischievous	41		( ) relaxed	35	22
(X) moderate	13		(X) reliable	34	
(X) modest	33		(X) resentful	26	
( ) moody	50	24	(X) reserved	17	
(X) nagging	19		(X) resourceful	18	
(X) natural	28		(X) responsible	33	
( ) nervous	46	64	(X) restless	45	
(X) noisy	18		( ) retiring	9	
(X) obliging	15		( ) rigid	8	
(X) obnoxious	12		( ) robust	6	
(X) opinionated	16		(X) rude	20	
(X) opportunistic	10		( ) sarcastic	23	35
(X) optimistic	17		(X) self-centered	24	
(X) organized	16		(X) self-confident	28	
(X) original	23		(X) self-controlled	32	
(X) outgoing	16		(X) self-denying	12	
(X) outspoken	22		(X) self-pitying	24	
(X) painstaking	13		(X) self-punishing	26	
(X) patient	28		(X) self-seeking	23	
(X) peaceable	27		(X) selfish	20	
(X) peculiar	20		( ) sensitive	36	58
( ) persevering	8		( ) sentimental	23	48
( ) persistent	18	27	(X) serious	46	
(X) pessimistic	14		( ) severe	8	
(X) planful	22		(X) sexy	21	
(X) pleasant	38		( ) shallow	5	
(X) pleasure-seeking	43		(X) sharp-witted	20	
( ) poised	11	20	(X) shiftless	11	
(X) polished	12		( ) show-off	28	20

shrewd	18	
shy	38	
silent	3	
simple	24	
sincere	33	46
slipshod	5	
slow	26	
sly	22	
smug	7	
snobbish	5	13
sociable	35	
soft-hearted	35	48
sophisticated	13	
spendthrift	16	
spineless	6	
spontaneous	8	15
spunky	20	
stable	17	
steady	30	
stern	14	
stingy	9	
stolid	5	
strong	36	
stubborn	38	50
submissive	12	
suggestible	17	
sulky	18	
superstitious	12	
suspicious	30	
sympathetic	26	45
tactful	22	
tactless	10	
talkative	36	49
temperamental	26	40
tense	18	45
thankless	12	
thorough	13	
thoughtful	31	44
thrifty	19	
timid	15	
tolerant	19	
touchy	29	44
tough	23	13
trusting	33	
unaffected	8	
unambitious	9	
unassuming	6	
unconventional	9	

undependable	14	
understanding	52	
unemotional	6	
unexcitable	6	
unfriendly	8	
uninhibited	8	
unintelligent	6	
unkind	10	
unrealistic	10	
unscrupulous	4	
unselfish	34	
unstable	9	16
vindictive	7	
versatile	16	
warm	52	
wary	12	
weak	19	
whiny	5	13
wholesome	20	
wise	31	
withdrawn	17	29
witty	26	
worrying	38	59
zany	16	

Appendix D

Footnotes

[1] "BR" refers to base rate or endorsement frequency of the total sample (middle column) where N = 834. The percentages for boys (N = 509) are in the left column and those for girls (N = 325) appear in the right column. Separate frequencies are given only for those descriptors where a significant sex difference was found. The symbol "(X)" indicates those items which were included in the statistical analysis of code types; excluded were descriptors which showed a sex difference, and those which had an endorsement frequency of <10% or >90%, as well as those referring to formal (psychiatric) diagnosis and psychotherapist data. Certain exceptions were made for descriptors whose content (*e.g.,* "suicide threat") was judged to be of exceptional importance. Note: All Q items were included in the analysis of codes (see discussion in Chapter 5).

[2] Primary and secondary referral reasons were not differentiated for purpose of this analysis.

[3] Identical to the list used in our study of adults reported in Chapters 3 and 4.

[4] Identical to the list appearing in the Personal Data Schedule completed by the patients.

Code Index[1]

---

[1]The *n* following a page number denotes citation appears in footnote of that page. Italicized numbers indicate entries appearing in the references.

Author Index[1]

Subject Index

Abnormal scores, 8, 78-79
Abortions, across codes, 256
Accessibility (in treatment), 248
"Acting out," 117
Actuarial
  prediction, 51
  processing
    accuracy *vs.* clinical, 45, 50-55
    attitude of clinicians toward, 46-49
    confusion about, 36-37, 38, 39, 41
    definition, 34, 35, 36
    description and prediction, 52, 53
    distinguished from automated, 35, 42, 43
    distinguished from clinical, 33, 34, 36, 44
    distinguished from mechanical, 35, 41, 42
    experimental derivation, 35, 36
    helping the clinician, 51
    levels, 40-41, 43, 44
    misconceptions concerning, 36-40
    questioned by Holt, 52
    questioned by Towbin, 59
    schematic representation, 38-39
Admission MMPI profile, 13-14, 78
Adolescent codes, 68
Adolescents
  abnormal sample, 137-142
  acceptance, 198, 203
  achievement orientation, 176, 190, 217, 231
  achievement, school, 202, 217, 227, 228, 230, 233, 237, 238, 239
  acting out, 177, 181, 192, 201, 206, 209, 212, 214, 216, 220, 222, 225, 231, 239
  affiliation need, 201
  agencies participating, 138
  alcoholism, 209, 210, 211
  alcoholism, parental, 173, 182, 210, 211, 218, 219
  anger, 187, 203, 210, 221, 222, 230, 231, 232, 233, 235, 239
  anxiety, 177, 179, 181, 187, 188, 190, 192, 193, 199, 200, 201, 203, 206, 209, 220, 223, 226, 229, 231, 233, 239
  assertiveness, 196, 229

average patient, 172, 175
  acting out, 174
  anger, 175
  attitude toward school, 173
  birth order, 173
  code type, 172
  dating, 173
  defense mechanisms, 173, 174
  denial, 173, 174
  depression, 175
  development, 173
  drinking, 175
  focal concern, 173
  friendships, 173
  immaturity, 174
  intellectual functioning, 174
  leisure time activities, 173, 175
  narcissism, 174
  opposite sex, view of, 175
  parental education, 173
  parental relationships, 173, 174
  typical father, 173, 174
  typical mother, 173, 174
  prognosis, 174
  self-report, 174, 175
  smoking, 175
  symptom pattern, 174
awkwardness, 199, 201, 231
bedwetting, 233
birth order, 196, 204
bizarre, 206, 230, 234
Case Data Schedule (CDS), 143
cheating, 211, 232
classifying profiles, 154
compulsive, 183, 201, 203, 204, 206, 229
concentration, 177
cross validation, 150-151
dating, 181, 192, 210, 212, 220, 224
defense mechanisms, 178, 226, 239
delusions, 181, 220, 222, 226, 231, 239
dependency, 178, 181, 196, 198, 204, 209, 211, 233, 236, 237
depression, 176, 179, 188, 190, 192, 196, 201, 203, 209, 231, 233
drinking, 176
drugs, 177, 179, 182, 186, 188, 190, 193, 195, 199, 201, 204, 206, 208, 210, 213, 218, 221, 225, 227, 231, 234
education, lack of, 177

317

DATE DUE

FEB 07 1996